DEVICES & DESIRES

DEVICES & DESIRES

BESS OF HARDWICK
and the BUILDING OF ELIZABETHAN ENGLAND

KATE HUBBARD

Chatto & Windus
LONDON

1 3 5 7 9 10 8 6 4 2

Chatto & Windus, an imprint of Vintage,
20 Vauxhall Bridge Road,
London SW1V 2SA

Chatto & Windus is part of the Penguin Random House group of companies
whose addresses can be found at global.penguinrandomhouse.com.

Penguin
Random House
UK

First published by Chatto & Windus in 2018

penguin.co.uk/vintage

A CIP catalogue record for this book is available from the British Library

ISBN 9780701188757

Map © Emma Lopes 2018
Typeset in 11.75/14.5 pt Arno Pro
by Integra Software Services Pvt. Ltd, Pondicherry

Printed and bound in Great Britain by Clays Ltd, Elcograf S.p.A.

Penguin Random House is committed to a sustainable future for
our business, our readers and our planet. This book is made
from Forest Stewardship Council® certified paper.

For Rebecca Nicolson
And in memory of my father

I have sene throwlie into your devices and desires.

Earl of Shrewsbury to Bess of Hardwick, 23 October 1585

Almightie and moste merciful father, we have erred and straied from thy waies, lyke lost shepe. We have folowed to much the devyses and desires of our owne harts.

Book of Common Prayer, 1552

Contents

List of Illustrations

Chapter headings: Masons' marks, used at Hardwick and still visible today

Picture section 1:

14. Design for a window at Longleat, *c.* 1568, Robert Smythson (RIBA Collections)

15. Designs for tools, Robert Smythson (RIBA Collections)

16. Hardwick Old Hall, 17th century, artist unknown (Historic England Archive)

17. Hardwick New Hall, 1959, Edwin Smith (Edwin Smith/RIBA Collections)

Picture section 2:

1. Architecture, Liberal Arts hanging, *c.* 1580 (National Trust Images/Brenda Norrish)

2. Design for Wollaton, 1580, Robert Smythson (RIBA Collections)

3. Wollaton Hall, *c.* 1880, Alexander Francis Lydon (Bridgeman)

4. Design for a screen at Worksop, Robert Smythson (RIBA Collections)

5. Variant ground floor plan for Hardwick, Robert Smythson (RIBA Collections)

6. Hardwick, north elevation, 1831, James Deason (RIBA Collections)

7. Long gallery, Hardwick, 1839, David Cox (Bridgeman)

8. Plasterwork frieze, High Great Chamber, 1590s (National Trust Images/Andreas von Einsiedel)

9. William Cavendish, 1st Earl of Devonshire, 1576, artist unknown (National Trust Images/John Hammond)

10. Arbella Stuart, 1577, artist unknown (Bridgeman)

11. Gilbert Talbot, 7th Earl of Shrewsbury, late 16th century, artist unknown (National Trust/Robert Thrift)

12. Mary Talbot, 16th century, artist unknown (National Trust/Robert Thrift)

13. Overmantel in Bess's bedchamber (National Trust Images/John Hammond)

14. Map of Hardwick, 1610, William Senior (Devonshire Collection, Chatsworth)

15. Faith and Muhammad hanging, 1580s (Bridgeman)

16. Drawing of Owlcotes, 1590, Robert Smythson (RIBA Collections)

17. Bess's silver livery badge (Devonshire Collection, Chatsworth)

18. Design for Bess's tomb, 1596, Robert Smythson (RIBA Collections)

19. Bess, 1590s, attributed to Rowland Lockey (National Trust Images/John Hammond)

Map of Derbyshire

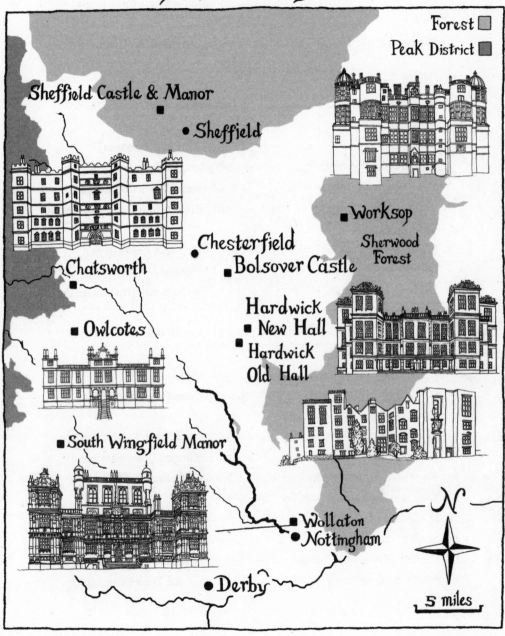

Forest ▢
Peak District ▢

Sheffield Castle & Manor

• Sheffield

Worksop

Sherwood
Forest

• Chesterfield
Bolsover Castle

Chatsworth

Hardwick
New Hall
Hardwick
Old Hall

• Owlcotes

• South Wingfield Manor

Wollaton
Nottingham

• Derby

5 miles

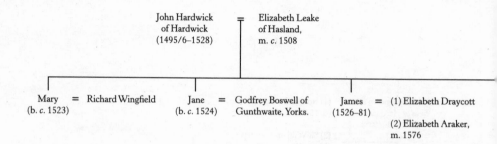

John Hardwick
of Hardwick
(1495/6–1528)
= Elizabeth Leake
of Hasland,
m. *c.* 1508

Mary
(b. *c.* 1523)
= Richard Wingfield

Jane
(b. *c.* 1524)
= Godfrey Boswell of
Gunthwaite, Yorks.

James
(1526–81)
= (1) Elizabeth Draycott

(2) Elizabeth Araker,
m. 1576

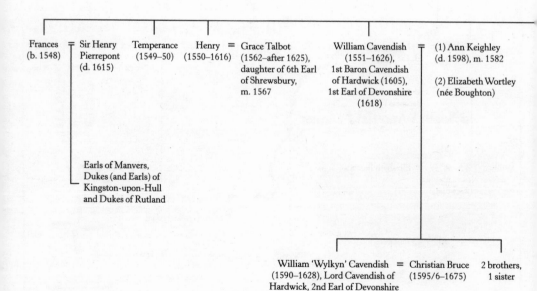

Frances
(b. 1548)
= Sir Henry
Pierrepont
(d. 1615)

Temperance
(1549–50)

Henry
(1550–1616)
= Grace Talbot
(1562–after 1625),
daughter of 6th Earl
of Shrewsbury,
m. 1567

William Cavendish
(1551–1626),
1st Baron Cavendish
of Hardwick (1605),
1st Earl of Devonshire
(1618)
= (1) Ann Keighley
(d. 1598), m. 1582

(2) Elizabeth Wortley
(née Boughton)

Earls of Manvers,
Dukes (and Earls) of
Kingston-upon-Hull
and Dukes of Rutland

William 'Wylkyn' Cavendish
(1590–1628), Lord Cavendish of
Hardwick, 2nd Earl of Devonshire
= Christian Bruce
(1595/6–1675)

2 brothers,
1 sister

HARDWICK
Family Tree

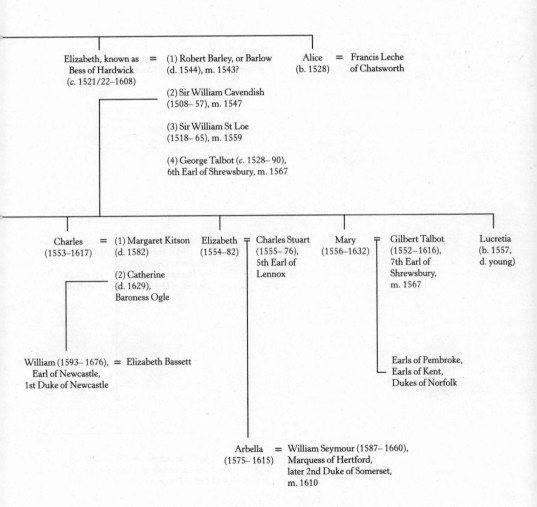

Elizabeth, known as = (1) Robert Barley, or Barlow
Bess of Hardwick   (d. 1544), m. 1543?
(c. 1521/22–1608)

Alice = Francis Leche
(b. 1528)   of Chatsworth

(2) Sir William Cavendish
(1508– 57), m. 1547

(3) Sir William St Loe
(1518– 65), m. 1559

(4) George Talbot (c. 1528– 90),
6th Earl of Shrewsbury, m. 1567

Charles = (1) Margaret Kitson
(1553–1617)   (d. 1582)

Elizabeth = Charles Stuart
(1554–82)   (1555– 76),
             5th Earl of
             Lennox

Mary = Gilbert Talbot
(1556–1632)   (1552–1616),
              7th Earl of
              Shrewsbury,
              m. 1567

Lucretia
(b. 1557,
d. young)

(2) Catherine
(d. 1629),
Baroness Ogle

William (1593– 1676), = Elizabeth Bassett
Earl of Newcastle,
1st Duke of Newcastle

Earls of Pembroke,
Earls of Kent,
Dukes of Norfolk

Arbella = William Seymour (1587– 1660),
(1575– 1615)   Marquess of Hertford,
               later 2nd Duke of Somerset,
               m. 1610

INTRODUCTION

If you find yourself driving north along the M1, twenty miles or so past Nottingham, and look up to the right, you will see a remarkable house sitting high and proud on an escarpment, gracing the Derbyshire skyline. This is Hardwick Hall, built in the 1590s by a woman in her seventies. You may note that its vast windows increase, rather than diminish, in height as they rise storey by storey; that its six turrets are crowned with what appear to be outsize 'ES's. These are the initials of the house's builder, Elizabeth, Countess of Shrewsbury, more commonly known as Bess of Hardwick.

According to William Harrison, an Essex clergyman, writing in 1577, the Elizabethan builder 'desireth to set his house aloft on the hill, to be seen afar off, and cast forth his beams of stately and curious work-manship into every quarter of the country'.[1] Bess's Derbyshire and Nottinghamshire neighbours would certainly have marvelled at the sight of Hardwick, but today the house still casts forth its beams, still astonishes. From the outside its masses seem to recede and advance, its towers to shift and regroup, and with its clean, regular lines and great grids of windows, it appears both sober and surprisingly modern.*

---

* The architects Caruso St John cited Hardwick as an inspiration for their design for the New Art Gallery, Walsall, 2000. Here, as at Hardwick, the highest ceilings are found on the top floor.

Yet there's something feminine about the lacy stonework along the parapet, with the delicate Hardwick stags (Bess's family arms) rearing up at the centre. And there's ego here too. At once romantic and austere, ostentatious and restrained, of its time and forward-looking, Hardwick is a house whose compact, regular exterior belies the ingenious and dramatic use of interior space, whose contradictions reflect the foibles and preferences of its builder.

'You shall have sometimes Faire Houses so full of Glasse, that one cannot tell where to become to be out of the Sunne or Cold', wrote Sir Francis Bacon in 1625.[2] Beside other so-called 'lantern houses' of the late sixteenth century – houses that gloried in large, expensive and status-enhancing windows, such as Sir Christopher Hatton's Holdenby or the Earl of Leicester's Kenilworth – 'Hardwick Hall, more glass than wall', could more than hold its own.* The sun, low in the sky, would have – and still does – set alight Hardwick's diamond panes, so the whole house glittered – or 'glistered', as the Elizabethans said – and shimmered gold. At night, lit by candles and torches, it became 'a great glass Lanthorne', much like those that hung throughout the house.

Standing on the 'leads' (the flat part of the roof) of Hardwick on a clear day is to survey Bess's domain. Down on the left can be seen the ruins of another great house – Hardwick Old Hall, also built by Bess, but not to her satisfaction. Looking westwards, across the park with its oaks and fish ponds, out over the valley of the Doe Lea river, towards the moors and hills of the Peak District, the view is not so very different today from that of four hundred years ago. Less wooded and more populated, of course, and bisected by the motorway, but the same open, rolling landscape. Sixteen miles to the north-west lies Chatsworth, Bess's first building project, undertaken with her second husband, Sir William Cavendish. Three miles north, just out of sight on the other side of the valley, is the site of Owlcotes, her final house,

---

* From 'Hardwick Hall? More window than wall', coined by Robert Cecil, 1st Earl of Salisbury, an admirer of Hardwick and a builder in his own right.

built for her son William. Six miles to the south-west is the imposing ruin of South Wingfield Manor, which belonged to her fourth husband, the Earl of Shrewsbury, a property never much loved by Bess, but a convenient base during the building of Hardwick. Further north along the ridge from Hardwick sits Bolsover, the enchanting castle built by Charles Cavendish, Bess's third son, who shared his mother's passion for building.

Looking east, the landscape has seen more change, although now, as then, on a particularly crystalline day, you might just glimpse the spires of Lincoln Cathedral in the far distance. But gone is the rough pasture of Bess's 'lawn', replaced by formal tree-planting in the eighteenth century. In the nineteenth coal, first mined by Bess, who had pits at Heath and Hardstoft, blackened the house and transformed the landscape. Up until the 1980s, the view eastwards from Hardwick's rooftop would have been dominated by colliery chimneys rising from flat Nottinghamshire farmland, at Teversal, Silverhill, Glapwell and Pleasley, with some to the west too, at Tibshelf and Holmewood: D. H. Lawrence country. In some respects, the landscape today appears returned to its pre-industrial state, apart from the very twenty-first-century wind turbines revolving gently on the horizon. But coal has left its traces: slag heaps, scars from defunct pits, disembowelled mining villages with their boarded-up shops and tanning salons. At Pleasley, once the oldest and deepest of the East Midlands coal fields, now optimistically rebranded as a 'country park', stands a lone chimney, from which Hardwick's towers can be seen floating in the distance.

Bess lived in an age of great builders, though Crown and Church, hitherto England's principal architectural patrons, played almost no part at all. Thanks to Henry VIII's enthusiasm for building – many of his forty-two houses and palaces had been bought, built or remodelled by the King himself – his daughter Elizabeth was positively over-housed. Ever careful and parsimonious, she chose to pass the building baton on to her subjects. Her courtiers, especially those newly ennobled, without inherited family seats, such as Sir Christopher Hatton, or Lord Burghley, risked bankruptcy by building enormous, spectacular 'prodigy houses', in the hope of entertaining the Queen (in fact this was a fearfully expensive honour that few actually sought). 'God send us both long to enjoy Her, for whom we both meant to exceed our purses in these', wrote Burghley to Hatton, referring to the building of Theobalds and Holdenby respectively.[3] At the same time the 'old' aristocracy, like the Earl of Shrewsbury, were busily improving existing houses or castles as well as building new: the fact that Shrewsbury inherited half a dozen very substantial houses didn't stop him from building several more.

These builders took a close and competitive interest in each other's projects. They visited, praised and criticised each other's houses, scrutinised each other's plans, recommended, exchanged and competed over sought-after craftsmen. They vied to outdo each other, to create buildings more extravagant, more original, more ingenious. Some patrons had travelled to France and Italy, or owned architectural works, or, later in the century, pattern books and engravings from the Low Countries, but few had any real understanding of the principles of Renaissance architecture. The Renaissance, as an intellectual movement, had barely touched sixteenth-century England, though some of its features – symmetrical design and classical ornament, both of which were employed at Hardwick – were borrowed by patrons and their craftsmen as architectural frills to be grafted onto an indigenous Gothic tradition. Elizabethan houses fire the imagination precisely because of their eclecticism, their lack of allegiance to any single controlling mind or architectural school, the magpie spirit with which their builders adopted and adapted.

But what motivated these Elizabethans to build so extravagantly and compulsively? Why build two great houses simultaneously in the same county; even, as did Bess, alongside each other? Some hoped to entice the Queen. Others wished to house children and heirs. A few, such as the recusant Sir Thomas Tresham, built to honour and celebrate faith and advertise learning. But most builders were aspirational and their houses concrete expressions of wealth and status: the twenty-first-century self-made millionaire, or multi-millionaire, might buy him- or herself a Tudor mansion; the sixteenth-century equivalent built one.

Bess built in the spirit of her times, as a materialist rather than an aesthete, though it mattered to her how things *looked*, and she was culturally literate too, drawing on classical and biblical sources for the decoration of Hardwick's interiors. However, as a female builder she was an anomaly. An ideal of Elizabethan womanhood posited a passive, obedient creature, producing children, managing her husband's household, tied to her embroidery. According to the 'Homily on Marriage', read in church every Sunday, a woman was a 'weak creature not endued with like strength and constancy of mind; therefore they be the sooner disquieted, and they be the more prone to all weak affections and dispositions of mind, more than men be'.[4] The reality, of course, was rather different, especially amongst the nobility. There were plenty of independent-minded, forceful women who defied their husbands, like Elizabeth Willoughby, wife of Sir Francis, builder of Wollaton; or interested themselves in their husbands' affairs, like Joan Thynne, who took on much of the running of Sir John Thynne's estates in the 1580s and 90s while he was in London. With husbands often away from home – attending Parliament, or court, or visiting other properties – wives were left in charge.

But however powerful and effective women might be in the domestic sphere, Tudor England was a strictly patriarchal society. Wives were legally and financially subordinate to their husbands. Those who wished to separate from their husbands couldn't expect any kind of restitution unless, in the rarest of cases, the Queen stepped in. Bess was only able to live apart from her estranged husband, the Earl of Shrewsbury, in the latter years of their marriage because she enjoyed an unusual degree of financial independence. She was a highly efficient manager of her husbands' houses and estates, but she went further, amassing property and estates of her own, pursuing her dynastic ambitions and business interests, extending her influence, and, as a four-times widow, capitalising and building on her inheritance with spectacular results.

Bess was not the first female architectural patron. In the fifteenth century, the building projects of Alice de la Pole, Duchess of Suffolk, included hospitals, a college for priests, parish churches, an almshouse, a market cross, and monuments to her husband. Lady Margaret Beaufort built a school, restored a church and founded two Cambridge colleges in the early 1500s. Margaret Clifford, Countess of Cumberland, built the circular Beamsley Hospital, in Yorkshire, as an almshouse for women in the 1590s (and also, like Bess, interested herself in mining works).[5]

The seventeenth century saw a number of women who commissioned buildings, or managed projects. Margaret Clifford's daughter, Lady Anne Clifford – perhaps Bess's closest rival in the building stakes – having fought a long battle to secure her father's estates in the north of England, set to work restoring her six castles, repairing her churches and chapels, and building a school, a bridge and a parish church. The widowed Mary Herbert, Countess of Pembroke, commissioned a house at Houghton, Bedfordshire, possibly designed by Inigo Jones. Alethea Howard, Countess of Arundel, Bess's granddaughter, oversaw many of her husband's projects, as well as building her own house in St James's Park.[6]

But generally all these aristocratic female patrons confined themselves to restoration, family memorials and public works. None of which much interested Bess, who did not come trailing a string of ancestral castles and churches, who was not motivated by piety, and who, although not uncharitable, did not have the benefactress's compulsion born of aristocratic privilege. Bess's motives for building were different, much closer in fact to her male contemporaries: she wished to make her mark, to leave a legacy in the shape of bricks and mortar, to honour and glorify the dynasty she founded. As a woman, and as the initiator and driving force behind four great houses in sixteenth-century England, she was unique.

Lytton Strachey had this to say about the Elizabethan world: 'With very few exceptions – possibly with the single exception of Shakespeare – the creatures in it meet us without intimacy; they are exterior visions, which we know, but do not truly understand … It is so hard to gauge, from the exuberance of their decoration, the subtle, secret lines of their inner nature.'[7] It's easy to feel baffled by the 'mystery of the Elizabethans', by their sheer strangeness, their unknowableness. Letters are curiously unrevealing and impersonal; their writers are solicitous over matters of health, occasionally tender, frequently furious, much preoccupied with financial and legal affairs. But what made these people laugh? What or whom did they love? What caused them pain? Or anxiety? Bess's own letters tell us much about her forcefulness and determination, much about what made her a brilliant manager and formidable woman of business, but little as to what made her attractive and lovable.

In an age of political and religious upheaval, of shifting alliances and sudden betrayals, obfuscation and concealment paid. Therein lay survival. It's hardly surprising that nothing delighted the Elizabethan mind more than the device – a trick or invention designed to intrigue and amaze, the harder to decipher, the more worthy of admiration. Artists scattered their portraits with emblems and symbols; poets wrote acrostic verse and employed conceits; letter-writers obscured meaning with convoluted courtesies; builders constructed houses in the shape of a letter, or inspired by biblical symbolism. Equally devices could be found in the wider arena of the personal and the political, in the pervasive love of intrigue and deception that animated Tudor England and proved irresistible to Bess.

Bess has been demonised, mostly by male historians, who seem to have taken their cue from the Earl of Shrewsbury. Horace Walpole was dismissive of Hardwick ('Vast rooms, no taste') and scathing about its builder: 'Four times the nuptial bed she warmed/And every time so well performed/That when death spoiled each husband's billing/He left the widow every shilling.' For Joseph Hunter, in 1819, Bess was a harridan.[8] For Edmund Lodge, in 1791, 'a woman of masculine understanding and conduct, proud, furious, selfish and unfeeling. She was a builder, a buyer and seller of estates, a money-lender, a farmer and a merchant of lead, coals and timber. When disengaged from these employments she intrigued alternately with Elizabeth and Mary, always to the prejudice and terror of her husbands.'[9] Lodge is absolutely right about Bess's multi-stranded businesses. And she was tough, ambitious, scheming and furious. She made enemies. But she also inspired devotion – two of her husbands loved her wholeheartedly, as did her fourth and last, before love turned to hate.

This book is an attempt to examine Bess's life as a builder within the context of the Elizabethan building world, dominated as it was by men – Sir John Thynne, Lord Burghley, Sir Christopher Hatton, the Earl of Leicester, Sir Thomas Tresham, some of them personal friends of Bess's as well as rival builders. It's about the building of Hardwick, but also of those houses that Bess knew, and visited, and coveted – Somerset House, Longleat, Kenilworth, Holdenby, Theobalds. Hardwick is not mentioned in any of Bess's surviving letters – there are no references to its building, no record of how she felt about it on completion. Nevertheless, she can be found *within* the house – in the towering top-floor rooms, the glass-walled turrets, the profusion of 'ES's, the bold and gorgeous textiles. Hardwick was certainly intended for the glory of Bess's heirs: it bristles with heraldry – Cavendish, Talbot and Hardwick arms – but it's the Hardwick arms that dominate, not those of any husband. Bess's identity is stamped, quite literally, all over her house, not only outside but in, where, like the doodling of a monstrous child, her initials are carved into overmantels and embroidered on hangings, tapestries and cushions. It's impossible not to feel that Hardwick is a celebration of self. It would have brought a smile to Bess's thin lips to know that she would become synonymous not with a husband, but with a house.

PROLOGUE

HARDWICK HALL, 1590

On the ground floor of Hardwick Hall is a small, vaulted room, cave-like, shadowy and lined from floor to ceiling with numbered oak drawers. This is the Evidence House (or Muniment Room), where for nearly four hundred years, in the drawers and in great iron chests on the floor, lay the 'evidence' of Bess of Hardwick's progress through Elizabethan England. Here, until the Evidence House was finally emptied in 1989, its contents removed to nearby Chatsworth, the principal home of the Cavendish family, lay title deeds, charters, bills, household and building accounts, letters, inventories, records of rent-gathering, land-buying, money-lending and legal suits, of sales of iron, glass, coal, lead and livestock.

It's at Chatsworth that we find the Hardwick building accounts today, in great leather-bound volumes, carefully itemised by a clerk in cramped and curling sixteenth-century script, and every two weeks totted up and signed with a large, emphatic 'E Shrowesbury'. Occasionally the clerk's arithmetic is corrected, or tart comments appear in the margin: 'Because the walls rise and be not well nor all of one colour they must be whited at the plasterer's charge.' Thus Bess kept a beady eye on the building of Hardwick New Hall, the greatest, and only survivor, of her four houses.

The first actual mention of the New Hall comes on 5 December 1590, when Thomas Hollingworth, a waller, was paid to set two steps in a top-floor room of the Old Hall – adjacent to the New – 'next to the leads towards the new foundations'.[1] Those foundations, together with cellars, had been dug that autumn, in advance of winter frosts. In October, extra labour had been taken on, up to forty men at one point, and shovels and spades paid for.[2] On 21 November, after four weeks of grinding work, the foundations were completed and the labourers dismissed. By the end of December, the 'fleaks' (hurdles), which formed a base for the scaffolding for the ground floor, were in place and masons began preparing stone for the walls. The great organisational engine required to construct a sixteenth-century house had been set in motion.

The start of work on the New Hall coincided with the death of Bess's fourth husband, George Talbot, Earl of Shrewsbury. On 18 November, Shrewsbury, crippled and twisted by gout and bitterness, died in the arms of his mistress, Eleanor Britton, at Handsworth Lodge, Sheffield. He was not mourned by Bess. Whatever had existed of tenderness and affection in their marriage – and there had been plenty of both – had long been extinguished by rage and recrimination. But the building of the New Hall was not, as is sometimes said, contingent upon the Earl's death. Bess was quite capable of funding her new house without Shrewsbury's money; indeed, she had been making plans for some time prior to his death. Now, however, an immensely wealthy widow of nearly seventy, she was able to devote her still considerable energies to the passion that shaped and animated her life, to the building of a house to inspire admiration, envy and awe.

By 1590, Bess was a seasoned builder. There was Chatsworth, on which she had worked for thirty years. And there was the Old Hall at Hardwick, very large, very grand and still unfinished. She could have made do, more than comfortably, with her existing houses. She could have sat back and congratulated herself on being rid of a troublesome husband, on her great wealth, on her position and status as family matriarch and Dowager Countess. Many – most – would have done just that. But Bess was dissatisfied. She hadn't done with building;

she had one more house in her. This could be the house that brought the Queen to Derbyshire; it could be for Bess's granddaughter Arbella, who herself had royal blood and for whom Bess nursed the highest hopes; or for William Cavendish, her second son, who needed a suitably impressive home. What it certainly would be was the house that Bess had always wanted, the house of her dreams.

The New Hall was carefully planned and considered. It was intended to dazzle; to display not only wealth and status, but wit and intelligence. Having acted as her own designer at the Old Hall, with decidedly mixed results, Bess now decided to engage the services of a man who could give shape to her vision, a man who had worked on some of the most romantic, dramatic and inventive houses to be found in sixteenth-century England, who came close to occupying the position of 'architect' at a time when such a term had no currency and little meaning: Robert Smythson.

'Architector and Surveyor unto the most worthy house of Wollaton with divers others of great account', reads the inscription on Smythson's tombstone – probably the first time he was so described. An architect in the modern sense was unknown in Elizabethan England and would remain so until the advent of Inigo Jones, in the early seventeenth century. When the term was used at all, it was done so loosely, in the sense of a 'supervisor', or of a craftsman capable of drawing up designs, and it carried no social status. It is used just once by Shakespeare, in *Titus Andronicus*, and then metaphorically. There was only one English book on architecture in existence, *The First and Chief Grounds of Architecture*, published in 1563, by John Shute, who had been sent to Italy in 1550 by his patron, John Dudley, Duke of Northumberland, specifically to study the subject (it was Shute who introduced the concept of the classical orders to an English readership).

Bess may well have read Shute, and she certainly knew something about architecture, but she would not have thought of Smythson as her *architect* – she simply needed his help in drawing up a plan. In 1590, Smythson was working at Wollaton, the house that he had built for Sir Francis Willoughby, near Nottingham. Wollaton was complete, though Smythson remained on the payroll, as a kind of bailiff. He was now known as *Mr* Smythson; plain 'Smythson the mason' no more. But his obligations to Sir Francis did not prevent him from taking on building projects elsewhere in the Midlands, including Worksop, a Shrewsbury property near Sherwood Forest, in whose early stages Bess was very likely involved. Those features particular to Smythson houses – prominent hilltop locations, an eye for the silhouette, height (often provided by turrets), a sense of order and symmetry, expanses of glass – were all things Bess wanted for Hardwick.

In the spring or early summer of 1590, Smythson rode northwards from Wollaton to discuss plans with Bess. He would have known the Countess by reputation. He would have known that she was sharp-tongued, but fair-minded; that she drove a hard bargain, but paid her bills; that she expected the highest standards of workmanship; that she personally inspected and scrutinised every stage of the building. He would have known that she'd already built one house at Hardwick.

From a distance, the Old Hall looked imposing, high on its ridge, and Smythson could see the possibilities of the site. Riding on, up the driveway, through great oaks and clusters of deer, he passed a man herding sheep, another with a cart of fish, a woman with a basket of plums, others digging ponds and erecting fences. The park was pleasing, but close up, he was dismayed by the house itself – its facade so plain, its silhouette so uneven and haphazard, its position (facing north) so misjudged, the whole so lacking in harmony. Inside, in the great hall, he was told that her Lady would receive him in her with-drawing chamber. He climbed the stairs to the fourth floor and found himself in a room panelled, he was quick to note, from floor to ceiling, and hung with fine tapestries. A small, slight figure rose to greet him: keen-eyed, hair still decidedly red, wearing a gown of black taffeta and several long ropes of pearls. She held out a hand: 'Good day, Mr Smythson.'

DERBYSHIRE BEGINNINGS

There is no lack of information about Bess in later life, when she had become a great personage, the wife of one of England's foremost earls, the friend of such as the Earl of Leicester and Lord Burghley, on (mostly) cordial terms with the Queen herself. But of her early years, the years of obscurity, we know little. As the daughter of a Derbyshire squire, who died young leaving his wife and six children in precarious circumstances, no one would have predicted great things for Bess. To marry into the local gentry, as did several of her sisters, was as much as she could have hoped for, and is indeed how she began her marital career. She would rise out of the ranks of the gentry, but it was precisely because she retained those traits particular to her class – energy, prudence and the kind of rigour she applied to her household accounts – just as she retained her flat Derbyshire vowels, that she prospered so spectacularly. That she defied her circumstances and from modest beginnings forged her way through the Elizabethan world, not merely by a judicious choice of husbands, but by shrewd exploitation of whatever assets those husbands brought her, is astonishing.

Bess's birth date is uncertain. Her monument in Derby Cathedral suggests that she was 'about 87' when she died, in 1608, but recent biographers have settled on 1527 as the year of her birth.* In fact she was probably born in 1521, or early 1522, at Hardwick, when Henry VIII was still, more or less happily, married to Catherine of Aragon and still in hopes of having a son.[1] Her parents, John and Elizabeth Hardwick, belonged to the minor gentry: respectable, not especially prosperous, part of a small network of gentry families – the Foljambes of Barlborough, the Frechevilles of Staveley, the Barleys of Barlow, the Leakes of Hasland, the Leches, the Babingtons, the Chaworths – interlinked by marriage, forever bargaining and bickering over land and money, all families Bess would come to do business with in the future. John Hardwick's family had owned land at Hardwick† since the thirteenth century, when the estate had been granted to them by the Savages of neighbouring Stainsby (they paid an annual peppercorn rent of 12d, one pound of cumin, one pound of pepper and a gillyflower).[2] By 1521, John Hardwick was farming over 400 acres, and enjoying rents from another 100 in Lincolnshire.[3] During the 1520s, he turned the original medieval farmhouse at Hardwick into a half-timbered manor.

Sixteenth-century Derbyshire was a remote, inaccessible county, a good five days' ride from London, varied and extreme in its landscape – craggy outcrops, rolling, thickly wooded hills and bleak expanses of moor, all criss-crossed by notoriously rough tracks and byways. Celia Fiennes, writing in 1698, a good hundred years after Bess's time, commented on 'the steepness and hazard of the Wayes – if you take a wrong Way there is no passing – you are forced to have Guides in all parts of Derbyshire.'[4] To southerners, it appeared a wild, uncivilised place. However, along with neighbouring Yorkshire and Nottinghamshire, it was also unusually rich in natural resources – lead, iron and coal. Upon such resources fortunes were founded and

---

* Gilbert Talbot, writing to Robert Cecil in 1604, refers to his 'unkind mother-in-law' as being 84 (HMC Salisbury, Vol. XVI, p.360).
† From 'de Herdewyk', meaning 'sheep farm'.

houses built. Sir Francis Willoughby's Wollaton was funded by coal; the Earl of Shrewsbury's Sheffield Manor and Worksop by lead and iron. It was no accident that the sixteenth century (and after) saw such a concentration of houses emerging in the north-east Midlands.

By 1507, when Bess's grandfather, another John Hardwick, died, his son and heir, though only eleven years old, was already married, to Elizabeth Leake, the daughter of a neighbouring squire, Thomas Leake of Hasland. The marriage would not have been consummated until both parties had come of age, but they went on to produce six children: five daughters, Alice, Elizabeth, Mary, Jane and Dorothy, and a son, James. Elizabeth (Bess) was most probably the second daughter, with her brother born three or four years later. Dorothy died young.

There are plenty of examples of highly educated Tudor women – Mary Sidney, Countess of Pembroke, the four brilliant daughters of Sir Anthony Coke, including Mildred, a Greek scholar, who became Lady Burghley, and Anne, who married Sir Nicholas Bacon, and of course the Queen herself. Bess was not one of them. Much has been made of the fact that only six books, kept in her bedchamber, are listed in the inventory made at Hardwick in 1601, including *Calvin upon Jobbe* (an edition of John Calvin's sermons on the Book of Job), *the resolution* (possibly by the recusant Robert Persons, though used by Catholics and Protestants alike), *Salomans proverbes* (one of the Books of Solomon), and *a booke of meditations*.[5] This doesn't mean that there were no other books at Hardwick (there certainly were – the inventory is incomplete and does not include clothes or jewels, and Bess's son William Cavendish bought a great many books*), or that Bess was unusually pious (she wasn't).[6] But, without being

---

* Including works by Montaigne and Chaucer, William Camden's *Britannia* and Sir Anthony Shirley's *Travels into Persia*, all bought from a London bookseller (Riden, *Household Accounts*). It was Thomas Hobbes, the philosopher, who came to Hardwick in 1608 as tutor to William's son, who created a library, on the top floor of the Old Hall.

uncultured, she was no bluestocking. As a gentry daughter, her education probably went little beyond reading, writing, needlework, the basics of accounting and herbal medicine. She most likely acquired her italic hand later – italic script, mercifully legible, unlike the secretary script practised by men, was generally the preserve of educated, aristocratic women and was not, for example, used by Bess's mother.

In 1528, John Hardwick died, aged thirty-three. Tudor landowners who died young, as so many did, leaving underage heirs, faced the great menace of wardship, whereby an estate became Crown property, administered by the Office of Wards, until the heir came of age at twenty-one. In the meantime, the heir became a ward, with a guardian who bought the wardship and could then arrange the ward's marriage – often to one of his own children, thereby securing the estate – as he saw fit. This iniquitous system carried over from medieval times, when the Crown awarded lands and property in return for knight service; since a child heir could not perform knight service, it was regarded as perfectly legitimate for the Crown to appropriate the heir's lands and revenues in lieu, until he reached majority.

By the sixteenth century, there was no call for mounted knights in creaking armour, but Henry VII and Henry VIII seized on wardship as a useful source of revenue and exploited it to the full. Bess's grandfather successfully foiled the Office of Wards by leaving his estate not to his eleven-year-old son John, but to sympathetic trustees, including Sir John Savage, who returned the lands to John when he turned twenty-one. In 1528, with little James Hardwick just three, John Hardwick tried the same ruse. In early January, presumably with intimations of mortality, he drew up, or so he claimed, a deed making over his estates to seven feoffees, or trustees. Ten days before he died, he made a will, referring to the deed (in point of fact, wills were solely for the leaving of goods and chattels, not land, which theoretically belonged to the Crown), stating that he wished those trustees to hold his land for the benefit of his wife and children until James came of age, and asking to be buried in Ault Hucknall church, close by

Hardwick. He also left a dowry of forty marks* (about £33) to each of his five daughters.[7]

Initially John's ploy seemed to have worked. In October, an inquisition post mortem – a standard procedure to examine the terms of wills and the leaving of land – found nothing to object to regarding the will. However, in August of the following year, a further enquiry was called for, and this time John Hardwick's deed was dismissed and his estate passed into the hands of the Office of Wards. John Bugby, a court official (officer of the pantry), bought James's wardship together with a quarter of the interest in the land.[8] For £20, he got land worth £5 a year and the right to sell the marriage of his ward. Bugby had no connection with the Hardwicks and no interest in their welfare; he simply saw an opportunity and took it.

For Elizabeth Hardwick, this was a calamity. She had her widow's jointure – the income from one third of her husband's estates for her lifetime – but this did not provide sufficient means to buy back the wardship, which she had the right to do. Bugby did not own the entire estate. Just over half of it, including Hardwick Hall, remained in the hands of the Crown and was rented back to Elizabeth, and she may well have also rented back the lands held by Bugby. She probably continued to live at Hardwick with her children, but her income, with rents to pay, was drastically reduced. Sometime after 1529, she took the only practical course of action open to her – remarriage.

Her second husband, Ralph Leche, was a younger son of the Leches of Chatsworth. Neither party had much to offer: Ralph an annuity of £6 13s., from Chatsworth, and a few leases in the Midlands; Elizabeth a home, at Hardwick, temporarily at least. It was at Hardwick that Bess most likely spent the remainder of her childhood, along with her siblings and younger half-sisters. The Leches had three known daughters (and possibly more): another

---

* A 'mark' being two thirds of a pound.

Jane, to whom Bess would be close throughout her life, another Elizabeth (Elizabeth Leche's stock of girls' names was apparently limited) and Margaret. The Leches' marriage does not seem to have been easy, with claims from Elizabeth in 1538 that Ralph had deserted her and the children, and there were financial problems from the outset.[9] Elizabeth struggled to pay her rent, while Ralph tried to make money from buying leaseholds and wardships, speculations that led to debts and legal suits.

While the Leches were squabbling and penny-pinching and producing more daughters, the King was ridding himself of Catherine of Aragon in order to marry his new love, Anne Boleyn. The alluring Anne had first caught Henry's eye in 1527, when eighteen years of marriage to good, dutiful, and now sadly stout Catherine had produced no more than one daughter, Princess Mary. Such was Henry's longing for Anne that it was easy enough to square his conscience by convincing himself that the Pope should never have granted him a special dispensation to marry Catherine, as his sister-in-law, in the first place (Catherine had been married to Henry's brother Arthur, though she emphatically denied consummation). In Henry's mind, his marriage to Catherine was cursed, and the proof was in the absence of a son. The Pope, he felt, must surely grant him an annulment, and he looked to Cardinal Wolsey, his Lord Chancellor, to bring it about.

When Wolsey failed, his downfall was inevitable, and in 1530, shortly after his arrest, he died. Henry promptly appropriated the Cardinal's properties, including Hampton Court and York Place (renamed Whitehall), and, with the encouragement of Anne Boleyn, began remodelling and expanding both. Henry, like Wolsey, who had acted as his architectural mentor, was an inveterate builder. He did not just commission buildings, he was actively involved in their design – he owned drawing instruments and was probably capable of drawing up basic plans. In 1532, impatient to see results at Whitehall, Henry had canvas tents put up over the works, so workmen could carry on in the rain, and on one occasion provided emergency midnight rations of beer, bread and cheese as they stood knee-deep in mud, digging foundations.[10]

Impatient with waiting for his annulment too, the King decided to take matters into his own hands. Without renouncing Catholicism, Henry, urged on by Anne, was open to new interpretations, and in particular to the evangelical ideas coming from the Continent. Evangelicals sought to reform the Catholic Church by taking it back to its bare essentials, by placing the word of God, as found in the Bible, over that of the Pope and scorning empty ritual. The seeds of the new faith were being sown. The first step in the break with Rome came in May 1532, when Thomas Cromwell, former right-hand man to Wolsey, now to Henry and a staunch evangelical (he had learned the New Testament, translated from the Greek by the Dutch humanist Erasmus, by heart), engineered the submission of the clergy to the King. In early 1533, Henry married Anne, who was already pregnant. That May, the new Archbishop of Canterbury, Thomas Cranmer, another evangelical and a firm ally of the Boleyns, declared Henry's marriage to Catherine null and void and Anne was crowned Queen. Four months later, she gave birth to a healthy baby – a girl, to Henry's chagrin – Princess Elizabeth. The following year, the Act of Supremacy made the King head of the Church.

Derbyshire was a long way from London, but the ripples following Henry's marriage to Anne and the break with Rome would have been felt. At Hardwick, the Leches were no doubt too preoccupied with the business of survival to take much notice of national events. Still, the shocking news, in May 1535, that a group of Carthusian monks, regarded as some of the holiest men in England, had been hanged, drawn and quartered (under the Treason Act of 1535, denial of royal supremacy was punishable by death) would have filtered its way to them; so too the executions of John Fisher, Bishop of Rochester, and Thomas More, who refused to accept the King as head of the Church or to support the Act of Succession, by which Princess Mary, Henry's elder daughter, was declared illegitimate.

But events moved fast at Henry's court. When Anne suffered a series of miscarriages, and with no sign of the male heir that Henry so badly needed, marital relations soured and the King began to look elsewhere. In May 1536, just eleven days after Anne's execution for alleged multiple adulteries and treason, Henry married Jane Seymour, who would, at last, produce a son. That autumn, the northern rebellion, known as the Pilgrimage of Grace, a riposte to Henry's perceived attacks on the Church, as well as a show of support for Princess Mary as his legitimate heir, began not far from Derbyshire, in Lincolnshire, before spreading north as far as the Scottish border. The scale of the rebellion took Henry by surprise, but merely hardened his determination to accelerate the process of Dissolution. Smaller monasteries, all over the country, went first. By 1540, in just four years, all England's monasteries had been suppressed; their libraries, art and relics destroyed; their monks and nuns pensioned off. The Dissolution and its after-effects left few corners of England untouched.

However, the King was busy constructing as well as destroying. 'Certainly, masonry did never better flourish in England than in his time', wrote William Harrison.[11] Aside from Whitehall and Hampton Court, Henry improved his palaces at Greenwich and Oatlands; he had work done at the Tower of London; and in 1538 he began to build the charmingly decorative Nonsuch, a glorified hunting lodge in Surrey, intended as a pleasure palace for informal entertaining. Nonsuch was timber-framed and constructed around two courtyards, with stucco plaster panels depicting classical and mythological figures lining the walls of the inner courtyard, and miniature onion domes. Its foundations were built of stone from Merton Priory. Former monasteries proved a rich resource for Tudor builders – they could be incorporated into and reworked as private houses, or demolished and used as quarries.

The building and maintenance of royal palaces, as well as of fortifications, throughout England was undertaken by the Royal Works. The Works was based in Scotland Yard, Whitehall, with an outpost at Berwick, on the Scottish border, and satellites at the Tower of London,

Windsor Castle and Chester. It was headed by a surveyor – the most powerful position in the Tudor building world – seconded by a comptroller, who oversaw financial and administrative affairs, then a master mason, master carpenter and master bricklayer, a chief joiner and chief glazier, a serjeant plumber and a serjeant painter, each of whom was responsible for his team of craftsmen.[12] A post in the Works brought status, security and a guaranteed income – salaries were modest, but as with court positions, there was ample opportunity to boost them with backhanders and bribes. Henry VIII kept the Works busy; under Elizabeth I they were not called upon for new royal buildings and simply maintained those existing. However, for private patrons they offered an extremely useful source of skilled craftsmen and draughtsmen (Lord Burghley used officers from the Royal Works to draw up plans for both Theobalds and his Chelsea house), bearing in mind that in theory such men could be commandeered at any time for a royal or military building project.[13]

Whitehall, Hampton Court, Nonsuch – all would become familiar to Bess. But as twenty-something Elizabeth Hardwick she would not have set her sights much beyond a husband. Marriage, for Bess and her sisters, was by far the best, indeed the only, option, but not one to be counted on, considering that all they had were their dowries of forty marks. The first step in Bess's marital career was unspectacular, no more than could be expected for a girl in her position, but presented with an offer, she took it. In about 1542, around the same time that her stepfather Ralph Leche was sent to the Fleet prison for debt (he died in 1549), Bess married Robert Barley (or Barlow) of Barlow, Derbyshire.[14] We know that the marriage took place within the lifetime of Robert's father, Arthur, and Arthur died in May 1543, when Robert was just thirteen and Bess twenty or twenty-one.

According to Nathaniel Johnson, the Yorkshire antiquarian, in his seven-volume history of the Earls of Shrewsbury, written at Chatsworth in 1692, 'some ancient gentlemen' told him that Bess and Robert

Barley met in London, in the household of Lady Zouch, where Robert lay sick with 'Chronical Distemper'. 'In which time this young gentlewoman making him many visits upon account of their neighbourhood in the country and out of kindness to him, being very solicitous to afford him all the help she was able to do in his sickness, by ordering his diet and attendance, being then young and very handsome, he fell deeply in love with her, of whose great affections to her she took such advantage, that for lack of issue by her he settled a large inheritance in lands upon herself and her heirs, which by his death a short time after she fully enjoyed.'[15]

Johnson was writing some 150 years after the event and the 'ancient gentlemen' may not have been the most reliable of sources. But his account probably has some truth in it. The Zouches came from Codnor Castle in Derbyshire, and Lady Zouch was distantly related to the Hardwicks. It was common practice for gentry sons and daughters of slender means to be placed in noble households, where they acted as obliging companions, performing light duties and acquiring some social polish along the way (Bess would have several such upper servants in her own household). Bess may well have been sent to attend on Lady Zouch, and Robert too, as a page.

In other respects, Johnson's account is quite wrong. Many Tudor marriages were political and economic contracts, and that of Bess and Robert Barley had a great deal more to do with money and property than with love, and was clearly arranged by their elders. The legal age of consent was twelve for girls and fourteen for boys, though early marriage was mostly favoured by the aristocracy, as a means of securing and consolidating inheritance. Bess, as a gentry daughter, would have expected to marry in her early twenties. For Robert, however, to be married so young, most likely in haste, was unusual.

At some point between 1533 and 1538, Arthur Barley had sold his son's wardship to Ralph Leche, along with part of the Barley estate (Ralph claimed that he had in turn sold on the wardship and marriage, though this was disputed).[16] Some years later, Bess explained how

Arthur Barley had contacted her mother and stepfather, seeking a match between Robert and Bess 'in consideration of divers great sums of money paid ... to the said Arthur for the same'.[17] 'Great sums' sounds like an exaggeration – the Leches were in no position to pay out great sums; Bess may simply have been referring to her own (modest) dowry. The marriage has every appearance of being an attempt to thwart the Office of Wards (as practised by Bess's own parents) and to secure the Barley estate. If the underage heir was already married at the time of his father's death, then at least he could not be married off by whoever bought the wardship. Arthur could die in the knowledge that his estate would remain within his family, while the Leches had a daughter off their hands and some additional land.

Where the Barleys lived as man and wife, if they lived together at all, is unknown – possibly with Robert's mother – but on 24 December 1544, Robert died. Given that he was still only fourteen, the marriage was probably unconsummated, or so at least family history had it – the Duchess of Newcastle wrote in her 1667 *Life* of her husband, the first Duke (and one of Bess's grandsons), that Robert 'died before they were bedded together, they both being very young'. Robert's younger brother George became the new heir, and the wardship was up for sale once again. This time it was bought by Sir Peter Frecheville, from Staveley, Derbyshire, who eventually married his daughter to George, so gaining permanent control of the Barley estates.

Bess, as Robert's widow, could expect her widow's jointure. Jointures, which were negotiated at the time of marriage, had a twofold purpose: to provide for the widow, and to preserve family estates for the heir. When a woman married in sixteenth-century England, her lands and property became her husband's for the duration of the marriage. Moveable property (plate, cash, livestock, etc.) was permanently lost to her; her freehold land could be sold off by her husband, but only with her consent; she might get back leases after her husband's death, if he hadn't already disposed of them. In return for her cash dowry, or 'portion', the groom and his family promised to convey specific estates, or pieces of land, to the couple, to be held jointly during their marriage, and solely during the life of the survivor. The income from these estates – generally a third of the total – was known as a jointure, and was intended to support a widow for her lifetime. This, at least, was the theory. In practice, heirs frequently proved reluctant to accept the widow's life interest in their estates, with the consequent loss of income. Chancery was clogged with jointure cases. Now, and not for the last time, Bess had a fight on her hands.

A document recording the Chancery case Bess brought in 1546 in pursuit of her jointure survives, torn on one side and the ink so faded in places as to be barely legible. Her voice is muffled by legalese, but her indignation, her sense of injustice still comes through. Here is a young woman of twenty-three or -four, demanding to be heard. She explains how she had applied to her brother-in-law George, through his guardian Sir Peter Frecheville, 'who hath the custody of the body of George', for her 'third part'. There was no one else she could look to for financial aid, since her mother was 'very poor and not able to relieve her self and much less' her daughter, and her stepfather was 'condemned in great sums of money'.[18]

Initially George Barley and Frecheville declined to pay up – 'they unjustly and against all the laws of equity refused'. Sir Peter threw up some obstacle and then tried to make a deal, offering Bess an annual sum if she would waive her rights to her jointure. Bess, on advice and for lack of alternatives, accepted the offer 'with misgivings', but then Sir John Chaworth, Robert Barley's uncle, made an objection and the agreement was overturned. In October 1546, Bess was awarded her third, though, so she claimed, it was somewhat less than her due. She was not prepared to give up. It took years of legal wrangling and three Chancery cases, but finally, in 1553, she received her full entitlement – about £24 a year – and damages of £14 as compensation for the delay.[19]

---

* By 1589, her Barley jointure was worth £100 a year (Durant, *Bess of Hardwick*, p.11).

This was hardly 'a large inheritance', but it was worth the having. A brief marriage had provided Bess with an income, small to be sure, but bringing a measure of independence. These early years of loss and financial insecurity help explain her drive to fortify herself with land, assets and cash, though for Bess the process of acquisition became compulsive, not merely a question of security, but of power and control. She had learned that the rights of a widow were considerably superior to those of a wife: as a widow, her goods and chattels were her own; she could hold, buy and sell freehold land and property; she could bring a lawsuit and write a will. She had discovered that she could expect no one to look out for her interests other than herself. And she had borne witness to the determined efforts on the part of both her parents to keep intact a small Derbyshire estate, Hardwick, a place that would come to exert a similar hold on Bess.

2.

SIR WILLIAM CAVENDISH

'Memorandum: That I was married unto Elizabeth Hardwick my third Wife in Leicestershire at Bradgate House the 20th August in the first year of King Edward the 6 at 2 of the Clock after midnight.'[1] So reads the entry in a notebook belonging to Sir William Cavendish. The year was 1547 and King Henry had died in January, succeeded by his nine-year-old son, Edward VI. It seems curious that Bess is 'Elizabeth Hardwick', not Barley, as though her first marriage has been excised. Did she choose to revert to her maiden name? Or, since an uncon-summated marriage was not legally binding, did she regard Barley as not worthy of record, although she had been quite prepared to go to court in pursuit of her jointure? Curious too to conduct a marriage at 2 a.m., though the hour was more likely chosen for astrological, than furtive, reasons.*

In the years following Robert Barley's death, Bess disappears from view. However, the mention of Bradgate House in William Cavendish's memorandum offers a clue to her whereabouts. Bradgate was the north Leicestershire home of Henry Grey, Marquess of Dorset, and his wife, Lady Frances, formerly Frances Brandon, the daughter of Henry VIII's younger sister Mary and Charles Brandon, Duke of Suffolk. The Greys

---

* Mary, Queen of Scots married Bothwell at 4 a.m., but in her case there were grounds for secrecy.

were very distantly related to the Hardwicks through Bess's mother and it seems likely that after Robert Barley's death, around 1545, Bess joined Lady Frances's household as one of her gentlewomen, much as she had Lady Zouch's, though the Greys were considerably grander. Bess would always maintain close ties to the Grey family, both to Henry and Frances, whom she would make godparents to her children, and to their three daughters, Jane, Katherine and Mary.

Bradgate was a substantial manor of diamond-patterned red brick, set in a great deer park six miles in circumference. The Greys were an attractive couple, passionate about hunting and gambling, presiding over an extravagant, sociable household, but they also placed the highest possible value on scholarship and religion, in their case, as reformers (evangelicals), on the 'new learning'. Reformers put the Bible, not the Mass, at the heart of their faith; since purgatory and transubstantiation were not mentioned in the Bible, so they did not exist; salvation could be attained by faith alone.

Frances was just a few years older than Bess, socially far her superior and officially her employer. Nevertheless, the two became friends. Henry Grey was not a man of any great ability as a statesman, regarded by his contemporaries as lacking in sense, naïve and easily led. However, he'd had the benefit of a first-class education (he had learned Latin from a pupil of Erasmus) and he wanted the same for his daughters – a humanist education, based on the classics. They were tutored in Latin, Greek and Hebrew, in addition to French and Italian, by John Aylmer, a brilliant young Cambridge graduate and protégé of Grey, who had paid for his schooling (Aylmer later became Bishop of London). Jane Grey grew to be a noted scholar, famously described by Roger Ascham, tutor to Princess Elizabeth, on a visit to Bradgate, as reading Plato in Greek while her family hunted in the park.

This high-minded scholarliness does not seem to have rubbed off on Bess, but she recognised its value (she did not see the need to provide a humanist education for her own daughters, but Arbella, her granddaughter, with her brilliant prospects, was a different matter). And it may well have been at Bradgate that she acquired her italic hand – bold and right-leaning – the hand practised by the Grey sisters. Nor does she seem to have been touched by the reforming zeal of the Grey household. Both Frances and Henry were committed to Protestantism, as the new faith came to be known, in whose cause Jane Grey would become a martyr. Bess too fell into line, but she would always be a dutiful rather than fervent Protestant: Hardwick had its own chaplain and chapel, where the household gathered for daily prayers, but this was standard for any great house. However, for an unsophisticated, uncultured young woman, a whole new world opened up at Bradgate. A world of ideas and learning, talk and glamour. A world Bess wanted to be part of.

It was at Bradgate that Bess probably first encountered William Cavendish. How else would a young widow from Derbyshire, with no fortune or prospects, have come to the attention of a rising man at court, a man based in London and Hertfordshire? The Greys had close court connections – Frances, after all, was the King's niece. They would certainly have known Cavendish, who was Treasurer of the King's Chamber, and to tempt him to Leicestershire, with the promise of fine hunting and hospitality, would have been easy enough. At any rate, the pair were married at Bradgate and launched themselves on an energetic programme of procreation and acquisition.

If Bess loved any of her husbands, it was probably the cheerfully materialist Sir William, the father of her children. In 1570, thirteen years after Sir William's death, she and Mary, Queen of Scots embroidered a hanging, now known as *The Cavendish Hanging*.* The central square shows tears falling onto smoking quicklime, with the motto 'EXTINCTAM LACHRIMAE TESTANTUR VIVERE FLAMMAN' ('tears witness that the quenched flame lives'); in the surrounding border are Bess and William's initials, the Cavendish arms and assorted

---

* Today *The Cavendish Hanging* is on display at Oxburgh Hall, Norfolk.

emblems of love – a cracked mirror, three broken rings and a glove. The Earl of Shrewsbury, Bess's husband of the moment, gets a heraldic acknowledgement, and Mary's hand can clearly be seen in the use of the emblems and mottos that she loved, but the hanging reads like a love letter from Bess to William Cavendish, the husband of her heart.

According to the Duchess of Newcastle, Sir William, 'being somewhat advanced in years', married Bess 'chiefly for her beauty'. Bess was in fact no great beauty, but she was spirited, vital and determined. It's a measure of her powers of attraction that Cavendish, a man on the make, chose a wife with little to recommend her in terms of social or material gain. But, at the age of thirty-nine, he found himself in the happy position of marrying a woman some thirteen years his junior, to whom he was temperamentally perfectly suited, and whose ambition, energy and pragmatism matched his own. He, like Bess, came from the landed gentry, by far the most vigorous and dynamic class in socially mobile sixteenth-century England. Members of the yeoman and merchant classes passed into the ranks of the gentry, and members of the gentry into those of the nobility. Such was the case with Cavendish, and along with him went his wife.

Tudor England offered unique opportunities for advancement. 'Never in the annals of the modern world has there existed so prolonged and so rich an opportunity for the businessman, the speculator and the profiteer', wrote John Maynard Keynes.[2] The Dissolution played a crucial part in this, changing forever the pattern of land ownership, freeing up property, redistributing wealth and boosting the rise of the gentry in the process. The prime beneficiary of the Dissolution was of course the King, whose coffers were swelled by the abbeys' enormous revenues, and who acquired great tracts of monastic land and property. But about a third of this land was redistributed, sold on to both courtiers and local gentry. With increased social mobility came increased class-consciousness. Newly won titles were proclaimed in heraldry, carved in stone, etched in glass and embroidered in textiles all over sixteenth-century houses, as they would be at Hardwick. And newly acquired land was fiercely protected and fought for. Here perhaps lies an explanation for why the Tudors were so obsessively litigious, so quick to sue, so jealous of their rights.

William Cavendish was born in 1508, the second son of a Suffolk squire, Thomas Cavendish, who had court connections as Clerk of the Pipe, a position in the Exchequer, under Henry VII. When Thomas died in 1524, he left William some land in Suffolk, but essentially he had to make his own way, though his older brother, George, was a gentleman usher to Cardinal Wolsey, to whom he was devoted and whose (anonymous) biographer he became, and was thus excellently placed to lend a helping hand. William probably became a gentleman servant in Wolsey's household, where he would have come across Thomas Cromwell, Wolsey's right-hand man. After Wolsey's fall, he swiftly hitched himself to Cromwell's coat-tails; by the early 1530s, he was working for Cromwell, as one of his agents in the appropriation of religious houses, and busily lining his own pockets in the process.

In 1536, when the Dissolution of the Monasteries got under way in earnest, William Cavendish was appointed one of ten auditors to the Court of Augmentations, which was set up to deal with the distribution of monastic land and property. He toured the country, mostly the Home Counties, sometimes with a Dr Thomas Leigh, another commissioner appointed to oversee the Dissolution. Typically, in June 1536, he wrote to Cromwell: 'we have been at the priory of Little Marlowe and have dissolved it. My lady takes her discharge like a wise woman and has made delivery of everything of which we send an inventory. She trusts entirely to you for a reasonable pension.'[3] Cavendish's salary was a modest £20, but the perks, the 'profits' of the office, were considerable, both in the shape of bribes* and in

---

* In 1538, Cavendish and Leigh were accused of accepting plate from the Abbot of Merivale 'to be good masters unto him and his brethren', but not prosecuted (L&P Henry VIII, Vol. 13.2B, p.514).

opportunities to hoover up parcels of land and property on favourable terms.[4] Cavendish assessed and audited the property of the immensely rich and well-endowed Abbey of St Albans in Hertfordshire (the King kept the Abbot's house at St Albans for his own use), which ultimately led to the grant of the freehold of the manor at Northaw, together with land and other properties in Hertfordshire. In similar fashion he acquired land and property in Lincolnshire, Shropshire, Norfolk, Staffordshire and South Wales.

In the early 1530s, he married Margaret Bostock, with whom he had three daughters. They made their home at Northaw, in prime hunting country but conveniently close to London, where Cavendish leased another house. Margaret died in 1540, the same year that Thomas Cromwell lost his head. This might have spelled trouble for Cavendish; however, he weathered the storm and was appointed one of three commissioners to survey Crown lands and oversee the surrender of religious houses in Ireland. Here he remained for over a year and prospered. In May 1542, Sir Anthony St Leger, Lord Deputy of Ireland, wrote to the King: 'Mr Cavendish took great pains in your said service, as well as with continual pains about the said accounts and surveys, as in taking very painful journeys about the same … to Limerick and those parts, where I think none of your Highness's English commissioners came these many years, and in such weather of snow and frost that I never rode in my life. And I note him to be such a man as little feareth the displeasure of any man in your Highness's service, wherefore I account him to be the meter man for this land.'[5] Back in England, in 1542, Cavendish married again, this time a widow, Elizabeth Parris, with whom he had three more children, all of whom died, as did Elizabeth herself, in 1546, while giving birth to her third child. In the same year he was appointed Treasurer of the King's Chamber (a position for which he paid £1,000), became a Privy Councillor and received a knighthood.

A prerequisite for survival, let alone advancement, at the Tudor court was a willingness to bow before the prevailing wind. Sir William showed himself more than willing. He'd survived the falls of Wolsey and Cromwell; now, after Henry's death in January 1547, he smoothly established himself in the new regime, making himself useful to the boy King, Edward VI, and retaining his position as Treasurer (Edward left him £200 in his will, suggesting that he valued Cavendish). It was in August, eight months after Henry's death, that Sir William and Bess married.

What kind of a man was William Cavendish? What kind of husband? Only one letter from him to 'good Besse' survives, a brief, businesslike note, written in 1550, asking his wife to pay eight pounds for some oats, and there are none of hers to him.[6] Judging from his career, we can assume that he was an efficient servant to Cromwell and Henry VIII; that he was ambitious, acquisitive and interested in money; that he was unscrupulous and opportunistic – not excessively so by the standards of the time, but a man not overly concerned with niceties or troubled by conscience. Judging from his portrait, hanging in the long gallery at Hardwick, he was florid and fleshy, with small, shrewd eyes, and luxuriant moustaches and beard merging into the extravagant expanse of his fur collar. He looks worldly, convivial, a man of hearty appetites. That he liked to live well is borne out by his household accounts and inventories: his table was well supplied, his cellar well stocked (he got through an impressive daily four pints of wine) and his homes lavishly furnished. Bess had married an unabashed consumer.

Marriage to Cavendish propelled Bess out of Derbyshire and into the worlds of London and court, where she had her first real taste of high life brought by wealth and royal favour. The Cavendishes set themselves up in two properties: the manor at Northaw in Hertfordshire, and a rented London house in Newgate Street, in the shadow of the great spire (which would be destroyed by lightning in 1561) of the medieval St Paul's. Newgate Street led into Cheapside, the busy heart of the city, crammed with goldsmiths, shops, lodgings and workshops, where the Cavendish servants, clad in their distinctive blue livery, would have been a familiar sight, scurrying about carrying out commissions for Bess. The Cavendishes kept at least fifteen servants, including a gentlewoman called Cecily, a nurse, a midwife – when Bess was giving birth – a cook, an embroiderer, a housekeeper, a footman, a couple of stewards, various maids, a stable boy and a porter. Some of these servants, such as Francis Whitfield and James Crompe,* stewards in London and Chatsworth respectively, would stay with Bess for many years.

While most of Cheapside was paved, the compacted earth of Newgate Street would have been frequently turned to dust or mud. The Cavendishes negotiated the streets on horseback – the city was just a few miles square – and Bess also had a horse litter, lined in green satin. But they made good use of the river too, hiring a barge and a bargeman to take them to King Edward's court at Whitehall, or to visit Frances and Henry Grey in their London mansion, Suffolk House, in Southwark.[7]

In London, Sir William and Bess were very much part of the Protestant elite, a small band of individuals bound by ties – of blood, marriage and faith – at once close and, when circumstances demanded, easily dissolved. Henry VIII had not wanted a protector, or regent, for his son, and to avoid power residing in any one individual had made a will appointing a regency council of sixteen to rule collectively until Edward's majority. But he died before his will was signed, which allowed for some reinterpretation, if not outright defiance. Three days after his death, the regency council named Edward Seymour, Earl of Hertford and the young King's uncle, as Lord Protector and head of the council. Seymour now became Duke of Somerset; his ally, John Dudley, became Earl of Warwick, and his younger brother, Thomas Seymour, Lord Admiral

---

* A room known as 'Crump's Chamber' appears in the 1601 Chatsworth inventory, though Crompe himself was long dead.

and Baron Sudeley (Sudeley was also appointed to the council). In May 1547, just five months after Henry's death, the attractive and ambitious Thomas Seymour married the Dowager Queen, Catherine Parr, who had been in love with him before she married Henry.

The Seymour faction held the reins of power and, as committed humanist reformers, like King Edward himself, set out to promote the cause of Protestantism. They were also, together with the Greys (whose eldest daughter, Jane, had been placed in the household of Thomas Seymour in 1547, in much the same way that Bess had been in that of the Greys themselves), the Warwicks and William, Marquess of Northampton (brother of Catherine Parr), and his wife, the men and women whom the Cavendishes visited, entertained, gambled with (3s. 4d was 'lost at play with my Lady and my Lord Admiral' – the Sudeleys), and made godparents to their children.

It was during these early years of marriage to Cavendish, when Bess was spending much of her time in London, and at Edward's court, that her cultural tastes were formed, crucially through exposure to humanism, in which many of her friends, including Frances Grey, Elizabeth Brooke (daughter of Lord Cobham and married to William Parr) and the Coke sisters (Mildred, married to William Cecil, Anne, married to Nicholas Bacon, and Elizabeth, married to Sir Thomas Hoby), were passionately interested. The study of ancient, in particular classical, texts lay at the heart of sixteenth-century humanism, and key to their dissemination was the printing press, which made available English translations of the Bible, classical and medieval texts and new European works, architectural books, prints, engravings and illustrations for herbals, all of which Bess would have come across in the homes of her learned friends and at court.[8] From such she absorbed images and references that would inform the design of her houses, both outside and in.

Designs for overmantels and textiles at Hardwick draw on Flemish pattern books, Continental prints and classical and biblical texts. So it was perhaps from Chaucer's *The Legend of Good Women* (his complete works were first printed in 1532 and the Northaw inventory lists a copy) that Bess first heard the stories of Cleopatra and Lucretia, who would feature in the Virtues hangings of noble women – great appliqué textiles made at Chatsworth and now at Hardwick. Here she would be able to display her familiarity with both classical texts and classical architecture – the noble women stand beneath arches, supported by fluted columns topped by Ionic capitals, with an entablature running above.

Bess would have witnessed classicism first hand in Somerset House, then known as Somerset Place, on the Strand. Now Lord Protector, Somerset was de facto ruler of England, and as such he required a suitably splendid London mansion. Work began in 1547, using materials from former monasteries. Built around two courtyards, with a triumphal arch and a classical facade, Somerset House is often cited as the first Renaissance building in England, although there is evidence that classical features were used earlier, from about 1515, in such houses as Southwark Place, Charles Brandon's house.[9] Nevertheless, Somerset House, as it emerged in the late 1540s, would have been a novel sight and certainly a talking point amongst the Cavendishes and their friends. By the time of Somerset's death in 1551, he had spent over £10,000, a huge sum, on his house.[10]

Somerset was a man of many parts: soldier, statesman, builder. His involvement in Henry VIII's military campaigns in Scotland and France and the building of fortifications meant he acquired an understanding of engineering, which fed quite naturally into the building of houses. He was a considerable private patron: in addition to Somerset House, he commissioned Syon House (a former Bridgettine abbey), outside London, and The Brails, a never-completed house at Great Bedwyn, Wiltshire. As a committed reformer, he was open to new ways of thinking, but equally to new developments in architecture and design coming from the

Continent. And, sophisticated and well travelled, he knew how to get his hands on the finest French craftsmen.

Somerset gathered around him a group of men who shared his love of building and would go on to become architectural patrons in their own right: Sir William Cecil, Sir Thomas Smith and Sir John Thynne. All were familiar with classicism, either because they had travelled in France and Italy, or because they had come across architectural books by such as Sebastiano Serlio (Serlio's six-part *L'Architettura* was *the* architectural manual of the Renaissance) and Vitruvius.* Cecil was Somerset's private secretary, later Lord Burghley, Elizabeth I's Secretary of State and Lord Treasurer, and the builder of Burghley House and Theobalds. Smith, Greek scholar, Cambridge don, ambassador to France and Secretary of State, knew as much as anyone in England about Renaissance architecture, owning no fewer than five editions of Vitruvius, supplying Cecil with French architectural books and building Hill Hall in Essex, complete with classical orders and entablatures. Thynne, Somerset's steward and a great friend of the Cavendishes, devoted over thirty years of his life to the building and rebuilding of Longleat. Each was something of an amateur architect: Cecil produced basic plans for Burghley and Theobalds; Smith made drawings for Hill Hall in collaboration with his carpenter-surveyor; Thynne was closely involved in the design of Longleat.

It's unlikely that any one individual was responsible for the design of Somerset House – like most Tudor houses it was a collaborative effort, to which Somerset, Thynne, Smith and the French masons all contributed. It played a key role in the Tudor building world, allowing would-be patrons to cut their teeth and see new ideas put into practice – classical features embellishing traditional design – and enabling craftsmen to hone their skills. It clearly influenced later houses, such as Longleat (the bay windows) and Burghley (the balustrading of the

---

* William Cavendish owned a copy of Vitruvius, inscribed with his name in 1557.

courtyard pavilions). Several craftsmen at Somerset House moved on to the Royal Works: John Revell, a master carpenter, became Surveyor of the Royal Works in 1560, and Humphrey Lovell became the Queen's master mason. Somerset House may also have provided a young mason, Robert Smythson, an apprentice to Lovell, with his first job.

3.

ACQUISITION

In marrying William Cavendish, Bess acquired three stepdaughters. Catherine and Anne, aged twelve and eight in 1547, lived with the Cavendishes and were treated generously by Bess. She bought them sugar candy and clothes: 'for my daughter Cateryn', ells of holland (fine linen) to make partlets (a kind of collar, or bib, covering the neck); 'for my daughter Ane', cloth to make sleeves, cambric and lace for kirtles, and white, red and yellow girdles.[1] However, Sir William's third daughter, Mary, lived elsewhere – regular payments were made 'to the woman that hath Mary' – most likely because she had some kind of disability (by 1556 she was dead). Bess kept close links to her own family: her younger half-sister, Jane Leche, was employed as one of her gentlewomen, as she would be throughout her life, and generously paid, at fifteen shillings a quarter; her aunt, Marcella Linnacre, was also a semi-permanent member of the household and helped with the children.

Bess lost no time in starting a family, giving birth to a daughter, Frances, in 1548, and efficiently producing a baby a year, more or less, for the next eight years. 'Frances my 9 Child and the first by the said Woman', read Sir William's memo, 'was born on Monday between the Hours of 3 and 4 at Afternoon, Viz the 18 of June. Anno 2 RE 6. The dominical Letter then G.'[2] Frances was named after Frances Grey, who was a godparent, along with Katherine Brandon, Lady Suffolk,

Frances Grey's very youthful stepmother (Charles Brandon's second wife, previously betrothed to his son), and Lord Suffolk, Charles Brandon's eldest son by Katherine, aged eleven. The Cavendishes could not have made a clearer statement of their loyalty to the Grey/Brandon family, and they continued to visit Bradgate – a payment to a 'poor man that wrought in the garden at Bradgate' is recorded in the household accounts.

These accounts were itemised daily by Bess herself (in later years, a clerk took over, though entries would always be checked and signed by his mistress, who made a point of keeping a close eye upon her affairs), while Sir William recorded other expenses and income from rents and fees. Probably for the first time, Bess had her own household to manage, and her accounts reveal something of the Cavendishes' domestic life. There are payments for quires of paper, straw for horses, a burden of rushes (for scattering on floors), faggots to light the oven, for mending a frying pan, sacks of coal, grinding kitchen knives, corn for the capons, hogsheads of claret, Rhenish (high-quality) wine, Malmsey (a sweet wine from Crete) and Muscadel, jelly bags, firkins of soap, loaves of sugar and candles. Quantities of linen were bought to make sheets and pillowcases and 'fine diaper' (expensive linen damask) for tablecloths and napkins. A woman was paid for scouring pans (using a mix of oil, chalk and sand), and a Mrs Pulforth for doing the weekly clothes wash. Baby Frances had a coral for her teeth, waistcoats, a red mantle, hose and 'neat caps'. A penknife, scales, weights, paper, wax and an inkhorn were bought for Bess's writing desk, and ginger, aniseed, liquorice and sugar to make a 'dredge' (comfit) for Sir William. Shopping was carted back to Newgate Street by a 'carryer'.

A grocer's bill, from a Robert Harrison, in December 1552, headed evocatively but presumably fancifully 'for all things from the beginning of the world to this day', comes to a hefty £6 11s. 10d. It gives some idea of the astonishing variety of foodstuffs to be found in London: the usual meats (mutton, beef, pork, rabbit, capons, veal), but many small birds too (woodcock, larks, blackbirds, sparrows) and quantities of fish (herring, whiting, eels, shrimps, oysters, lampreys, sole, plaice, cockles, mussels, crab, dabs). There was suet, oatmeal, flour, eggs, 'sweet' and salt butter, fruit according to the season – strawberries, apples, pears, figs – verjuice (crab apple juice, used for preserving) and comfits, to be served at the end of the meal. Yeast went into the 'potech' (pottage) – all Tudor kitchens featured a simmering pot of stock, or broth. Manchet, high-quality white bread, made from wheat flour, was bought expensively from a baker. A flourishing trade with North Africa and the East meant currants, sugar, dates, 'rasings off the sonne' (dried raisins), cinnamon, mace, ginger, almonds, oranges, lemons and 'bay salte' (from the Bay of Biscay, coarse-grained and good for preserving) were all available. Eggs and sack (a sweet white wine from the Iberian peninsula) were bought to make a posset, milk for Frances, with saffron (expensive, but produced in England in the sixteenth century), or sometimes garlic, to flavour it, and ale for Bess's mother and Sir John Berends, the family priest, who often visited Newgate Street.

The Cavendishes, as a rising young couple, eager to know and be known, were busy, social and hospitable. Besides new Protestant reformer friends, Bess kept up with old Derbyshire friends and neighbours. Godfrey Boswell, who had married her sister Jane Hardwick, visited, as did Thomas Babington and Sir James Foljambe, who came with Bess's brother James, and Sir John and Lady Port (Lady Port was from a Derbyshire family and Sir John became sheriff of Derbyshire in 1553). When guests came to dine at Newgate Street – dinner was eaten early, at dusk – the parlour was decorated with 'bowes and flowers and garlands' and sweetened with herbs, and diners were serenaded by a harpist and two minstrels. Not much seems to have been eaten in the way of vegetables, save 'coleworts' (a kind of cabbage) and 'hartechokes', but there were plenty of 'sallats', made with cooked vegetables as well as raw and dressed with herbs, oil and vinegar. Salmon was boiled in ale, eels were soused in brine and apples were roasted or turned into fritters. Shops were open every day until late, so in the event of short rations a servant could be sent out 'at nyghtt' for emergency supplies of cakes or cracknels (hard biscuits).

It was a household of free-spending and largesse. The Cavendishes' annual expenditure, in London between 1552 and 1553, was about £500, while their income, from rents and fees, stood at around £1,000.[3] They could afford to be extravagant. Both Bess and Sir William liked to gamble, and large sums of money – as much as £2 in an evening – were 'lost at play' (to put this in perspective, the rent of the house in Newgate Street, leased from the Marquess of Northampton, was £3 16s. 8d a year). Presents were regularly made: 'my sister Wingfield' (probably Bess's half-sister Elizabeth to whom she was close, or possibly her full sister Mary, who also married into the Wingfield family) had 26s. and 8d 'to buy her a carpet'; Cecily, Bess's gentlewoman, was given, variously, a petticoat, an apron and a pair of shoes; Nan, a maidservant, had 5s. to buy herself a petticoat; Bess bought a 'stele glas', 'bone combe' and brush for her stepdaughter Anne, and in December 1551 (a New Year's gift, perhaps) a needle case, silver thimble and two pairs of gloves for Catherine. In 1550, Sir William presented Bess with a magnificent book 'of gold ... set with stones', including ten rubies and a diamond, containing portraits of the pair of them, a token of esteem and affection, but also of wealth – it cost £14 6s. – cherished by Bess all her life and left to her daughter Frances.

Since Bess and Sir William were mixing in court circles, they had to look the part – sumptuous clothes figure prominently in the household accounts. Cloth was bought to make shirts for Sir William; 'the skinner' (probably of rabbits) was paid 'for furring' his gowns and jerkins; there was bone-work for his shirts and Bess's smocks, lace for her sleeves and collars, and silver and gold metal thread for edging her purse and sleeves, with silk thread to couch (hold down) the metal thread. Metal thread embroidery was highly skilled, the province of professional male embroiderers – 'Angell', in the Cavendish household, later replaced by 'Barnet'. A goldsmith supplied buttons and 'work' for Bess's cape, while 12s. and 4d went to a furrier 'for furring' her 'gown of mole taffeta', and another 12s. for two ounces of gold 'to make lace for handkerchiefs'.

In the summer of 1548, Catherine Parr died in childbirth. Thomas Seymour, just as Catherine had feared, promptly set about plotting to marry Princess Elizabeth and to overthrow his brother, the Duke of Somerset, which led to Seymour's execution in March 1549. There was dissatisfaction with Somerset, too. That summer, Archbishop Cranmer authorised a new Book of Common Prayer, written in English and laying down a religious service along reformist lines (the revised 1552 edition would be more evangelical still). This provoked furious protests and calls for the return of the Mass, which Princess Mary stubbornly continued to celebrate. An uprising began in the West Country, spreading east, and was only suppressed with great brutality and loss of life, for which Somerset was blamed. His fellow members of the Privy Council seized their chance to remove him. Somerset was sent to the Tower and replaced by John Dudley, Earl of Warwick, who now headed the Council and was given the title of Lord President a few months later.

In November, Henry Grey, Marquess of Dorset, the Cavendishes' old friend, was appointed to the Privy Council, probably on account of his reputation as a reformer rather than his political acumen. Grey, along with Dudley and William Parr, Marquess of Northampton, pushed forward with reform: clergy were given permission to marry, stone altars were destroyed, organs ripped out, books burned. Somerset, however, was by no means vanquished. After his release from the Tower in February 1550, he set about trying to oust Dudley, while Dudley took counter-action, persuading King Edward, now twelve, to strengthen his own position, and that of his supporters. In October 1551, Dudley became Duke of Northumberland, while Henry Grey became Duke of Suffolk (the title had become available after the young Brandon brothers had died from the sweating sickness*) and William Parr's brother-in-law, William Herbert, was made Earl of Pembroke (Parr himself, as Marquess of Northampton, hardly needed further elevation). Somerset found himself back in the Tower; his execution in the new year was supervised by Henry Grey.

In the shifting sands of the Tudor court, fortunes rose and fell with terrifying speed. Such fluctuations can be charted in the Cavendishes' choice of godparents for their growing family, as they endeavoured to square loyalty to old friends with strategic currying of favour with the new men. A second daughter, Temperance, was born in June 1549, at Northaw, with Bess's aunt Marcella Linnacre in attendance and presents of nourishing brawn and capons sent by her mother from Derbyshire. Lady Warwick, wife of the on-the-rise John Dudley, was made a godmother, together with Jane Grey, while the Earl of Shrewsbury – a friend of Sir William and father of George, who would become Bess's fourth husband – stood as godfather.

Temperance died within the year, while in December 1550 Bess gave birth to her first son, Henry – 'my bad son Henry' as he was destined to become, the source of much trouble and disappointment. This time the Cavendishes set their sights a little higher in the godparent stakes, choosing Princess Elizabeth (the beginning of a long if occasionally strained association between Bess and the future Queen), the Earl of Warwick, now Lord President and the most powerful man at court, and their old friend Henry Grey. William, born in 1551, got Elizabeth Brooke (Elizabeth's brother married Cavendish's daughter Catherine), the second wife of William Parr, Marquess of Northampton, as a godmother, and William Herbert, the newly ennobled Earl of Pembroke. The

---

* Highly contagious and fatal, this swept through England in a series of epidemics during the first half of the 16th century.

Cavendishes could hardly have allied themselves more closely with the Protestant regime.

In Bess, William Cavendish found a highly competent manager of his family and household as it moved between Northaw and Newgate Street. Indeed, the gift for managing, both husbands and households, would stand Bess in good stead, and would contribute greatly to her desirability as a wife. In 1549, she succeeded in 'managing', or persuading, Sir William into acquiring a further house and household: the manor of Chatsworth, in Derbyshire, together with that of Cromford, and some surrounding land, bought for £600. Although materially, socially and culturally, Bess had left Derbyshire far behind her, it was by no means forgotten.

Chatsworth manor and estate had belonged for several generations to the Leche family, who were well known to Bess, not only because Ralph Leche had been her stepfather, but also because his nephew, Francis, married her younger sister Alice. In 1547, Francis discovered that Alice had been unfaithful to him. Enraged by her 'lewdness', he sold the manor and estate to a Thomas Agard, 'rather than let bastards be his heirs'. Once he'd cooled down, Francis realised he'd been foolish and tried to back out of the sale. Agard insisted that he'd made a legal 'bargain' and the case went to the Duke of Somerset, who ruled in favour of Leche, despite the fact that the sale stood.[4] When Thomas Agard died, his son Francis Agard, rather than holding on to a property that would always be subject to dispute, and to silence the claims of the Leches, sold Chatsworth to the Cavendishes.[5]

Over the next few years, they pursued a determined programme of land-buying, consolidating and expanding on their new purchase. In 1550, the manor of Ashford, a few miles north of Chatsworth, which would later provide Bess with blackstone for Hardwick, was bought from the Earl of Westmorland, and the rectory at Edensor, adjoining Chatsworth, from William Place and Nicholas Spakeman. Further blocks of land were added later, acquisitions that were funded in part by the sale of property in Hertfordshire.[6] Rents, from land and property, would provide a steady stream of revenue.

In 1551, Sir William seemingly decided to move his power base entirely to Derbyshire. That December, Crown commissioners arrived at Northaw to assess its value. The Cavendishes, as a sweetener, sent gifts of capons, conies (rabbits) and woodcocks to Northaw, together with a lavish consignment of fish: one 'great ling', whiting, forty herrings, flounders and a pike. In June 1552, Sir William made what proved to be an extremely profitable deal. Northaw and other Hertfordshire property, together with estates in Wales and Lincolnshire, were sold to the Crown, and in return he received extensive estates in Derbyshire – most of them formerly monastic property – as well as land and property in Lincolnshire, Nottinghamshire, Dorset, Devon, Cornwall, Northumberland, Kent and Herefordshire.[7] The core of the estate, however, lay in Derbyshire.

What prompted this move? Was Sir William so enamoured of his wife that he simply fell in with her plans, giving up his Hertfordshire home, which, on the Great North Road, was so conveniently close to London and court, and relocating to a remote corner of the Midlands? Or were there considerations of security, rather than sentiment, at work? Northaw's proximity to London also made it vulnerable in the event of unrest or civil war, and with a Protestant boy king on the throne and the fervently Catholic Princess Mary as the next in line, that was a real possibility. There were fears, too, that should Edward die, Mary might hand back confiscated Church property, out of which Sir William had done so well. Still, the possibility of Church land being returned did not stop him from acquiring more, and it seems more likely that he simply saw a good deal and took advantage of it, urged on by Bess. Sir William, shrewd speculator that he was, would never have embarked on a property-buying spree in Derbyshire if it hadn't made sound business sense. But the impetus surely came from his wife, who had probably been tipped off about the Chatsworth sale by her mother or sister. All these new estates were cannily bought in the names of both Sir William and Bess, thus ensuring that in the event of Sir William dying and his heir being underage, they would come under the control not of the Court of Wards, but of his wife. This was unusual, and though we don't know for sure, it's tempting to see Bess's hand at work again – she was not going to fall into the clutches of the Court of Wards for a second time. She also, with Chatsworth, now had a foothold in Derbyshire, and her first building project.

'Every man almost is a builder', wrote William Harrison, 'and he that hath bought any small parcel of ground, be it never so little, will not be quiet till he have pulled down the old house (if any were there standing) and set up a new after his own devise.'[8] So it was with the Cavendishes.

Today's Chatsworth, freshly gilded, sitting massively in its parkland, retains almost nothing of Bess's house. This was demolished in the seventeenth century by her great-great-grandson, William Cavendish, the 4th Earl and 1st Duke of Devonshire, who in its place, on the same foundations, built the present house (later enlarged by the 6th Duke). Of the Elizabethan original mere traces remain: the hunting tower, known as 'The Stand' (from which to watch the hunt, also used as an occasional banqueting house); a moated structure in the park called 'Queen Mary's Bower'; and some cellars. However, within the solid ducal splendour lurks 'the ghost of the Elizabethan house', detected in Chatsworth's unusual height and the configuration of the interior, especially the positioning of the state rooms on the top floor.[9]

'He that builds a fair house upon an ill seat committeth himself to prison.' So wrote Francis Bacon.[10] Site mattered to Elizabethan builders, and that of Chatsworth, in the valley of the Derwent, with the river below and the drama of the moors as a craggy backdrop, could hardly be bettered.* It was decided that the existing crumbling manor would be demolished and a new house built on an altogether grander scale, a house that would proclaim the Cavendishes' wealth and status, a house that would announce their arrival in Derbyshire in no uncertain terms.

In the meantime, however, they simply patched up the old manor as best they could. In November 1551, ironwork for two 'portalls' (doors) was sent up from London, with 'old Alsope the caryer', along with thirty dozen candles, wrapped in blankets, and quantities of oranges and lemons.[11] The following month, a carpenter carried out repairs, and on 26 December Roger Worde (or Worthe), a mason, was paid 20s. for drawing a 'platt' (plan) of the new house.[12] Worde was clearly no ordinary mason: like Robert Smythson, he could draw. Five years later, now 'Mason to Sir W. Cecil', he was writing to his patron asking for clarification as to the design of the windows at Cecil's house, Burghley: 'I shall desire you to draw your meaning ... both the width of the light and the height, with the fashion of all the molds ... I would be very glad to know your pleasure for your steps forth of your base court up to the terrace, the proportion of them and for the gate at the end of the terrace.'[13]

The worldly, wily Cecil, who would become a loyal friend to and supporter of Bess, had risen, like Cavendish, from the ranks of the gentry (in Cecil's case, minor and Welsh). His father and grandfather had served in the households of Henry VII and Henry VIII and used their fortunes to buy estates in the Midlands. Cecil, again like Cavendish, negotiated the reigns of Edward VI and Mary I, and would make himself indispensable to Elizabeth I, whose coolness and caution matched his own. But he lacked a country seat. In 1553, he began remodelling an existing manor at Burghley, Lincolnshire, which would be improved upon and expanded over more than thirty years.[14]

---

* Daniel Defoe, looking over the moors above Chatsworth in the 1720s, saw 'a waste and howling wilderness' (Hey, p.12).

Work on the new Chatsworth probably began in the spring of 1552. Like Burghley, it was a courtyard house, originally two storeys high and one room deep. A needlework cushion of the 'platt of Chatesworth house', which Bess later kept in the long gallery at Hardwick, shows the west (main) front of the house, complete with the extra storey that she added in the 1570s, and four towers, one at each end and one either side of the gatehouse, through whose arch you can just glimpse a fountain in the courtyard.[15] Architecturally there was nothing very original about the Cavendishes' Chatsworth; indeed, it was a rather old-fashioned building, looking back to the quadrangular fortified mansions of the past. In its height, compactness and towers it belonged to the court Gothic tradition, recalling the likes of Richmond Palace, built by Henry VII.[16] What was unusual, though not without precedent, was the placing of the state rooms (high great chamber, long gallery, withdrawing chamber, best bedchamber), with their lofty windows and ceilings, not on the first floor, as was conventional, but on the second. Here, in the Elizabethan Chatsworth, was 'the first expression of a passion for high buildings' that stayed with Bess throughout her life and would be recreated in both Hardwick Old and New Halls.[17]

However, in the early 1550s, the complete three-storey Chatsworth was some way off and the Cavendishes were making do in the old house. Court business kept them in London for lengthy periods, so the management of their new estate and building frequently had to be conducted long-distance, with the inevitable frustrations and misunderstandings. In November 1552 comes Bess's first surviving letter, a characteristic mix of instruction and admonition, written to the steward at Chatsworth, Francis Whitfield: she has spoken to Sir William and he's happy that the carpenter should have whatever 'cleats' (boards) he needs, provided that 'you take such as will do him no soreness about his building at Chatsworth' – it's most important that repairs to the old house don't compromise the building of the new. Francis is ordered to 'look well to all things at Chatsworth' until Bess's aunt Linnacre comes home, and to 'let the brewer make beer for me forthwith for my own drinking and your master and see that I have good store of it, for if I lack either good beer or charcoal or wood I will blame nobody as much as I will do you. Cause the floor in my bed chamber to be made even either with plaster, clay or lime and all the windows where the glass is broken to be mended and all the chambers to be made as close and warm as you can.' She is extremely put out to hear that her sister, Jane Leche, who had been left at Chatsworth, was not being properly treated – 'if it be true you lack a great [*sic*] of honesty as well as discretion to deny her any thing that she has a mind to ... I would be loathe to have any stranger so used in my house as then assure yourself I can not like it to have my sister so used. Like as I would not have any super-fluity or waste of any thing so like wise would I have her to have that which is needful and necessary.' With this last sentence we have Bess in essence: excess and waste were abhorred, yet things had to be done properly, with due care. 'At my coming home I shall know more', she finishes, 'and then I will think as I shall have cause.'[18] Francis Whitfield must have quailed.

In February 1553, King Edward succumbed to a chill that he seemed unable to shake off, and by the spring it was clear that he was suffering from tuberculosis. Edward faced the problem that beset Tudor monarchs – the lack of an heir, and specifically a male heir. Possibly encouraged by the Duke of Northumberland, he decided to draw up 'My Device for the Succession', a startling document that overrode Henry VIII's Third Act of Succession and passed over the claims of Mary and Elizabeth on the grounds of their illegitimacy, though Edward's primary concern, reasonably enough, was that Mary would undo his Church reforms. Instead, the throne was left to the sons who might be born to Frances Grey, now thirty-five, and failing that the sons of Jane, Katherine or Mary Grey. Mary Tudor, however, remained by far the strongest claimant, and the Cavendishes, knowing this, took pains to cultivate her, paying visits to 'my Lady Mary's Grace' and making small gifts – a 'glass' (mirror), 3s. and 4d 'towards her purse'. At times of such uncertainty, when thrones, faith and heads all looked precarious, it was as well to hedge your bets.

William Cecil, who had become Edward's Secretary of State, claimed that it was William's Parr's wife, Elizabeth Brooke, who suggested that fifteen-year-old Jane Grey marry Northumberland's fourth son, Lord Guildford Dudley. At the same time, Katherine Grey was to marry Henry, Lord Herbert, son of William Herbert, Earl of Pembroke. These were strategic alliances, to shore up the Protestant regime. But in May, shortly after the double marriage had taken place, Edward's health took a turn for the worse and he made a further change to his will: the throne was to go to Frances Grey's male heirs, but if none such were born before Edward died, it was to go to Jane Grey and her male heirs. In effect, Jane was named as future Queen.

The Cavendishes would have known that Edward was dying. They would also have been aware of the turmoil that his death might bring – the now very real risk of civil war. They could, of course, count on the goodwill and favour of Jane Grey, but her accession was far from a certainty. As, if not more, likely was the prospect of a Catholic queen, Mary, and Mary might not look kindly on Sir William, gifts or no gifts. It was only prudent for the Cavendishes to remove themselves to a safe distance from London. In June 1553, with Bess pregnant once again, they set out for Chatsworth.

4

'EVERY MAN ALMOST IS A BUILDER'

The Cavendishes were at Chatsworth when Edward VI died in July 1553. News would have filtered its way to them of the proclamation of Jane Grey as Queen, which was swiftly followed by Princess Mary's own claim. The people of England had by no means embraced Protestantism and there was a great deal of popular enthusiasm for Mary – she was, after all, Henry's daughter, and a Tudor, and the Tudor lineage exerted a powerful hold. Then too, Jane's *éminence grise* John Dudley, the Duke of Northumberland, was a much-hated figure. Support for Jane melted away, just as, in the east of England, where Mary had estates, it swelled for the Princess. Once it was clear that Jane didn't have the backing of the people, courtiers and councillors, beginning with William Herbert, Earl of Pembroke, fell over themselves in their haste to declare allegiance to Mary. Jane Grey, sixteen years old, the 'Nine Days' Queen', who had never sought the throne, found herself imprisoned in the Tower, together with her husband Guildford Dudley and her father Henry Grey. Northumberland, godfather to little Henry Cavendish, was executed in August; the following month saw the coronation of Mary, England's first female monarch.

The Cavendishes no doubt congratulated themselves on being out of the way, but these would still have been highly alarming events. The Protestant elite, to whom they'd bound themselves so closely, stood in disarray. They might well have been tainted by association, but those little attentions to Princess Mary seem to have paid off. Sir William found himself called back to court. Once again, probably against all expectation, and unlike most of Edward VI's courtiers, he held on to his position as Treasurer.

It was something of a coup, and incontrovertible proof that Queen Mary bore Sir William no ill will, that she agreed to stand as godmother to the Cavendishes' third son, Charles, born in November 1553. Stephen Gardiner, Bishop of Winchester, and long-term supporter of Mary, was a godfather, together with, for the second time, Henry Grey. The latter seems an oddly tactless, indeed reckless, choice, given that Grey had worked directly to supplant Mary with his own daughter. At a time when alliances changed with the wind and self-preservation was all – the Pembroke family, for example, lost no time in distancing themselves from the Greys, by seeking an annulment of the marriage between Henry Herbert and Katherine – the Cavendishes remained steadfast. But Mary had always been close to her cousin Frances Grey, despite their religious differences, and initially she chose to see Northumberland as the villain of the piece. Henry, thanks to his wife's pleas, had been pardoned and released from the Tower with a fine, presumably to the relief of the Cavendishes, allowing them to conciliate all parties, to demonstrate allegiance to the throne and loyalty to the Greys. The christening took place just two weeks after Jane Grey and her husband were tried and found guilty of high treason.

Shortly before Bess was due to give birth once again, in March 1555, Sir William wrote to his friend Sir John Thynne. Thynne and Cavendish had a certain amount in common – both demonstrated a gift for riding the cross-currents of Tudor politics, and both were keenly interested in money and building. Even their portraits share something, not so much a matter of feature as of atmosphere: a high-coloured forceful-ness, an air of tightly controlled energy. They had probably met at court and they certainly visited each other, at Longleat, Thynne's

Wiltshire house, and Chatsworth. Now Sir William hoped Thynne could help him out of a fix.

He was in need of a house, near London, an alternative to Newgate Street, 'for the repose of myself, wife and children', and having searched fruitlessly had remembered Thynne's house at Brentford, which Thynne had built in 1549. Might he be able to lease it? Bess, apparently, was 'not disposed, as women be' – here Cavendish became jocular – '(if I durst say) fantastical, to lie in' at the Newgate Street house, on the grounds that Sir William's previous wife had died in childbirth there. This seems surprising: Bess does not come across as a woman inclined to the 'fantastical', but she apparently had a streak of superstition. Childbirth was always risky, and the birth of her last baby, Charles, may have been particularly difficult. 'Beseeching you good Mr Thynne', continued Sir William, 'to take it in good part and to consider if you were not my friend I would not so boldly have asked you … And for your stuff within your house shall be so handled and used that if any thing be lacking … I will either buy new or supply the lack and default with money.' He hoped to be able to keep the house until Bess had been delivered and churched, and ideally to stay for at least a year, since court business required that he 'tarry' in London for a while.[1]

Thynne was agreeable, and Elizabeth Cavendish was born at Brentford on 31 March. This time the Cavendishes made Katherine Grey, Jane's younger sister, godmother, despite the fact that by now, after the Wyatt rebellion the previous year, the Greys were thoroughly disgraced. Henry Grey had hardly been released from the Tower in July 1553 before he was plotting, with Sir Thomas Wyatt and others, to place Princess Elizabeth on the throne (Mary's betrothal to the Catholic Philip of Spain was deeply unpopular with all, and the Protestant reformers in particular). The rebellion was planned as a series of revolts, led by local bigwigs – Sir Thomas Wyatt in Kent, Sir James Croft in the Welsh Marches, Sir Peter Carew in the south-west, and Henry Grey in Leicestershire – which would converge on London.

But the plot was betrayed and Grey, along with the other conspirators, was arrested once again.

Mary could hardly be expected to show mercy to the Greys now, and one can only wonder why Henry Grey imperilled himself and his daughter by involving himself in the Wyatt rebellion at all. He was executed in February 1554, eleven days after the executions of Jane Grey and Guildford Dudley. In March, his brother Thomas also lost his head, for carrying messages from the conspirators to members of Princess Elizabeth's household. It was a dangerous time to be a Grey, or indeed to know one. Three weeks after her husband's death, Frances married her Master of the Horse, Adrian Stokes, a loss of status that saved her skin – as plain Mrs Stokes, she forfeited any claim to the throne and no longer represented a threat to Mary.

What did Bess make of Frances's hasty marriage? An act of prudence, or folly? Given that the Cavendishes reasserted their friendship with the Greys by making Katherine a godmother, the latter seems more likely. What we can be sure of is that, for Bess, the death of Jane Grey, whom she'd first met as a precocious eight-year-old at Bradgate and whom she'd made godmother to her second daughter, Temperance, must have brought deep shock and sadness. Jane, just seventeen years old, met her death with courage and grace, but as she fumbled, blindfolded, for the block, crying, 'What shall I do? Where is it?' few could have been unmoved. Bess, though not a witness, would have heard the reports. She kept a portrait of Jane in her bedchamber at Chatsworth for the rest of her life.[2]

In 1555, ensconced at Brentford, where Bess was recovering from the birth of Elizabeth, and Sir William found 'ease and quietness', another letter was dispatched to Thynne and his 'good lady your bedfellow'. Cavendish had a further request: 'I understand that you have a cunning plasterer at Longleat who hath in your hall and in other places of your house made diverse pendants and other pretty things. If your business be at an end or will be by the next summer after this that cometh in

I would pray you that I might have him in Derbyshire for my hall is yet un-made.'[3] Sir William's duties at court curtailed time at Chatsworth, but work on the new house was continuing. Having seen, or heard of, the decorative plasterwork at Longleat, which Thynne had been building for several years, the Cavendishes wanted something of similar quality for their great hall. A good deal of exchange of and competition for craftsmen went on between patrons. Highly skilled men, especially plasterers and masons, were in short supply and much sought after.

An aerial view of England during the latter half of the sixteenth century would have revealed something of a frenzy of construction. 'Prodigy houses' may have been the most visible face of the building boom, but they were a minority phenomenon. Houses of every shape and size appeared all over the country: houses built in the shape of a letter, or employing elaborate geometry and symbolism, manor houses, banqueting houses, lodges, almshouses. Building mania took hold right across the social scale, from old and new nobility to gentry and yeomen. A stable government and a flourishing economy meant standards of living rose, and with them a growing interest in domestic comfort. At the same time, labour was cheap. And in the wake of the Dissolution, land came up for grabs and social structures loosened. This was the era of the self-made man: canny lawyers, civil servants, merchants, sheriffs and adventurers made fortunes, and what better way to display your fortune than to build a house?

A new breed of builder and a new kind of house. The fortified courtyard homes of medieval England began to make way for more compact, outward-looking houses, houses that experimented with new ideas about design and decorative detail coming from Europe, houses that were more about comfort than security, but which also pleased and intrigued the eye. 'Curious' became a term of approbation. They were lived in differently too. An increasing desire for privacy meant that rooms became more specialised in their uses, whether for eating, or entertaining, or sleeping, and that servants and family were increasingly separate. The great hall, once the noisy heart of the house, was now relegated to the servants, while their employers moved upstairs. And the service buildings (bakehouse, brewhouse, wash-house, etc.), instead of cluttering the forecourt, were removed to a distance.

William Cavendish, William Cecil and John Thynne, newly ennobled and newly rich, were all new builders. Thynne would have been regarded by the Cavendishes not just as a friend, but as something of an authority in the building game. He had been closely involved in the various architectural projects undertaken by the Duke of Somerset, whose steward he had become in 1536, probably contributing to the design of Somerset's proposed Wiltshire house, The Brails, and possibly that of Somerset House. According to a satire written about Thynne by a neighbour in 1575, he was responsible for 'infesting his Master's head with plattes and forms and many a subtle thing'.[4] After Somerset's fall in 1549 (on his execution, in January 1552, Somerset House remained unfinished), Thynne found himself out of a job and spending ten months in the Tower. However, like Cavendish, he was a survivor, and despite having to stump up a hefty fine of £2,000, he managed to hold on to much of the fortune he'd accumulated while in Somerset's employ, as well as his estates, most of them in the West Country. Released from the Tower, he retired to Wiltshire, to personally oversee the building of Longleat, a former Carthusian priory that he'd acquired in 1540, during the Dissolution.

Thynne had plenty of money to pour into his project, his own fortune boosted by an advantageous marriage to Christian Gresham, daughter of the wealthy Sir Richard Gresham and sister of Sir Thomas, who built the Royal Exchange (after Christian's death in 1566, Thynne married Dorothy Wroughton). But he hadn't just profited financially from his years in Somerset's household; he also understood the mechanics of building a great house, as well as the basic principles of Renaissance architecture, and he'd acquired some expertise in drawing up plans and designs. All of which made him unusually qualified among Tudor patrons.

The first phase of building work at Longleat began in 1547 with a straightforward conversion of the existing monastic buildings into a house. For much of this period, Thynne was in London with Somerset, or, after Somerset's fall, in the Tower, which meant long-distance supervision of the work. He was a micro-manager par excellence and he bombarded his steward at Longleat, John Dodd, with daily – sometimes twice-daily – letters, a barrage of instruction, exhortation and complaint: John Berryman, Thynne's chief mason, was to come to London to receive his orders; the joiners must 'make as much haste as they may', so the wood had time to season; the plumber was to set Thynne's arms on the pipes of the tower, as well as on the other pipes around the house; the whereabouts of the glazier must be discovered; the young apricot and cherry trees were to be watered.[5] In June 1547, Thynne, keen to make progress, wanted extra rough-layers and masons taken on, which, he felt, shouldn't present any difficulty, because the war with France, and hence the building of fortifications, was now over and craftsmen were no longer subject to impressment: 'they shall be in no danger of the commissioners now it is peace'.[6]

In winter, exterior building work largely came to a halt and many found themselves out of a job. Those working on country houses, beyond the umbrella of a trade guild, were entirely dependent on the whims of their employers. Thynne certainly had no compunction when it came to laying off men. 'I will not keep one workman that shall work day work [those paid by the day, usually labourers] after Michelmas ... but you shall not need to let the workmen themselves know it', he wrote to Dodd in August 1547.[7] That October, Dodd was ordered to make sure that the tower and porch were rough-cast (the rough plastering of external walls) before the frosts and that the window in the chapel was put in before 'the men go'. However, work on the interiors of the house *could* proceed through the winter: the joiners were to carry on with the parlour and the chamber above it, while the masons were to prepare stone for the following spring.[8]

'To my servant John Dod at Longleat haste haste haste' is a familiar refrain. And 'I may command what I will and you will do what you do list, but trust to it you shall pay hereafter' pretty much sums up Thynne's attitude towards his workforce.[9] He's a hard man to warm to and was clearly impossible to work for – demanding, impatient, suspicious, capricious and mean. However, such qualities were accompanied by a restless energy and perfectionism that served him well as a patron, driving him to build and rebuild until he had the house he wanted. Dodd assured his master that Longleat was shaping up to be 'the first house and handsomest that is or shall be … within the compass of four shires … and so doth all the country report, some grieved and some pleased'.[10] But Thynne was not easily mollified, preferring to believe himself cheated and taken advantage of at every turn. He was forever 'marvelling' at some instance of incompetence or neglect: 'I marvel that I should now lack lead for if it be not stolen or bribed away I know I should have had sufficient … as I have always said I am served with words.'[11] After 1549, the stream of letters dries up. And by 1553, when the next phase of building began, Thynne was on site to boss and bully in person.

The Cavendishes were eager to inspect Longleat's progress, but by 1556, Sir William's health had deteriorated. In June, a few months after Bess had given birth to her seventh child, Mary (Lucretia, her last, born in 1557, would die young), he told Thynne that 'god willing having my health which I thank God I have partly recovered', he and Bess hoped to visit Longleat before Bartholomew's Fair, held in mid August, or earlier if he could get away from court.'[12] But a few weeks later, he wrote again: 'I am fallen into my old disease and sickness and

---

* Bartholomew's Fair was one of the largest and most popular fairs, held in the fields beyond Smithfield, outside London.

am so sick that I shall not be able to ride.' The Longleat visit was postponed. He sent a present of larks by way of apology and signed off 'from Chattysworth my pore house'.[13] This was no more than a figure of speech – Chatsworth by now was anything but 'poor'.

The new house, though by no means finished, was already a very substantial two-storey building, for which the Cavendishes were steadily accumulating magnificent furnishings. Wealth and status in Elizabethan houses were displayed not in fine furniture, but in plate and textiles – tapestries, hangings, cushions and carpets. So a bed was judged by the splendour of its hangings, rather than by the bed itself. According to an inventory of William Cavendish's goods (dated 1553, but in fact drawn up in 1559, after his death) Chatsworth had no fewer than forty-eight tapestries, two enormous 'Turkey' (Turkish) carpets (twenty-one and fifteen feet long respectively), nineteen smaller carpets (laid over tables and cupboards), quantities of napkins and tablecloths made of 'fyne diaper' and even greater quantities of gold and silver plate – basins, ewers, porringers (shallow bowls), spoons, snuffers, casting bottles, standing cups and goblets. The Cavendishes' marriage bed had black velvet hangings embossed with cloth of gold and silver and embroidered with gold and pearls, five curtains of yellow and white damask, and a black velvet cover, worked with silver and embroidered with purle (a form of embroidery, using coiled metal thread) and pearls.*[14] If there was nothing very remarkable, architecturally, about Chatsworth's exterior, its interiors, swathed in richly coloured textiles, shimmering with plate, would have dazzled.

While some of these furnishings – beds, for example – had come from Sir William's Northaw manor, much must have been bought or made specifically for Chatsworth. The Cavendishes were living in considerable style. Then too, they had been steadily building up their

---

* The bed was later removed, by Bess, to Hardwick, where it gave its name to the Pearl Bedchamber.

landholdings around Chatsworth. How had all this been paid for? Not, it seems, exclusively from Sir William's revenues.

In the spring of 1557, Sir William received a bombshell: a commission of privy councillors, headed by the Lord Treasurer, William Paulet, had been appointed to look into his accounts, as Treasurer of the Chamber, and had found a discrepancy to the tune of a very substantial £5,237 5s. Sir William was called to account, although why is not altogether clear. He had bought his office; his salary (£100) was modest; boosting it with the sale of favours, or some discreet siphoning-off of revenues, was no more than standard practice at the Tudor court. Perhaps he had simply overstepped what was considered acceptable. Perhaps Queen Mary was in need of money to finance the war against France into which she had been, reluctantly, dragged, as Spain's ally, by her husband Philip, who had by now more or less deserted her. Perhaps someone at court had their own reasons for wanting to get rid of Cavendish.

There was no denying the accusation, and Sir William grovelled. He offered various excuses and explanations: a servant, Thomas Knot, whom he'd inherited from the previous Treasurer, had absconded during 'the time of my sickness', taking £1,231; there had been several instances, under Henry VIII and Edward VI, when he'd incurred expenses for which he'd never been repaid; he even cited £700 that he'd supposedly spent on raising a force against Northumberland, in defence of Mary in 1553.[15] He offered lands, fees and goods in payment of the debt, though claiming these were of no value. And he begged for mercy. If he was forced to repay the whole sum he, his 'poor wife' and 'innocent Children' would be 'utterly undone, like to end our latter days in no small penury'.[16] Sir William was due to appear before the Privy Council, to answer charges, in October. He was facing a crisis, his health was failing and he wanted Bess by his side. On 20 August, she set out from Chatsworth to join him.

Bess travelled fast – three days, on horseback, with stops at Northampton, St Albans and Barnet. Her accounts record the expenses of the journey: new shoes for the horses, and, at Northampton, famous for its shoemakers, new shoes for two footmen and for Bess's daughter Elizabeth; canvas to provide padding under a saddle; drink for the men; a fire for Bess's chamber at an inn (it must have been a chilly August).[17] Once in London, she set about stocking up the larder and cellars, buying beef, veal, rabbits, chickens, butter, salt, pepper, nutmeg, mace, mutton, damsons, pears, a pie for 'Master Harry's' breakfast, pigeons, sparrows, calves' feet, oysters, shrimps, cherries, strawberries, rushes, coal, candles, and a great many gallons of ale, and pints of wine and sack for 'my master'.[18]

Cavendish had seemingly lost none of his appetite, but he was not well enough to appear before the Council in person in October, appointing two clerks, William Cade and Robert Bestnay, to appear in his stead. On 12 October, Bestnay handed over a book containing an account of his master's debts and his pleas for mercy. The following day, Bess's household accounts come to a halt. Perhaps Sir William had taken a turn for the worse. He died on 25 October (an outbreak of influenza killed thousands over the autumn and winter of 1557–8, but Cavendish probably died from whatever 'sickness' he'd been suffering from over the previous couple of years). He was buried at St Botolph's church, Aldgate, joining his mother and first wife.

For Bess, this was a devastating loss. Cavendish was only forty-nine, and, despite recent poor health, a man with the kind of vigour that seemed to defy mortality. Theirs had been a life of common purpose, a joint enterprise – the amassing of a great estate in Derbyshire, the building of a great house, the production of children. And now that life, a decade of happy marriage, was over, leaving Bess a widow at thirty-six, with seven young children – Lucretia, the baby, just a few months old* – and one unmarried stepdaughter (Catherine Cavendish had married Thomas Brooke), without the protection and the

---

* Lucretia was still alive in June 1558, when Bess had velvet shoes made for her, but then disappears from the record (Devonshire MSS, Chatsworth, HM/3, f.20).

direction of Sir William. No letters from Bess to Cavendish survive and we have no record of her feelings, but if love can be inscribed by the embroiderer's needle, then *The Cavendish Hanging* tells its story. As does Bess's entry in the notebook in which Sir William had noted the hour of their marriage: 'Memorandum. That Sir William Cavendish Knight my most dear and well beloved Husband departed this present Life of Monday being the 25th day of October between the Hours of 8 and 9 of the same day at Night in the year of our Lord God 1557. The dominical Letter then C. On whose Soul I most humbly beseech the Lord to have Mercy and Rid me and his poor Children out of our great Misery.'[19]

5

'MY HONEST SWETE CHATESWORTH'

Everything that Bess and Sir William had built together suddenly looked under threat. Bess did not have to fear the Court of Wards, since Cavendish's portfolio of land and property had been bought in their joint names, and as a result Chatsworth and its estates, though entailed on Bess's eldest son Henry, were hers for her lifetime, to be presided over and improved upon. And she had a reasonable income from rents, calculated in 1558 as around £300, while her outgoings stood at about £200, though 1558 was a particularly expensive year as much of it was spent in London.[1] However, there were large amounts owing, too: money had been borrowed to extend the Chatsworth estate, not to mention Sir William's £5,000 debt, which was now hanging over Bess's head. It looked as though she might be 'utterly undone', as Cavendish had feared.

In January 1558, a bill came before Parliament, which, if it became law, would allow lands to be confiscated for the recovery of debts such as those left by William Cavendish. This would directly affect Bess and threaten her Derbyshire estates. She could, of course, have raised money to settle her debts by selling off some of those estates. But this she was not prepared to do. Instead she tried to marshal support from powerful friends such as Sir John Thynne.

'I am now driven to crave your help', she wrote to Thynne in February. 'There is a bill in the parliament house against me ... it doth touch many and if it pass it will not only undo me and my poor children but a great number of others.' The bill had been read twice in the 'Lords' House', and was to be read in the 'Lower House' (the Commons) in the next few days. It was short notice, but could Thynne get to London to vote against it? 'If you be here of Friday you shall stand me in good stead', she added in a postscript, and in the margin, in a rare moment of whimsy, she doodled a ewer, holding a flower.[2] We don't know if Thynne made it to London, but the bill was opposed, as Bess explained in a letter written on the 25th: 'hitherto I have taken no hurt by the parliament, yet do I still stand in great fear and shall do until such time as the parliament ends which I wish daily, for the bill has as yet been but once read and is so evil liked of the house that I trust through the help of such as you and other true ... friends it shall take small effect'.[3] She was right – the bill, on the Queen's orders, was abandoned.

In March, Bess felt able to return to Chatsworth, after a six-month absence. The journey, on horseback, after winter rains, along mud-bound tracks, was, as she told Thynne, long and 'foul', with her horse struggling to 'pass through the tough mire'. She had been ill, too – 'I have escaped one of my fits since my coming home and doubt not in short time to recover my health' (this is the only reference to Bess suffering from 'fits'). Things had not been well looked after at Chatsworth, which was in a state of disarray, but for all that she could not but delight in the house itself – 'for the good order and kindliness of it I dare compare it to any within this realm'.[4]

During her marriage to Cavendish, Bess had learned to run several households, but estate business had been Sir William's province. Newly widowed and not yet confident as a woman of property, she felt in need of advice and turned to Thynne, who arranged for one of his servants, a Mr Hyde, probably a steward or lawyer, to visit Chatsworth. 'Master Hyde' proved most helpful, as Bess reported: 'he has taken much pain to bring my disordered things in to some good order. I shall by his means be able so to use my tenants as I trust they shall not much deceive me'. She did her best to induce Thynne to come to Chatsworth: 'I would I could persuade you that your nearest way to London were to come to Chatsworth or else that you would choose this time to go see your land in Yorkshire. If any occasion might bring you hither so that it were not ill to you I would be very glad of it ... I will cease troubling you with my scribbling, from my poor house at Chatsworth.'[5]

Having set Chatsworth to rights, Bess returned to London, with the children joining her in June.[6] Once again, she rented Thynne's Brentford house. That summer, the talk in London would all have been of Queen Mary's deteriorating health – another false pregnancy in the spring had left her suffering from headaches, depression, insomnia and poor vision. She could expect no comfort from Philip, who was in Spain, as he had been ever since his last visit to England the previous year. By the autumn, it was clear that Mary was dying, and she named Elizabeth, her half-sister, though still a bastard in Mary's eyes, as her successor. Elizabeth was living at Hatfield, Hertfordshire, a few miles north-east of St Albans. When Bess left London for Chatsworth at the end of September, it would have been but a short detour off the Great North Road to visit Hatfield. She may well have taken the chance to pay her respects to Elizabeth; with Mary dying, it was important to position herself to advantage with the incoming Queen.

Bess would have first come across Elizabeth as a teenager, on her visits to Edward's court with Sir William, and they were on friendly enough terms for the Cavendishes to make the young princess godmother to their firstborn son, Henry. Now twenty-five, Elizabeth was a little over ten years younger than Bess. Both were strong-willed, fearless redheads. Both would have recognised something formidable in the other, a glint of steel. Both were prepared to take on a man's world on their own terms. If Bess needed an example of what a woman could achieve, then she needed to look no further than Elizabeth – a female monarch who chose not to be answerable to either a husband or her councillors. However, where the Queen's unique position was largely defined by her unmarried state – marriage was a trap to be avoided, a curtailment to independence – Bess's ascent was only made possible *through* marriage. And where Bess, though by no means averse to scheming, was decisive and forthright, Elizabeth was the mistress of vacillation and equivocation, supremely artful and subtle in her dealings with others. But there is nothing to suggest that in the early years relations between the two were anything but cordial, founded on mutual, perhaps wary, respect.

On 17 November 1558, Mary died, aged forty-two. Four days earlier, Bess, anxious to be at the centre of events, had arrived in London and reopened the Brentford house. She opened a new account book too – 'the charges for my house begun the 26 of November' – engaged a boy to look after her sheep (Brentford was no more than a village) and went shopping. All the children and Bess herself needed new clothes, which meant the purchase of ells* of buckram, ells of holland, yards of black fustian and of gold and black sarcenet (a fine, soft cloth, often used for linings), mockado (deep-piled velvet), lace and black and white feathers. 'Harry' (Henry) had a pair of shoes to dance in and 'Wyll' (William) had gloves and hose.[7]

On 14 January, under heavy grey skies, huddled against flurries of snow, Bess's daughters, Frances and Elizabeth, stood in new clothes, their hair freshly dressed, to watch Elizabeth I process in a horse litter from the Tower to Westminster.[8] Bess does not seem to have been with them, probably because she had been invited to the abbey to witness the coronation the following morning, along with her sons Henry and William, whose hair had been especially 'polled' by a barber in honour of the occasion. Also in the abbey would have been one of the new Queen's most loyal servants – Sir William St Loe.

---

* A measure of length: one ell being equivalent to six hand breadths, or 45 inches.

William St Loe, born in 1518, was the eldest son of Sir John St Loe, of Sutton Court, Chew Magna.[9] The St Loes were an old Somerset family, with a history of service, both royal and military. William had three younger brothers, Edward, John and Clement, and a sister, Elizabeth. As a boy he was tutored by the distinguished scholar John Palsgrave, who had also taught Henry VIII's sister Mary, and Henry's illegitimate son Henry Fitzroy, and who thought highly of William's intelligence. William made his first appearance on the public stage in 1536, when he became a gentleman usher in the household of Henry Courtenay, Marquess of Exeter, but two years later Courtenay was convicted of high treason – for plotting against the King – and executed. William, now married to Jane Baynton, the daughter of a family friend, followed his father into the army; by 1545, he was serving in Ireland, as a grand captain, along with his father and his uncle William, and received a knighthood for good service. In 1549, his wife died, leaving two daughters, Mary and Margaret.

In the spring of 1553, William returned to England and was put in charge of Princess Elizabeth's security by Edward VI. On Edward's death, the St Loes, Sir John and his sons, firm Protestants all, were involved in the attempt to put Jane Grey on the throne, raising a force in her support. More damagingly, months later, William took part in the Wyatt rebellion, several of whose leaders, though not Henry Grey, were personal friends – both Sir Peter Carew and Edward Courtenay were West Country men. Wyatt's confession implicated St Loe, who was sent to the Tower, where he 'came in with a wonderful stout courage, nothing at all abashed'.[10] He continued to be 'stout' under interrogation, divulging nothing.

Princess Elizabeth was also in the Tower, accused of treason and fearing for her life – the memory of Jane Grey's execution so recent and raw. But she vehemently denied all knowledge of the rebellion and indeed was exonerated by Wyatt himself, in a last speech as he went to the block. Mary chose to believe in her innocence, and in May 1554, Elizabeth was released and placed under house arrest at Woodstock. Her servant William St Loe remained in the Tower, but in June was removed to the Fleet prison. Six months later, a free man, he was given a command on the south coast, though the Somerset lands granted to him by Edward VI were confiscated. Unlike his father and his brother Edward, Sir William was not involved in a further plot, in 1556, to put Elizabeth on the throne. By 1558, he was serving in her household at Hatfield.

It was there that he and Bess might have met. Equally, they could have been introduced by Sir John Thynne, who was a friend and neighbour of St Loe. Bess was in need of a husband. She had six children, a large, unfinished house, and an even larger debt. And Sir William St Loe had much to offer. Socially, from an old and titled Somerset family, he was William Cavendish's superior. On his father's death in December 1558, he inherited the St Loe Somerset and Gloucestershire estates (he appeared as a member of Parliament for Somerset in the parliament of 1559), which brought in an annual income of about £500.[11] His loyalty to Elizabeth was rewarded on her accession with two court posts: Captain of the Guard and Chief Butler of England, positions that required near constant attendance at court. Here was a man who was solidly wealthy, highly respectable, well connected and a widower.

On 15 August 1559, William St Loe wrote to his old friend John Thynne with the news that his marriage to Bess was to take place 'upon Sunday this sevennight', as ordained by the Queen. He and Bess hoped that Thynne would be there. 'She hath with terrible threatenings commanded me not to forget making her hearty commendations unto you and to my Lady your wife' – Bess was clearly hovering at his elbow.[12] The invitation to Thynne suggests that the marriage took place in Somerset, but September saw the St Loes in London, as William had been called back to court to take part in a ceremony at St Paul's to honour the memory of Henry II, King of France, who had died in a jousting accident. The new French King, Francis II, was just fifteen, and his wife Mary, who would loom large in Bess's life, a year older. In the first happy flush of marriage the St Loes handed out presents: William's sister Elizabeth St Loe, one of the Queen's ladies of the privy chamber, was given two gold chains, costing £21 20s., while his brother Clement had five marks (£4).[13]

There is no surviving portrait of St Loe, but he was said to be unusually tall, like all the men in his family.[14] What little we know of him rests on a handful of letters and an account book, kept over five months by one of his servants. But from such slim pickings something can be gleaned: he was partial to nuts – filberts and walnuts in particular; he loved lyre music; he was open-handed and generous – a present-giver, with a teasing humour and graceful manners; and he was a devoted husband. His letters to Bess are spiked with longing – court business kept him in London for much of the time, while building kept her at Chatsworth – and syrupy with endearments. 'My own, more dearer to me than I am to myself', he wrote, 'most heartily farewell by thine who is wholly and only thine.'[15]

That St Loe was willing to take on a woman no longer young – by sixteenth-century standards – encumbered with children and debt, says much about Bess's capacity to charm and allure. We must take this on trust. Reading her peremptory letters – husbands are frequently addressed in much the same tone as stewards – charm is not to the fore. What comes across is force of will, steely determination, powers of organisation and control. But spirit and energy are attractive, and Bess had plenty of both. And as a consummate manager, she found in St Loe a husband who was happy to be managed.

A portrait of Bess, painted about 1560 by a follower of Hans Eworth, when she was nearly forty and newly married to St Loe, shows her gazing benignly into the middle distance. Her cheeks are plump, her hair red, her eyes blue and rather small and her nose long. Her loose black velvet gown – worn over a bodice and skirt – is lined with mink, trimmed with bands of bone-work and fastened with gold aiglets (metal pins, used in place of buttons). Her sleeves and partlet are elaborately embroidered in red silk. She wears enamelled bracelets, a pearl choker, a French hood (made fashionable by Anne Boleyn) decorated with black pearls – Bess would always love pearls – and a gold billament (headdress) set with diamonds. In her beringed, capable-looking hands she holds a pair of leather gloves, a traditional wedding gift. It's not so much a record of beauty as a portrait of wealth and status. Here, it says, is a woman of consequence.

In January 1560, William Marchington, one of Bess's stewards along with James Crompe, reported the news from Chatsworth. Bess's daughters, Frances, Elizabeth and Mary, as well as 'Mistress Kniveton's' children (Jane Leche, Bess's half-sister, had married Thomas Kniveton), had all recovered their health, but did 'not prosper well in learning'. The orchard had been hedged and ditched and hay had been given to the cattle since Christmas. Preparations for building work were in train, with the arrival of timber, and marble from Ashford. Should Thomas Allen (one of Bess's long-serving labourers and still working at Chatsworth, quarrying blackstone, in the 1570s), asked Marchington, work 'by the day or by the great'?[16]

Labourers generally received a daily wage, but the more skilled craftsmen, plasterers and joiners for example, were paid either according to the job, on a contract basis, known as 'bargains-in-great' (or 'piece work'), or by 'measure', according to the quantity. A 'bargain' drawn up in 1580 between Bess and Christopher Sedgefield, a joiner, for the 'parlour' at Chatsworth, gives a sense of how such contracts read. Specifications, both in terms of what was to be done and what was to be provided, are precise: Sedgefield is to lay the floor, make a doorway and doors, put up French panelling to a height of four feet ten inches, and set an architrave and cornice. On top of his wage, he is to get food, drink and lodging for himself and his 'folks' (men), materials – timber, nails and glue – and money for candles.[17]

Marriage to St Loe brought an injection of funds, and with that, building work at Chatsworth could resume after a two-year hiatus. This was partly a question of finishing off – there were floors to be laid, roofs and doors to be made, and walls and ceilings to be plastered. But it was probably at this point that Bess added a long gallery, on the first floor, so making the west front two, rather than one, rooms deep.[18] Long galleries, used to display family portraits and for wet-weather exercise, were becoming fashionable – John Thynne was building his at Longleat – and whatever was most current and desirable Bess wanted for Chatsworth. It was important that Chatsworth should measure up against other great houses under construction – Longleat, or Burghley. That Bess hoped the Queen might grace her house is unlikely – Elizabeth didn't venture much further north than Warwickshire on her summer progresses, and Chatsworth was particularly remote – but Chatsworth would pass to Henry Cavendish, and future generations of Cavendishes. It had to be worthy.

Gearing up for building in the spring of 1560, trees (mostly oak) were felled, sawpits dug and limestone and coal procured for the lime kilns.*[19] Lime kilns, originally introduced by the Romans, were a feature of any large-scale Tudor building site – domed, beehive-like structures, made of brick or stone. Limestone was burned in the coal- or wood-fired kilns, which needed tending twenty-four hours a day, to produce lime – also known as 'quicklime' or 'burnt lime'.† The lime was 'drawn' from the kiln, 'slaked' (mixed) with water, beaten well to make a lard-like substance – lime putty – and left to rest. When needed, the putty was mixed with sand, resulting in mortar and, with the addition of strengthening chopped straw or horse hair, plaster. It was a labour-intensive but cost-efficient process – lime could also be used to make lime-wash, for whitening walls, while ash from the kilns could be mixed with water to make hard-wearing floors, like those on the upper storeys of Hardwick. Lime had an agricultural use too – as a fertiliser.

---

* Sawpits, a 16th-century innovation, allowed timber to be sawn on the spot – tree trunks were marked with chalk, then fastened with wedges over a pit and cut with a two-handed saw, one man above, the other below.

† Today limestone is no longer burned, but simply ground to a powder.

William St Loe's duties at court kept him mostly in London, and wifely duty kept Bess, for some of the time at least, by his side. But when St Loe visited his estates, and his mother, in Somerset, he was not accompanied by Bess, who remained in Derbyshire. Just as with Cavendish, the husband accommodated himself to the wife. St Loe understood and accepted that Bess's heart lay at Chatsworth – 'my honest swete chatesworth', he addressed her in one letter. He acknowledged her as 'chief overseer of my works' and confined himself to offering advice about estate matters, such as fishing leases and horses. 'Trust none of your men to ride any your housed [stabled] horses but only James Cromp or William Marchington but neither of them without good cause ... for nags there be enough about the house to serve other purposes. One handful of oats to every one of the geldings at a watering will be sufficient ... you must cause someone to oversee the horsekeeper for that he is very well learned in loitering.'[20]

Whilst away from Chatsworth, Bess fretted about the progress of the building work. Her stewards kept her informed, but as always, there were problems with unsatisfactory, unreliable or absent workmen. In March, Bess told Crompe not to listen to a certain Worth, 'for where he doth tell you that he is to any penny behind for work done to Master Cavendish he doth lie like a false knave, for I am most sure he did never make any thing for me but two vanes to stand upon the house'. She was glad to hear that Crompe had sent 'sawyers' to cut up timber at Pentrich and Medowpleck, 'for that will further my works', and keen that Thomas Mason (trades could stand in for surnames) should come to Chatsworth. 'I will let you know by my next letter what work Thomas Mason shall begin on first when he does come.' However, she was losing patience with another mason, recommended by Sir James Foljambe, a neighbour: 'if he will not apply his work you will know he is no meet man for me and the masons work which I have to do is not much and Thomas Mason will very well over see that work.'[21]

Within towns, at least those with a corporation granted by a royal charter, trade guilds operated – apprentices were trained, usually for seven years, before becoming members, and standards of work were regulated and supervised. But the monopoly of the guilds did not extend into the country – you might find craftsmen working on a house like Chatsworth who had been trained in, and were members of, a guild, but were outside of the guild's control, something that on the whole suited patrons who could hire and dismiss at will, so long as quality wasn't compromised. Skilled craftsmen, like Thomas Mason perhaps, tended to be itinerant, moving around the country, singly or in groups, from site to site (hence the term 'freemason'), according to demand. However, they could also remain in one area with a high concentration of building, such as the north Midlands, for many years. At least sixteen craftsmen who worked on Chatsworth went on to Hardwick.

The basic construction of a sixteenth-century house was straight-forward enough, and there was certainly no shortage of cheap, unskilled labour, but the quality of the finishing and detailing of the interiors depended on skilled craftsmanship, and here plasterers and masons were key. Demand for such, however, outstripped supply, and finding them, let alone keeping them, was no easy matter. In April, Bess wrote to John Thynne – once again she was after the plasterer 'that flowered your hall'. Presumably Thynne hadn't been able to spare him back in 1555, or he had, but she needed him again. She wanted him either sent to her in London, or directly to Chatsworth, where Crompe would instruct him as to what was to be done. 'I pray you if your man cannot be had to send me yet some other, wherein you shall do me great pleasure for that my house is much imperfect in that respect and lacketh meet men for the same.'[22]

By 1560, Thynne was reaching the end of the second phase of his building at Longleat – a new wing and the great hall so admired by Bess (and eventually replaced). For this second phase, he'd taken on more sophisticated craftsmen, like John Chapman, a decorative stone carver. In 1553, Thynne had begged Chapman off Sir William Sharrington, for whom Chapman had been working on Lacock Abbey, also in Wiltshire, where Thynne had presumably seen his work. Sharrington explained that Chapman had temporarily gone to Dudley Castle, to install a chimney-piece he'd been carving for the Duke of Northumberland – Thynne would have to 'take patience for a time'.[23] Patience was not Thynne's strong suit; Chapman was with him within the year.

Key among Thynne's craftsmen was William Spicer, a local mason, though clearly, like Roger Worde and Robert Smythson, a great deal more than that. In 1559, when work began on a suite of grand rooms, including a great chamber, a dining chamber and a long gallery, Spicer was given the contract to oversee 'the new piece of building' according to a 'platt' drawn up by himself and Thynne. Thynne was to provide all materials – stone, lime, sand, scaffolding, timber, ropes – as well as lodging for the men and as much beer 'as they shall have need of'.[24] Spicer was also made bailiff and rent-collector of Thynne's manor, Lullington, in Somerset. However, relations deteriorated, and after numerous rows, he left in 1563, his contract unfinished, £34 of the Lullington rent money in his pocket and the house still pretty much a shell. To fit up the interiors, Thynne took on two Frenchmen, Alan Maynard, a sculptor and mason, and Adrian Gaunt, a joiner, both of whom came armed with knowledge of and experience in classical detail. Longleat, much like Somerset House, was becoming 'a school or magnet for talent'.[25] As for Spicer, he subsequently flourished, going on to work for the Earl of Leicester at Kenilworth Castle in the 1570s, becoming Surveyor of the Queen's Works at Berwick in 1584, and, in 1596, Surveyor of the Royal Works, *the* plum job in the Elizabethan building world.

When it came to her house, Bess was clearly making decisions herself, rather than deferring to her new husband. In fact it was easy to forget she had a new husband at all. 'Elizabeth Cavendish', she signed off her letter to Thynne, in a moment of inattention, before correcting herself: 'Seyntlo'. And it wasn't only decisions about which craftsmen were employed, but how the work was to be carried out, how the house was to *look*. Instructions came thick and fast: 'I will not now have the porch botched', she told Francis Whitfield, 'seeing I have been at so great charges.' The battlement was not to be started before the porch was 'covered' and dry, and the crest, she felt, should be made of the same stone as the porch.[26] She was thinking about the garden too, on which Crompe was to tell aunt Linnacre to begin work. 'I care not whether she bestow any great cost thereof but to sow it with all kinds of herbs and flowers and some piece of it with mallows. I have sent you by this carrier three bundles of garden seeds all written with William Marchington's hand and by the next you shall know how to use them in every point.'[27] Her children, however, were not entirely forgotten amongst the bricks and mortar, and interspersed with instructions to the stewards were messages for them: 'tell Bessie Knowles and Frances that I say if they play their virginals that they are good girls'.

June 1560 saw Bess back at Chatsworth, with St Loe joining her in August. She must have cracked the whip, as her arrival brought a surge of activity: plasterers, joiners, glaziers, carpenters and painters were all hard at work on the 'new building', in which the St Loes were living, despite what must have been a good deal of chaos.[28] A plumber leaded the roof over the buttery window, while a slater mended the roof on the old house, parts of which were still in use.[29] At the end of August, stone-breakers, rough-wallers and masons appear on the payroll, suggesting that construction – the gallery perhaps – was under way.[30] Inside, tailors were busy making bed hangings.

Building work took place alongside the steady rhythms of agriculture – by 1560, the Chatsworth estate supported large numbers of livestock, particularly sheep: forty drawing oxen, forty milk cows, twenty heifers, twenty steers, five hundred ewes and six hundred wethers (castrated male sheep).[31] A new cog-wheel was made for the mill; pasture at Ashford was enclosed; a boy was paid for keeping the cows. In the summer, extra labour – including a number of women – was drafted in for mowing and haymaking, threshing and binding corn into sheaves.[32] Labourers moved easily between house and farm – a woman might be carrying water to the plasterers one week and making hay the next.* Bess's house was taking shape, her estates were flourishing, her children healthy and her husband doting. Not all, however, delighted in her good fortune or wished her well.

---

* Bess rarely employed women, and only for light work – polishing stone, collecting rubbish, weeding – at 1d a day (Durant and Riden (eds), *Building of Hardwick Hall: Part II*, p.xlix). Some builders made more use of women – at Wollaton they carried limestone, and Sir Thomas Tresham had them tending the lime kilns.

6

'THIS DEVIL'S DEVICES'

Bess's letter to Thynne in April 1560 makes no mention of the drama of the previous months: an attempt by Edward St Loe, William's brother, to poison her. Edward St Loe was a rogue. He had been imprisoned, for an unknown offence, in 1556 (the St Loes seem to have had a strain of criminality – Edward's uncle, another William, another bad hat, was accused of murder and poaching), and had done his best, according to William, to make trouble between William and their father. And he had form when it came to poisoning.

In 1557, Edward had married Bridget Scutt, 'a very lustye yonge woman', the widow of John Scutt, owner of an estate at Stanton Drew, near the St Loe family home, Sutton, in Somerset.[1] According to William St Loe, when John Scutt died, aged ninety, 'the world both spoke and suspected his poisoning'; William pointed the finger at his brother, Edward. Not long after Scutt's death, Edward and Bridget, who was pregnant, were married, and Edward, already looking to the future, set about cajoling Bridget to settle the manors of Stanton Drew and Stanton Wick, with some other estates, on him for his lifetime. He also persuaded his brother William 'not to marry the gentlewoman his father had provided for him'.[2] But within two months Bridget too was dead, possibly also poisoned (she left a twelve-year-old son, Anthony Scutt, whose wardship was bought by William St Loe in March 1560), whereupon Edward promptly married the selfsame 'gentlewoman' who had been marked out for William. Further muddying already muddy waters, this was Margaret Scutt, a relative of old John Scutt.[3] In early 1560, Edward, now married to Margaret, visited William and Bess, who were lodging at a house they sometimes used, belonging to a John Mann, in Red Cross Street, London. Shortly afterwards, Bess was poisoned.

Margaret St Loe, William's mother, had been staying with the St Loes at the time and her later letters to Bess provide the best account of what transpired in John Mann's house. She had been visited by a cousin of Edward's, who was seemingly in cahoots with him and anxious to discover what Margaret knew – 'I told her I was sure you were poisoned when I was at London and if you had not had a present remedy you had died.' She distrusted both the cousin and Edward: 'I perceive their heads to be full of this matter, as they have little grace so god send them little power to do my son Sayntlo or you any hurt.' And she was under no illusions as to the character of her younger son: 'this was the goodwill he bore you when he came up to London to see you, as he said was none other cause his coming, which I know the contrary for he liked nothing your marriage. His good friendship to you and to me is all one. The living god defend us all from such friends. I pray you madam send me word how this devil's devices began and how it came to light.'[4] Edward himself countered all accusations by claiming they were simply Bess's 'devices and practices'.

Whether or not Edward was the 'devil' his mother believed him to be, he was not charged with poisoning. Probably nothing could be proved, or perhaps William was unwilling to press charges. In March 1561, John Mann, who presumably felt to some degree responsible, accused a Bristol tavern keeper, Hugh Draper, a self-styled 'astronomer', of practising 'necromancy' against William and Bess. Draper was sent to the Tower, where he was joined by one Francis Cox and one Ralph Davis. All three were released within the year. On the wall of the Salt Tower, above a drawing of a sphere for casting horoscopes,

Bess, *c.* 1560, by a follower of Hans Eworth

Central square of *The Cavendish Hanging, c.* 1570,
worked on by Bess and Mary, Queen of Scots

Sir William Cavendish, *c.* 1550,
Bess's second and best-loved husband

Penelope, a classical heroine from the
Virtues hangings, with whom Bess
liked to identify

Needlework cushion 'of the platt of Chatesworth House',
in the long gallery at Hardwick in 1601

Elizabethan Chatsworth, before 1750, by Richard Wilson

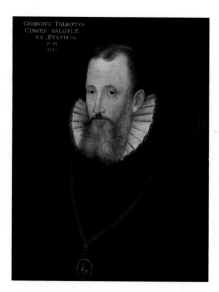

George Talbot, 6th Earl of Shrewsbury,
1580, Bess's fourth husband, before love
turned to hate

Mary, Queen of Scots, *c.* 1578, by or
after Rowland Lockey, probably
painted during her captivity

Elizabeth I, *c.* 1599, commissioned by Bess for Hardwick

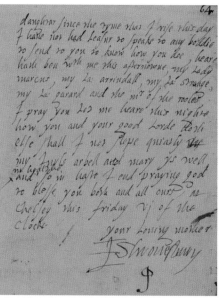

Embroidered panel, decorated with
cloth-of-silver strapwork and gold
and silver thread

Letter from Bess to her daughter,
Mary Talbot, 1580s

The Evidence Room at Hardwick

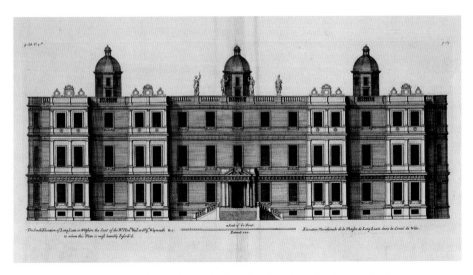

Longleat, the south front, showing Robert Smythson's rooftop banqueting houses

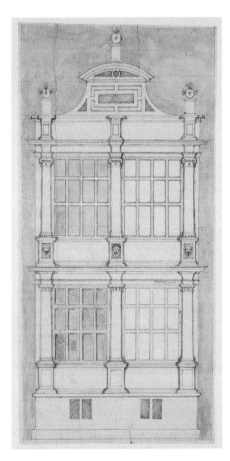

Smythson's design for a two-storeyed
bay window at Longleat, *c.* 1568

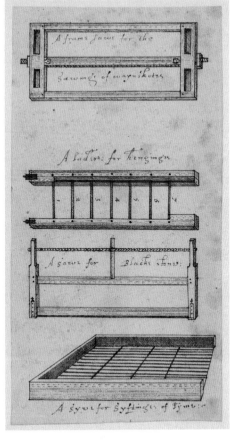

Smythson's designs for tools, including a saw
for blackstone and a sieve for sifting lime

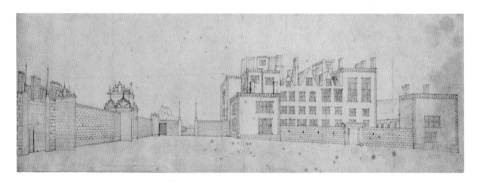

Hardwick Old Hall, the north front, with the New Hall to the left,
anonymous 17th-century drawing

The New Hall, the west front, 1959, by Edwin Smith, showing the house
battered and blackened by coal dust

is a piece of graffiti: 'Hew Draper of Bristowe made thys spheer the 30 daye of Maye anno 1561'.[5]

This is a knotted and murky story, impossible to fully unravel. Did Mann's accusation relate to the poisoning? What was the link between Edward St Loe and Draper and his associates? Had they supplied, or dispensed, the poison? But it's clear enough that Edward was motivated by greed, envy and dislike of Bess. John St Loe had left his Somerset and Gloucestershire lands to William; Edward, as the second son, was the next in line, so long as William had no male heirs. Edward had thwarted William's marriage once, but he was unable to prevent his union with Bess, who, though in her late thirties, could very possibly give William a son. Edward saw the St Loe estates lost to him forever.

William St Loe insisted that Bess 'bore his said brother Edward very good will' and claimed that she had in fact persuaded William, in the event of the St Loes having no children, to entail his lands on Edward. Only when he 'perceived his brother to much unnaturalness and unseemly speeches of him and his wife' did William change his mind and his will.[6] In March 1563, he left 'all ... my leases, farms, plate, jewels, hangings, implements of household, debts, goods and chattels ... to my most entirely beloved wife' and her heirs thereafter. Edward was cut out completely.[7] He continued to make trouble for the St Loes, bad-mouthing Bess and claiming that the manor of Chew Stoke had been left by Sir John St Loe to Edward's wife Margaret, for her lifetime.

Other dramas touched the St Loes during 1560. The previous year, Katherine Grey, the pretty second daughter of Frances and Henry Grey, had fallen in love with Edward Seymour, Earl of Hertford, son of the former Lord Protector. Seymour, described by a contemporary as a 'little man and a great bladder', was not a young man of great distinction, but Katherine was infatuated. However, according to an Act passed in 1536 by Henry VIII, those of royal blood required royal permission to marry and Katherine was a great-granddaughter of

Henry VII. Elizabeth was not likely to look kindly on a marriage between Katherine and Hertford. Katherine won the support of her mother, Frances Grey, but Frances died in November 1559, aged forty-two. The Queen paid for her Westminster Abbey funeral, which, if she had been in London, and given their long association, was very likely attended by Bess.

To the consternation of her councillors, Elizabeth had announced on her accession that she had no desire to marry. John Aylmer, the scholar and bishop, had sought to allay fears about a female monarch – an aberration in the eyes of many – by insisting that as a queen was subject to law and Parliament, there was no great cause for alarm: 'A woman may rule as a magistrate and yet obey as a wife.' But crucially, Elizabeth was not a wife, nor did she wish to become one. Why that was so is a matter of speculation. The fates of her father's wives, especially that of her mother, were hardly an advertisement for marriage. Mary's disastrous union with Philip of Spain (who had already proposed himself as a groom for Elizabeth) was enough to put her off a foreign consort, while marriage to a subject would only create factions and tensions. Perhaps having been subject to the will and whims of her father, brother and sister, she was now simply enjoying her freedom too much to relinquish it. But at the same time, she showed no inclination to name an heir; to do so, she claimed, would be 'to bury herself alive'. It was a position from which she never wavered.

The lack of an heir was an open invitation to those with a claim, however tenuous. Potential claimants, all descended from Henry VII, included the Grey sisters, Katherine and Mary, who according to the term's of Henry VIII's will legally had the best claim, and Mary Stuart, who stood closest in blood. Mary, the daughter of James V of Scotland and a granddaughter of Margaret Tudor, Henry VIII's elder sister, was currently married to the new young King of France, Francis II, and the French were already proclaiming her, provocatively, as Queen of France, Scotland and England. There was also, more distantly, Margaret

Douglas, Countess of Lennox, Margaret Tudor's daughter, who, amongst a dearth of male heirs, did at least have two healthy sons. None of these were ever recognised by the Queen; all were known, or would be known, to Bess, who, like many, would seek to exploit the question of the unresolved succession.

In late 1560, Katherine and Hertford married in secret, and by the following March, Katherine knew she was pregnant. In July, with Hertford in France and knowing she could no longer conceal her pregnancy, a desperate Katherine confided in Elizabeth St Loe, William's sister, one of the Queen's privy chamber women, who was no help at all and simply 'fell into great weeping saying she was very sorry she had done so without the consent or knowledge of the Queen's Majesty or any other of her friends'. Katherine then appealed to Robert Dudley, the Queen's Master of the Horse, who went straight to his mistress. Predictably, Elizabeth was furious and Katherine and Hertford were sent to the Tower, where, in September, Katherine gave birth to a son, Edward Seymour, Lord Beauchamp. The Queen had the Seymour marriage declared invalid, thereby making little Edward Seymour illegitimate, and negating his claim to the throne. Katherine and Edward, though held separately in the Tower, clearly had sympathetic gaolers, since Katherine gave birth to a second son the following year.

Her end was wretched – released from the Tower, she was kept under close house arrest, barred from all contact with Hertford and her elder son. She sank into a deep depression and died in 1568, possibly from anorexia. For failing to inform the Queen of the Grey/ Hertford marriage, Elizabeth St Loe was dismissed from the privy chamber and spent six months in the Tower. Several biographers have mistaken Elizabeth St Loe for Bess. Aside from the fact that Bess was never a gentlewoman of the privy chamber, she would not have fallen 'into great weeping' on hearing Katherine's confession. Hysterical tears were not Bess's style; she would merely have been exasperated by Katherine's foolishness. But given her relationship with the Greys, she must have followed the story closely. She had probably heard the rumours about Katherine and Hertford long before the Queen.

In September 1560, William St Loe, who had been called back to court, wrote to his wife from Windsor, where he visited his stepsons Henry and William Cavendish at Eton and paid their fees (nineteen shillings a term).[8] He reassured Bess that according to the Eton almoner, 'no gentlemen's children in England shall be better welcome nor better looked unto than our boys'. St Loe, however, was much 'troubled' at being parted from his wife and suffered 'continual nightly dreams'. Alsope, the carrier, had not been able to satisfy him 'in what estate thou nor thine is, whom I tender more than I do William St Loe, therefore I pray thee as thou dost love me, let me shortly hear from thee for the quieting of my unquiet mind how thy own sweet self with all thine doeth'. He hoped 'shortly to be amongst you all'.[9] The Queen, however, came first. Wherever she went – Winchester, Hampton Court, Windsor, Whitehall – St Loe followed. When she took a fancy to his horse, he obligingly handed over the animal, an act for which he received 'many goodly words'.

If Elizabeth was resistant to marriage, she was certainly not indifferent to flirtation and the attentions of a handsome man. That September court was gripped by scandal, after the death of Amy Robsart, the wife of Robert Dudley, whose relationship with the Queen had recently been the subject of much speculation and the source of acute anxiety for William Cecil, Elizabeth's Secretary of State, who longed for nothing more than to see the Queen safely married. Amy had been found at the foot of a flight of stairs, her neck broken. It was said that she had been suffering from depression, and possibly from breast cancer, and the official verdict was one of death by misadventure. Gossip, however, had it otherwise. Wasn't her death all too convenient, clearing the way for Dudley to marry the Queen? Dudley appeared deeply shocked, and was soon restored to royal favour, but whatever hopes he'd entertained of the Queen receded. Of this drama St Loe said not a word in his (surviving) letters to Bess. Instead he complained about the cost of 'hired court stuff', and asked her to send hand towels, linen and shirts.[10]

St Loe owned a London house, in Tuthill Street, though he apparently preferred to stay at Somerset House (now the property of the Queen), or to lodge with John Mann, whose wife acted as a housekeeper – useful when leading a bachelor life in London. He made good use of the river, hiring boats to carry himself and his horses from Somerset House to Blackfriars, Westminster or Hampton Court, or to transport 'stuff' for the Cavendish boys at Eton. He dined out with Lord Cobham, whose wife Frances was a lifelong friend to Bess, or Lady Throckmorton, whose husband was ambassador to France. But he missed Bess badly and consoled himself by buying presents, which were parcelled up in boxes and baskets and carried to Chatsworth. Three French grammars, a copy of *Cosmografie de Levant*, and psalms in French went to the children. Spanish gloves, Spanish leather shoes, velvet shoes and 'a bone grace of the new fashion' were bought for Bess, and goods and delicacies not available in Derbyshire: a barrel of sturgeon, a firkin of olives, a basket of plums, artichokes, 'cowcombres' (cucumbers), Spanish silks, red frisado (a silk fabric), wire for stringing a virginal, lemons, oranges, hops, frankincense, ten pomegranates at 8d each. Probably on Bess's orders, St Loe spent 12s. on 'a grate and knocker for the great gate at Chatsworth'.[11]

It wasn't only his duties to the Queen that kept St Loe in London 'against my will'. He was also trying to settle the question of Bess's £5,000 debt, 'our chequer matter', as he called it, which was dragging on and delaying his return. 'My reward as yet is nothing more than fair words with the like promises', he told Bess on 12 October, having bought paper the same day 'to write home', for 2d. But he did at least have leave to come to Chatsworth, along with his brother Clement, the following week.[12]

After Chatsworth, St Loe visited his mother in Somerset, bearing presents – 'half a yard of red and white stool-work', to make sleeves, and gold and silver thread.[13] On returning to court, he found Elizabeth displeased: 'The Queen hath found great fault with my long absence', he told Bess, 'saying she would talk with me further and that she would well chide me thereunto, I answered that when her highness under-stood the truth and the cause she would not be offended whereunto she said very well very well howbeit hand of hers did I not kiss.' He had been suffering from 'extreme pain in my teeth since Sunday dinner, thus with aching teeth I end, praying the living to preserve thee and all thine'. His heart ached too – 'Your loving husband with aching heart until we meet.'[14] Bess joined him in November, remaining over Christmas.

It's hard to fault William St Loe as a husband, a model of generosity and forbearance, happy to bend before the greater will of his wife, prepared to base himself in Bess's home county rather than his own. In Derbyshire, he became both a justice of the peace and a member of Parliament. He didn't add to Bess's Derbyshire estates, but he funded the building work at Chatsworth. In 1563, he finally succeeded in settling the matter of Bess's debt – paying a fine of £1,000 on behalf of Bess and Henry Cavendish, in return for a royal pardon. And he took responsibility for her children and stepchildren, providing a dowry (William Cavendish did not apparently make provision for dowries for his daughters) of 1,000 marks (£666) for Anne Cavendish, Bess's stepdaughter, who married Sir Henry Baynton, the younger brother of St Loe's first wife, in 1562.

Bess was partial to matchmaking – a pursuit involving intrigue and speculation – amongst her acquaintances as well as family. In 1561, it was the turn of her eldest daughter, thirteen-year-old Frances, for whom Bess selected a husband in the shape of Henry Pierrepont, aged fifteen. The Pierreponts were a local family, with a large estate, Holme Pierrepont, near Nottingham. Henry's father, Sir George Pierrepont, was extremely rich and in poor health. It had the makings of an excellent match. In the autumn of 1561, the St Loes rode over to Holme Pierrepont, where they were able to make themselves useful to Sir George by offering support and advice in a suit he was bringing against a certain Master Whalley, as well as discussing the proposed marriage. The matter of a dowry must have been raised, and presumably William St Loe obliged. In November, Sir George wrote to Bess in London, thanking her for 'your great pains taken with me at Holme' and assuring her that 'if your ladyship and the gentlewoman your daughter like our boy upon sight as well as I and my wife like the young gentlewoman, I will not shrink one word from what I said or promised'.[15] It was important that the young couple 'liked' (each other); as a way of finding out Frances joined the Pierrepont household as a gentlewoman.

By May 1562, all was settled. Sir George wrote to Bess, thanking her for the 'bounteous goodness and cost' bestowed on his son Henry in London and lamenting that he was unable to accept her invitation to Chatsworth to 'make merrie', as the 'pain of my disease' (arthritis, perhaps, or gout) made it impossible to ride.[16] The marriage took place soon after.

The dramas and anxieties of the early 1560s – Edward St Loe's skulduggery, the Katherine Grey affair and the disgrace of Elizabeth St Loe, the question of Bess's debt – had kept Bess in London more than she would have liked. But as life became more settled, she was able to spend longer periods at Chatsworth. By October 1564, the house was nearing completion and a St Loe cousin wrote to congratulate her: 'I am glad you are in health and I trust the sight of your near finished building will continue it.' William St Loe 'must now tarry by it, to render his credit of negligent waiting. It will stand you in hand to forbear him more than you have' – a hint that St Loe's friends felt he received less than his due from his wife.[17]

By now, Chatsworth was looking very splendid both inside and out. Thirteen bedchambers boasted magnificent beds, with en suite furnishings – this very rare at the time – chairs, stools and cushions upholstered in matching fabric (cloth of silver and gold, black and white velvet, white and tawny damask, gold and purple taffeta). Bess's own room, on the first floor, was a profusion of reds, blues and greens. She slept in 'a bed of red cloth, trimmed with silver lace', hung with five curtains of red mockado (a woollen velvet). There was a great chair of green checked silk, a small chair of blue velvet, long cushions made of black velvet, red velvet and blue taffeta, and six blue hangings. Green satin curtains hung at the windows, and portraits of Sir William Cavendish, Sir William St Loe, Lady Jane Grey and Bess herself on the walls.[18]

Bess's London friends also regretted her preoccupation with Chatsworth. In October 1564, Frances, Lady Cobham, wrote wishing she saw more of Bess in London: 'would you had as good cause to come to lie in these parts as I could wish and then you should be as great a stranger in Derbyshire as now you are in London'. Lady Cobham, the wife of William Brooke, Baron Cobham, and a gentle-woman of the privy chamber (and soon-to-be Mistress of the Robes), was writing from the Cobham family home in Kent, where she was awaiting the birth of her second child. She and Bess were working together on a dress, to present to the Queen as a New Year's gift. Present-giving, for the Elizabethans, took place at New Year rather than Christmas, and as far as the Queen was concerned, money or plate were perfectly acceptable, but imaginative effort was appreciated (such was not expected of Her Majesty, who invariably gave plate). 'I have basted the sleeves', Lady Cobham told Bess, 'of that wideness that will best content the queen … they are fine and strange. I have here sent you enclosed the braid, and length of caulle [netting] for the queen of the same work for to suit with the sleeves, you may send it up unmade for that the fashion is much altered since you were here. Ten yards is enough for the ruffs of the neck and hands.'[19] Gifts of clothing went down especially well with the Queen, the finer and stranger the better, and, crucially, made in accordance with the very latest fashions, with which Lady Cobham felt, quite reasonably, Bess might not be entirely au fait, marooned as she was in Derbyshire.

Chatsworth provided a permanent or temporary home and refuge for Bess's extended family, her mother, brother, sisters and half-sisters (when smallpox swept through Derbyshire, her mother sent some of her daughters from her home at nearby Hardstoft, to Chatsworth, which was smallpox-free). Within her family, Bess, at forty-three, was firmly established as matriarch, both deferred and appealed to. James Hardwick, her brother, who did not share her head for business, was a regular supplicant. James was living in the old family home at Hardwick. Due to lack of funds, he made few improvements to the house – although there is some evidence that he began building a new wing, to the east – but he did add substantially to the estate, buying land and manors in Derbyshire and Nottinghamshire, mostly around Hardwick.[20] To finance these acquisitions, he borrowed heavily and was soon in debt and appealing to Bess for help.

In December 1564, James was testing the waters, with vague references to a Master Clark, whom he hoped might bail him out, especially, he suggested, if urged on by a letter from Bess. He was otherwise preoccupied by ill health – since he had the 'emeroydes', the pain in his head had gone, 'but I feel age [he was thirty-nine] were upon me for I may not abide cold'.[21] James Hardwick was either rather sickly or rather hypochondriacal. By the new year, his health and finances had both taken a turn for the worse. He explained that he would have come to Chatsworth, but for having had 'such hoarseness that never could you hear me speak', not to mention a 'coughe of the longes that hath put me in marvellous pain'. The hoarseness had improved, but not the cough – 'specially in the night it holdeth me sore' – so he would wait until the weather became 'fair' before seeing Bess. Meanwhile, all hopes of Master Clark had come to nothing. Could Bess lend him £100? Even £50? As security he offered the lease of a coal mine at Heath, or a mortgage on his land at Aldwark (acquired in 1561).[22] There's a note of desperation here – he needed the money by 27 January, only a week away.

Bess, who in later years established a lucrative line in money-lending, did not immediately oblige. She was not lacking in family feeling, and was indeed clearly fond of her sisters, but family feeling was not allowed to trump good business sense. A bad deal was a bad deal. Nor was she likely to have been particularly sympathetic to James's plight, brought about as it was by poor judgement and reckless borrowing.

Elizabeth Leche, Bess's mother, who was certainly more indulgent towards James than his sister, waded in to lend support. After thanking Bess for the 'great kindness' she'd showed her daughter Margaret (Bess's half-sister), she continued: 'I perceive that my son stands in great need of money for payments he has to make. Daughter, seeing my son and you cannot agree of the price of the land at Aldwark it were much to my comfort if you would be so good to lend so much money as you think it to be worth and if the money be not paid by the day appointed, the land to be full bought and sold to you.' Alternatively, Bess could buy James's estate at Little Hallam – 'I assure you it is very good land and better than Aldwark and the tenants handsome men and the land stands upon coal which I think is very good for you daughter.' She admitted that she was particularly anxious to prevent a neighbour and relation, Sir Francis Leake, who had been negotiating with James, from buying the land himself. 'I heartily pray you good daughter somewhat to strain yourself for my sake.'[23] Whether or not Bess strained herself and provided the money, we don't know. But James Hardwick continued to borrow.

Shortly after Elizabeth Leche's plea on her son's behalf, around February 1565, Sir William St Loe died in London. It was seemingly quite sudden – if he had been seriously ill, one might have expected Bess to have been at his side, rather than, as she was, at Chatsworth. On the other hand, during six years of marriage she had clearly *always* preferred to remain at Chatsworth. Instead, during his last days,

William had the dubious pleasure of the company of his brother Edward, though there is no reason to think that Edward was making free with the poison once again. It seems unlikely that Bess greatly grieved. In St Loe she could hardly have had a more devoted or obliging husband, yet there's a definite sense that their frequent separations pained her rather less than they did him. If many marriages have an adorer and an adored, in this Bess was certainly the latter. St Loe was buried in the church of Great St Helen, at Bishopsgate, beside his father.

Bess was left a wealthy, and highly eligible, widow. Now in her early forties, she was probably past childbearing, but she was still vigorous and attractive. The St Loe western lands, in Somerset and Gloucestershire – valued, in the 1580s, as bringing in at least £500, and possibly as much as £700, a year – were all, according to the terms of St Loe's will made in 1563, now hers. And this of course in addition to her life interest in the Chatsworth estates and her jointure from her marriage to Robert Barley. Bess's income in 1566 stood at around £1,600 a year.[24] These were assets that considerably upped the ante in the marriage market, as she well knew. Since she was a great deal more likely to acquire a new husband, or at least a husband worth the having, in London than in Derbyshire, it was to London that she decamped for much of 1565 and 1566.

7

COUNTESS OF SHREWSBURY

By 1565, Bess had not travelled very far geographically – she remained based in her beloved Derbyshire – but materially and socially she had come a very long way indeed. She was now a woman of considerable wealth and property. She had powerful friends and allies at court, such as William Cecil and Robert Dudley (now the Earl of Leicester), and the good opinion of the Queen herself. With such advantages came notoriety, and she found herself the subject of gossip and speculation. There was talk about the terms of William St Loe's will and, unsurprisingly, noisy objections on the part of the St Loe family – from Edward, naturally, but also from Margaret, William St Loe's younger daughter by his first marriage, who contested the will, although it was upheld by the Court of Probate. There was some sympathy for Margaret, who was married to Thomas Norton, and her sister Mary – a feeling that they had been unfairly cheated of their inheritance.

Edward would not be silenced, claiming that all had been 'unnaturally given and bestowed upon' Bess, who had enriched herself at the expense of the St Loe family.[1] If nothing else, Edward was determined to hang on to Chew Stoke. He claimed that he had an indenture, signed by Sir William before his death, giving him and his wife Margaret a lifetime's interest in the property. He also claimed that William had forgotten legacies due to Edward and his siblings under their father's will. Bess countered by insisting that the counterpart of the conveyance of 1564 had gone missing in London at the time of William's death, when Edward was with him and she in Derbyshire. She also pointed out, rightly, that Sir John St Loe had left nothing to Edward. Quarrels rumbled on. Edward stopped paying Bess rent; Bess stopped making payments against backdated sums that Sir William had agreed to give to Edward. It finally went to court, where it was settled that Chew Stoke was Margaret St Loe's for her lifetime but would revert to Bess and her heirs after Margaret's death (not to the St Loe family, as Edward had wished). In 1566, Edward was sent to Ireland, in the Queen's service, for which Bess can only have been thankful.

Bess was quite as capable of defending her inheritance as she was of managing her own affairs in general. In March 1565, shortly after St Loe's death, she was negotiating with Henry Babington, a Derbyshire neighbour, over land that Babington was clearly hoping to sell. Bess was not to be rushed into a deal until Babington provided more information. She wanted 'notes of the whole value of your lands, how much is assigned for jointure, or otherwise, which shall descend to your son immediately after you ... so as I may understand truly your estate'. With such details, and given sufficient time, she would 'very gladly proceed into further talk, as I well hope to a good end, otherwise being destitute of counsel for so weighty a matter I dare not talk further'.[2] In reality Bess hardly needed 'counsel'.

With Bess in London, Chatsworth was left in the care of her stewards, who supervised building works, oversaw estate matters (the grievances of tenants, the care of livestock), kept Bess supplied with money, and reported on the progress of the children. By the winter of 1565, Henry and William Cavendish had left Eton (William went to Cambridge in 1567) and Charles was being tutored at Chatsworth. In November, James Crompe told Bess that William, who already seemed to be putting himself forward as head of the family, felt that it would be a mistake to send 'Master Charles' to a new school (Tideswall), since then 'all this learning that he now hath shall do him small pleasure, for the schoolmaster that he should go to will teach him after another sort so that he shall forget these teachings which he hath had' at the hands of his present tutors, Masters Jackson and Taylor. William, according to Crompe, would see that Charles 'applies his book'. William himself needed no such urging: he 'doth study and apply his book day and night, there need none to call on him for going to his book'. There is no mention of Henry Cavendish's scholarly habits; he was due to come to London soon, but 'hath no boots that will keep out water, so there must be a pair made'.

As regards other Chatsworth news, Crompe reported that the 'fat wethers' were not yet sold, and the paving, outside the house, was nearly completed, except for one 'piece before the garden door'.[3] Building work was drawing to an end, apart from finishing off the long gallery. In early 1566, Bess told Crompe that she wanted a door made between the gallery and the great chamber. 'You did write that you would not have the end of the great gallery next the great chamber seeled [panelled]', he replied, 'but a portal [door] there to be made. James Joiner is in hand with the portal ... I do not understand your meaning for the cornice, I am sure you will have the cornice to be as the rest is and of like height. Let me know your pleasure further therein.'[4] The gallery was eventually panelled from floor to ceiling.

The smooth running of Chatsworth depended on competent servants, but such could not always be counted on. Word reached Bess in December 1565 that her warrener, Edward Fox, had been neglecting his duties. Rabbit skins were highly valued, and the warren (or 'cuningree') played an important part on the Elizabethan estate. Sir Thomas Tresham (of whom more later) built his Triangular Lodge, an exquisite slice of a building, at Rushton, Northamptonshire, for the use of his warrener, though Edward Fox was housed less elaborately, in a simple 'lodge' in Bess's warren. Fox had received a sound ticking-off for being absent for three days about his 'pleasure'. Feeling himself unfairly maligned, he put up a spirited defence: 'if the report of them that have no knowledge is better to be credited than mine, I am not meet to be in an office.' There were, he assured Bess, a great many conies (mature rabbits), as anyone could see. As for burrow-making, a group of neighbours were all set to 'cast burrows' after Christmas, and in the meantime he himself had made two burrows and covered them with thorns. Moreover, he had seen off two pairs of hounds that had found their way into the warren: 'I ran up and down the wood and were angry at them ... and at length I with my bill cut three of them very sore that I think they will not live.'[5]

There was trouble from an old employee, too. Henry Jackson, recently a fellow at Merton College Oxford, and former tutor to the Cavendish boys (the same mentioned in Crompe's letter), began spreading 'scandalous reports' about Bess. What these were is unclear. It sounds as though Jackson bore a grudge, for dismissal from his post perhaps, and had been reviving the old tales of Bess unjustly appro-priating the St Loe inheritance. Or possibly it was something more defamatory – some impropriety on Bess's part during the months that she had spent alone at Chatsworth. At any rate, whatever he was claiming was considered serious enough for Cecil, on behalf of the Privy Council, to inform the Archbishop of Canterbury (Jackson had become a minor canon at St Paul's Cathedral) that 'the matter' was to be examined 'thoroughly and speedily ... that the good lady's name may be preserved'. The Queen, mindful that this was the widow of her valued servant William St Loe, waded in too: if Jackson had defamed Bess, who 'has long served with credit in our Court', then he should face 'extreme punishment, by corporal or otherwise'.[6] What form, if any, of 'extreme punishment' Jackson received is not recorded. But that Bess could command such high-placed defenders of her reputation says much about her standing.

Gossip of a more harmless nature also swirled around court – who might become Bess's fourth husband? In January 1566, William Cecil received a letter: 'either Lord Darcy or Sir John Thynne shall marry Lady St Loe and not Harry Cobham'.[7] Harry Cobham's brother had married Bess's stepdaughter Catherine, and Thynne of course was an old friend. There is no evidence that Bess had any intention of marrying any of them.

In April 1567, a great fire swept through John Thynne's Longleat, raging for five hours and virtually destroying the house that he'd been working on for twenty years.* Thynne seemingly took this in his stride: he moved into another house on the estate and started building again. For this third Longleat, he took on a new mason – Robert Smythson. In March 1568, Humphrey Lovell, the Queen's master mason, wrote to Thynne: 'According to my promise I have sent unto you this bearer Robert Smythson freemason, who of late was with Master Vice Chamberlain [Sir Francis Knollys], not doubting him to be a man fit for your worship.' Smythson, stipulated Lovell, was to have 16d a day and a 'nage' (horse), kept at Thynne's expense, while his men – the five masons who came with him – were to have 12d day; Thynne should pay for their travel expenses and the carriage of their tools.[8]

Smythson is one of those fascinating Elizabethans of whom we know all too little. We have the legacy of his houses – high, compact, full of drama and light – and his drawings, but Smythson the man remains elusive. We do know that he was born in 1534 or 1535, that his family came from Westmorland and that he was probably brought up in or near London, where he was apprenticed to a member of the London Masons' Company.[9] Somewhere along the line he learned to draw, exceptionally well. He may have worked on Somerset House, as an apprentice under Humphrey Lovell; by the 1560s, he was certainly working for Sir Francis Knollys on Knollys' house at

---

* Sir Thomas Smith, who had known Thynne from the Somerset House days, wrote to commiserate on his 'mischance'. Smith, who had just returned from his ambassadorship in Paris, was about to embark on the building of Hill Hall in Essex, transforming the existing timber-framed courtyard structure into a classical house (Longleat Building Records, Vol. II, f.261).

Caversham, near Reading. Lovell clearly rated Smythson highly and thought he could be of use at Longleat.

Smythson and his family rented the parsonage and farm at Monkton Deverill, with Smythson presumably commuting the six miles to Longleat on his 'nage'. He was joining a crack team of craftsmen, including the French mason Alan Maynard and the joiner Adrian Gaunt, but he had plenty to contribute himself. Craftsmen who could turn their hands to design were not uncommon – men like Roger Worde, or William Spicer, or Richard Kirby, who worked on Thomas Smith's Hill Hall. Kirby was a carpenter, from the London Carpenters' Company (whose members built London's theatres), but he also worked closely with Smith on the design of his house. When Smith died, in 1577, Hill Hall unfinished, he left a will appointing Kirby 'as chief Architect, overseer and Mr of my works for the perfecting of my house'.[10] Smythson was similarly multi-skilled. He combined his mason's training, in a late-medieval indigenous tradition, with a familiarity with classical ornament and detail gleaned from working with foreign craftsmen. From studying architectural works coming from the Continent by such as Sebastiano Serlio and Jacques Androuet du Cerceau, he learned about symmetry, geometry, order and proportion. And to such disparate influences he brought his own ideas and preferences.

Longleat's eight charming rooftop banqueting houses, with their domes and stone fish-scale tiles, capped by miniature classical lanterns, are Smythson's earliest known works. Banqueting houses, where diners repaired after the main meal to eat a dessert course, such as 'comfits' made from seeds, spices and fruits covered with sugar, were a desirable feature of any great Tudor house. Generally they were separate from the main body of the house and involved an element of surprise, delight or discovery – an ascent culminating in a view, as at Longleat (the 'prospect' room in the gatehouse of Henry VIII's Nonsuch was an early prototype), or a meandering walk, as at Hampton Court, where little banqueting houses were dotted around the gardens.

On 27 August 1567, Bess wrote to Thynne: 'I have earnestly moved my lord to grant your suit which I can not obtain [perhaps this was in connection with the loss of his house] ... in the mean time I will not fail to do for you what I can for the furthering of your desire therein.'[11] She was writing from Sheffield Castle, one of the many properties belonging to her 'lord', George Talbot, Earl of Shrewsbury.

The exact date of Bess's marriage to Shrewsbury is unknown, but it was most likely in the summer of 1567 shortly before her letter to Thynne. That October, Elizabeth Wingfield, one of Bess's half-sisters, married to Anthony Wingfield, a gentleman usher to the Queen, informed Bess that her husband had safely delivered the Shrewsburys' venison to Her Majesty. The Queen had spent an hour talking about the Earl and Countess in the most flattering terms, anxious to know when they intended to come to court and full of praise for Bess – 'I have been glad to see my Lady St Loe, but now more desirous to see my Lady Shrewsbury ... there is no lady in this land that I better love and like.'[12]

In marrying Shrewsbury, Bess allied herself with one of the great northern earls, a Midlands magnate, a man of immense wealth and assets. George Talbot was born in 1528 and was thus some six or seven years her junior. In 1560, on the death of his father, Francis, he became the 6th Earl of Shrewsbury. He held a number of high offices, including Lord Lieutenant of Yorkshire, Derbyshire and Nottinghamshire, Chief Justice in Eyre, Chamberlain of the Receipt of the Exchequer and Knight of the Garter. His first wife, Gertrude Manners, a daughter of the Earl of Rutland, died in January 1567, leaving four sons and three daughters.

Shrewsbury owned vast tracts of land in Derbyshire, Yorkshire, Nottinghamshire, Shropshire and Staffordshire. Profits, from rents and the sales of corn, cattle, sheep, wool and hides, were substantial: in 1591, sales from just one of his estates brought in over £3,000.[13]

With land came property: Sheffield Manor, Sheffield Castle, South Wingfield Manor, Rufford Abbey, Welbeck Abbey and Tutbury Castle, the latter leased from the Crown. He owned two houses in London – one at Cold Harbour near London Bridge, and another, smaller, near Charing Cross – and one outside it: Shrewsbury House, in Chelsea. Once married to Bess, he became an enthusiastic builder in his own right, embarking on major works at Sheffield, a hall to accommodate visitors to the baths at Buxton, improvements to Shrewsbury House and finally the great Worksop Manor. Competing building programmes would be just one source of friction between husband and wife.

'I knew a nobleman of England', wrote Francis Bacon, 'that had the greatest audits of any man in my time, a great grazier, a great sheep-master, a great timber-man, a great collier, a great corn-master, a great lead-man, and so of iron, and a number of the like points of husbandry; so as the earth seemed a sea to him in respect of the perpetual importation.'[14] It has been said that he was referring to Shrewsbury – and if he wasn't, he could have been. The Earl was not just a great landowner, but an industrialist-in-the-making, a producer of coal, iron, lead and glass, a trader in foreign goods.

Taking advantage of new technology – water-powered smelting – the Earl became the largest supplier of lead in England, with, by the 1580s, four smelting mills, producing 600–750 fothers (a fother was just over a ton) of lead a year.[15] From the smelting works, lead was sent to the Earl's storehouse at Bawtry (an inland port), then on by river to Hull, where it was sold to London merchants or exported directly, on one of Shrewsbury's three ships, to Rouen. From Rouen he imported luxuries such as wine and silks (in 1575, 14 lb of 'fine sleyed silk' – floss silk, used for embroidery – in 'all colours', costing a hefty £22 8s., was bought for Bess).[16] Other goods – cloth, carpets, foodstuffs – were imported from the Far East. The *Talbot*, the largest of the Earl's ships, became a privateer and was sent on two commercial voyages to Newfoundland. And Shrewsbury had regular dealings with the

London merchants Sir Richard Staper and Sir Edward Osborne, who began trading with Turkey in the 1570s.*

By 1566, there were two Talbot iron furnaces and a forge, near Sheffield, which by the early 1590s were producing up to 160 tons of bar iron per year, with further furnaces and forges in Shropshire. The Earl also built a steelworks, to furnish the expanding cutlery trade of Sheffield. Sheffield knives were highly prized – when Shrewsbury sent a case of knives to William Cecil, Cecil thought them so 'well wrought' that he kept them in his bedchamber.[17] By the 1590s, the steelworks was producing between thirty and forty-five tons a year, with a cash profit of £200–400.[18]

Shrewsbury did his best to keep a grip on his businesses – watching the pennies, scrutinising accounts and reports sent by stewards and bailiffs, sending detailed orders and instructions himself. When it came to letter-writing, whether to servants, friends or family, he was indefatigable – he wrote often, at enormous length and quite illegibly. Amongst impossible sixteenth-century hands, Shrewsbury's is notorious, and all the more so for the 'gout' (probably arthritis or rheumatism) that crippled his hands as the years went on (when the 'pain and stiffness' were insupportable, he resorted to a scribe). His letters range from the affectionate to the furious, with a persistent undertow of complaint – the gout that plagues him, the tenants who malign him, the wife who undermines him, the children who disappoint him. 'Toiling' is a much-used verb – the Earl is forever 'toiling'.

In a portrait from 1567, Shrewsbury appears slim of build, with a high, narrow forehead, a feeble beard, and an air of anxiety. With all the trappings of a tycoon, he lacked the temperament, the requisite

---

* The Earl started doing business with Osborne, a member of the Clothworkers' Company, in the 1560s. In a letter from September 1585, accompanying a delivery of nutmeg, Osborne, now governor of the Turkey Company and Lord Mayor of London, wrote of the arrival of a ship from Turkey carrying carpets – did the Earl want any? (Shrewsbury MSS, LPL, 695, f.27). The following month the Earl asked Osborne for a loan and was refused (Shrewsbury MSS, LPL, 698, f.83).

toughness and ruthlessness, the confidence to know when to delegate and when to step in, the ability to distinguish between the important and the trivial. He was a worrier and a neurotic: emotional – given to public weeping – immensely sensitive, especially where his honour was concerned, quick to take offence and easily overwhelmed. Conscientious, dutiful and honest to a fault, he proved a most loyal servant to the Queen, but he was no more cut out for the duties that Her Majesty would impose upon him than for managing a great empire. He was certainly no match for the cool head and implacable will of his wife.

Bess would have known Shrewsbury. His father, the 5th Earl, had been a friend of William Cavendish, and a godfather to their daughter Temperance. They were neighbours of a kind – the Earl's main residence at Sheffield was not a great distance from Chatsworth. They would have met in London, at court. Shortly after the death of his first wife, Shrewsbury must have turned his attentions to Bess.

In an age when so many died young, remarriage was common enough, whether for financial security, social advancement or love and companionship. Bess had found all these in William Cavendish, while William St Loe's chief attraction was most probably his ample means and the generosity with which he dispensed them. However, it was not unknown for women, having made one advantageous match, to marry again for love. Frances Grey may have married her Master of the Horse, Adrian Stokes, a younger man and a commoner, to distance herself from the disgraced Henry Grey, but she may, as some believed, have simply been carried along on a love tide. Similarly Frances's stepmother, the Duchess of Suffolk, took humble Richard Bertie, her gentleman usher, as her second husband.

The Shrewsburys' marriage, though, like most sixteenth-century unions, especially amongst the aristocracy, was not a love match, but primarily an economic and dynastic contract, a practical and mutually beneficial arrangement. To Shrewsbury went Bess's property and estates, many of which adjoined his, and her £1,600 a year (he lost £550 of this when Henry Cavendish came of age in 1571 and took possession of the Chatsworth lands settled on him by his father). Her Derbyshire lead mines, including one at Barley, part of her jointure from Robert Barley, would provide ore for his smelting works, while the St Loe lands would give him a presence in the West Country. For Bess, remarriage brought loss as well as gain. Why did Lady St Loe, with her splendid house, her extensive estates and her handsome income, choose to take another husband, thereby forfeiting control of said house, estates and income, not to mention her independence and her freedom? It was true that Chatsworth was entailed on Henry Cavendish, but since Bess had a life interest, she could have lived there in style and comfort, mistress of her own home and her own means.

Many years later, in 1586, when the Shrewsbury marriage had irretrievably broken down, the Earl, harking back to the old gossip peddled by the tutor Henry Jackson, would claim that he had both rescued and elevated Bess: 'where you were defamed and to the world a byword when you were St Loe's widow, I covered those imperfections (by my intermarriage with you) and brought you to all the honour you have and to the most part of that wealth you now enjoy'.[19] He may have helped restore Bess's reputation, or at least silenced the tongue-waggers, though she could surely have managed that herself. Nor was she lacking for wealth, though since a few years later, in 1572, there was mention of her debts, it's possible that she did need Shrewsbury's money. More powerful, surely, was the lure of an earl. Lady St Loe did well enough, but as Countess of Shrewsbury, Bess entered a different league entirely. And, crucially, she saw a chance to further the interests of her children, only one of whom, her daughter Frances, was married.

The Shrewsburys' marriage settlement, most likely negotiated by Bess herself, on favourable terms, has vanished, and with it details of her jointure – the third of the Earl's estate that she would receive on his death. This, however, would only be for her lifetime, and Bess would not have expected to have more children with the Earl. But there was a way of ensuring that not all the Shrewsbury lands and properties were lost to the Cavendishes after her death. The union between Bess and the Earl was cemented by the intermarriages of four of their children.

The indenture for this, dated 7 January 1568, survives: Gilbert Talbot, the Earl's second son, aged fourteen, was to marry Mary Cavendish, aged twelve, before Easter. If Mary died before the marriage, or 'before carnal knowledge betwixt them', then Gilbert was to marry Elizabeth Cavendish.[20] If anything happened to Gilbert, then Mary was to marry either Edward or Henry Talbot. Lip service was paid to the feelings of the parties concerned, with the insertion of if 'Mary agrees', but the point about this arrangement was that it should be absolutely watertight. Furthermore, Henry Cavendish, Bess's eldest son, aged seventeen, was to marry Grace, the Earl's youngest daughter, aged eight – and various alternative siblings were put forward in the event of untimely deaths. All parties apparently agreed, though they could hardly have done otherwise, and the double wedding took place on 9 February 1568 at the church of St Peter and St Paul, in Sheffield. The lands involved in these marriages were to be enjoyed by the Earl and Bess for their lifetimes, then by the two couples and their heirs. The marriage of Gilbert and Mary Talbot proved successful enough; that of Henry and Grace Cavendish wretched.

Some historians – hostile and male – have claimed that Bess made this marital package deal a condition of her acceptance of Shrewsbury.[21] They may well be right, though in point of fact, in marrying Grace Talbot to Henry Cavendish, Bess's heir, the Talbots had much to gain. And at a time when marriage amongst the nobility was designed to preserve and consolidate inheritance, such cold-blooded arrangements were common enough – Shrewsbury had already married his eldest son, Francis, to the Earl of Pembroke's eldest daughter, and his eldest daughter, Catherine, to Pembroke's son.

* * *

If the Shrewsbury marriage was conceived as a merging of assets, familiarity bred affection and in the early days the Earl's letters were unfailingly loving. 'My dear none' (a contraction of 'my own'), he wrote to her in June 1568, from Wingfield Manor, 'though weary in toiling about yet thinking you would be desirous to hear from me, scribbled these few lines to let you understand I was in health and wished you anights with me.' He hoped to join her at Chatsworth the following day, 'and in the meantime as occurrences befall to me you shall be the partaker of them. I thank you sweet none for your baked capon and chiefest of all for remembering of me.'[22] Bess was good about sending foodstuffs and treats.

Six months later, in December, Shrewsbury was at Hampton Court, where the Queen had decamped to avoid the plague that was raging in London, leaving Bess at Tutbury Castle. Having not heard from her for some time, 'which drove me in dumps', he was 'now relieved' by her letter and grateful for her venison and puddings, some of which he'd given away to Bess's friend Lady Cobham, to the Lord Steward and to the Earl of Leicester, keeping the rest for himself. He told her that he'd thanked the Queen for having 'little regard to the clamorous people of Bolsover' – some of his tenants who had drawn up a petition against him – and Her Majesty had replied that 'she did so trust me as she did few', a reference, he suspected, to 'the custody of the Scots Queen'. 'As the pen writes', he finished, 'so the heart thinks that of all the earthly joys that have happened unto me I thank God chiefest for you, for with you I have all joy and contentation of mind and without you death is more pleasant to me than life, if I thought I should be long from you ... farewell dear sweet none from Hampton court this Monday at midnight, for it is every night so late before I go to my bed being at play in the privy chamber at primero [Elizabethan poker] where I have lost almost a hundred pounds and lacked my sleep.'[23]

The question of 'the custody of the Scots Queen' was one that had been preoccupying Elizabeth ever since Mary Stuart had arrived in

England in May. Shrewsbury, as he must have known, was in the running for the custodianship and Tutbury for a possible place of custody. Tutbury was horribly damp and dreary, by far the least comfortable of Shrewsbury's houses and generally used as a hunting lodge. Bess was there to assess its suitability.

8

THE SCOTS QUEEN

In the summer of 1561, eighteen-year-old Mary Stuart returned to Scotland, a country that she'd left thirteen years earlier to go to France as the betrothed of the young Dauphin, Francis. Her mother, James V's widow, Mary of Guise, as capable and shrewd as any amongst the Guises (one of France's most powerful and ambitious families), was left to rule Scotland as regent. In 1559, Henry II died in a jousting accident and fifteen-year-old Francis, now married to Mary, became King. But just a year later, Mary suffered a double bereavement: the deaths of both her mother and her husband. Her brief reign as Queen of France, a position for which she'd been groomed for most of her life, was over. With Francis succeeded by his ten-year-old brother and his mother Catherine de Medici as regent, there was no place for Mary in France. She decided to return to Scotland to take up her throne.

Still grieving, Mary was propelled from the luxury and sophistication of the French court into a brutal and barbarous Scotland, a place she could scarcely remember, where the Protestant lords, a ruthless, self-seeking lot, headed by the Earl of Moray, James V's illegitimate son, held sway. The lords had led a Protestant rebellion against Mary of Guise as she lay dying in 1560, and, with the backing of English forces, had driven out the French, who, according to the treaty of Edinburgh, agreed to recognise Elizabeth, not Mary, as the legitimate Queen of England. Now the lords appeared biddable enough, and

Moray successfully concealed his own designs on the throne. For her part, Mary accepted Scotland's Protestantism so long as she, as a Catholic, was allowed to celebrate Mass privately. Negotiations began between the respective Queens' advisers. If Mary would ratify the Treaty of Edinburgh and thereby renounce her claim to the English throne, then she would be recognised as Elizabeth's successor, providing Elizabeth had no children. Mary declined. Could Mary have an audience with her cousin? Elizabeth demurred.

Elizabeth was now faced with a Catholic claimant to the throne just across the border. And not just any claimant, but one whose claim was nearest in blood, who was unmarried, young and famously attractive. For many Catholics, in England and Europe, Elizabeth was a bastard and a usurper and Mary the rightful Queen. For William Cecil, Elizabeth's Secretary of State, Mary was, and always would be, a mortal threat: to exclude her from the succession and thus safeguard Protestantism, the true faith, and at the same time persuade Elizabeth to marry and produce an heir became his life's work.

Cecil was an ideologue; the Queen a hedger. There was ambivalence in her feelings about religion, and even more so about Mary. The 1559 Act of Uniformity, which compelled the clergy to use the 1552 Book of Common Prayer, officially established Protestantism in England, but Elizabeth, for whom souls were not to be examined too closely, chose to adopt a policy of moderation – if Catholics continued to practise their faith, privately and discreetly, that was a matter of conscience. Elizabeth was equivocal about Mary too: she could never entirely disregard the fact that Mary was Queen of Scotland, and nor could she dismiss Mary's claim to the English throne. At the same time she couldn't bring herself to recognise Mary as her successor. To do so was simply too dangerous: how could she love her 'own winding sheet'? There was personal rivalry too. Elizabeth was avid for details about Mary's looks, yet shrank from meeting her face to face.

It is generally held that Mary was ruled by her heart, and Elizabeth by her head, which, like many simplifications, has a good deal of truth in it. Mary was no scholar, unlike Elizabeth, but she was intelligent, energetic, impulsive and brave – sometimes recklessly so. Where Elizabeth preferred to sidestep decisions, Mary careered headlong into disastrous ones. Having reclaimed the Scottish throne, Mary, not unreasonably, wished to remarry. Marriage – to the right husband – was one way of clipping her wings, and Elizabeth even considered Leicester, a Protestant and a loyal subject, as a possible candidate, though no one, least of all Leicester himself, seems to have entertained this very seriously. As far as Elizabeth and Cecil were concerned, Mary's actual choice of groom could hardly have been worse.

As the son of the Earl of Lennox and Margaret Douglas (Henry VIII's niece), Henry, Lord Darnley, like Mary herself, was a great-grandchild of Henry VII. A match between Mary and Darnley united two individuals with claims to the throne and was therefore doubly threatening to Elizabeth, who had the Countess of Lennox sent to the Tower for her part in promoting it. Hardly had the marriage taken place, in July 1565, than Darnley revealed himself to be as worthless as he was (excessively) handsome – a 'polished trifler', spoilt, vain and dissolute. Initial infatuation soon palled, though not before Mary had conceived.

In the spring of 1566, a group of men, including Darnley, burst into the room where Mary was dining with some friends at Holyrood, Edinburgh, seized her Italian secretary David Riccio, Darnley's former lover – whom Darnley now chose to believe was also his wife's – and stabbed him fifty-six times. Despite this, Mary gave birth to a healthy son, James, in June, which further strengthened her claim to the English throne. Then, in February 1567, Darnley himself was found dead after an explosion at his lodgings at Kirk o' Field, Edinburgh, killed not by the explosion but by strangulation.

Just three months later, in one of her many catastrophic errors of judgement, Mary married the swashbuckling, vicious Earl of Bothwell, but only, so she said, after he had abducted and raped her. She may have hoped that Bothwell would act as a protector and help her control the Protestant lords – her traitorous half-brother and Bothwell's sworn enemy, the Earl of Moray, in particular. She insisted that she did not know that Bothwell was one of the chief suspects in Darnley's murder. The lords, who loathed Bothwell, rose up in protest. That Mary largely still had the support of the Scottish people was not enough; after surrendering, she was imprisoned in the island fortress of Lochleven and forced to abdicate in favour of her baby son James. Moray was declared regent; Bothwell fled. Eleven months later, in May 1568, Mary escaped her prison. Briefly it looked as if the tables might turn, as she gathered an army of supporters that outnumbered Moray's own. But defeat followed and Mary took what she felt to be her only course of action: she fled to England, where she threw herself on the mercy of her cousin and fellow Queen.

This put Elizabeth in an impossible position. In the short term, she dispatched Sir Francis Knollys to Carlisle to take charge of Mary. But what to do with her thereafter? She was unwilling to send her back to Scotland, to certain death. But nor did she want to go to war with Scotland on Mary's behalf. It was too dangerous to let her go to France or Spain, and equally so to leave her at liberty in England, especially in the predominantly Catholic north. As usual, Elizabeth prevaricated: the question of whether or not Mary should be restored to her throne was made contingent upon that of her guilt of Darnley's murder. To this end an inquiry opened in October in York, not far from Bolton Castle, where Mary had been moved.

The evidence that Mary had committed adultery with Bothwell and conspired in Darnley's murder was based on the Casket Letters, which, produced by the Earl of Moray who had every reason to see her condemned, were almost certainly forgeries. When the inquiry failed to reach any conclusions, it was moved south, to Westminster, and five more commissioners appointed, including Cecil and his brother-in-law, Sir Nicholas Bacon, both of whom were determined on Mary's guilt. On 6 December, Mary, allowed neither to defend herself nor to see the Casket Letters, had her advocates withdraw. The Queen, who wanted her found innocent, now intervened. The inquiry was suspended once again and yet more judges added, including the Earl of Shrewsbury, with Elizabeth herself overseeing proceedings at Hampton Court. The Casket Letters were examined for the last time. Mary demanded an audience with Elizabeth and was refused.

On 13 December, Shrewsbury wrote to Bess again, still full of yearning: 'me thinks time longer since my coming hither without you, my only joy, than I did since I married you, such is [the] faithful affection which I never tasted so deeply of before'. The inquiry had failed to reach any kind of verdict – nothing could be proved against Mary, but nor could Elizabeth allow her her liberty. 'Things fall out very evil against the Scots Queen', wrote Shrewsbury, 'what she shall do yet is not resolved of.' And then, later that day, came a hasty post-script: 'now it is certain the Scots Queen comes to Tutbury to my charge'.[1]

The custodianship of the Queen of Scots would have seemed an honour to the Shrewsburys in 1569, a mark of Elizabeth's regard and trust. The Earl would never have imagined that his charge would continue for fifteen years, to the detriment of his fortune, his health, his peace of mind and his marriage. In the eyes of Elizabeth, Shrewsbury was the ideal candidate for the post – thoroughly Protestant and utterly loyal. He also, crucially, owned several properties that were both suit-able for accommodating a queen and also in the geographically secure Midlands, at a safe distance from London, Scotland and the English ports. And he was newly married, and thus, it could reasonably be expected, less susceptible to Mary's fabled charms.

Shrewsbury, who was still at court, received his instructions from Elizabeth: the Scots Queen was to be treated with proper reverence and allowed all ceremony, but most definitely not to escape; none but her immediate retinue were to see her, and Bess might do so only if Mary was sick, or asked to speak to her, and then 'very rarely'; no other gentlewoman should visit; unnecessary members of Mary's household were to be dismissed.[2] Bess, waiting anxiously at Tutbury, was unsure as to when to expect Mary, finally receiving a letter, on 20 January from the Earl of Leicester, with information about her arrival. She replied the next day, grumbling that his letter hadn't reached her sooner: 'I was much grieved because there was no more haste with delivering of the said letters considering the weight and great causes depending thereupon.' Tutbury, she felt, was 'unready in many respects for the receiving of the Scottish Queen coming at sudden'. She had put men to work and was raiding Sheffield for furnishings and hangings for Mary's quarters – 'I will lack furniture ... for myself' rather than fail 'the trust reposed by the Queen's Majesty'.[3] In fact the Queen stepped in too, sending 'Turkey carpets', beds, chairs, linen and plate from the Tower of London.[4]

While marooned in Derbyshire, Bess relied on family (Gilbert Talbot, Elizabeth Wingfield) and friends (Leicester) to keep her informed about events in London and at court. But she had private informants too. One such was Hugh Fitzwilliam, a distant relation, who wrote regularly, with both national and foreign news. On 23 January, Fitzwilliam told Bess that Shrewsbury had been made a privy councillor and that Mary was on her way to Tutbury, 'something against her will'.[5] Her journey, from Bolton Castle southwards to Tutbury on the Staffordshire/Derbyshire border, took a painfully slow ten days – 'the ways being long and foul' and one of her ladies falling ill. She finally arrived on 4 February, to be received by the Shrewsburys.

Tutbury had been chosen for reasons of security – it was surrounded by high walls, with only one entrance, and was therefore easy to defend. Despite Bess's best efforts to instil a little comfort, it remained a deeply cheerless place. Mary herself was scathing: 'I am in a walled enclosure, on the top of a hill, exposed to all the wind and inclemencies of heaven. Within the said enclosure, resembling that of a wood of Vincennes, there is a very old hunting lodge, built of timber and plaster, cracked in all parts ... situated so low that the rampart of earth, which is behind the wall, is on a level with the highest point of the building, so that the sun can never shine upon it on that side, nor any fresh air come into it. For which reason it is so damp that you cannot put any piece of furniture in that part without its being, in three or four days, covered with mould.' Her own apartments consisted of 'two little miserable rooms ... excessively cold'; the 'garden' in which she was allowed to exercise was no more than a 'potato patch'; and the privies had no drains, which meant 'a continual stench'.[6]

A visitor to Tutbury, Nicholas White, one of Cecil's minions, did not paint quite such a dismal picture. White reported to his master that he'd found Mary in one of her two main rooms, sitting beneath the canopy of her cloth of state, which was embroidered with the words 'In my end is my beginning' (her mother Mary of Guise's motto). When asked how she passed the time, 'she said that all day she wrought with her needle, and the diversity of colours making the work seem less tedious, she continued so long at it till the very pain made her to give over, and with that laid her hand upon her left side, and complained of an old grief increased there'. Embroidery, at which Mary excelled, became a distraction and consolation during captivity, and the pain in her side one of several persistent ailments. White, like most men, found Mary fascinating: 'she had withal an alluring grace, a pretty Scottish accent, and a searching wit, clouded with mildness'.[7]

Was Shrewsbury similarly allured? Without being a classic beauty – her nose a trifle too long – Mary, now twenty-six, was immensely attractive. Even John Knox, the fiery Scottish minister and reformer, and hardly one of Mary's admirers, recognised in her 'some enchantment whereby men are bewitched'.[8] She was unusually tall – just under six foot – slim, glamorous and beautifully dressed. Her complexion was creamy, her eyes almond-shaped and her hair somewhere between chestnut and auburn. But her appeal resided in manner as much as looks – she was warm and winning; she knew how to listen. Adroit deployment of feminine wiles had become Mary's principal strategy for survival.

In his instructions from the Queen, Shrewsbury had been explicitly warned to steel himself against Mary's charms, though Bess, in later years, affected to believe that he'd succumbed. This seems unlikely. But the Earl was far from cold-hearted, and while he might declare Mary to be 'a stranger, a Papist and my enemy', in letters to Cecil, he could not but be moved by her plight, nor, over the course of fifteen years, fail to respond to her personally. In the early years, relations between the Queen of Scots and both Shrewsburys were decidedly cordial.

Mary presented them with a number of expensive gifts – bejewelled pomanders, a collar of gold set with agates and pearls, gold and pearl bracelets, partlets with bejewelled ruffs.[9] She and Bess spent many hours gossiping over their embroidery. The Earl, while assuring Cecil and the Queen of the sternest vigilance, tried to allow his charge what diversions he could – occasional rides, perhaps, or visits to the baths at Buxton. Tutbury was admittedly a dismal place, but Shrewsbury's other properties – Wingfield Manor, Sheffield and Chatsworth, between which Mary was shunted – were comfortable and well furnished, indeed grand, and she was kept in some style. Mary may have been a prisoner, but she was quite insistent that she be treated as a queen. Throughout her long years of captivity, she dined in state, at her own table, with her 'diets' maintained at two courses for dinner and supper, each consisting of sixteen dishes, all prepared by her own kitchen staff. She had a large household, she kept her own horses, though she was rarely allowed to ride them, and her sheets were washed by her own laundresses.

The Earl made regular attempts to cut back Mary's retinue, beginning, on her arrival at Tutbury, by reducing her servants from sixty to thirty, besides her women. Mary reluctantly agreed, whilst at the same time asking for more horses and grooms. But Scottish supporters and hangers-on endlessly gravitated to her. By May 1569, numbers had crept up to eighty and the Earl was protesting to Cecil that this was far in excess of his allowance, not to mention the fact that more Scots meant more guards.[10]

The large number of people that the Earl was expected to accommodate was not just expensive, it also placed immense strain on sanitation and supplies of water, food and fuel. The lack of a sewage system, or plumbing, meant houses quickly became noxious – 'noysome', as the Earl put it – needing to be vacated in order to be 'sweetened': the stinking business of carting away the contents of the latrines. By the end of February 1569, the well water at Tutbury was 'evil and scant', fuel was scarce and Mary had a fever. The Earl asked for, and was granted, permission to move her to Wingfield, and Bess was sent ahead to prepare the state apartments.

South Wingfield Manor, built in the fifteenth century, on a hilltop site, around two courtyards (the state apartments, accommodating Mary, were in the inner court), has long been ruined, but even in outline it is possible to appreciate how grand and impressive a house it once was. However, in little over a month, Mary was complaining about the 'very unpleasant and fulsome savour' in the room next to her chamber, which was 'hurtful to her health', and the Earl was asking permission to move her once again, this time to Chatsworth for a few days, so the Wingfield apartments could be 'made sweet'.[11] Over the fifteen years of Shrewsbury's custodianship, Mary was moved forty-six times, and each move meant packing up and trundling her retinue, wardrobe, dogs, jewels and canopy of state over the ruts and potholes of the Derbyshire byways.

Shrewsbury reported faithfully on his prisoner to Cecil and the Queen. Mary was 'quiet' on arrival at Tutbury, but for much of the time she was 'unquiet'. There were frequent storms of tears, much dreaded by the Earl. She wept when any of her servants, to whom she was very attached and who were equally attached to her, were dismissed. She wept 'exceedingly' when Alexander ('Sandy') Bog, one of her servants, who had been sent on a reconnaissance to

Scotland, returned with the news that there was little or no support for her return. She complained constantly of her treatment at the hands of the Queen, of unsavoury smells, of lack of exercise, and of ill health – variously the pain in her side (probably a gastric ulcer), neuralgia, headaches, digestive problems, swollen legs and rheumatism. Some of these ailments were neurotic and most likely due to too much food and too little exercise. For a young woman as physically energetic as Mary – she adored riding, dancing, archery, even golf – confinement was a particular torment. However, what the Earl did not report were the times when Mary was merry and light-hearted and at her most charming, out on a ride, perhaps, or gossiping with Bess.

In March 1569, the Earl told Cecil that Mary 'daily resorts to my wife's chamber, where with Lady Leviston [Agnes Livingston] and Mary Seton [the only one of the 'Four Marys', Mary's childhood playmates, still with her], she sits working with the needle, wherein she much delights and devising works – her talk altogether of indifferent trifling matters, without any sign of secret dealing or practise I assure you'.[12] This was of course in violation of Shrewsbury's orders – Mary was not supposed to be fraternising with Bess in the ordinary way of things. But during the early days of her captivity, the two were very much together. This was hardly surprising. Mary was naturally gregarious and welcomed company. She was also avid for information about Elizabeth, the cousin she would never meet and in whose hands her fate lay. The two women may have talked of 'trifling matters', but as Mary would later claim in her 'Scandal Letter' (of which more later), such matters included a great deal of scurrilous gossip about the Queen. Nor were they averse to a bit of 'secret dealing'.

Bess was a source of information for Mary, and Mary an object of fascination for Bess – a figure of glamour and romance, but also one hung about with intrigue. Her twenty-six years had been shadowed, even by the standards of the age, by an unusually high quota of tragedy and brutality. She'd lost a kingdom, a son, and three husbands, in the murder of one of whom she had quite possibly connived and another by whom she had been abducted and raped. Here was a woman who was everything Bess was not – impulsive, reckless, fatally lacking in good judgement. Something they shared, however, was a love of 'working with the needle'.

Needlework, using silk or wool on a linen canvas background, was a sociable, communal activity, practised by the lady of the house together with her gentlewomen and servants. More complex techniques – metal-thread embroidery or appliqué work – were undertaken by men. (Bess employed various professional male embroiderers throughout her life, including Angell and Barnett during the years of marriage to William Cavendish, and later on, Thomas Lane, a man known as 'old Freake' and John Webb, who had his own room in Hardwick Old Hall.) Needlework was extremely popular in France, and Mary an accomplished needlewoman. Bess was less skilled, but she supervised the large-scale production of embroidered cushion covers, panels, table carpets and hangings during the 1570s, originally made for the adornment of Chatsworth, and eventually finding their way to Hardwick.

It is impossible to determine precisely the extent of Mary's involvement. But here was an activity she adored and excelled at – her knowledge and taste, acquired and refined at the French court, could be put to good use, as Bess was quick to note and exploit. Mary had fabric and sewing silks sent to her from France. She had at least one highly skilled embroiderer among her gentlemen, Bastian Pagez, a valet. It was Mary who introduced the practice of embroidering flowers, or 'slips', on canvas, which were then cut out and applied to a fabric background.[13] She may well have taught Bess and her ladies particular techniques, such as coloured cut-work, a painstaking process where embroidery forms a lacy effect against a contrasting background.[14] And she certainly had input when it came to design.

Designs were often taken from books of engravings, or woodcuts, and herbals – scenes from the Old Testament or classical mythology, prints of animals, plants and flowers. Bess probably owned some such books herself, and Mary certainly did – Conrad Gesner's *Icones Animalium*, for one, with its woodcuts of animals, birds and fish, published in 1560. Once chosen, designs were drawn onto canvas, which was stretched over frames, known as 'beams' or 'tents', then filled in using cross- or tent-stitch.* An embroidered panel, still at Hardwick, of 'A Catte' shows a marmalade cat – a sly allusion to Elizabeth's red hair – wearing a coronet, keeping a beady eye on a mouse (Mary). Neither coronet nor mouse is in Gesner's original – embroidery allowed Mary to indulge her love of coded messages, ciphers and emblems. Together she and Bess worked on a series of octagonal panels of plants and flowers, copied from a herbal by the botanist Pietro Andrea Mattioli.[†15] Mary's French sophistication and eye for design must have helped form Bess's own tastes.

The hours spent by Bess and Mary closeted over their needlework soon gave rise to talk, and the Earl found himself firing off assurances to Cecil and the Queen. Surely, he pointed out, 'no man of understanding can think that I or my wife "wittingly" should be glad of such tedious hourly attendance to the want of our own liberties, as we fain would have, and where none of us can talk or hear without suspicion!' He was all too aware though of 'the perils of envious tongues'.[16]

In fact, there was nothing enviable about the Earl's position. If ever there was a man caught between a rock and a hard place, it was he. On the one hand, there was Elizabeth, with her suspicions, her stinginess, her paranoia about Mary, her insistence that her cousin be treated with the respect her rank demanded but kept in conditions of the

---

* 'Nine pairs of beams' for the embroiderers were listed in the Hardwick inventory of 1601.

† Most of those worked by Mary are now at Oxburgh Hall, Norfolk, while those at Hardwick, all but two initialled by Bess, have been mounted on screens.

strictest restraint; on the other, Mary, with her intrigues, her complaints and her blandishments. To please both Queens required immense diplomacy and was a task the Earl felt increasingly unequal to. And then of course there was a third demanding woman in the mix – Bess, determinedly pursuing an agenda of her own.

9.

A DUBIOUS HONOUR

Shrewsbury found himself as much a prisoner of the Queen of Scots as she of Shrewsbury: required to be in permanent attendance; required to ask permission every time he needed to move her to another property (not always granted), or to come to court (usually refused), or simply to entertain his own children. That their children were not supposed to live under the same roof as Mary was a source of regret for the Shrewsburys – 'it seems her Majesty has no liking our children should be with us ... a great grief unto us'.[1] It meant that the Earl had to fund separate establishments for his sons, as well as maintaining two households, his own and Mary's.

The size of Mary's household fluctuated alarmingly and its costs were a constant bugbear. Officially Shrewsbury had a weekly £52 for Mary's 'diet' – her expenses – with an extra sum for those of the guards. But this was paid intermittently, and was anyway insufficient, as the Earl repeatedly and plaintively pointed out. Mary had a pension from the French Crown, but she had no intention of using this to fund herself whilst in captivity. It soon became abundantly clear that Elizabeth expected Shrewsbury to defray Mary's costs from his own pocket. By 1574, the Earl reckoned that he was spending an extra £300 a year on wages alone. In 1580, he set out the 'hidden charges' involved in keeping Mary: £1,000 a year on wine, spice and fuel; another £1,000 on the plate, pewter and 'household stuff' that was routinely 'spoiled' and had to be replaced; £400 on bonuses to his servants to ensure their loyalty.[2]

Most painful of all was the fact that Shrewsbury felt his honour to be impugned. And honour was paramount, the benchmark by which he defined himself. Having taken on the burden and expense of guarding Mary, he felt personally affronted when Elizabeth begrudged him Mary's allowance or questioned his treatment of his prisoner. Not only was he inadequately recompensed, but he was regarded with suspicion, constantly required to justify his conduct to Cecil and the Queen.

Mary would never forgo her plotting and intriguing, in the hope of gaining her freedom and restoration to the Scottish throne. And she would never cease reiterating her claim to the English throne and looking not just to English Catholics, but to Spain, France and the papacy, to help her. Shutting off all channels of communication between Mary and her supporters was an impossible task. Letters were found hidden in bags with false bottoms, or under stones, or within the hollow staff of a visitor; they were smuggled out by servants, despite Shrewsbury's cash bonuses, bringing further criticism on his head. Naturally prone to paranoia, the Earl felt increasingly aggrieved: 'I could be right well contented to be discharged ... if I could see how the same might be without any blemish to my honour and estimation.'[3]

In June 1569, Bess reported to the Queen that her husband, while at Chatsworth, had 'fallen into extreme sickness' and had to be carried back to Wingfield on a litter. The Earl, unlike his wife, was not robust and suffered regular bouts of ill health – gout, colic, mysterious agues – probably exacerbated by nervous strain. This time he felt 'so grievously tormented with the gout and a hot ague' that he longed for death.[4] The Queen, anxious that he wasn't up to the job, ordered that Mary be bundled off to a neighbour, Sir John Zouch (the same family to whom Bess had been sent as a young woman).

Mary wrote to Bess, her 'very good friend and cousin', enquiring after the Earl, relaying 'such news' as she had – allusions to obscure plots against her on the part of the Earl of Mar, who had custody of her baby son James, and 'five or six particular men', who were 'bound to all extremity against me and mine' – and complaining of the 'double dealing' of the Earl of Moray, the Scottish regent.* She begged Bess to send 'word of your well doing both'.[5] The tone of the letter is confiding, though Mary failed to mention her most interesting piece of 'news' – the fact that she was busy plotting to marry the Duke of Norfolk.

This plan had the backing of many at court, including Leicester, though the Queen, fatally, was kept in the dark. Marriage to Norfolk, England's premier nobleman, immensely rich and, nominally at least, Protestant, was seen as a way of neutralising Mary – once safely married, she could then be restored to the Scottish throne. Mary seized on the idea with enthusiasm – here was a route to freedom and Scotland. Norfolk, who had buried three wives, could not quite resist the prospect of a Scottish queen as a fourth. The two were soon exchanging love letters. There was of course the small matter of Mary's marriage to Bothwell (Bothwell had lost his wits and was languishing in a Danish jail), which, to Mary's frustration, had been voted by the Scots as legal and binding, but she hoped for an annulment.

By July, the Norfolk marriage plan was common knowledge; when it came to the ears of the Queen, she, predictably, flew into a rage. In October, Norfolk, despite a great deal of frantic back-pedalling, found himself in the Tower. And Shrewsbury, who had recovered sufficiently to be able to walk from his bedchamber to his gallery (hardly much of a recovery), came in for blame too. 'I have found no reliance on my Lord Shrewsbury in the hour of my need, for all the fine speeches

---

* Moray was killed in January 1570 and replaced by the Earl of Lennox, who suffered the same fate a year later.

he made me formerly, yet I can in no wise depend on his promise', huffed the Queen.[6]

She ordered Mary back to Tutbury, where her rooms were thoroughly searched, her servants were once again reduced to thirty and the sending and receiving of letters was forbidden. The Earl of Huntingdon and Viscount Hereford were sent to Tutbury as reinforcements, implicitly casting doubt on Shrewsbury's competence. Huntingdon was soon causing trouble, claiming that the Earl had been overly lenient towards his charge, and there was talk once again of Bess's partiality and rotten apples amongst the Shrewsbury servants. The Earl wrote to Cecil in October of his 'grief that suspicion is had of over nice good will born by my wife to this Queen, and of untrue dealings by my men'. Bess, he insisted, had 'not otherwise dealt with this Queen than I have been privy unto, and that I have had liking of'. Far from urging him to continue in his post, since his 'sickness' she had been calling for his 'discharge'. But, the Earl assured Cecil, 'I am not to be led by her otherwise than I think well of'.[7]

In fact, in the honeymoon days of their marriage, Shrewsbury was more than happy to be 'led' by Bess. 'Of all joys I have under god the greatest is yourself', he wrote soon after the Norfolk fiasco, assuring her that he'd burned her last letter, as she'd wished.[8] He had questioned Mary as to whether she had been writing to her 'friends', and though she had insisted that 'of her honour she hath not', the Earl was taking 'small account' of her denial. He had told his son Gilbert how lucky he was 'to have such a mother' as Bess. There is no suggestion that Shrewsbury was anything but entirely devoted to his wife, and entirely indifferent to the Queen of Scots. Nevertheless, a third person had been introduced into a marriage that had scarcely had time to find its feet – a woman some twenty years younger than Bess, and an unusually alluring woman at that. Mary, with her love of intrigue and powers of attraction, could not help but be a divisive presence.

* * *

November 1569 saw one of Elizabeth's worst fears realised – a Catholic rebellion in support of the Scots Queen. The northern rising was led by the Catholic Earls of Westmorland and Northumberland, both supporters of the Duke of Norfolk (Norfolk's sister was married to Westmorland). Shrewsbury and Huntingdon, having heard that a rebel army six thousand strong had set out from Durham Cathedral and was marching south towards Tutbury, hastily moved Mary to Coventry. In fact the rebellion was a damp squib, crushed within six weeks, but the reprisals were brutal – over eight hundred went to the gallows – and the Queen was shaken. The northern rebellion marked a shift in religious policy. For a decade, Elizabeth had favoured toleration, but now attitudes to Catholics hardened, especially when, a year later, the Queen was excommunicated by the Pope, who called on Catholics to withdraw their allegiance to her. No longer could one claim loyalty to both Queen and Pope (though many, like the recusant Sir Thomas Tresham, continued to do so). To be a Catholic was to be a 'papist' and a traitor.

The new year found the Scots Queen back once more at the hated Tutbury. Bess had no more love for Tutbury than Mary, and by the spring of 1570 she had taken herself off to Chatsworth, still the house closest to her heart, and certainly preferred to any Shrewsbury property. Of her children, only Elizabeth and Mary – the latter, though married, did not yet live with Gilbert Talbot as his wife – remained at home. William and Charles were studying at Cambridge. Henry was already attracting trouble – one of his servants, a certain Swinnerton (a 'vain, lewd fellow' according to Bess), had killed a man in a sword fight. Perhaps to remove him from undesirable influences, Henry, together with Gilbert Talbot, had been packed off on a kind of grand tour of France and Italy.

Hugh Fitzwilliam kept Bess informed about events in London and abroad with regular bulletins. In July, he described how the French King, Charles IX, had told Elizabeth that he hoped the Queen of Scots (his former sister-in-law) 'might enjoy her own realm and to govern it and to see the bringing up of her own child' (with the implication that it was Elizabeth's duty to facilitate this). The Queen's reply was tart: 'she marvelled the King would trouble himself in matters so far from him, having so much to do at home'. As regarded herself and Mary, 'they could agree well enough'. The Duke of Norfolk, said Fitzwilliam, had 'utterly renounced the marriage with the Scottish Queen'.[9] The following month, he reported on the treason trials, in the wake of the northern rising, at Norwich. Several rebels were to be hanged, drawn and quartered; others faced life imprisonment and the loss of their goods and lands. He had also heard that the Earl of Leicester was employing a great many workmen to make Kenilworth Castle 'strong', furnishing it with 'armour, munitions and all necessaries for defence'.[10]

In 1563, Leicester had been given Kenilworth, in Warwickshire, and in 1570 he embarked on an ambitious remodelling of the existing medieval buildings, supervised by William Spicer, formerly of Longleat, including a gatehouse, a new wing and a huge lodging tower. Why he would have concerned himself with fortifying Kenilworth is unclear – it may have been thought to be vulnerable after the northern rising, but that aside, Leicester had military aspirations and liked to see himself not merely as a great patron, but a great soldier, who would lead his forces into battle in defence of his Queen. In fact, Kenilworth became known not for its forti-fications, but for its dazzling expanses of glass, a 'lantern house'. Windows, during the 1570s, were growing ever larger.

If Shrewsbury's letters to Bess in the early years of their marriage are scattered with professions of love and gratitude, hers to him, though not unaffectionate, are more notable for their demands, and their note of impatience. 'You forget your none', she wrote from Chatsworth, 'send the plumber with speed I pray you.' Hanks, her brewer, was unable to brew beer and ale for lack of malt and hops – 'either there must be better provision made or else I shall think my none means not to come here this summer'. As a sweetener, she sent him lettuces and butter.[11] The Earl was not of course free to come to Chatsworth to please Bess, but in May 1570 he was granted permission to move Mary there.

Chatsworth, being remote from any town, was considered particularly secure. Bess was planning a major new phase of building work, but even in its present state the large and comfortable house, with its river and gardens, was a very great improvement on Tutbury, and for the first time, the conditions of Mary's confinement were somewhat relaxed. The Queen agreed that she could 'take the air for her health', ride on the moors, hawk, send and receive letters and have a few visitors.[12] It even appeared that she might be considering Mary's restoration to the Scottish throne.

In September, Cecil and his wife Mildred came to Chatsworth, along with Sir Walter Mildmay, the Chancellor of the Exchequer, and John Lesley, Bishop of Ross, a Catholic and former lawyer, who acted as Mary's representative. They were there to discuss the possibility of Mary giving up her claim to the English throne and returning to Scotland as Queen, leaving her son James in England as a hostage to good behaviour, a plan that came to nothing since it was rejected by the Scots, who had no desire to have Mary back. What did Cecil and Mary make of each other, these two so implacably opposed? For Mary, Cecil was the agent of her destruction; for Cecil, Mary was a threat to the English throne and the Protestant faith, and thus needed to be removed, ideally by death. Of their interview, which ended with Mary in tears, neither left any record. Cecil did write a 'leaving letter' to Shrewsbury, assuring him that Elizabeth had perfect confidence in both Shrewsburys as custodians of the Queen of Scots. Bess had showered Lady Cecil with gifts and Cecil could only regret 'that my Lady should have bestowed such things as my wife cannot recompense as she would, but with her hearty goodwill and service'.[13]

Plots and intrigues rumbled on. That summer, at Chatsworth, a half-baked attempt was made to free Mary, led by a local Catholic squire, Sir Thomas Gerard. Initially the plan was to kidnap her while she was out riding, but when this was vetoed by John Beaton, her master of the household, as too risky, it was decided that she would be lowered from a window. The plot was discovered by the Shrewsburys, but had never had Mary's backing in the first place. One of the plotters was a former disaffected servant of the Earl, John Hall, who claimed he had left Shrewsbury's service because he 'did mislike my lord's marriage with his wife, as divers of his friends did', a hint that Bess was not universally popular within the household.[14]

The Shrewsburys were plagued by disloyal servants, who seemed only too willing to be conscripted into Mary's service, a measure of her capacity to win sympathy. In October 1571, Bess received a letter from William Cecil, now Lord Burghley,* about a certain Hersey Lassels, a former servant. Lassels, said Burghley, had confessed that he'd been 'dealing' with the Queen of Scots, having been approached by her and John Beaton. He had smuggled letters between her and the Duke of Norfolk, and had done so with Bess's knowledge. 'I have thought good to advertise your Ladyship thereof', continued Burghley smoothly, 'and withal to pray you to let me understand the truth of such matter as your ladyship doth know of the said Hersey Lassels dealings.'[15]

This letter must have struck a chill into Bess's heart – she was, after all, being accused of 'dealings' herself, of using Lassels to spy on Mary's 'doings and devices', and such dealings were potentially treasonable. But she defended herself robustly: it was true that the moment she had heard that Lassels had 'some familiar talk' with Mary, she had asked him to report to her. When Lassels told her that Mary had showed him 'great good will' and promised to make him a lord, Bess disabused him – Mary actually hated him and he should beware of her. He was then dismissed by the Earl, for being 'both vain and glorious'. However, she flatly denied that she had ever known of any

---

* In 1572 Burghley became Lord Treasurer.

'dealing between her [Mary] and the Duke of Norfolk by the said Lassels or any other'.[16]

Whether or not Bess knew of it, Mary had not given up hopes of Norfolk and was still trying to have her marriage to Bothwell annulled by the Pope. In September 1571, Norfolk was once again imprisoned in the Tower. Bess, desperate to learn more, sent word to Hugh Fitzwilliam, who supplied what information he could: Norfolk, it seemed, had been sending money to Scottish lords, supporters of Mary; letters from Mary, as well as the cipher, had been found hidden 'in the roof amongst the tile stones' of Norfolk's house; Norfolk's servants were being racked.[17]

This all led to the uncovering of the Ridolfi Plot. Roberto Ridolfi, who had been involved in the earlier plan to marry Mary to Norfolk, was a Florentine banker and double agent, working for both the Spaniards and Walsingham, the Queen's spy-master. This time, with the backing of the Spanish, Elizabeth was to be deposed and replaced by Mary, with Norfolk as her husband. So serious a threat was this that Parliament – rarely summoned under Elizabeth – was called to debate the Queen's safety. Burghley and his supporters lobbied for Mary, like Norfolk, to be tried for treason, but without any absolute proof that she had endorsed the plot, the Queen stalled. For Elizabeth, executing an anointed queen was a step too far. She was not even willing to exclude Mary from the succession. Shrewsbury was merely ordered to confront his prisoner and get her to admit her guilt. Mary, however, was admitting nothing.

She was being held at Sheffield, where conveniently Shrewsbury had two properties – the castle and the manor, just a mile apart, so Mary could easily be shunted from one to the other, allowing for 'cleansing'. The Earl assured Burghley that she was under the strictest surveillance, only permitted to walk on the 'leads' of the castle, or in the dining chamber or courtyard. He had increased her guard, and either he or Bess was always with her.[18] When Shrewsbury went to London in January 1572 – as Lord High Steward he had to preside at Norfolk's trial – Sir Ralph Sadler came to Sheffield to take charge of Mary, who refused to leave her rooms in the castle and would have nothing to do with him. Bess, according to Sadler, hardly left Mary's side. This may have been Mary insisting on Bess's company, but it could equally well have been Bess keeping a watchful eye on Mary.

Norfolk was found guilty of high treason and sentenced to death. Shrewsbury, who would take on Norfolk's title of Earl Marshal, wept as he pronounced the verdict. At Sheffield, Sadler asked Bess to inform Mary of Norfolk's execution. Mary, who already knew, was found 'all to be wept and mourning'; when, somewhat callously, Bess asked her what the matter was, she replied with dignity that 'she was sure my Lady could not be ignorant of the cause'. Sadler had not relished his duties at Sheffield, confessing himself 'never so weary of any service as I am of this'. Bess, he thought, could hardly look forward to the Earl's return 'more than I do'.[19]

Shrewsbury's return to Sheffield, where Mary was now generally held, brought no let-up. He was still regularly called on to defend himself and Bess in the face of 'doubts' on the part of the Queen. In December 1572, the Earl wrote to Burghley, aggrieved by accusations of 'undutiful dealing' and defending his habit of 'riding abroad sometimes (not far from my charge) in respect of my health only'. Occasional rides were nothing new, and 'I trusted none in my absence but those I had tried'.[20] Earlier that year, a 'device' had been uncovered for 'the stealing of' Mary from Sheffield and the Earl had laid on an extra thirty guards and forbidden her to walk outside the castle.[21] In 1573, yet another attempt to spirit her out of a castle window was foiled. Gilbert Talbot, when questioned by a member of the Privy Council about his father's competence, replied that it was quite impossible for Mary to escape 'unless she could transform herself to a flea or a mouse'.[22] The following year, several of the Earl's servants, including his sons' tutor Alexander Hamilton, of whom he thought highly, were, yet again, found to be smuggling letters for Mary.[23]

Bess, who was by now tiring of the Queen of Scots and her duties as gaoler's wife, spent increasingly less time at Sheffield, preferring to base herself at Chatsworth, away from Mary and therefore apart from her husband. In November 1571, Thomas Kniveton, who was married to Bess's half-sister Jane, and who also worked for Shrewsbury, wrote to tell her that the Earl, still not entirely recovered from his collapse in the summer, was 'very quiet and reasonably well but cannot so continue ... I think his lordship minds your honour shall abide at Chatsworth till near Christmas, but that I like not if I might be heard.'[24] This sounds a note of warning – Kniveton, as family, felt able to offer Bess some brotherly advice. Remaining at Chatsworth for long periods of time was not necessarily for the good of the Shrewsbury marriage.

If the fault lines were in place, they stayed largely hidden during the early 1570s. It suited Bess in many ways to have the Earl tied to Mary at Sheffield, leaving her free to pursue her own projects, and her plans for Chatsworth in particular. While at Chatsworth, she looked to her husband to supply her needs, be it money, iron, timber, plate, beer, oats, barley or venison pasties. He didn't always oblige, or at least was dilatory. 'You haste not to supply any want I have', she wrote testily, 'the two bottles of sack you sent hither will do small service here, the one is the smallest that ever I drink, like as though it were half water, the other much worse ... it savours so of the vessel ... Farewell unkind none.'[25]

Shrewsbury's letters to Bess, on the other hand, remain unfailingly uxorious, even clumsily flirtatious: 'the true and faithful love you bear me is more comfortable to me than any thing I can think upon and I give God thanks daily for the benefice he has bestowed upon me and greatest cause I have to give him thanks [is] that he hath sent me you in my oldest years to comfort me ... I thank you for the fat capon and it shall be baked and kept cold and untouched till my sweetheart comes. Guess who it is? I have sent you a pheasant cock ... farewell my sweet true none and faithful wife.'[26] He sent horses so that she could come to him the following day, 'for that I think it long till you come'. He provided snippets of news – Sheffield was 'greatly troubled with measles', Mary 'keeps much to her bed' – and bulletins on his health: his colic was 'grievous', he had 'been too bold with the herring' and made himself sick.[27]

Ailments aside, the Earl was feeling the pinch. The costs of keeping up multiple households, not to mention those of keeping Mary, were huge, and these on top of the large settlements that had to be made on the occasion of his children's marriages, especially that of his eldest son Francis to the daughter of the Earl of Pembroke. Francis was also constantly in debt and applying to his father for handouts. Shrewsbury saw money leaking away in every direction, and it panicked him.

Lack of ready cash led him to sign a deed of gift, on 22 April 1572, whereby he was let off from paying 'great sums of money which he the said Earl standeth chargeable to pay as well to the younger children of the said Countess as also for the debts of the said Countess [what these were is unclear] and for diverse other weighty considerations'.[28] Under the marriage settlement, the Earl was due to make large payments (about £20,000), which he could ill afford, to his stepsons, William and Charles, when they came of age (William was twenty-one in 1572, hence the urgency). In return for not doing so, all the estates that Bess had brought to her marriage (the western lands for example), which brought in a little over £1,000 a year in rents, were now settled on William and Charles, with Bess retaining a life interest. Later, the Earl would do his best to wriggle out of this deed – the source of the bitterest wrangling between the Shrewsburys – but in the short term it brought financial relief. For Bess, its benefits were immense: all that she had given up on her marriage was returned to her, and she now had financial independence and a profitable core of estates on which she could build and expand over the coming years.

10.

'CLOSE DEALING'

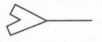

In 1574, at Sheffield, Mary, Bess's youngest daughter, married to Gilbert Talbot, gave birth to her first child, a son, named George after his paternal grandfather. The Queen, fearing that strangers might have been present, soon made her displeasure felt. Shrewsbury hastened to reassure her – none had attended the birth apart from the midwife, and he himself, with two of his children, had christened the child. The previous week the castle had been shaken by an earthquake, which had greatly alarmed the Queen of Scots – God 'grant it may be a forewarning unto her', wrote the Earl sententiously.[1] By now he was heartily sick of his charge, confessing to Burghley, 'I wish with all my heart I had never dealt withal.' A 'bruit' reached his ears, relayed by Elizabeth Wingfield, Bess's half-sister, 'of this queen going from me'.[2] It turned out to be false, but it would have been welcome enough.

For the Earl, the constant alarms and the resulting criticism and suspicion that he felt directed at him presented an increasing strain. He had Mary's complaints to contend with too. Lack of exercise was taking its toll on her health. She tried regular bathing with herbs, but when the 'hardness in her side' worsened, she began agitating to be taken to the baths at Buxton – 'La Fontayne de Bogsby' as she called them. In August 1573, royal permission was finally granted, on the condition that Mary be kept well away from any strangers.

Taking the waters at Buxton, both bathing and drinking, became highly fashionable during the 1570s. At Buxton one could pursue good health and meet friends, activities that were not necessarily complementary. Leicester was a regular, as were Shrewsbury and Burghley, both in search of relief from their gout. So too was Sir Christopher Hatton. 'Mr Hatton by reason of his great sickness is minded to go to the spa for the better recovery of his health', Francis Talbot told his father in May 1573.[3] Hatton was a gentleman's son from Northamptonshire, who rose to become a member of the Privy Council, and, eventually, Lord Chancellor. According to a contemporary, he was 'a mere vegetable of the Court that sprung at night and sank again at noon', but, partly on account of his good looks and his dancing prowess, he was a great favourite with the Queen, who, reported Gilbert Talbot, visited him daily on his sickbed.[4] Gilbert saw little hope for Hatton, but perhaps Buxton worked its magic, for he made a full recovery, going on to build his great houses Holdenby and Kirby Hall.

According to William Harrison, the Buxton waters were said to be the finest in England, unsurpassed when it came to 'strengthening the enfeebled members' and 'assisting the lively forces'.[5] Some of the springs were hot, in theory, though the Earl of Sussex found the water so cold in 1582 that he could hardly bear to get in, and settled on drinking it instead – three pints, rising to eight, a day.[6] Buxton was part of the Cavendish estate, and in the early 1570s Shrewsbury began building a hall over the baths, described by a Dr Jones, who wrote a treatise on the waters in 1572, as 'a very goodly house, four square, four stories high, so well compact with houses of office beneath and above and round about, with a great chamber and other goodly lodgings to the number of thirty, that it is and will be a beauty to behold'.[7] There were seats around the baths and fireplaces for the airing of clothes. Buxton was not entirely a spa for the rich: fees operated on a sliding scale, ranging from £5 for an archbishop to 20s. for an earl and 12d for a yeoman; one half of the fee went to the doctor in charge, the rest into a fund for the use of the poor, who were lodged in wooden sheds.[8] By 1573, Shrewsbury's hall was finished, ready to receive the Queen of Scots.

Besides the hall at Buxton, the Earl was building at Sheffield on a grand scale. This presented yet another drain on his finances, but was at least one of his own making. Prior to his marriage to Bess, Shrewsbury had shown no particular interest in building; however, spurred on by, and possibly in competition with, his wife, he soon caught the bug. To what degree Bess, who was busy with her own building works at Chatsworth, was involved with those at Sheffield is hard to gauge, but she would surely have advised and she would certainly have had views. 'Your plan has not come down according to your promise', the Earl complained in 1574.[9] This could have referred to Chatsworth, but equally to Sheffield, where an extensive remodelling of the manor, including the addition of a grand gatehouse with twin octagonal towers, had been going on for a couple of years. In 1573, the Earl told his bailiff, William Dickenson,* that the pain in his leg prevented him coming to Sheffield to inspect the works, but Dickenson was to make the workmen *believe* that he was coming – it was important to keep them up to the mark.[10]

Sheffield Manor, from its hilltop site, once overlooked a great deer park, eight miles in circumference and bordered by two rivers. The park, where Mary longed to hunt, was known for its walnut avenues and giant oak trees, one so vast, it was said, that two hundred horsemen could take shelter beneath its branches.[11] All traces of the park have long gone. Today the ruins of the manor – nothing of the castle survives – are hemmed in by post-war housing estates and, beyond, the sprawl of the city. However, a turret house, built in 1574 as a banqueting house or hunting tower, remains intact. In January 1574, William Dickenson drew up an agreement between the Earl

---

* Dickenson was building his own house in Sheffield, timber-framed, with panels of wattle and daub.

and two masons for a year's work.[12] In addition to their wage, the masons were to get a coat each but were expected to provide their own tools.

The Turret House is three storeys high, with two small rooms on each floor, and a corner stair rising to the turret. On the top floor is the banqueting room, where the Shrewsburys and their guests would have decamped, after dinner in the manor, to eat comfits and chat and admire the view. This is a jewel of a room: a grand fireplace with an overmantel of great muscular Talbot hounds (known as Talbots); an elaborate plasterwork ceiling with more hounds, coronets, lion heads, Etruscan masks, vines and sprays of lilies and roses; windows of glowing red and yellow heraldic glass. It's finer than anything at Hardwick (where there is no heraldic glass) and gives some measure of the former glories of the manor.* Did Mary have a hand in the decoration? Was the plasterwork drawn from images in her pattern books? What of the lilies of France? Or the crowned 'M's in the window glass? It's hard to believe that the Scottish Queen wasn't consulted, or that she didn't occasionally enjoy the banqueting room herself, or stand on the leads, looking out across the expanse of the park towards the hills of 'Hallamshire' (Yorkshire).

For the Queen of Scots, intrigue was life, the only means she had of exercising some degree of free will and autonomy. Intrigue, practised judiciously, appealed to Bess too, and matchmaking was just one form. Back in 1571, she had been intriguing with a John Lenton about a match for 'Master Pierrepont', presumably a relation, perhaps brother, of the Henry Pierrepont to whom her daughter Frances was married. They must proceed carefully, thought Lenton: 'therefore he must handle the matter wisely and silently, that must put his hand without

---

* Sheffield was lavishly furnished. A 1582 inventory mentions a great six-piece tapestry of the story of Hercules and eight 'long Turkey carpets' (*Journal of the British Archaeological Association*, 1874, Vol. XXX).

harm between the bark and the tree ... I beseech you good madam, use the young gentleman as gently as you can, that we may win him.' Bess had apparently had plans for Anne Pierrepont too, but Anne was in love with 'one Teyvle', so Lenton thought Bess's hopes of 'Master Chaworth' (the Chaworths were cousins of Bess's) would be dashed. 'By close dealing a man will come to a kingdom', he added in a post-script, a piece of gnomic wisdom with which Bess would have concurred.[13]

'Close dealing' was the order of the day in 1574. Some of this involved the Queen of Scots, of whose intrigues Bess was at the very least aware.* In 1574, she wrote to Mary, thanking her for remembering her 'little poor creature', who 'showed more gladness than was to be looked for in one double her years'. This most probably refers to Bessie Pierrepont, Bess's granddaughter, who had been taken into Mary's household in 1571, aged four, and who was a great favourite with the Queen of Scots – she called her 'Mignonne' and made her pretty dresses. Then Bess, who must have known of the danger of Mary's correspondence being intercepted by agents of Walsingham or Burghley, becomes cryptic: she has sent four letters, which she hopes can be 'showed'; if Mary feels that *she* can write 'as required' – and Bess assures her 'no harm' will come of it – she begs her to send her letter with 'this bearer', and, for safety's sake, to address it to Bess's son.[14] In an accompanying note, she asks Gilbert Curle, Mary's secretary, to deliver the letter and 'procure answer with that speed you may'.

As to the nature of the four letters sent by Bess, or the letter she hoped that Mary would write, we are in the dark. But it's clear enough that she was attempting to enlist Mary's help, perhaps in connection with her principal project of 1574 – the marriage of her daughter Elizabeth. Of Bess's daughters, only nineteen-year-old Elizabeth

---

* A few years later, c.1577, Gilbert Talbot would alert Bess to a couple of Scots, one the brother of Mary's secretary Gilbert Curle, who were heading for Sheffield, posing as cloth-sellers and bearing letters for Mary (BHL, ID 84).

remained unmarried. We know little of Elizabeth Cavendish – just two creatively spelt letters survive, one thanking her mother for the loan of a horse litter, the other anxious that 'false bruits' about her have incurred Bess's 'displeasure'.[15] But she seems to have been of a mild, amenable disposition – certainly in comparison to her sister Mary – happy to fall in with her mother's plans.

Bess had been casting about for a husband for Elizabeth. According to Shrewsbury, there had been 'few noblemen's sons in England that she hath not prayed me to deal for at one time or other'.[16] The Earl had been digging his heels in when it came to stumping up a dowry, and although eventually Bess 'by brawling did get three thousand pounds', various candidates – Lord Rutland, Lord Sussex, Lord Wharton – fell by the wayside.[17] One, however, looked promising – Peregrine Bertie, the son of Katherine, Duchess of Suffolk, by her second marriage to Richard Bertie. The Duchess, previously married to Charles Brandon, Duke of Suffolk, and reluctant to relinquish her title for plain Mrs Bertie, was known to Bess of old – she was godmother to Frances Cavendish. She and Bess had been discussing the match for the past year and the Earl was in favour – young Bertie would do well enough.

In February 1574, Hugh Fitzwilliam wrote to tell Bess that he was trying to engineer a 'meeting of the parties'. The Duchess wanted to set this up at Huntingdon, her Northamptonshire house, but Fitzwilliam thought this too public 'considering both sides require secrecy' (why this should have been so is a mystery). Bertie had now come to Gray's Inn, where William Cavendish was studying law, and if he and his father were to meet William, and all were agreeable, it 'may further the matter much'.[18] However, it seemed that the feelings of the young couple had not been taken into account – young Bertie loved another and the match came to nothing.

Bess had to think again. The details are murky, but over the summer of 1574, in cahoots with the Duchess of Suffolk, who perhaps felt badly that Elizabeth had been 'disappointed of young Bertie', and

Margaret, Countess of Lennox, she cooked up a plan. Margaret Lennox was a woman much battered but unbowed by misfortune and loss. Six of her eight children by the Earl of Lennox had died young, and Darnley, married so disastrously to the Queen of Scots, had been killed at Kirk o' Field. Only nineteen-year-old Charles Stuart remained, by all accounts an unsatisfactory and sickly youth, described by even his mother as 'my greatest dolour'. The passion and recklessness of Margaret's youth had been tempered by age – she was now a widow of fifty-nine – but for wiliness and force of will she was certainly Bess's equal. Margaret was anxious to find a wife for young Charles, ideally one with a substantial dowry to boost the dwindling Lennox fortunes.

While Bess schemed at Chatsworth, Shrewsbury, at Sheffield with Mary, was not consulted. By August, a note of impatience creeps into his letters – Bess's long absences and her endless demands were beginning to grate. His 'only joy' and 'sweet true none' is now addressed merely as 'Wife', and her various 'wants' wearily listed: a book, a dozen pigeons, items of plate, a billament costing £23, pheasant pullets, 'pastes of a stage' (venison pasties), beer and ale, boxes of comfits, lemons and oranges. In a postscript he adds darkly, 'great turmoil doth two houses breed'.[19] The logistics and expense of maintaining two separate, and very large, households, at Sheffield and Chatsworth, was taking its toll on the Earl. He longed for a little *tendresse* from his wife; he longed for her company; he longed to be regarded as something more than a purse and provider.

During the summer of 1574, Margaret Lennox asked for the Queen's permission to visit her Yorkshire estate, Temple Newsam. This was granted on the condition that she didn't visit the Queen of Scots either at Sheffield or Chatsworth, or indeed go within thirty miles of her. Margaret affected indignation, insisting that she had no intention of doing any such thing, 'for I was made of flesh and blood and could never forget the murder of my child' – though in point of fact she no longer believed Mary guilty of Darnley's murder and was on friendly enough terms with her former daughter-in-law.[20] Rumours swirled about court as to her real motives in visiting Yorkshire – some said she intended to bring her little grandson James back from Scotland.

In September, the Countess, together with her son Charles, set out for the north. She broke her journey with a stay at Huntingdon, and the Duchess of Suffolk then accompanied the Lennoxes as far as Grantham before returning home. At Newark, Margaret received a message from Bess, inviting her to Rufford Abbey, once a Cistercian abbey, acquired by the 4th Earl of Shrewsbury during the Dissolution and subsequently converted into a house. Bess, who had conveniently positioned herself at Rufford, which, on the edge of Sherwood Forest, was but a short distance from Newark, rode out to meet the Lennoxes. Once at Rufford, the Countess fell ill and promptly took to her bed for five days, during which time Charles Stuart and Elizabeth Cavendish, responding either to the romance of their surroundings* or to the wishes of their mothers, obligingly fell in love and were promptly married in Rufford chapel.

This was possibly very fortuitous, but more likely very carefully stage-managed. It was presented, however, as a *coup de foudre*, with all parties insisting loudly that there hadn't been any underhand 'dealing', that love had simply carried the day. Shrewsbury, giving Burghley a full account 'of these ladies and their dealings at my houses', claimed that the young man was so in love that 'he is sick without her'.[21] Personally, he was relieved to have Elizabeth off his hands.

For Bess, it was no small triumph; she might find herself grand-mother to a future king, or queen. Since the direct line from Henry VIII ended with Elizabeth, if, as seemed increasingly likely, she died childless, the throne could then pass to the descendants of Henry's elder sister, Margaret, or his younger, Mary. From Mary Tudor came the Grey sisters, of whom Jane and Katherine were dead, Mary the youngest was childless and Katherine's two sons had been declared

---

* D. H. Lawrence based Wragby Hall in *Lady Chatterley's Lover* on Rufford.

illegitimate by the Queen. From Margaret came Mary, Queen of Scots, her son James VI of Scotland – whose Scottish birth by rights nullified his claim – and Charles Stuart, who thus stood third in line to the throne. This of course was precisely why a match between Charles and Elizabeth Cavendish would not find favour with the Queen; indeed it would feel a threat. Not only would a child born to Charles and Elizabeth take its place in the succession, but he or she would also have the Queen of Scots as an aunt. Closer ties between the Shrewsburys and Mary were not to be encouraged. The benefits for the Lennoxes were less obvious – Elizabeth Cavendish was no great catch in terms of birth – but there were powerful financial incentives: a loan from Bess (over the next four years Margaret made annual repayments of £500) and Elizabeth's £3,000 dowry, though in fact, with Shrewsbury arguing that he'd never consented to the marriage in the first place, this was only paid many years later, long after Elizabeth herself was dead.[22]

For the Queen, the succession was, and would remain, a subject of acute sensitivity, and one with which she refused to engage. By 1574, she had been on the throne for fifteen years and, in defiance of all doubts and apprehensions about her sex, found herself greatly loved by a people who were enjoying stability, prosperity and peace – the religious wars that were convulsing France and the Netherlands left England untouched. Only her lack of husband or heir presented, at least for Burghley and his fellow councillors, a cloud of anxiety. The possibility of the Duke of Anjou (the future Henry III) as a husband had been mooted four years earlier, in 1570, when the Queen was thirty-seven – still within childbearing age – and when, in the wake of the Ridolfi Plot and the Queen's excommunication, a French alliance, as a bulwark against Spanish and papal aggression, looked particularly appealing. But Anjou, an energetically bisexual yet fervently religious nineteen-year-old, was unenthusiastic about the match; when he refused to renounce his Catholicism, it foundered. At forty-one, the chances of Elizabeth producing an heir looked slim.

When the Lennox marriage came to the Queen's ears in November, it brought a storm. Margaret Lennox was ordered back to London, together with Charles and Elizabeth. Once there, all three were placed under house arrest in the Lennox house in Hackney, and following an inquiry, the Countess was sent to the Tower, this for the third time, and all, as she said plaintively, 'for love matters'. Thomas Fowler, her secretary, was interrogated as to what he'd known and whether, when he'd been at his mistress's house at Temple Newsam the previous summer, he'd been to see Bess.[23] Nobody really believed that there was anything very spontaneous about the marriage – rather, it had every appearance of having been planned for some time.

By now, Shrewsbury was in a spin of alarm, assuring the Queen that as far as he was concerned, the marriage had been 'dealt in suddenly and without my knowledge'.[24] In all likelihood, he hadn't been consulted – he would never have condoned a marriage that he knew would anger the Queen, as Bess would have been well aware. Bess herself, almost certainly the chief architect of the match, surprisingly went unpunished. Over an acquaintance of more than twenty years, she had always been careful to cultivate the good opinion of the Queen, irreproachable in conduct, thoughtful with gifts. Her credit stood high enough for a single breach of loyalty to be overlooked. Besides, as the wife of Mary's gaoler, she had made herself indispensable – the Queen needed her by Shrewsbury's side, not in the Tower.

By the following year, whatever 'dealings' had taken place over the Lennox marriage had been forgiven and the Earl was writing affection-ately to his wife: 'My dear heart, as you long to be with me so assuredly I am as desirous to have you.' Bess was to be sure to tell Elizabeth Stuart to eat fruit, 'which she loves well'.[25] The Earl's concern about Elizabeth's diet had particular significance – she was pregnant.

In November 1575, the Countess of Lennox, now released from the Tower and back in her Hackney home, wrote to the Queen of

Scots, who took a kindly interest in the young Lennoxes, to thank her for her 'good remembrance and bounty to our little daughter – her who some day may serve your highness', with Elizabeth Lennox adding her thanks in a postscript.[26] Elizabeth had just given birth to a daughter, Arbella. The baby's sex no doubt came as a relief to the Queen and a disappointment to Bess, who would nevertheless campaign for what she saw as Arbella's rights.

Conscious that with the Lennox marriage she had sailed very close to the wind, Bess took particular trouble over her 1576 New Year's gift to the Queen. She was seeking advice from friends and family at court as early as October 1575. Her brother-in-law, Anthony Wingfield, told his wife Elizabeth that he had consulted the Countess of Sussex and Lady Cobham, Bess's old friend, who had suggested a travelling outfit of a safeguard (an outer skirt) and cloak made of watchet (blue) or peach satin, 'embroidered with some pretty flowers and lined with sundry colours', made with gold spangles and silks. 'Such fantastical things will be more accepted than cups or jewels.'[27] He wrote again, in December, with further advice about colours and design – the Queen particularly favoured pansies.[28]

Bess's efforts paid off, as Elizabeth Wingfield reported in January: 'Her Majesty never liked anything you gave her so well … the colour and strange trimming of the garments … and great cost bestowed upon it hath caused her to give out such good speeches of my Ld and yr La as I never heard of better.' In her view, if Bess had given £100 – as she often did – 'it would not have been so well taken'. After such gratifying comments, Elizabeth slipped in a request for 'the rest of the money' (presumably a loan from Bess) and, in a postscript, added that 'all are well at Hackney and my La Arbella a good child'.[29]

All was not well for long. In April 1576, Charles Lennox, who had probably been suffering from tuberculosis, died and Elizabeth was left a widow, with a small daughter, after just eighteen months of marriage. This immediately raised the question of the Lennox earldom and estates. The Scottish government argued that the title and the Scottish lands now reverted to the Crown, to be awarded as it saw fit. Bess claimed the Lennox inheritance for her daughter and Arbella. She had the support of old Margaret Lennox, and also the Queen of Scots, who drew up a draft will stating: 'I give to my niece Arbella the earldom of Lennox, held by her late father; and enjoin my son, as my heir and successor, to obey my will in this particular.'[30] But the will, unsigned, was worthless, and in this, as in so many things, Mary's wishes were ignored.

In June, Bess came to court, hoping to persuade the Queen and the Privy Council to back her claim and put pressure on the Scottish regent. She stayed at Leicester House, courtesy of the Earl, who wrote to Shrewsbury, 'without flattery, I do assure your Lordship that I have not seen Her Majesty make more of anybody, than she has done of my Lady'.[31] Her Majesty was sympathetic enough, as were the likes of Leicester and Walsingham, but it brought no result. Elizabeth Lennox and her little daughter may have had the support of two powerful grandmothers, not to mention the Scottish Queen, but such counted for little in the face of the indifference of the Scots.

11

'GREAT TURMOIL DOTH TWO HOUSES BREED'

In August 1573, Lord Burghley told Shrewsbury how much he wished he could be at Chatsworth, 'where I think I should see a great alteration, to my good liking'.[1] Bess had been building again, this time extending the house upwards, with a third storey. In addition, galleries were built around the inner courtyard, the great hall was enlarged, rooms were refitted and work began on the garden and outbuildings. This was not a matter of a few home improvements, but a major programme of construction. The extra storey provided a complete second suite of state rooms. These may have been intended to accommodate the Queen of Scots, but the existing rooms served perfectly well, and besides, Mary was rarely kept at Chatsworth. Bess's ambitions for her house were her own.

Burghley, keen builder that he was, was naturally eager to see the new Chatsworth. During the previous decade he'd been occupied not only with building a London house on the Strand,* but with the hugely ambitious project of Theobalds, a Hertfordshire manor acquired in 1563, work on which had put a temporary halt to Burghley House.

---

* Sir Nicolas Bacon, writing to Cecil about the London house in 1560, felt that the privy had been put 'too near the lodging, too near an oven and too near a little larder', and that it would have 'been better to offend your eye outward than your nose inward' (quoted in Airs, p.5).

Theobalds, just ten miles north of London, was convenient for royal visits, and begun, wrote Burghley, 'with a mean measure but encreast by occasion of her Majesty's often coming' (she came, expensively, thirteen times).[2] And increase it did, with the new house eventually spreading over four courtyards, with an open two-storey gallery or loggia (this was imported from Flanders, through Sir Thomas Gresham's mason, Henryk), a great chamber with a famously fantastical interior, turrets covered in blue slates topped by lions bearing weather vanes, and huge gardens.[3] The costs escalated too, peaking at £2,700 during 1571–2. In 1573, with Theobalds still unfinished, Burghley restarted work on Burghley House, building, now on a grander scale, the west front with its turreted gatehouse, the north front and a third storey.

Burghley followed the progress of his building projects closely – scrutinising and annotating plans, making decisions, directing operations. For design expertise he looked to the Royal Works. So Henry Hawthorne, the Queen's Surveyor at Windsor, provided plans for parts of Theobalds, and William Spicer, when Surveyor of the Royal Works, did the same for the remodelling of Burghley's great Chelsea house, in the 1590s, but Burghley also contributed basic designs of his own. He had already amassed a large collection of architectural drawings – houses, lodges, harbours, fortifications. In 1575, he received a new addition: a plan of Longleat, sent by Thynne.[4]

By the early 1570s, the exterior of the third Longleat was finished, though the interiors still had to be fitted up. However, Thynne, being Thynne, was not satisfied. In 1572, the fourth and final phase of building began, under a team of masons headed by Smythson and Maynard. They set to work wrapping the existing house round with a new classical facade. Thynne remained a ruthless employer, and relations with his chief masons were fraught. In 1574, Smythson was away from Longleat – probably working on another job at Wardour Castle – and in his absence, even though Maynard was still on site, the carving of one of the new bay windows was given to three lesser masons, who were paid at a lower rate. Smythson and Maynard had been undercut; they saw their work being taken over by inferiors (who botched the job and were never actually paid) and their income slashed. They wrote a desperate, pleading letter (Smythson's only known letter) to Thynne: they were very sorry for his 'displeasure'; they were no longer able to pay their debts; they considered themselves better able to do the work than their replacements 'for the ordinance [design] thereof came from' them. 'We have been instruments to serve other men's terms for a great while and our own always unserved' – the rights of the craftsman were non-existent. Such, however, was their desperation that they caved in and offered to do the work at a lower rate than anyone else.[5] Thynne had his way.

Thynne would always extract his pound of flesh, but when it came to craftsmen and materials, he made sure he got the best. No longer was local stone good enough. Now he wanted Bath stone – a quarry was acquired, near Box, from where stone was dragged by oxen, on wheel-less drags, for twenty-five miles, at great expense. Glass, nails and panelling came from London. In 1573, the house was roofed with 13,000 Cornish slates, partly transported by sea.[6] It was a plan – probably a collaboration between Maynard, Smythson and Thynne himself – of this final Longleat (still unfinished on Thynne's death in 1580) that was sent to Burghley.

Bess was a no less firm but much fairer employer than Thynne. The Chatsworth building accounts for the early 1570s have vanished, so the precise chronology of the building is impossible to determine. What we do know is that Bess spent as much time there as she could, overseeing the work, and that this provoked a great deal of marital friction. Whereas William St Loe had been indulgent of her attachment to her house, as well as willing to fund its building, Shrewsbury greatly resented Chatsworth, not just for its expense, but for taking up Bess's time and attention.

By 1575, Shrewsbury was feeling harried from every side, by the Queen, Mary, Bess, his children and his tenants. The Queen proposed that Mary's household should be reduced, and in consequence the Earl's diet money cut, from £52 to £30 a week. The Earl took this hard. 'When I received her into my charge at your Majesty's hands, I understood very well it was a most dangerous service, and thought over-hard for any man to perform, without some great mischief to himself at least; and as it seemed most hard and fearful to others, and every man shrunk from it, so much the gladder was I to take it upon me ...'[7] Having undertaken so thankless a task, he was not even adequately, let alone generously, rewarded. The original sum had been little enough; now he was to receive even less. And this when he had just spent over £300 on a voyage to Rouen, to stock up on fine French goods for Mary, including twelve tons of wine, red and white wine vinegar, thirty ells of damask for table napkins, twenty-two ells of diaper 'of Rouen making', forty-two pounds of comfits and forty-eight dozen quails with cages to keep them in.[8]

In addition, some of the Earl's tenants from Derbyshire's Peak District were protesting about the enclosure of pasture and rights of way in the forest, for which they blamed Bess.[9] Gilbert Talbot told his stepmother that 'those lewd fellows of the Peak' had come to court with a petition.* Gilbert had a petition of his own, for a house for himself, Mary and their baby son George, who was greatly adored by his grandparents. Although the Earl had agreed to provide a house, and had indeed sought Bess's advice, he then stalled. In October, Gilbert reported to Bess, whose support he counted on, that his father was 'very often in exceeding choler of slight occasion, a great grief to them that love him to see him hurt himself so much'. Gilbert, living at Sheffield with his family, was growing restive – 'in all my life I never

---

* The tenants of the Peak Forest were *still* petitioning about 'common pasture' in 1604, their claims dismissed by Bess as 'altogether untrue' (BHL, ID 100).

longed for any thing so much as to be from hence, truly madam I rather wish myself a ploughman than here to continue'.[10]

When the Earl did finally offer the Talbots the dilapidated Goodrich Castle in Herefordshire, he made difficulties about furnishing it. Bess provided some furniture, from Chatsworth, including beds and pieces of tapestry. 'That which your Ladyship has given us', wrote Gilbert, was worth more than anything that had come from Sheffield. Indeed, the Earl had been deliberately obstructive, forbidding the delivery of 'the bed of cloth of gold and tawny velvet', refusing to pay for cloth to make sheets because he considered it too 'dear' and denying the Talbots the plate that had been set aside for them by Bess.[11] Shrewsbury's conviction that he was being taken advantage of, especially when it came to his own family, was coupled with inherent meanness, and this kind of behaviour – penny-pinching over trifles like sheets – would become familiar.

Further aggravation came from the fact that the Earl's building works at Sheffield were being held up because Bess was monopolising workmen at Chatsworth. 'Assure yourself', he told her, 'I cannot like to have you undo your self and hinder me and my works to bestow my men in work there and you to keep so many men as you do considering my building.' He would now be unable to provide her with corn and beef until his works were finished. In the meantime, there were Mary's requirements to be met – he needed Bess to order plate, sheets and damask and diaper napkins for Sheffield. But he ended affectionately enough – 'farewell my only love'.[12]

Joining the workforce at Chatsworth was a plasterer borrowed from Leicester's Kenilworth Castle. By 1575, Kenilworth was complete, in time to receive the Queen on her summer progress. Leicester laid on an extraordinarily lavish ten-day extravaganza, including an enormous artificial lake complete with its own Lady of the Lake and a papier-mâché swimming dolphin concealing an orchestra in its belly, rosemary bushes whose individual needles had been specially gilded, spectacular fireworks and masques. A guest at the festivities described 'the rare beauty of building that his Honour had advanced; all of the hard quarry-stone; every room so spacious, so well belighted, and so high roofed within; so seemly to sight by due proportion without; at day time on every side so glittering by glass; at nights, by continual brightness of candle, fire and torch-light, transparent through the lightsome windows'.[13] Bess very likely attended herself and, prompted by the 'rare beauty' of the castle, begged Leicester for the loan of his plasterer.

She would certainly have followed the building of Kenilworth with interest. Leicester was some ten years the younger, but, as the son of John Dudley, Duke of Northumberland, he and Bess had known each other from the days of Bess's marriage to William Cavendish. Besides their building projects, both shared a love of hangings and textiles, of which Leicester had an impressive collection, including many very costly gilt leather hangings and over eighty Turkish or Persian carpets.[14] Leicester proved a loyal friend to both Shrewsburys, offering the use of his rooms at court and his London house on several occasions, insisting: 'command and dispose of house and all that is in it even as you would of your very own and I pray you think that next her Majesty there is no two in England better welcome than your lord and your self is'.[15] And he did what he could to further not just their own interests, but those of their children too.

In May 1577, Bess wrote to Leicester thanking him for 'an infinite number of goodnesses to me and mine', and especially for his efforts to find a match for Elizabeth Lennox, whose 'well bestowing' was her mother's 'greatest care'. Having failed to secure the Lennox inheritance for her widowed daughter, Bess was anxious to find her a new husband, no doubt aware that as long as she remained unmarried, financial support would have to be provided by the Shrewsburys. Leicester had proposed various candidates, but Elizabeth was apparently no longer quite so obliging – 'she says ever to me she can not determine herself to like of any for a husband whom she never saw nor knoweth not his liking of her'.[16]

Bess repaid Leicester's hospitality and kindness in whatever ways she could. When his sister, Lady Mary Sidney, mother of the poet Philip, was in need of a London house over the winter of 1576, Bess begged her husband for the loan of his at Coldharbour, near London Bridge. She assured Shrewsbury that Mary would only take the house on condition that if he wanted it himself, 'you may have it upon two days warning to be made ready for you', but she must have known that the Earl's duties as the Queen of Scots' gaoler made it virtually impossible for him to come to London.[17]

In the early summer of 1577, Leicester proposed a visit to Chatsworth, following a sojourn at Buxton. Now in his mid forties, Leicester remained highly attractive to women, a fact that did not go unnoticed by the Queen. A few years earlier, Gilbert Talbot had reported to his father how two sisters at court, Lady Sheffield (with whom Leicester had an illegitimate son) and Frances Howard, were vying for Leicester's affections 'and the Queen thinketh not well of them and not the better of him'.[18] He was currently, secretly, courting Lettice Knollys, widow of the Earl of Essex. But middle age and good living were taking their toll; Leicester, anxious lest he 'grow high-coloured and red-faced', had hopes of Buxton's waters.

Bess, in anticipation of Leicester's visit, determined that Chatsworth should look its best, and cracked the whip. Major construction was at an end; it was now a question of finishing off – plastering, panelling, carving chimney-pieces, etc. Blackstone was acquired to make fire-places; sawyers were paid to cut timber for doors and floors; 'wiskets' (baskets) were bought for carrying mortar, and 'strickes of heare' (bundles of hair) and a 'heare sive' (sieve) for making plaster.[19] A new screen (screens, made of stone or wood, divided the great hall from the service areas) was carved for the hall, and the parlour and several bedrooms were panelled (Chatsworth, when it was finished, had thirty rooms panelled, six right up to the ceiling, some inlaid with alabaster and coloured stones, an extravagance that was not repeated when it came to the more restrained decoration of Hardwick). There was landscaping too – a new orchard was walled and stocked with fruit trees, 'tarris' (balustrading) was added to the bridge, and ponds were dug. Over the summer of 1577, Bess employed as many as eighty-two labourers, some of them working overtime; just before Leicester's arrival, Thomas Accres (a stone and marble carver, who would contribute much to the interiors of Hardwick) and two others were paid extra for working on a Sunday and through one night.

Leicester had nothing but praise for the hospitality of the Shrewsburys, at both Buxton and Chatsworth. He had certainly been well fed. At Buxton, which was after all a spa of sorts, excessive eating and exercising were frowned upon as undermining the benefits of the waters. Moderation was all. Whilst at Buxton, Leicester had written to Burghley claiming that he and his brother, who had accompanied him, were diligently drinking and bathing, restricting themselves to just one or two dishes at each meal, and taking only the gentlest exercise, unlike Burghley, who, so Leicester had heard, on *his* last visit to Buxton had dined lavishly and ridden up to twelve miles a day.[20] The list of foodstuffs sent by Bess to Buxton during Leicester's eight-day stay rather belies such claims. A hogshead of clear wine, two hogsheads of beer and two of ale had been laid down in advance, and supplies for his first day included '1 buck, 24 rabbits, 4 fat capons and 12 quails', supplemented by bread, clotted and sweet cream, sweet butter, partridges and peascods (pea pods), venison pasties, artichokes, puddings and radishes.[21] Such indulgence must have continued at Chatsworth and led to Leicester developing a painful boil on his calf and being carried home on a horse litter, for which he was much teased. Was Buxton supposed to send 'sound men halting home'?[22]

News of Leicester's fine dining reached the Queen's ears. In skittish mood, she composed a letter thanking the Shrewsburys for entertaining her favourite (she was as yet unaware of Leicester's affair with Lettice Knollys) and acknowledging her indebtedness to them both. She continued with some playful allusions to both Leicester's diet and Shrewsbury's pleas for diet money for the Queen of Scots: unless Leicester's consumption was reduced, she would be bankrupt and unable to discharge her debts to Shrewsbury, so in future she recommended Leicester's diet be limited to 'two ounces of flesh' a day, though for dinner on festival days he might be allowed 'the shoulder of a wren and for his supper a leg of the same'.[23] However, she clearly thought better of writing so facetiously – the ever-sensitive Earl was not likely to appreciate jokey references to diets and debts – and the letter was never sent. Instead, she wrote another, in more sober vein: 'In this acknowledgement of new debts we may not forget our old debt, the same being as great as a Sovereign can owe to a subject, when through your loyal and most careful looking to the charge committed to you both we and our realm enjoy a peaceful government.'[24] Whatever her reluctance to reach into her pocket, the Queen knew full well the value of the service the Earl was performing.

Over the summer of 1577, Shrewsbury hoped to move Mary to Chatsworth for a few weeks, while Sheffield was cleaned, and he invited Burghley to break his journey from Burghley to Buxton with a stay there in August. He wanted Burghley's advice too on a 'lodge' he was building (Handsworth Lodge, on the edge of the park at Sheffield Manor), for which he'd sent a 'platt'.[25] The exchange of advice and materials between patrons was reciprocal: Burghley cast his eye over Shrewsbury's 'platt', and the Earl supplied him with large quantities of lead for Theobalds (lead, a particularly valuable and expensive commodity, was used for roofing, pipes and windows). 'I think some unkindness in you being a builder and hath need of lead and will not send to me to be your purveyor', wrote the Earl in 1578, adding Bess's pleas: 'my wife desires your lordship should end that house as you have begun'. A dozen fothers of lead were sent from Hull to Theobalds, a further ten fothers a few months later.[26] In the 1580s, the Earl would supply Lord Ogle and Sir Christopher Hatton with lead for their building works.

Bess's own needs were not of course to be forgotten. As chatelaine of Chatsworth, overseeing the completion of the house and the entertainment of guests, she looked, as always, to the Earl to supply her with building materials and provisions. Her tone, in 1577, was distinctly high-handed: 'If you cannot get my timber carried I must be without it though I greatly want it ... I pray you let me know if I shall have the ton of iron, if you cannot spare it I must make haste to get it elsewhere. You promised to send me money before this time to buy oxen, but I see out of sight out of mind with your unkind none ... I will send you the bill of my wood stuff ... here is neither malt nor hops, the malt come last is so very ill and stinking as Hanks [her brewer] thinks none of my workmen will drink it.'

It was not entirely a letter of complaint and demand; she also mentioned Gilbert's health – he had been 'ill in his head' ever since he'd come from Sheffield – and alluded to the ongoing dispute between her Derbyshire neighbours, Sir John Zouch and Sir Thomas Stanhope, in which Shrewsbury, siding with Stanhope, was embroiled. She thought the Queen would grant permission for the Earl to bring Mary to Chatsworth, but since the Earl had failed to provide the necessary provisions, she assumed 'you mind not to come'. And then came a postscript: 'I have sent you lettuce for that you love them, and every second day some is sent to your charge and you. I have nothing else to send. Let me know how you, your charge and love do and commend me I pray you. It were well you sent four or five pieces of the great hangings that they might be put up and some carpets.'[27] What did she mean by 'your charge and love'? This must be an allusion to Mary. But was it merely a light-hearted tease? Or more barbed – real, not feigned, jealousy? Shrewsbury saw rather more of his 'charge' than he did of his wife. Bess had now reached an age – fifty-six – when her physical and sexual confidence was a little less sure, when a woman twenty years younger than herself, a woman known for her powers of attraction, might well feel a threat. Relations between the Shrewsburys were souring over the summer of 1577.

Bess's request for 'four or five pieces of the great hangings' probably included at least one set of the Virtues hangings, made in the 1570s for Chatsworth, and later removed to Hardwick (today they are to be found in the Great Hall and on the chapel landing and are some of the rarest and most valuable textiles in the house). The larger set of five hangings (of which four survive) features women of the Ancient World, flanked by personifications of their virtues: Penelope stands between Patience and Perseverance, Lucretia between Chastity and Liberality, Cleopatra between Fortitude and Justice, Zenobia between Magnanimity and Prudence, and Artemisia between Constancy and Piety. The second set, of three, which was probably only completed after Bess left Chatsworth for Hardwick in 1584, depicts the theological virtues of Faith and Hope and the cardinal virtue of Temperance (suggesting Bess valued temperance over charity), together with their opposite vices.[*]

Together the two sets celebrate powerful women, several of them female rulers, but also women who were devoted wives, as well as virtues – patience, constancy, fortitude, wisdom, generosity, temperance – that Bess prized, if did not always practise (it should be remembered that her two daughters who died young were named Temperance and Lucretia). She clearly identified in particular with the patient Penelope, who featured in the decoration of both the Old and New Halls at Hardwick, and the virtuous Lucretia, but Shrewsbury, by the 1570s, would have held a rather different view. Patience was not a quality that he would have recognised in his wife. The Virtues hangings say a great deal about their creator – her eye for design and dramatic effect, her learning, her moral code – but more importantly, they say something about Bess's idea of herself and how she wished to be seen.

The hangings are very fine, large-scale examples of appliqué work. Bess may have seen, and been inspired by, a set of such hangings at

---

[*] These were based on Flemish prints published by Hans Collaert in 1576, after designs by Crispin van der Broeck (Levey, *Embroideries at Hardwick Hall*, p.109).

Nonsuch, Henry VIII's Surrey palace, made of red Turkey silk, embroidered with horsemen and figures, each of them fourteen feet square. Appliqué work was the province of professional, male embroiderers; according to Bess, hers were in the main made by her 'grooms, women and some boys she kept', together with Thomas Lane, an in-house embroiderer. A patchwork effect was created using pieces of velvet, cloth of gold and patterned silk, cut from late-fifteenth-century ecclesiastical vestments (orphreys and cope hoods) acquired by William St Loe, and possibly William Cavendish, during the Dissolution, and brought to Chatsworth.*

The hangings would be fought over during the unravelling of the Shrewsbury marriage; in July 1577, their makers provoked the couple's first major public row. This is relayed, in some detail, by Gilbert Talbot, who had his father's penchant for prolix letters and his own gift for recalling dialogue. He told Bess of a conversation between himself and the Earl while the two men were riding the fifteen miles or so from Bolsover, a Shrewsbury property close to Hardwick, back to Sheffield. Bess and Gilbert were at this point on excellent terms. Bess had taken the Talbots' part in their efforts to secure a home of their own. Gilbert positioned himself as a go-between in his parents' battles – he was essentially sympathetic to his stepmother, but, perpetually short of cash, he could not afford to alienate his father. His letter, he says, is written 'plainly and truly', though 'bluntly and tediously'.

The latest quarrel had taken place at Sheffield, where Bess's embroiderers had been locked out of the lodge overnight by John Dickenson, Keeper of the Earl's Wardrobe. The Earl, when questioned the next morning by Bess, flatly denied any involvement and flew into a rage, using many 'hard speeches'. These, however, as he told Gilbert, were as nothing compared to the 'cruel speeches' he'd had from Bess, who 'scolded like one that came from the bank' (the mouth of a coal pit).

---

* Pieces showing biblical scenes, which were not appropriate for classical heroines, were carefully cut away and stored. They are now on display at Hardwick.

His wife, he said, was surrounded by 'varlets' who did nothing but tell tales, and he singled out Owen, one of her grooms, and the embroiderers in particular. He was expecting to find Bess back at Sheffield, and when Gilbert broke the news that she'd left the day before for Chatsworth, he 'seemed to marvel greatly and said is her malice such she would not tarry one night for my coming ... After he had seen all his grounds about Bolsover and was coming into the way homewards, he began with me again, saying that all the house might discern your Ladyship's stomach against him by your departure before his coming.'

Gilbert tried to defend Bess, citing business she had at Chatsworth, but the Earl 'allowed not of any reason or cause'. Gilbert went on to explain how 'grieved and vexed in mind' Bess was, how she felt that Shrewsbury's 'heart was withdrawn from her'. At this, his father 'melted and although I cannot say his very words were that he had injured and wronged you, yet both by his countenance and words it plainly showed the same ... I know, quoth he, her love hath been great to me and mine hath been and is as great to her, for what can a man do more for his wife than I have done, and daily do for her.' Nevertheless, replied Gilbert, Bess believed 'that you love them that love not her and believe those about you which hate her', and that Shrewsbury was 'gladder of' Bess's 'absence' than her 'presence'. 'You know the contrary,' protested the Earl, 'and how often I have cursed the building at Chatsworth for want of her company.' That night, back at Sheffield, Gilbert felt convinced that his father's 'heart desired reconciliation, if he knew which way to bring it to pass'.[28]

Here is marital breakdown vividly dramatised – two irreconcilable versions of a single event. On the one side is Bess: all innocence and distress and forbearance, the personification of Patience, Fortitude and Temperance. And on the other, Shrewsbury: all resentment and rage and irrationality. The Earl, always acutely sensitive about matters of honour and his reputation in the eyes of the world, is mortified by Bess's leaving Sheffield without waiting for his return – he will be diminished before his household. And she treats him so insultingly when he's done so much for her. As always, it's Chatsworth that comes first, that comes between them. But he loves her still.

Bess's feelings are more opaque. She presents herself, to Gilbert, as the injured party – bewildered that her husband's 'wonted love and affection is clean turned to the contrary', ignorant of the crime she's supposed to have committed, professing herself willing to take on his 'grieves' if it would give him some relief. 'When she told me', wrote Gilbert, 'of her dear love towards you and now how your Lordship had requited her, she was in such perplexity as I never saw woman.' Yet this is the same woman who 'scolded like one that came from the bank'. Gilbert's letter is revealing in other ways – the incident with the embroiderers is merely the latest of many quarrels, which have now extended beyond the protagonists to their households, fuelled by the gossip and backbiting of servants.

On 1 August, after visiting Bess at Chatsworth, Gilbert wrote to her again. The Earl had questioned him less closely, but was keen to know when Bess was coming to Sheffield. Gilbert had told him that she was willing to dismiss Owen, her groom, as the Earl was 'so offended with him', but she still 'knew not what offence he had committed'. To which the Earl had replied curtly, 'it was his will for diverse causes'. In a postscript, Gilbert gave news of little George, Bess's grandson, who 'drinketh every day to his Lady grandmother, rides to her often but yet within the court and if he has any spice I tell him Lady grandmother is come and will see him, which he then will either quickly hide or quickly eat and then asks where Lady Danmode is'.[29]

Just over a week later, on 10 August, two-year-old George Talbot, having apparently been in perfect health, died quite suddenly. On the 12th, the Earl wrote to Burghley, preferring that his friend should hear the news from him personally rather 'than by common report ... though it nips me near'. He made no attempt to hide his own grief, but sounded impatient with that of his wife: 'I doubt not my wife will show more folly than need requires, I pray your lordship write your letter to her which I hope will greatly relieve her.'[30] He told Walsingham that Bess was 'not so well able to rule her passions, and has driven herself into such a case by her continual weeping as is like to breed in her further inconvenience'. And he asked permission to go to her at Chatsworth, taking Mary with him.[31] This was granted. For the moment, the Shrewsburys came together in their grief.

12.

'THE OLD SONG'

The Shrewsburys were still presenting a united front in March 1578, when Margaret Lennox died. Arbella, her granddaughter, should have now inherited the Lennox estates in England and Scotland, and the Lennox title. But the Queen, who, in an uncharacteristic act of generosity, had paid for Margaret's state funeral in Westminster Abbey, promptly recouped the costs by appropriating most of the Lennox lands in England, while those in Scotland remained with the Crown. Furthermore, in May, the Scottish regent awarded the Lennox title to the elderly and childless Bishop of Caithness, brother of the 4th Earl of Lennox and uncle to Charles Stuart (on the Bishop's death, it passed to Esmé Stuart, James VI's cousin). Even the Lennox jewels, which the Countess had left to Arbella, to be held by Thomas Fowler, her secretary and executor, until Arbella was fourteen, were lost. Fowler took off to Scotland and the jewels found their way into the greedy hands of James VI. Clearly Arbella could not expect any kind of restitution from the Scots. She had been roundly cheated of her entire inheritance; it was left to Bess to fight for her rights.

The Shrewsburys set about enlisting the support of Burghley, Walsingham and Leicester – who, it was hoped, would persuade the Queen to look kindly on Elizabeth and Arbella – as well as petitioning the Queen herself. They had some success. Custody of Arbella was granted to her mother, rather than her wardship being sold outside of the family, and the Queen agreed to provide an annual pension of £400 for Elizabeth and £200 for Arbella. For Bess, however, this was not sufficient. She continued to badger Leicester, who that summer made another visit to Buxton, where Gilbert Talbot acted as his host. Leicester, as Gilbert told his parents, felt it was 'better for him to defer her [Elizabeth Lennox's] suits to her Majesty till his own coming to court', when, he promised, he would be an 'earnest solicitor'.[1]

A portrait of two-year-old Arbella, commissioned by Bess, hangs at Hardwick. It shows a solemn, round-eyed child, stuffed into an elaborate dress, clutching a doll; around her neck is a triple gold chain, with a pendant shield bearing a countess's coronet and the Lennox motto, 'To achieve, I endure', in French. Bess was making no bones about proclaiming her granddaughter's rightful inheritance. In the autumn of 1578, she came to court, bringing Arbella with her, and took up lodging in two rooms, lent by Leicester, within his own apartments at Richmond Palace, where the court had decamped to avoid the plague. Bess was more than happy: 'I had rather have albeit never so little a corner within the court than greater easement further off.'[2] If she had hoped that the Queen would soften at the sight of little Arbella, such hopes were dashed, but she continued to petition for an increase to her granddaughter's pension.

By Christmas, Bess was back in Derbyshire, where she deposited Arbella at Chatsworth before joining the Earl at Sheffield on Christmas Eve. On 29 December, she told Walsingham that since her arrival, the Queen of Scots had kept to her bed, except for Christmas Day, and that she was 'grown lean and sickly and sayth want of exercise brings her to that weak state. I see no danger in her of life and whatsoever she writes in excuse of herself I hope there will be advised considerations in believing her.'[3] In fact, Mary's complaints of ill health were real enough. She had recently sat for Nicholas Hilliard – a surprising bending of the rules on the part of the Queen – and his portrait shows her as still attractive, but with features beginning to blur and soften, and a lurking double chin. Mary was now thirty-six; age and nearly a decade of captivity were taking their toll.

In February 1579, Gilbert Talbot wrote to Bess from London with news from court: 'Her Majesty continues her very good liking of Monsieur Simier and all his company and he hath conference with her three or four times a week.'[4] This was Jean de Simier, who had been sent to England by the Duke of Anjou to discuss a possible marriage between Anjou and the Queen. Anjou was the younger brother of Henry III, King of France, who had himself been proposed as a groom for Elizabeth some ten years earlier but had been unwilling to put aside his Catholicism. Anjou, who was puny, pockmarked and less than half the Queen's forty-five years, had no such scruples and appeared enthusiastic about the match. Simier, Anjou's 'chief darling', was a smooth-talking scoundrel (he had murdered his brother for having an affair with his wife, who had recently poisoned herself), but the Queen was enchanted with him, so much so that tongues at court were wagging about their frequent late-night 'conferences'. Anjou would be the last serious candidate for the Queen's hand, but the proposal, like those before it, came to nothing.

Aside from court gossip, Gilbert reported on the works at the Earl's Chelsea property, Shrewsbury House. This had been built, of brick, in 1519, around three sides of a quadrangle, backed by a large garden, on the river at Cheyne Walk. The Earl had been carrying out improvements, particularly in the Great Chamber, where coats of arms were being carved into the plasterwork ceiling and set into stained-glass windows (Shrewsbury loved heraldic glass, which was much used at Sheffield). The heraldic decoration at Shrewsbury House had been devised by William Jones, the 'finisher',* and Robert Cooke, the Clarenceux King of Arms. Jones, reported Gilbert, was to be given

---

* A 'finisher', sometimes called a 'furnisher', was a new profession, combining literal 'finishing' (present-day 'snagging') with interior decorating.

'good glass' and a room in which to work and sleep; once he'd finished the glass, he was to oversee the rough-casting and panelling of such rooms as needed it. Gilbert thought that the 'arms in glass that Clarentius the herald did bespeak' would be 'the fairest glasswork that is ... anywhere in England to be found'.[5] Richard Topcliffe, the Queen's psychopathic rack-master, a Nottinghamshire man and friend of the Shrewsburys, came to inspect Cooke's work and felt similarly about the plasterwork in the Great Chamber: it would 'exceed in rareness of device and beauty' any house in England.[6]

A few months later, William Jones informed the Earl that his Great Chamber would be ready by the time Shrewsbury came to London, but that he was in urgent need of payment – 'I am like to be put in prison for your lordship's debts.' Several noblemen, including the Earl of Derby and the Earl of Surrey, had been to see the house, and two nights in a row the Queen's barge had moored close by and 'stayed there with musicians playing'.[7] Shrewsbury House clearly did excel 'in rareness of device and beauty'.

Bess was there for a few months in 1580. She had been suffering from rheumatism, as she told her daughter Mary: 'Swete harte ... I have been continually greatly pained in my head, neck, shoulders and arms and think it much worse in the moist weather, this day I thank God I am somewhat better and ventured to go into the garden where I was not this 5 or 6 weeks ... I thank God that your Lord, you and all our little ones are well ... I heard not from the court since Monday nor know nothing worthy the advertising.'[8] She had had a number of visitors – Lady Arundel, Lady Strange, Lady Marcus and the Master of the Rolls. 'I pray you let me hear this night how you and your good Lord do else I shall not sleep quietly, my jewell Arbell is well.'[9]

Bess's letters to Mary, her youngest and best-loved daughter, with their titbits of gossip, bulletins on health and enquiries after the children, are the affectionate, mundane letters of a mother. The two would always be close, even after relations with Gilbert Talbot deteriorated. Of her other daughters, Frances was long established at Holme

Pierrepont with her husband, and Elizabeth, despite the fact that Arbella, and so presumably her mother, spent much of her time with Bess, never quite comes into focus. Mary, darkly handsome, with sharp, defined features, was the daughter temperamentally most like Bess – spirited and combative – though she lacked her mother's prudence and in later years made no secret of her Catholicism. Mary, like Bess, could be a formidable foe. Writing to Sir Thomas Stanhope, a Derbyshire neighbour with whom the Talbots, like the Zouches, had a long-running feud, she didn't hold back – Stanhope was 'more wretched, vile and miserable than any creature living and ... more ugly in shape than the ugliest toad in the world'. She hoped that he would be 'damned perpetually in hell fire'.[10]

Shrewsbury believed that Bess's children were entirely 'ruled' by her, and they were certainly kept on the shortest of reins. However, she was also capable of being a fond, even indulgent mother (and an even fonder grandmother), solicitous over health and generous with handouts. And, as Shrewsbury acknowledged and appreciated, she treated her stepsons kindly – supportive of Gilbert and giving Henry and Edward Talbot £10 each when they set off to study in France in 1581.[11]

But possibly her stepchildren found her easier than her own: Bess inspired fear as much as love, and her children dreaded her disapproval and anger. Elizabeth Lennox wrote anxiously: she could not imagine that she would have 'continued' in Bess's 'displeasure so long a time', unless Bess had heard some 'false bruits'.[12] When, during a mock duel, Charles Cavendish injured the eye of the servant of a friend with his rapier, he appealed to Shrewsbury to intercede with Bess: 'I beseech you to appease my Lady's mislike to me through this crooked misfortune, which was but ill luck.' The man was recovering and in no danger, but 'I desire not to have the least frown of her, much less to be in her disgrace.'[13] Bess's children, her sons in particular, could ill afford to incur her displeasure – she held the purse strings.

Of all her children, Henry was the most troublesome, not merely evading Bess's control but actively opposing her. Henry was no scholar as a boy, and did not, unlike William and Charles, go to Cambridge. Soon after his marriage to Grace Talbot, he was dispatched on a tour of Europe, travelling through France and Italy with Gilbert. Back home in 1572, he became an MP for Derbyshire, being returned for six consecutive elections, and in 1574, he went off to fight in the Dutch wars against the Spanish, with a letter of recommendation from Leicester and '500 tall men', mostly drawn from his estates. Bess perhaps hoped that this would be the making of him – in 1576, she asked Leicester if he could send 'earnest letters' to William of Orange, on Henry's behalf.[14] Whether Henry had a distinguished military career, we don't know, but in Bess's eyes he remained a wastrel – overly fond of gambling, racking up debts (by 1584 he was in debt to the tune of £3,000) and womanising.[15] His marriage to Grace was child-less, though he fathered numerous illegitimate offspring* – not for nothing was he known as 'the common bull of Derbyshire and Staffordshire'. Grace had to endure his faithlessness without the con-solation of children of her own. By the 1580s, the pair were living, miserably, at Tutbury, which had been given to them by Shrewsbury.

Henry himself resented his mother's disapproval. In 1585, he wrote refuting reports that he'd come to London 'to play at dice, to seek ease and dalliance and for any other vain delight'; in fact, he was seeking 'virtue and honour in arms', and if others, with their 'babbling tongues', sought to make trouble with Bess, he was not to be blamed. 'My study is to please your ladyship', he claimed.[16] This rings hollow. Henry, perhaps believing that having forfeited his mother's good opinion he had nothing to lose, went out of his way to thwart her, siding with the Earl in his battles with her, and, later, with Arbella in hers. Grace tried to act as a mediator and conciliator. In 1585, she

---

* From one of whom, another Henry, descended the Lords Waterpark.

wrote, humbly, to Jane Kniveton, Bess's half-sister, asking her to pass on a letter from Henry to Bess, 'a suit he has to her honour which I trust she will not be offended with him for'. Perhaps hoping to soften her mother-in-law, she sent her 'two fat capons which are not so good as I desire they were but I hope to have better shortly', as well as a hundred wardens (cooking pears), 'the best fruit our country will afford this year'.[17]

Capons and wardens notwithstanding, Bess saw no need to bail out Henry. He was not, after all, without means – he had the Chatsworth lands settled on him by his father, and he would eventually inherit Chatsworth itself.[18] Bess could do nothing to prevent this, but having written off Henry as a bad lot, she looked to William, her second son, as her de facto heir. At the age of fifteen, William had gone to Clare Hall, Cambridge, and from there to Gray's Inn to study law – his legal skills would be put to good use when managing the Cavendish estates. He was knighted in 1580, and in 1582 he married Anne Keighley, the daughter of Henry Keighley, of Keighley, Yorkshire, who came with a gratifyingly large collection of estates in Lancashire. The pair lived with Bess, at Chatsworth and later at Hardwick, an arrangement that must have had its strains but meant that William had his mother's ear.

It's hard to get much sense of William, or to greatly warm to him. We have a mere handful of letters between him and Bess, partly because for much of the time they shared a roof; such as there are are dull and businesslike. With a lawyer's clear and tidy mind, William was the safe pair of hands who could be trusted to look after Bess's interests and to manage and expand her estates, and he received large sums of money with which to do so (by 1584, he was enjoying £700 a year from lands bought in his name). He had his mother's red hair, her caution and her head for business, but there's little evidence of her spirit and singularity, and he had a reputation for meanness (something that, for all her aversion to waste and excess, was never said of Bess). His accounts, however, from the early 1600s, tell a rather different story: an interest in music and books; a taste for milk baths and fine underwear; a willingness to indulge his second wife's love of clothes, jewels and fine furniture.[19] And he had the imagination, or simply the good fortune, to employ the philosopher Thomas Hobbes as tutor to his son.*

Of Bess's three sons, Charles, the youngest, appears the most attractive – open-hearted, generous, loyal and brave. In 1575, Shrewsbury felt Charles was 'easily led to folly', having spent a night poaching with some servants, and that Bess should 'advise him from those doings'.[20] But this was no more than a young man's escapade. He was a fine horseman and swordsman. He loved music, and was a patron of the madrigalist George Wilbye, who dedicated a book of airs to him. He also shared his mother's passion for building and was something of an amateur architect. Although Charles had a home, Stoke Manor, just north of Chatsworth, bought by Bess in 1573, he started (but did not finish) building a house at Kirkby-in-Ashfield, just a few miles from Hardwick, and later the enchanting Little Castle at Bolsover, which was completed by his son. To Gilbert Talbot, his stepbrother, he was a steadfast friend, 'always at his elbow, politic and having great sway with him'. Gilbert was not the easiest of friends: Charles found himself drawn into his feuds, and to help relieve his debts he took Bolsover and Welbeck Abbey off his hands.

When it came to what she perceived to be her children's rights, Bess fought hard whether it was a question of a pension or a marriage settlement. In 1581, Charles married Margaret Kitson, the daughter of Sir Thomas Kitson of Hengrave Hall, Suffolk. Bess had been closely involved in the negotiations, carefully going through the marriage 'articles' and noting in the margin her 'answer and mind to every such particular'. She felt the Kitsons' demands were excessive, as she told

---

* Since Hobbes was only two years older than young William, master and pupil had a companionable relationship and did much travelling together. After William's death, in 1628, Hobbes remained employed by the Cavendishes, dying at Hardwick at the age of 91.

Sir Thomas Cornwallis, Sir Thomas Kitson's father-in-law, whose help she had enlisted. She said the same to William Cavendish and Gilbert Talbot, who had been petitioning for an increase to Charles's £400 allowance.[21] Bess was having none of this: 'I say and am sure that four hundred pounds a year is as large a proportion as any Earl allows his eldest son.' Sir Thomas Kitson could surely do something for the couple. Charles would have £2,000 from her, but as to a further £5,000, 'this is so great a sum as I know not which way to turn me for discharge of so much'. She was willing to promise that on her death he would have £5,000 'either in money or land ... and yearly as I live care shall be had therein', but 'to depart with so much presently, or in short time, that can I never do except I should utterly spoil myself'.[22] But she was very keen that the marriage shouldn't founder over the question of the £5,000, and in the end, when Shrewsbury refused to stump up the money, she paid it herself, or so at least she claimed.[23] Reluctant though she was to provide more than Charles's due, Bess was equally determined that the Kitsons should do the right thing by him, and when the settlement of lands on Charles and Margaret (part of her dowry) was obstructed by a member of the Kitson family, she promptly went into battle on their behalf.[24]

In July 1582, after little more than a year of marriage, Margaret died. Bess's immediate concern was that Charles should still receive what was owed to him under the marriage settlement. She asked Cornwallis if he could use his influence with Sir Thomas Kitson to ensure that Charles was treated 'as much to his commodity as that by her life might have come to him'. Sir Thomas was now left with just one daughter 'and none else near to him'; surely he would treat Charles 'as his own child and even so deal with him'? 'I have always had so good liking of him as I hold him no less dear than one of my own', she added unconvincingly.[25] Whether Sir Thomas fell into line we don't know, but Charles's second wife, Catherine Ogle, the daughter of Baron Ogle, brought with her substantial lands and property – he was well provided for.

* * *

In 1578, Nicholas Booth, a Shrewsbury bailiff, told his master that servants of Bess and William Cavendish were trying to stir up the Glossopdale tenants, in Derbyshire's Peak District, against him.[26] They succeeded. The following year, John Kniveton, one of Bess's servants, said that he'd heard 'very evil speeches' of the Earl, who 'had put out a number of tenants lately to their utter decay'.[27] The Glossopdale tenants were up in arms, soon to be joined by those at Ashford, which belonged to Bess, under the leadership of the splendidly named Otwell Higgenbotham (later a slater at Hardwick). In protest at leases being revoked and rents being raised, they brought a petition to court, where they were examined before the Privy Council. The Earl was indignant: those few tenants who had been evicted had been causing trouble; it was a matter of a few 'lewd persons' inciting the rest and they deserved to be punished.[28] The Council, however, found in favour of the 'lewd persons'. Discontent amongst the Shrewsbury tenants posed a risk to the security of the Queen of Scots – a risk they could not afford. For the Earl, it was another slight.

'I consider myself very hardly dealt withal', he wrote to Burghley in 1580. And this after eleven years of faithful service as Mary's custodian. He was still out of pocket, regularly shelling out £1,000 'over the shoulder', but costs aside, there was 'the loss of liberty, dangering of my life, and many other discomforts which no money could have hired me to'. Still, he added, ever loyal, 'the desire I have to serve my Sovereign makes peril and pain a pleasure to me'.[29] The Queen had granted permission for the Earl to take Mary to Buxton in the summer of 1580, but she would not allow him to take her to Chatsworth, where Mary Talbot was awaiting the birth of her second child.

'Commend me to the great belly', the Earl wrote to Bess. He felt that she was wrong in not allowing Elizabeth Lennox to be with her sister for the birth – 'it were not amiss she should be with her now and Grace also' – but in fact he had been making difficulties about Gilbert visiting his own wife at Chatsworth.[30] This came out of the Earl's growing paranoia, his sense of being maligned and exploited by those around him, and in particular his conviction that Gilbert and Mary were in cahoots with Bess against him.

That the Shrewsbury marriage was in trouble was by now a matter of common knowledge, and their servants were taking sides. In April 1580, Nicholas Booth told Thomas Kniveton, Bess's brother-in-law, that Shrewsbury had been full of 'great speeches' about Bess and had written to the Queen and the Privy Council 'touching some hard and indirect dealing [regarding revenues] by my lady and Mr Harry Cavendish'. He did not see much hope of reconciliation.[31] After his summer sojourn at Buxton, Leicester, at the Queen's request, went to see Bess at Chatsworth, 'to let her know how sorry' Her Majesty was to hear of a 'breech' between the Shrewsburys. Leicester, as he reported to the Earl, found Bess 'in very great grief'. When asked whether there was any truth in the rumours that she had been threatening the Earl, 'as though she knew things by you that she could harm you if she listed', she replied 'calmly saying I think there is no man able to say it of me'. Rather, she claimed, she had been subjected to such treatment 'as were enough to alienate the heart and duty of any wife', including being 'slighted' in front of the Earl's servants.[32]

Behind Bess's threats – most likely made – lay her suspicions about the Earl's relations with the Queen of Scots. But the more immediate and obvious cause of conflict was money, for which, as the Earl complained to his steward Thomas Baldwin, he was being continually pressed by his wife – 'the old song'.[33] Bess was far from without means of her own: in addition to her £1,000 yearly allowance, she had, since 1572, the income from the St Loe lands. How she used that income is unclear (to buy more land, Shrewsbury would claim), but she certainly looked to the Earl to meet her expenses. In June, he told her that he was only able to provide £50 of the £150 she wanted, since he was waiting in vain for various creditors to pay up. 'You have stopped my mouth for bringing of you any, your want being so great and therefore in that matter I cannot help you, so many breaking promises with me.'[34] 'Your want being so great' – there was no end, it appeared, to Bess's demands.

The state of the Shrewsbury marriage worried the Queen, not out of any great personal concern, but because dissension between the Earl and Bess, like that amongst the Shrewsbury tenants, might be exploited by supporters of the Queen of Scots. In 1579, Gilbert Talbot, apropos of rumours at court of 'no good agreement' between the Shrewsburys, had warned that if Elizabeth came to believe 'that there were jars between them, she would be in such a fear as it would sooner be the cause of the removing of my Lordship's charge than any other thing'.[35] However welcome Mary's removal might be, it could not be seen to reflect badly on the Earl, as a stain on his conduct.

In November 1581, Elizabeth dispatched Robert Beale, Clerk of the Council and Walsingham's brother-in-law, to Sheffield. He was to assess the situation there, to discover, if possible, Mary's intentions (she had been busily corresponding with the King of France about her restoration to the Scottish throne, where she would co-rule with her son James) and to remind her that 'the usage she receives' was 'much better than she deserves'.[36] For much of his three-week visit, Mary was bedridden, complaining bitterly of the old pain in her side. During one especially bizarre interview he found the Queen of Scots and her women, all of them weeping, in complete darkness, with Mary claiming, faintly, that she was dying. When Bess was sent to see her, her verdict was tart: 'in her opinion she had known her far worse than she presently was'.[37] Beale was nonplussed: 'the parties are so wily with whom a man deals'. Who, if anyone, could be believed? All he could say for certain was that Mary was genuinely ill. He came away with her assurances that she would recognise Elizabeth as the lawful Queen of England, and would have no more dealings with foreign powers, but such assurances counted for little. And Mary won some concessions – permission to ride out in a coach and horses in Sheffield Park.

Bess saw Mary infrequently, on her occasional visits to Sheffield, and the days of gossiping over embroidery were long gone. Her public stance on the Queen of Scots was one of sceptical impatience – there was nothing much wrong with her and whatever she said should be treated with caution – but privately she was quite prepared to use Mary to further her own ends. In July 1582, in a 'secret letter' to Bess, Charles Cavendish asked whether Mary could write a letter on his behalf saying she had known a certain individual 'in the duke's time' – this would somehow hobble the man, rendering him harmless. The request was passed on and Mary replied: she was glad to hear of Bess and her 'little niece' (Arbella), but she didn't have an 'acquaintance with the old man', and felt that if she wrote she would put both Charles and Bess 'in hazard by my letters rather than to do him thereby any good at all'.[38] This is an opaque exchange – the identity of the old man and what exactly Bess and Charles were after is a mystery, but it reveals Bess as neither so indifferent to, nor so distant from, the Queen of Scots as she professed.

The Shrewsburys were together at Sheffield for the Christmas of 1581. During the Twelfth Night celebrations, Elizabeth Lennox fell ill, and on 21 January, she died. In her will, made a few days before her death, she hopefully left the lands from which her £400 pension was paid to her daughter Arbella, and, presumably to reinforce that hope, her 'best jewel set with great diamonds' to the Queen. Leicester, Burghley, Walsingham and Sir Christopher Hatton were asked to continue their goodwill to the 'smale orphant'. Elizabeth's white sables went to Bess, and a gold salt cellar to Shrewsbury, as a token of thanks for being a good father to her.[39]

Bess, always an odd mixture of the hard-headed and the sentimental, had been happy enough to use Elizabeth as a marriageable commodity, but was greatly distressed by her death. The Earl told Walsingham that 'the poor mother takes her daugther's death so grievously and so mourneth and lamenteth that she cannot think of ought but tears'.[40]

Grief, however, did not get in the way of practicalities – the question of six-year-old Arbella's maintenance. On the 28th, Bess wrote to both Walsingham and Burghley, hoping that Arbella would get her mother's 'portion' (Elizabeth's £400 pension, in addition to Arbella's £200), 'for her better education and training up in all good virtue and learning and so the sooner may she be ready to attend on her Majesty'.[41] This was the key point – Arbella's proximity to the Queen. A 'better education' was simply her due.

Her Majesty recognised no such requirement and did not oblige. In May, Bess tried again, with further letters to Burghley and Walsingham. She could not remember her daughter 'but with a sorrowful, troubled mind'; now she was pleading the case of the 'poor infant, my jewel Arbella, who is to depend wholly upon her majesty's bounty and goodness'. She hoped that the Queen would 'confirm that grant of the whole six hundred pounds yearly for the education of my dearest jewel'.[42] This education, the 'dearest jewel' being of royal blood, not to mention keeping Arbella 'with such as are fit to attend upon her and be in her company', was, she pointed out, an expensive business, though Arbella was proving to be a gifted child, a child worthy of investment and 'of very great towardness to learn anything'.[43] The Queen remained unmoved, but Arbella now became the focus of Bess's ambitions – watched over, cosseted and groomed, so she hoped, for a glorious future.

13.

'SEND ME ACCRES'

'I pray you send me Accres so soon as you can for I may spare him no longer', wrote Shrewsbury peremptorily to Bess in October 1580.[1] 'Accres' was Thomas Accres, the great stonemason, who had been working at Chatsworth and was now required by the Earl for his new building project at Worksop. He had decided to remodel a hunting lodge, built by his father, on the edge of Sherwood Forest.

Nothing of Worksop remains – it burned to the ground in 1761 – but drawings show an extraordinary building, compact, immensely tall (incorporating the existing lodge necessitated a narrow site, so it was decided to build upwards; the parapet was some ninety feet above ground and the turrets higher still) and wrapped around by great bands of windows. It looks monumental and fortress-like, but softened and lightened by the expanses of glass and the domed turrets. These, with their circular glass walls, would have made thrilling prospect rooms, from which to look down on the surrounding forest and watch the hunt.

As at Chatsworth and Hardwick, Worksop's second floor was taller than the first and almost entirely taken up by the long gallery – 212 feet long and 36 feet wide, with ranges of huge windows on three sides. It was much admired at the time, and set something of a gold standard for galleries. In 1590, Burghley's son, Robert Cecil, wrote to Gilbert Talbot: 'It were a much more ease for a man's coach or horses to visit you at Chelsea with a fair pair of oars from London than to come through your craggy stoney lanes where in seeking for the fairest gallery in England a man shall meet never a cup of good drink."[2] Getting to Worksop took some doing, but it was worth the effort.

Worksop was a great house, but one can't but wonder why Shrewsbury built it at all. He was hardly short of houses, what with South Wingfield Manor, Sheffield Manor and Castle and the new lodge, Tutbury Castle, Rufford Abbey, Welbeck Abbey and his London homes. Improvements at Shrewsbury House were barely completed and building work at Sheffield was ongoing, with more work on the manor from 1583. This came at a cost. And all the while the Earl was complaining bitterly about the parlous state of his finances – so much so that he told Thomas Baldwin, his London steward, that he was contemplating selling off plate and his ship, the *Talbot*, just to raise cash.[3] Why then did he embark on an enormous, expensive and superfluous house?

It may have been to rival Chatsworth and outdo Bess. Having watched the expansion of Chatsworth, that 'devouring gulf of mine and other your husbands goods', Shrewsbury might simply have wanted to spend his money on his own house rather than see it swallowed up by his wife's. He now saw an opportunity to build something bolder and more contemporary. However, besides an element of marital one-upmanship, there was also the spur of a new house under construction in Nottinghamshire, a house that would have been the talk of the Midlands in the 1580s – Wollaton.

From its hilltop site, Wollaton now looms over the sprawl of Nottingham, but once this was farmland, whose inhabitants would

---

* Ben Jonson, visiting Worksop in 1618, during his great walk from London to Edinburgh, remarked on 'the bigness and beauty' of the gallery, which 'exceedeth most that I have seen', and on the eight vast windows set, as at Shrewsbury House, with heraldic glass (*Ben Jonson's Walk to Scotland*, ed. James Loxley, Anna Groundwater and Julie Sanders, 2015, p.55).

have marvelled at the emergence of a great glittering edifice, topped by a kind of giant conservatory (the glass prospect room), 'standing bleakly', in the words of William Camden, 'but offering a very goodly prospect to the beholders far and near'.[4] Wollaton was built by Sir Francis Willoughby, a complicated, curious man – highly cultured, brilliant, uncomfortable and quarrelsome. Willoughby was a 'projector' (speculator), in coal (profits, as much as £1,000 a year, from the coal fields that surrounded Wollaton funded its building), iron, woad and property, but he managed his affairs badly, overextending himself with compulsive land-buying, disastrous investments and grandiose schemes.[5] He was a much less successful businessman than Bess, to whom he would turn to for loans in the 1590s.

The Willoughbys were originally Nottinghamshire gentry, prosaically named 'Bugge', who, thanks to some judicious marrying, accumulated large estates rich in coal and, to a lesser extent, iron. Having been orphaned at the age of two, Francis was shunted about between relatives, including several years with his uncle, Henry Grey, Marquess of Dorset, at Bradgate (Grey had bought the wardship of Francis's older brother Thomas), though at a later date than Bess. Along the way, probably encouraged by Grey, he acquired an excellent classical education. When his brother died in 1559, Francis, at the age of thirteen, became heir, and his wardship was bought by Sir Francis Knollys, Treasurer of the Queen's Chamber.

The young Francis, already showing a certain contrariness, refused to marry Knollys' daughter, and when the executors of his father's will bought out the wardship, he became independent. In 1564, he married Elizabeth Lyttelton, with whom he had six daughters, and a son who died young. The lack of heir, Elizabeth's chronic ill health and her habit of running up debts and running down to London made for incessant quarrels and a wretched marriage. Elizabeth was said to be wilful and fiery. During one of her many visits to Buxton, Sir Francis wrote hoping that 'with the recovery of her health she may also put on a tractable mind and let her self-will give place to reason'.[6] The quarrels went on, and, in much the same way as those of the Shrewsburys, were exploited by their servants. In 1582, Elizabeth petitioned the Queen for a separation (Sir Francis was ordered to pay her £200 a year maintenance), though she returned to Wollaton in 1588.

Sir Francis fought not just with his wife, but with everyone around him – daughters, son-in-law (Percival Willoughby, a cousin, married Sir Francis's eldest daughter Bridget, and became his heir), servants – all of whom also fought with each other. Wollaton was a house of turbulence and discord, riven by distrust and rivalries, something that seems reflected in its exterior (the interiors were almost entirely remodelled by Jeffry Wyatville in the nineteenth century). In many ways Wollaton is a monstrous building, heavy and hectic, overcrowded with ornament, overwhelmed with glass. The prospect room, known at the time as the 'High Hall', is astonishing but was utterly impractical – reached by the narrowest of stairs, with no fireplace or furniture, a space for Sir Francis and his guests to walk in and admire the view but not to sit, linger or relax.

Wollaton is a restless house built for a restless patron. But a patron who wanted his house to be noticed. Willoughby, 'out of ostentation to show his riches' (Camden again), 'built at vast charges a very stately house, both for the splendid appearance and curious workmanship of it'.[7] For help in building something splendid and curious, he turned to Robert Smythson.

Sir Francis would have known of Smythson through his sister Margaret, who was married to Sir Matthew Arundell, for whom Smythson had worked at Wardour Castle during his years at Longleat. In 1580, after the death of Sir John Thynne, Smythson came north, to Wollaton. He was employed as a 'Surveyor', drawing up plans for Sir Francis's new house (a plan for the ground floor and gardens, and drawings of a turret and the hall screen, survive), and he remained at Wollaton, living in the village and acting as a kind of bailiff – collecting rents and drawing up inventories of bedding – until his death in 1614.

Along the way he became a gentleman, meriting a 'Mr' in the building accounts. His name first appears in those accounts in 1584, paying wages to the masons at the quarry at Ancaster. He also ordered and paid for materials. Aside from the design, he oversaw and managed the whole project.

Smythson was a highly skilled and versatile draughtsman, as can be seen from his surviving drawings, exquisite things in their own right. Besides plans and elevations for houses, he turned his hand to the design of windows, chimney-pieces, hall screens, beds, tools, tombs, summer houses and gardens. He learned from the buildings he worked on, the craftsmen he worked with and the architectural manuals that came his way. Since the 1560s, pattern books and engravings showing architectural ornament had been coming off the printing presses in Antwerp, while the persecution of Flemish Protestant craftsmen meant that many made their way to England. This led to strapwork (stone carved into interlaced ribbons or straps), for example, inspired by Hans Vredeman de Vries, becoming increasingly common. Strapwork was used extensively at Wollaton, and later at Hardwick (amongst the Smythson drawings are copies of details from Vredeman de Vries's *Varia architecturae formae*). Smythson would also have had access to Sir Francis's extensive library, which contained a great many architectural books and prints by such as Sebastiano Serlio, Vitruvius, Palladio, Jacques Androuet du Cerceau and John Shute. In Serlio (published in separate books from 1537 and in a single edition in 1575), Smythson would have discovered illustrations, derived from Roman builders, of classical features such as order, proportion and symmetry, as well as plans for villas with towers containing prospect rooms. In du Cerceau's handbooks, he would have come across the kind of geometrical devices that he would employ in houses like Hardwick.

Having worked at Longleat, alongside his fellow mason the Frenchman Alan Maynard, Smythson had plenty of experience of classical ornament. However, the excesses of Wollaton – the proliferation of ornament – probably shows the hand of Sir Francis, a patron with wide-ranging intellectual interests. Wollaton, in all its strangeness, stands as a synthesis of ideas, influences and styles, filtered through Willoughby, Smythson and the craftsmen.

Craftsmen, and masons in particular, moved about the country in groups, from site to site, wherever the work took them. Thus Smythson brought some of his Longleat team with him – Christopher Lovell (son of Humphrey) and John Hills, both masons, and Richard Crispin, a carpenter. They were joined by men who had been employed else-where in the Midlands – the mason brothers John and Christopher Rhodes, who had been working on Sheffield Manor and William Dickenson's (Shrewsbury's bailiff) house, and Thomas Accres, who was at Wollaton in 1584, presumably 'spared' by either Shrewsbury or Bess. The Rhodes brothers, Accres and Hills would all go on to Hardwick.

By the time it was finished in 1588, Wollaton had cost around £8,000, though this did not include some boon work (free labour extracted from Willoughby tenants) and the fact that stone was traded for coal – carriers bringing the Ancaster stone with which the house was faced (on a brick core) from Lincolnshire, forty miles away, had their panniers reloaded with coal.[8] Wollaton was the first house that Smythson designed from scratch, and his least harmonious, though that was probably due in large measure to the influence and interfer-ence of his patron. But it was a new kind of house – an outward-looking house, rather than an inward-looking courtyard house – which got him talked about and brought him to the attention of the Shrewsburys.

Wollaton didn't stop Smythson from taking on other projects.* Bess would have known of Smythson through her old friend Sir John

---

* During the 1580s, he drew up plans for Barlborough Hall, Derbyshire, now a school, and possibly for Heath Old Hall, Yorkshire (Girouard, *Robert Smythson*, p.120).

Thynne, and once he was established at Wollaton, it would have been easy enough to seek him out. The Stand at Chatsworth, above the house, at a fine vantage point for hunt-viewing, may have been designed by Smythson. Built in the early 1580s, it's a square tower, with four domed turrets that recall the banqueting houses at Longleat and prefigure those at Worksop, and exquisite plasterwork ceilings.

How much of a part Bess played in the building of Worksop is unclear, but the Shrewsburys, though often at loggerheads, were not estranged when work began. Bess made regular visits to Sheffield, and Worksop must have been discussed; it may well have been on her suggestion that the Earl brought in Smythson, though he would have been much occupied with Wollaton during the early stages of Worksop. By 1583, when the Queen of Scots stayed there (the Earl was ticked off for allowing Mary to walk in Sherwood Forest, a charge he denied), Worksop was clearly habitable, but it was probably no more than a ground and first floor.[9] Smythson came in for the second floor, with its great gallery and projecting bays, the glory of the house. Surviving drawings include a survey plan of Worksop by his son John, and a design for a hall screen, by Robert, that was never executed. Stylistically, Worksop shows distinctive Smythsonian features – domed turrets, bay windows, height, expanses of glass. As the architectural historian John Summerson put it: 'It was as if Longleat had been compressed into one of its shorter sides and then built upwards half as high again.'[10]

The house was pretty much complete by the summer of 1585, when Richard Torre, the Worksop bailiff, told Shrewsbury that 'all your Lord's things at Worksop and your Ld's lodging at Worksop are well'. Work was ongoing in the gardens. Torre had taken delivery of thirty orange trees, sent from London by ship to Hull, but found all but two to be dead on arrival.[11] And the plumbers had made the pipes for the waterworks, though Torre was scandalised at the cost of the lead. Inside the house it was a question of finishing touches – in the gallery,

Giles Greve, a mason, had almost set up the chimney-piece, which was then to be plastered, and the panelling was very nearly complete.[12] Bess, however, was never to enjoy Worksop's sky-high gallery, or water features, or orange trees. By 1585, the Shrewsburys had long since ceased to share a roof.

'I am most quiet when I have the fewest women here', wrote Shrewsbury wearily to Thomas Baldwin in February 1582. He was at Sheffield Castle, where Mary Talbot had recently given birth to a second daughter. Bess had returned to Chatsworth, having failed to persuade her husband to take on Elizabeth Lennox's servants. The Earl felt that he already had 'too many spies' in his house.[13]

Shrewsbury was feeling more than usually beleaguered. His eldest son, thirty-two-year-old Francis, died in the summer of 1582, leaving no heir and a great many debts, in addition to which came a demand from the Earl of Pembroke, the brother of Francis's widow, for his sister's jointure to be paid to him, and if possible increased, according to the terms of his father's will.[14] Gilbert now became Shrewsbury's heir; always a 'costly child', he was shaping up to be no less profligate than his brother. He was also, so his father believed, hopelessly under his wife's thumb and therefore would inevitably side with her, and Bess, against him. The Earl dated his alienation from Bess to the loss of his eldest son: 'till Francis Talbot's death she and her children sought my favour, but since those times they have sought for themselves and never for me'.[15] It was less important to solicit Shrewsbury's goodwill now that Gilbert and Mary were destined to become the next Earl and Countess – their inheritance was secure.

And yet again, the Earl was facing criticism for showing too much leniency towards the Queen of Scots. A letter came from Burghley informing him that Elizabeth had heard that he allowed Mary to hunt and fish 'and that she is more lusty now than she was these 7 years and that she hath her mind in all things'.[16] Shrewsbury, writing to Walsingham, 'from the bottom of my afflicted spirit', could only insist that Mary 'hath showed herself an enemy unto me and to my fortune'.[17]

Mary, who was nothing if not manipulative, would have been perfectly aware that the Earl was increasingly at odds with Bess – here was a chance to play the husband off against the wife. As anyone who had any contact with her attested, she had a great gift for listening, for directing the full beam of her attention on the speaker, for making him, or her, feel that no one could be more interesting; it was key to her charm. If the Earl was occasionally tempted to unburden himself, to allow himself the luxury of a little feminine sympathy, it would hardly have been surprising.

The Shrewsbury servants were no less willing than the Queen of Scots to exploit the differences between their master and mistress, who both complained of their insulting behaviour. The state of the Shrewsbury marriage and the atmosphere at Sheffield are spelled out in a letter from Marmyon, a servant loyal to Bess – and therefore a spy in the eyes of Shrewsbury – to Sir Francis Willoughby. Marmyon described the 'civil wars' at Sheffield, which was 'a hell' thanks to 'a broil or kind of tragedy betwixt my Lord and Lady'. The Earl had accused Bess and Marmyon of being 'devisors for the disabling of his service to Her Majesty'; if Bess didn't dismiss Marmyon, he had threatened to 'shut her Ladyship up without suffering any servants about her than of his own placing'. This, thought Marmyon, would have consequences: 'the sequel is in doubt to breed afterclaps'.[18] He begged Sir Francis for a position in his household, apparently unaware that the backbiting and tale-telling amongst the Shrewsbury servants was as nothing compared to that at Wollaton (by 1584, he had joined the Willoughby household, a move he may have lived to regret).

Yet affection between the Shrewsburys had not entirely dried up, and the Earl could still be solicitous towards his wife. In May 1582, he instructed Thomas Baldwin to procure her a 'very handsome' horse litter. He took trouble with the details – it was to be large, light, covered with leather, able to open on both sides, with curtains, a small chair, and a long rein so she could 'both rise and steer herself'.[19]

With the Earl chained to the Queen of Scots at Sheffield, he relied on Baldwin to carry out commissions, transact business and keep an ear to the ground. Baldwin reported on news from court; he arranged loans for the Earl's sons, and for Bess to have £100 as the Queen's New Year's gift; he escorted Henry and Edward Talbot on their trip to France (after a year at Oxford); he had the Earl's cloak mended; he dispensed venison pasties,[†] sent from Sheffield, amongst court officials; he arranged for lead to be transported to Lord Burghley at Theobalds; he commissioned satin nightcaps for the Queen of Scots; he purchased black rabbit fur for a nightgown for the Earl.[20] And, on Shrewsbury's instructions, he bought goods not readily available outside London – yards of 'scarlet' (the most expensive variety of woollen cloth, often dyed scarlet), almonds, saffron, mace, cloves, pepper, garden seeds, cinnamon, canary seed, cassia, plate, glasses, candlesticks, tons of claret, a jerkin of Spanish leather, feathers for mattresses, copper pans, and oil of roses for the Earl's feet – and had them sent up to Hull, by sea, then on to Sheffield. When, in 1583, a bride was being sought for Edward Talbot, Shrewsbury's third son, Baldwin was dispatched to Bothal Castle to assess the suitability of Jane Ogle, the daughter of Lord Ogle (Charles Cavendish was married to Jane's sister Catherine); he considered her rather short, but 'of very good complexion'.[21] In the smooth running of Shrewsbury's affairs, from arranging loans,

---

* It may well have been this litter that Francis Willoughby asked for the loan of in 1589, to bring his wife back from Buxton, as she was too weak to ride or travel by coach, 'wherefore I am humbly to desire your Ladyship to lend her your horse litter and furniture' (Folger X.d.428 [126]).

† The pastry in the pasties was used to preserve the venison in transit and was probably not eaten.

to obtaining soothing foot oil and looking over brides, Baldwin was key. It must have been a blow when, in 1584, he was arrested for 'having secret intelligence with the Queen of Scots' (accepting coded letters from Mary's secretary Gilbert Curle).[22] Shrewsbury's paranoia was not entirely unfounded: Mary, her servants, his own servants, his wife, her children, all appeared to be working against him.

In February 1583, Bess was at Sheffield, from where she wrote, somewhat nervously, to Walsingham. She had heard that the Queen was displeased by the marriage of Bess's nephew, John Wingfield, to Susan Bertie, the widowed Countess of Kent (this sounds like Bess matchmaking), that had taken place without royal consent. She hoped that Walsingham would do what he could to bring the Queen round.[23] And she was back at Sheffield in the early summer, for Mary Talbot's lying-in – she had a baby boy, John, who died young.

Bess's subsequent departure to Chatsworth would be a point of much dispute between the Shrewsburys. Did she go 'voluntarily' (the Earl's version), or was she sent away, on the pretext of the 'littleness' of his (very large) house, and a lack of beds for her grooms and women? According to Bess, the Earl 'picked no quarrel' when she left and assured her that he would send for her again within a month.[24] He didn't, and Bess would never return to Sheffield. From this moment, the Earl stopped paying her £1,000 annual allowance. He also claimed that she had broken the terms of the 1572 deed of gift by selling land without his agreement, thereby rendering the deed null and void; henceforth he intended to appropriate the rents from Bess's lands – those that had been settled on William and Charles in 1572 – since they had now reverted to him. When the tenants of the western lands, who recognised no allegiance to Shrewsbury, refused to comply, the bailiffs were instructed to tell them to pay the Earl, not Bess, 'at their uttermost peril'.[25] Shrewsbury had declared war.

Something of his state of mind comes across in a letter from Gilbert to Bess, in which Gilbert reported a conversation he'd had with his father at Worksop in September. The Earl had raged incoherently, at times 'so out of purpose as it were in vain to write it', with occasional lurches into sentimentality. He saw all around him as ranged either with him, or against him. He didn't want Gilbert to take his wife Mary to London because he was convinced that Bess would join them there and then they would all join 'in exclaiming against him' (the Earl was petitioning desperately for permission to go to London himself). William Cavendish was demanding £1,800 for 'lott and cope' (lead mining dues), which presumably the Earl had appropriated. Henry Cavendish was 'commended exceedingly … for maintaining his honour', as was the Earl's servant George Bentall, a 'traitor' according to Bess, but 'the truest and faithfullest servant that ever he had' in Shrewsbury's eyes (Bentall was a gentleman porter at Sheffield, who later came under suspicion for carrying letters for the Queen of Scots). Whenever Gilbert tried to speak, he was cut off, but his father assured him that he loved him best of all his children, and that Gilbert had never given cause for offence 'but in tarrying so long at chatsworth'.[26]

Those around Shrewsbury urged him to reconcile with Bess. The Queen wrote with the sympathetic concern of a kindly aunt, enquiring after her 'good old man', though no doubt she was most anxious about how the turmoil at Sheffield, and the Earl's erratic behaviour, would affect Mary. Leicester, who was a friend to both Shrewsburys and had been called in as mediator before, wrote in July 1583 sending his compliments on the return of the Earl's youngest sons Edward and Henry from France and hoping 'in God's name to hear better of these matters between my Lady and you and it would be no small sorrow to me if she should justly give your Lordship any ill causes both because she is your wife and a very wise gentlewoman'.[27] This fell on deaf ears. The Earl told Baldwin that he wanted the boys to come to Sheffield, where they were to be 'stout' with Bess and their stepbrothers, since Bess had 'set her children to give evil speeches against him' and Charles Cavendish had been spreading 'false rumours'.[28]

Bess, naturally, was keeping her cards close to her chest. Privately she must have seethed at the withholding of her allowance and at the Earl's decision to disregard the deed of gift and appropriate her rents. But her public stance was one of bewildered distress. A letter to Walsingham sounds a most uncharacteristic note of defeat. Having done all she could to placate her husband, she could now only look to the Queen for justice. She hoped that Her Majesty would allow her sons 'to seek their livings in some other place', keeping only their deer. 'Their banishment will I trust pacify his [Shrewsbury's] indignation, for my self I shall find some friend for meat and drink and so end my life'.[29] She did not of course intend anything of the sort.

14.

'CIVIL WARS'

The breakdown of the Shrewsbury marriage, played out over four long years, grew out of resentments and jealousies, escalated into an ugly battle over money and property – the issues on which both Shrewsburys sharpened their knives – and ended mired in pettiness and trivia. That it was treated as a matter of national importance, with several inquiries ordered by the Queen, may seem surprising, but it wasn't unknown for Elizabeth to step in and adjudicate between estranged couples – as with the Willoughbys. Shrewsbury was a great earl and a loyal servant, but more importantly, dissension between him and Bess threatened the security of the Queen of Scots. An entire volume of State Papers charts the dissolution of the Shrewsbury marriage: letters, appeals and counter-appeals, accusations and rebuttals, charters, lists of expenditure made and losses sustained (a typical list sets out 'his griefs' and 'her griefs' in two long columns). Much hinged on the terms of the marriage settlement – now lost to us – and the 1572 deed of gift. Much is tortuous, impenetrable and repetitive, the same old grievances resurrected, the same old arguments rehashed. However, two leitmotifs come through: Shrewsbury's conviction that Bess and her sons were out to bleed him dry, and Bess's determination to hold on to what she believed was rightly hers.

Both Bess and the Earl were enthusiasts for pecuniary nit-picking, and both had very long memories – no expense was too minor to be raked up and added to the balance sheet: servants' wages, New Year's gifts for the Queen, building work at Chatsworth, supplies of timber, iron and lead, payments of debts, gifts of plate and linen, Elizabeth Lennox's dowry, twenty pounds here and forty pounds there.[1] The Earl claimed he'd given Bess 'over and above' £27,000 in money, chattels, timber, lead and iron during their marriage; Bess insisted that since being separated from her husband she'd suffered £22,700 worth of losses (her allowance, rents appropriated by the Earl, expenses of servants, etc.).[2] These are huge sums; by way of perspective, Charles Cavendish lived very comfortably on his £400 annual allowance.

A portrait of Shrewsbury from 1582, when he was fifty-four, shows a man aged beyond his years, worn-looking and pained, his eyes shadowed and his forehead deeply lined, a man hollowed out by rage and bitterness, a man who struggled to hold a pen in hands twisted and swollen by arthritis as he composed page after page of bile directed at his wife. There is something unbalanced about Shrewsbury's behaviour in the face of the collapse of his marriage, about the extremity of his feelings, which so often seem disproportionate to their purported causes. There may have been some physiological explanation – incessant pain from the gout that plagued him, or possibly he'd suffered minor strokes that made him irascible and irrational.[*] There is something of Lear in the violence of the Earl's language, in his 'ungoverned rage', his self-pity, his resistance to reason.[†] 'How sharper than a serpent's tooth it is to have a thankless child.' And not just a thankless son – Gilbert – but a thankless wife too.

As Shrewsbury flailed around, hurling accusations and abuse, Bess, at the centre of the storm, remained still, calm and resolute, holding her course. Whatever financial depredations she was suffering at

---

[*] In a letter written in September 1583, Gilbert refers to a 'swellinge' in 'my Lord's boddy' (BHL, ID 86).

[†] *King Lear* was first performed at James I's court in December 1606.

Shrewsbury's hands, they were not such that prevented her from buying the Hardwick estate in June 1583, for £9,500, in William Cavendish's name (as a wife, she could not buy freehold property in her own). Shrewsbury, who was applied to for the money, refused.[3] Two years earlier, Bess's brother, James Hardwick, whose grandiose land-buying, using borrowed money, ended in bankruptcy and the Fleet prison, had died.* Bess had had Hardwick in her sights for some time, even exercising some kind of occupancy, on the expectation that James's ownership was doomed (from about 1578, his estate was in the hands of the receivers).[4] In 1577, her daughter Elizabeth addressed a letter to her at Hardwick, and three years later, Bess asked, or rather ordered, Shrewsbury to have timber carried there, indicating some kind of building work, or repairs. Hardwick, the place of Bess's birth, the home that she could enjoy independently of any husband, was now hers. Whatever became of her marriage, she was looking to the future. And to that of her granddaughter, Arbella, too.

Bess was plotting a match between Arbella and Leicester's two-year-old son Robert, Lord Denbigh, by his second wife, Lettice Knollys. During the unravelling of the Shrewsbury marriage, Bess had regularly sent Arbella to Gilbert and Mary Talbot (Arbella's godmother), who could offer a calmer, more congenial home for a little girl, and the company of their own daughters. But she had by no means abandoned her ambitions for her. A match between Arbella and Robert would unite royal blood on her part and powerful connections on his, and for those very reasons it was not likely to be welcomed by the Queen, who was kept in the dark. It certainly infuriated the Queen of Scots. She had been willing enough to lend support to Arbella's claim to the Lennox inheritance, but Bess pushing her granddaughter towards the English throne was quite another matter.

---

* Bess hadn't entirely turned her back on James – in 1582, she paid off £100 of his debts.

'Nothing has ever alienated the Countess of Shrewsbury from me more', she raged to the French ambassador in March 1584, 'than this imaginary hope, which she has conceived, of setting this crown on the head of Arbella, her granddaughter, by means of marrying her to the son of the Earl of Leicester.'[5]

However, the match came to nothing, as little Robert died in July. This, as Leicester wrote to Shrewsbury, in reply to his letter of condolence, was 'a great grief... for that I have no others [sons] and more unlikely to have any, growing now old'. This was not strictly true, as he had an illegitimate son by Douglas (named after Margaret Douglas, Countess of Lennox, her godmother) Sheffield, of whom he was very fond. He felt the Earl was too hard on Gilbert – sons, after all, were there to be cherished.

But Shrewsbury couldn't stop himself from railing against Gilbert, who as he told Leicester was claiming that he was being forced to either 'forsake' his father or 'hate his wife'. The Earl denied this, though admitted that he had asked Gilbert to keep away from his 'wicked and malicious wife, who has set me at nought in his own hearing', but that contrary to his wishes Gilbert had been seeing Bess regularly and carrying letters for her. The Earl put this down to Mary Talbot's 'wicked persuasion and her mother's together, for I think neither barrel better herring of them both ... to be plain, he shall either leave his indirect dealings with my wife, seeing I take her as my professed enemy, or else indeed will I do that to him I would be loth, seeing I have heretofore loved him so well'.[6] That Gilbert, his favourite child, should side with Bess was a source of particular bitterness.

In the summer of 1584, the Earl began a campaign of harassment aimed at Chatsworth and the Cavendishes. At Ashford, which had been returned to the Cavendishes by the deed of gift, the Earl's men, led by Nicholas Booth, took rents and lead ore, and attacked Charles Cavendish, who was forced to take refuge in the church steeple. The walls around Charles's pastures at Stoke were demolished and some of his servants wounded. One of Bess's servants was attacked by Booth in Chatsworth park, while the house had windows broken and tenants had their livestock impounded, because they'd already paid rent to Bess and saw no reason to pay the Earl.

Bess, feeling under siege, retreated to Hardwick, where furnishings, hangings and plate from Chatsworth had been carried off by William Cavendish, presumably acting on his mother's orders, during two nocturnal raids.[7] This must have been some feat. The finest furnishings would have been in the state apartments on Chatsworth's top floor; plate was extremely heavy, as were hangings, such as the Virtues hangings. These would have had to be rolled up and carried down several flights of stairs, in the dark, before being loaded onto wagons and trundled the sixteen miles to Hardwick, which was hardly in a fit state to accommodate them. None of this could have been done without the cooperation of the Chatsworth servants, but many of them, like James Crompe, were long-serving and loyal to Bess. Furthermore, since it cost considerably more to furnish a house than to build it, the contents were immensely valuable, and their removal an indisputable act of aggression. Shrewsbury certainly took it as such and, accompanied by forty armed men, arrived at Chatsworth, where – if his own account is to be believed – he was refused 'a night's lodging' by William Cavendish, who, armed 'with halberd in hand and pistol under his girdle', insulted him with 'lewd language'.[8] Naturally the Earl was quite incapable of overlooking such an affront to his honour, and immediately made an official complaint to the Privy Council; William was sent to the Fleet gaol for 'insolent behaviour'.

On 2 August, a 'distressed' and 'sorrowful' Bess wrote to Burghley from her new home at Hardwick, hoping that he and the Queen might use their influence with the Earl for her 'better usage'. 'Quietness is the thing I most desire in these my latter days', she claimed, not entirely convincingly. Her husband was trying 'to take away Chatsworth and those poor goods and living which were mine which himself assured to my two younger sons under his hand and seal about 11 years since'. Since she had not received her allowance for over a year, she was 'driven to live on my children'. Those children, barring Henry, who had been 'won' by the Earl 'to deal most unnaturally with me', would 'rather lose their life' than be deprived of what was rightfully theirs, and Bess herself was 'not without fear' of her life.[9] She was laying it on thick.

She wrote the next day to Shrewsbury, apparently in similar vein. Her letter (since lost) displayed a 'fair and unaccustomed show of dutifulness and humility of spirit', but did not have a mollifying effect. Rather, the Earl suspected 'it to be a siren's song set for some other purpose than it pretends', for Bess had shown herself his 'bitter enemy, seeking by your ministers of false suggestions everywhere my infamy and overthrow, then the spoil of my goods and of mine and your own children by your unnatural means and malice and lastly the sack of Chatsworth house that devouring gulf of mine and other your husbands goods'. He had willingly funded Chatsworth for the sake of future heirs and he was now going 'to proceed by due order of law with those my adversaries your sons ... thinking it in conscience most dishonourable unto me to stand and look upon the ruin of that house with the utter undoing of your eldest and best deserving son'. Henry, by taking Shrewsbury's part against his mother, had found favour with his stepfather. William Cavendish's raids on Chatsworth, argued the Earl, deprived Henry of his inheritance.[10]

In August, while lodging in Chancery Lane, where Bess had come on behalf of William Cavendish, who was languishing in the Fleet (after the case against him had been heard, he was released), she wrote: 'My lord, the innocency of my own heart is such and my desire so infinite to procure your good conceit as I will leave no way unsought to attain your favour ... my heart notwithstanding what I have suffered thirsts after your prosperity and desires nothing so much as to have your love ... I know my Lord that hatred must grow of something and how I have deserved your indignation is invisible to me.'[11]

Was she sincere? Bess, said a contemporary, was 'humble in speech and stout in actions'.[12] It was a policy that served her well. While more than capable of fighting her corner, viciously if necessary, she was also careful to present herself, especially to those that counted – the Queen, Burghley, Walsingham, Leicester – as the wronged but ever-dutiful wife. There lay her best chance of redress. And why should she seek the dissolution of a marriage that had, on the whole, suited her for many years, that had allowed her to operate within the umbrella of Shrewsbury's wealth and position, to promote the interests of her children and to lead a largely independent life at Chatsworth? Bess had lost the ability to manage the Earl, largely because he had become unmanageable. There was, however, another factor in the mix, also beyond Bess's control – the Queen of Scots.

In March 1584, Frances Battell, one of Bess's gentlewomen, had written to Lady Paulet (the wife of the Marquess of Winchester) from Chatsworth, where Bess was still living. She claimed she was being victimised by Shrewsbury, who 'gives out hard speeches of her to her great discredit' and was agitating for her dismissal and all because the Scottish Queen disliked her. How could Mary 'abide her when she is with all hatred bent against her mistress [Bess]?' Frances recalled an incident when one of Mary's gentlemen said that Mary should be Queen of England, whereupon Bess replied 'that it were better that the Scottish Queen were hanged before that time should come to pass'. The Earl had taken great offence at such disrespect and 'since that time ... deals hardly with' Bess. Frances did not want to leave Bess's service, but felt she would have no choice if the Earl continued his campaign against her.[13] This letter was given to Burghley by Bess's half-sister Elizabeth Wingfield, possibly as evidence of Bess's loyalty to the Queen, or of the Earl's unreasonable behaviour. It makes it abundantly clear that Bess had made an enemy of Mary, that the Earl was taking his prisoner's part against his wife and that the Shrewsbury household had become polarised in consequence.

Any goodwill between Bess and Mary had long vanished. Where both women had once hoped each might be of use to the other, both had been disappointed. Bess had ceased to be a source of court gossip or information about the Queen, and her ambitions for Arbella had infuriated Mary. By 1584, rumours of an affair between the Scots Queen and Shrewsbury, and indeed of a child or two, were rife.[14] Both Mary and the Earl firmly pointed the finger at Bess and her sons as the source of such rumours. Mary was certainly out to make trouble for Bess. In January 1584, she told the French ambassador, de Mauvissière, that she sought 'to implicate indirectly the Countess of Shrewsbury'.[15] This was followed by claims that Bess had offered to help her escape should her life ever be in danger, that Charles Cavendish had offered to act as a spy for her in London (Charles certainly had asked favours of Mary and probably offered them in return), and that Bess's servants and Bess herself had delivered ciphers to her.[16]

Whether or not Bess believed the rumours, it suited her to appear to do so, and she may well have authorised her sons to see to their spreading, as part of a campaign to undermine the Earl, to besmirch his reputation. On the other hand, if she really hoped for reconciliation, why would she have gone out of her way to further enrage Shrewsbury? That the Earl had conducted an affair with Mary seems highly improbable – he was far too neurotic, as well as deeply loyal to his Queen, to take such a risk. That Bess was jealous, very possible. At the very least, she would have resented what she perceived as a partiality on her husband's part, a sympathy between him and his prisoner. According to the Earl, Bess believed that 'the Scottish Queen could rule me in all things against her'.[17]

For Mary, time was running out and with that came a growing sense of desperation, as any hopes of liberty, let alone of restoration to the Scottish throne, fell away. Her son James, having declared in 1583, aged seventeen, that his minority was at an end, was now King James VI of Scotland. And he had made it perfectly clear that he had no interest in co-ruling with his mother. In fifteen years of captivity, Mary had not so much as had an audience with Elizabeth. All the intriguing, all the plots and attempts to spring her free had come to nothing. Since Walsingham had by now become adept at intercepting Mary's correspondence, virtually no communication passed undetected. In November 1583, the Throckmorton Plot, by which an invasion of England and Scotland, backed by Spain, the Pope and the Duke of Guise, would place Mary on the throne, had been uncovered. Mary was clearly implicated, but once again the Queen baulked at putting her on trial, though she agreed to the execution of Francis Throckmorton. Then in July 1584, Protestants throughout Europe were deeply shaken by the assassination, by a Catholic, of William of Orange, who had led the Dutch Protestants against the Spanish. Fears for Elizabeth's safety grew. Anti-Catholic feeling had never run higher. And the noose tightened around Mary.

The 'scandal letter', from the Queen of Scots to Elizabeth, undated but most probably written in early 1584, lobbed a series of small grenades – pieces of gossip supposedly relayed to Mary by Bess – in the Queen's direction. Elizabeth, according to Bess, was an insatiable nymphomaniac, whose lovers had included Leicester, Hatton and Jean de Simier; she was 'not as other women' – suggesting some kind of sexual deformity; she took so much 'pleasure in exaggerated flattery, such as that none dared' look her 'full in the face because it shone like the sun'; when Bess and her daughter Elizabeth had been at court, they had been unable to 'look at each other when addressing' the Queen 'for fear of bursting out laughing'; the Queen had broken the finger of Mary Scudamore, one of her ladies and Bess's cousin, in a fit of rage and then blamed it on a falling chandelier; Bess had tried to marry her daughter Elizabeth to Sir Christopher Hatton, but he had held back for fear of the Queen's wrath (Elizabeth did not look kindly on her favourites marrying, and Hatton, who would have been a great match for Elizabeth, remained a bachelor); the Queen had stepped in to stop Charles Cavendish marrying Lord

Paget's niece because she had another groom in mind.[18] And so it went on, a document steeped in venom, much of it pure invention. But Bess certainly *had* gossiped to Mary and some of this has the ring of truth: the Queen's vanity and susceptibility to flattery; Bess's irritation at being thwarted in her matchmaking plans for her children. The letter was most probably never sent, only finding its way into Burghley's hands after Mary's death (any earlier and he would have used it against her). But it says a great deal about Mary's desperation and frustration, her desire to besmirch Bess, her desire to have an *effect*.

By the summer of 1584, the decision had been taken to relieve Shrewsbury, after fifteen years, of Mary's care.[19] His health was poor, his temper worse and his marriage in ruins, all of which inclined the Queen to doubt both his judgement and Mary's safety. Sir Ralph Sadler was appointed to take over (Sadler's custodianship would be short-lived – he was seen as too soft and replaced by the hard-line Puritan Sir Amyas Paulet in 1585). Sadler found Mary 'much altered' since he had last seen her in 1572 – stout, stooped, her grey hair hidden beneath a wig, her legs so inflamed and swollen that she could hardly walk. She was only forty-two. In September, on the Queen's orders, Shrewsbury and Sadler escorted Mary to South Wingfield (subsequently she would be moved back to the hated Tutbury), where the Earl made his farewells, a moment that must have brought very mixed feelings, of sadness and relief.

Shrewsbury was finally free to come to court, for the first time in twelve years. He arrived at Oatlands in September and was so overcome on seeing the Queen, and kissing her hand, that he burst into tears.[20] He showed himself to be as proud and prickly as ever, refusing to take a seat at his first Privy Council meeting until 'he knew if any of them would charge him with any lack of duty to her Majesty'. Only having been 'declared by them all to be both honourable and loyal' did he sit.[21]

Bess too had come to court, and in November, she and William and Charles Cavendish appeared before the Privy Council to answer the charge that the allegations about Mary and Shrewsbury had originated with them. Naturally they denied everything. They were not 'the authors, inventors or reporters' of the rumours about the Queen of Scots having had a child, or several, by the Earl. Such were 'very false, scandalous lies'.[22] Of course they remained guilty in Shrewsbury's eyes.

In December 1584, a commission of inquiry into the Shrewsbury marriage was conducted by the Lord Chancellor and two chief justices. At the centre of the Shrewsburys' disputes stood the 1572 deed of gift, which the Earl initially claimed to be a forgery, and then said he thought had been made for the benefit of Bess alone, not for William and Charles Cavendish. According to the Earl, Bess's sons had spent more than £25,000 on buying land in Derbyshire, Nottinghamshire and Staffordshire over the twelve years since the deed of gift, with Hardwick being the largest single purchase. Bess, he said, was enjoying an annual income of £5,000, five times the amount that had been agreed as her marital allowance, while William Cavendish had £700 a year from estates bought since 1572.[23] And all this at his expense. Bess countered by claiming that William and Charles had been buying land with their own money, that they were now in debt as a result, and that besides, the total sum was much less than that alleged by the Earl.

This, however, was disingenuous – William and Charles were funded by Bess. Her accounts, in the early 1580s, record a steady stream of payments: £100, £200, £400, £345 'out of my jewel coffer at Chatsworth', all 'to Wyll', sometimes delivered by James Crompe, sometimes given to 'my daughter Cavendish' to pass on to her husband.[24] Charles received a quarterly allowance of £100, as well as the revenues from the Somerset portion of the western lands, which were made over to him in 1586, with Bess keeping the Gloucestershire share (this too went to Charles after her death).'[25] Were such sums paid entirely from Bess's income? Or was she dipping into the Talbot coffers? Wherever the money came from, it was used by William and Charles to buy land, on their mother's behalf, consolidating and expanding the Cavendish estates in Derbyshire and beyond.

The commission resulted in an 'order' from the Queen and a victory for Bess: Shrewsbury was to take her back; William and Charles were to keep the lands bought over the last twelve years, as well as those settled on them in 1572; the Earl was to return the £2,000 he'd seized in rents; he was to drop all the legal suits currently pending against William and Charles and Bess's servants. As a sop, he was to receive £500 a year from Bess for lands that she occupied, according to the marriage settlement, but which belonged to him.

Shrewsbury complained to Leicester, in April 1585, about the Queen's 'hard sentence against me, to my perpetual infamy and dishonour, to be ruled and overrun by my wife, so bad and wicked a woman'.[26] To be ruled by Bess 'and her servants', to be made 'the wife and her the husband' – this was key to Shrewsbury's resentment, to his sense of being humiliated. William Cavendish and William St Loe had, it seemed, willingly submitted to Bess's rule, but possibly she had been careful to rule by stealth, to operate within the bounds, or maintain the appearance, of wifely duty. With Shrewsbury she had overstepped the mark and lost control. He felt *unmanned*. Nevertheless, he assured Leicester that he would abide by the Queen's order, 'though no curse or plague on earth could be more grievous to me'.

---

* Bess didn't forget her daughters -- Frances and Mary both had regular cash gifts (Devonshire MSS, Chatsworth, HM/5).

15.

MOCKING AND MOWING

'My riches they talk of are in other men's purses', wrote Shrewsbury to Thomas Baldwin plaintively.[1] The Earl's expenses were huge, as were his debts, but so was his income from rents and sales, estimated at £10,000 a year in the 1580s. Like many rich men, he believed himself to be less rich than he actually was, and there was nothing he liked less than parting with money. Shrewsbury was mean and Bess and his children suffered for it. Gilbert Talbot in particular was constantly in debt and constantly applying to his father for relief. In 1585, the Earl gave him £1,000, which all, including the Queen, saw as a cause for celebration. Sir Christopher Hatton, with no sons of his own, felt that Gilbert could be 'a comfortable staff in your old years' and deserved some help.[2] Burghley, who did have a 'son or two', agreed and repeatedly urged Shrewsbury to deal generously with Gilbert.

Burghley and Shrewsbury were friends of old and united by their 'joint enemy', gout. They exchanged reports and commiserations, suggested remedies, sent soothing ointments, and in Burghley's case, offered the use of Burghley House, which was on 'drier soil' than Sheffield.* Both were sometimes unable to write at all, so crippled

---

* Gilbert Talbot, with the help of his upholsterer, 'devised' a gout-friendly upholstered chair with a leg-rest, giving one to his father and offering another to Burghley (CP 165/17).

were their hands, but as Burghley put it touchingly, 'I pray you make more account of my heart than my hands.'[3] 'I am as lonely as an owl', claimed Burghley. This was no doubt true enough of Burghley the public figure, but privately he was a devoted husband and a humane and kindly father: 'we fathers must take comfort in our children, to see and provide for them to live agreeable to our comforts'. Debt, he told the Earl, was 'a cancer growing', and without relief, Gilbert's estate would simply be 'eaten with burden of interest'. 'No deed', he thought, was 'more charitable than to help a man out of a deep pit of debt, wherein the longer he shall be the deeper the pit will be'. And it would only take 'a small portion' of Shrewsbury's 'favour and purse' to relieve his son. He knew that the Earl saw Gilbert as in league with Bess, but he, Burghley, believed that in actuality Gilbert had 'worked for reconciliation', and besides, he could hardly be blamed for seeing Bess, given that she was his wife's mother.[4]

Far from abiding by the Queen's order, Shrewsbury continued to make trouble, carrying on his suits against Bess's servants and sons, and stirring up her Derbyshire tenants. Both he and Bess came to court during the spring and summer of 1585, anxious to further their cases. Bess lodged in Chancery Lane, and, as Henry Talbot reported to Shrewsbury, she, together with William, Charles and Mary Talbot, attended 'very diligently at Court', where they commanded 'little respect' (this may well have been a case of telling the Earl what he wanted to hear).[5] By October, Bess was back at Wingfield, where, according to the order, she was based (she had the use of Wingfield for her lifetime, under her marriage settlement). From here she told Burghley that her husband made 'a sport of this broken reconcilement', that she had hardly seen him, and, despite his promise to the Queen to 'send often' for her, he refused to let her come to any of his other houses. She had now endured 'these extreme wrongs' for three years.[6]

Bess needed Burghley's support. She assured him that she counted him as one of her few true friends, though she must have been aware that Burghley's loyalties were divided between the Shrewsburys. Marital breakdown tests friendship, and Bess felt let down by many – a certain 'noble man', for example, whom she had 'found at the time of my need much less than he professed'; others who offered nothing but 'general words, referring my comfort to hope'.[7] There was sympathy for Bess – the Earl's behaviour was, after all, highly unreasonable at best – but she did not command the kind of power and connections that Shrewsbury relied on. Living at Wingfield, a house she had little love for, was isolating, both geographically and emotionally. When she signed herself off to Burghley 'your Lordship's poor friend greatly oppressed', it was probably no more than the truth.

A few days later, she wrote to her husband, repeating her desire to return to him: 'I see your love is withdrawn from me, but my constant duty and affection continues so to you, that if my time were long, as it is sure to be short, I shall never cease to seek and sue by all good means, that I may live with you as I ought.'[8] These of course were the stock expressions of the dutiful wife. Lady Willoughby, when pleading with Sir Francis to be allowed to return to him in 1586, wrote in similar vein, vowing 'to perform all good duties that do become a loving and obedient wife towards her husband'.[9] Lady Willoughby's case was rather different to that of Bess – she had left her husband and thus suffered from the loss of the 'good opinion' of her peers, as well as of financial security. The Queen had ordered Sir Francis to pay his wife £200 a year in maintenance, but the Willoughby finances were so rocky, with Sir Francis renegotiating her jointure four times, to raise money, that she was probably lucky if she received anything at all.

Bess enjoyed significant financial independence and she had been careful to preserve her reputation. She was certainly not prepared to abjectly prostrate herself before her husband. She reminded Shrewsbury that just two months before he sent her away from Sheffield, back in 1583, he had expressed a desire to put their differences behind them, promised to 'become a new man', and vowed that he loved her 'so well' that he 'also loved the steps' she trod on. And she claimed that she couldn't be blamed for defending herself when she had barely £300 a year to live on and when her children would be forced 'to sell all they have for my maintenance and to pay my debts'.[10]

The Earl dismissed Bess's 'fair words' – 'though they appear beautiful yet they are mixed with a hidden poison' – and replied with an outpouring of invective: 'there cannot be any wife more forgetful of her duty and less careful to please her husband than you have been … I have seen thoroughly into your devices and desires, your insatiable greedy appetite did betray you, you own living at my hands could not content you, nor yet a great part of mine, which for my quietness I could have been contented to give you.' She would always 'favour' her children over him, and it would therefore be 'dangerous … to be compassed about with you and them when after me you shall leap into my seat'. But, as often, in amongst the wild hyperbole are small nuggets of truth. Bess claimed to have been 'in misery', yet she was 'sufficiently furnished to buy lands' for her children.[11]

'You loved me so well that you also loved the steps I trod on.' The extremity of Shrewsbury's loathing for Bess was directly proportionate to the love he'd borne her: she only became a devil because she had once been an angel. But was she the devil Shrewsbury believed her to be? Bess could justly be accused of many things – she was rapacious, self-seeking, ruthless. But for all her capacity for feuding, she had an equal capacity for love, whether for husbands (some), children (similar) or grandchildren. And malice – too impractical an impulse, its effects too uncertain – was not part of her make-up. Her schemes were framed by the long view, which did not allow for small-minded vengefulness. That she left to Shrewsbury.

As Christmas approached, Bess consulted Elizabeth Wingfield about her New Year's gift for the Queen (with her affairs in such disarray, it was more important than ever to get this right). Elizabeth, after talking to Lady Cobham, advised that a 'fine, rare thing' would definitely be preferred over money, and added that Lady Cheke had talked to the Queen 'of my lord's hard dealing' and she had given 'many good words what she would do for your honour'.[12] The Queen, who was not insensible to Shrewsbury's loyalty and the service he'd performed for her, and who besides disliked warring couples, was indeed doing her best to bring the Shrewsburys together. She told the Earl how she 'had long desired for your own good and quiet, that all matters of difference between the Countess your wife, your sons and you, might be brought to some good composition', and she asked him to drop legal proceedings against Bess's servants and sons.[13] But even Her Majesty's pleas had little effect.

Since the first commission had clearly brought no kind of reconciliation between the Shrewsburys, it was decided to hold another. At Ashford, in January 1586, Sir Francis Willoughby (a supporter of Bess) and John Manners (Shrewsbury's brother-in-law) heard allegations from both sides. Much the same ground was covered, with much the same outcome – a second order from the Queen, in May, reiterating the first, with the added stipulation that Shrewsbury was to be allowed to sue William Cavendish for the plate and hangings that he'd taken during his raids on Chatsworth. The Queen followed this up with a letter to the Earl – it was not right for 'two persons of your degree and quality to live in such a kind of discord. As also for the special care we have of yourself, knowing that these variances have disquieted you, whose years require repose, especially of the mind.'[14]

Many around Shrewsbury felt that his obsessive vendetta against his 'wife and her imps' was undermining his mental and physical health and that he should simply swallow his pride and take Bess back. Many shared the view of William Overton, Bishop of Coventry and Lichfield, who wrote urging reconciliation and offering some marriage guidance: 'if shrewdness and sharpness may be just cause for separation I think that few men in England would keep their wives long, for it is common jest yet true that there is but one shrew in the world and every man hath her'.[15]

The new order brought some result. Shrewsbury, as Bess wrote, paid William and Charles £850 of the £2,000, though otherwise he was still displacing 'sundry tenants' and continuing his legal suits.[16] The order was reinforced in August, when the Queen saw the Shrewsburys together at Richmond Palace: the Earl was bound by the colossal sum of £40,000 to end all conflict with Bess; he was to accompany her to Wingfield, where he would supply provisions and bear all expenses, as he would in any of his other homes occupied by her; he was to content himself with his £500 a year while Bess was 'to hold to herself all the rest of her living'; William and Charles Cavendish were to be sure not to give any cause for offence; the items removed from Chatsworth were to be returned. The official version had it that the Shrewsburys 'both showed themselves very well contented with Her Majesty's speeches and in good sort departed together, very comfortable to the sight of all their friends'.[17] Privately observers took a rather different view – 'in common opinion', wrote one, it was 'more likely' that the wars in the Low Countries would come to an end 'than these civil discords between him and her'.[18] Roger Manners told his father, the Earl of Rutland, that Shrewsbury intended to 'rule my lady, but she says little and yet plainly thinks to govern him'.[19]

Shrewsbury was certainly not having much success in ruling Bess, though he seized on the question of the Chatsworth goods and furnishings as a chance to gain the upper hand and promptly submitted a lengthy list of items he claimed as his: plate, New Year's gifts, linen, jewels, sheets, hangings, household utensils, and feather beds. In her 'Answer to the Demand of Plate', Bess went through his list, adding her own crisp comments in the margin. Various items of plate had been at Chatsworth at the time of the deed of gift and had thus gone to William and Charles Cavendish. 'One great bason and ewer, fashioned like a ship', was dismissed with 'bought by the Earl of purpose for the Countess to give away, which she did, as he well knoweth'.* Various items

---

* Bess regularly gave 'parcels of plate' as gifts: a 'gilt basin and ewer, the ewer like a ship' to Leicester, a 'gilt basin and ewer' to Walter Mildmay, a 'crystal cup trimmed with gold' to Gilbert Talbot, etc. (Devonshire MSS, Chatsworth, H/143.8, 143.6).

of plate – 'six candlesticks fashioned like boats, two cups of alabaster bound about with silver', etc. – given by Bess to the Earl as New Year's gifts had been returned to her, 'he misliking of them'. 'Rich hangings' (including the Virtues hangings) had been made at Chatsworth and the Earl hadn't contributed a penny towards their making. Sheets and pillow cases were 'worn out, made 17 years ago'. At the bottom of the page she wrote: 'these parcels above demanded by the Earl are things of small value and mere trifles for so great and rich a nobleman to bestow on his wife in 19 years'. Besides, if the Earl wished to stoop to such pettiness, she could match him – what about the 'pots, flagons, chafing dishes, chamber-pots, porringers, warming pans, boiling pots, and many other things', not to mention over £1,000 worth of linen, that she had provided for his various houses over the years?[20]

It was no surprise to anyone that the Queen's second order was scarcely more successful than the first. Shrewsbury continued to be irascible and unpredictable, allowing Bess a brief audience in London, when he made 'favourable and loving speeches' before reverting to his 'former wrath and heavy displeasure'.[21] He told Burghley that while he was prepared to bear Bess's living expenses, he would 'neither bed nor board with her'.[22] Drawing up a list of 'causes ... why he should not cohabit with the Countess', he claimed that Bess 'doth deadly hate him and hath called him knave, fool and beast to his face and hath mocked and mowed at him'.[23]

In the autumn of 1586, the Shrewsburys' 'civil wars' came to a temporary halt, and the Earl's attentions were diverted, as the last act in the unhappy life of the Queen of Scots played itself out. Walsingham had devised a system by which nothing written by Mary went unread: her letters, which were smuggled out of Chartley Manor, where she had been moved from Tutbury, in waterproof containers slipped into beer barrels, came straight into his hands and were decoded before being sent on to the recipient. It was simply a question of waiting for Mary to condemn herself, and with the discovery of the Babington

Plot, the moment came. Burghley, who had always believed that only Mary's death could secure the English throne and the Protestant succession, finally had his chance.

Anthony Babington came from a family of Derbyshire Catholics. The Babingtons were known to Bess – she had negotiated for land with Henry Babington, Anthony's father, back in 1565 – and Anthony himself had served Shrewsbury as a page, at Sheffield. He was young, charming and entirely out of his depth – the plot to which he gave his name, but of which he was not the chief architect, involved a revolt by English Catholics, a Spanish invasion, the assassination of Elizabeth and the liberation of Mary. It differed little from previous plots, and it never posed a serious threat, but crucially, it was known about and condoned by Mary, who was desperate enough to seize at the slenderest of straws. On the letter, a reply to Babington, in which Mary fatally incriminated herself, Walsingham's decipherer drew a small gallows. She was trapped.

According to the Bond of Association, drawn up in October 1584, anyone who threatened the life of the Queen was to be put to death. This was modified, the following March, by the Act for the Queen's Safety, which insisted on a legal process: a claimant to the throne who was involved in a plot or rebellion against the reigning monarch was to be tried by a commission, and if found guilty, would face death. Nevertheless, it still smoothed the way for Mary's destruction. At Fotheringhay Castle, she was put on trial by thirty-six commissioners, including Shrewsbury, who lodged nearby, at Orton Longeville, with his son Henry Talbot. Mary, claiming that she was 'a Queen and not a subject', at first refused to appear before the commission; when she did, she defended herself with dignity and denied any intention to kill Elizabeth. The commissioners returned to London to consider their verdict, though Shrewsbury, who was too unwell to travel, remained at Orton Longeville, where he received a letter from Burghley informing him that the Queen deplored his absence, 'less there may be some malicious sinister interpretation' (a reference to the old rumours about the Earl and Mary). Burghley advised the Earl to write a letter reiterating his belief that Mary was guilty.[24] Whether or not Shrewsbury truly believed so, or whether he simply had to be seen to believe, his fellow commissioners were of the same opinion – in the Star Chamber, on 25 October, the Queen of Scots was pronounced guilty.

But when it came to signing the warrant for Mary's execution, Elizabeth, true to form, prevaricated. Accepting her guilt was one thing; regicide quite another. She was no longer willing to 'cherish a sword to cut my own throat', but her feelings for Mary were as ambivalent as ever. She wanted Mary dead. Yet how could she take on the responsibility for executing an anointed queen? The warrant was signed, but still Elizabeth held back. Hoping to pass the buck, she let it be known that she would count it as a service if Sir Amyas Paulet quietly did away with Mary, a service that Paulet declined. In the end, Burghley and the councillors made the Queen's decision for her and sent the warrant to Fotheringhay.

Shrewsbury and the Earl of Kent, who had been chosen to supervise the execution, arrived at Fotheringhay in early February. On the 7th, the two earls, together with Robert Beale, told Mary that she was to die the next day. On the morning of the 8th, in Fotheringhay's Great Hall, it was Shrewsbury, as Earl Marshal, who had to give the signal to the executioner, whereupon he looked away and wept. He may not have seen the first fall of the axe into the back of Mary's head, the second that failed to cut through her neck, the sawing it took to finally sever her head, but during those long minutes he would have heard the grunts of the executioner, the dull thud of the axe, Mary's cry of pain, the weeping of her ladies. It was a scene to which even the most hard-hearted of men could not have been indifferent, and the emotional Earl was certainly not that. That Mary had been Shrewsbury's mistress can surely be discounted. Nevertheless, for fifteen years he had shared a roof with her, her gaoler but also her protector; there had scarcely been a day when he hadn't been in her company and many times when her company must have been a pleasure, even a balm. However exasperating Mary could be, however much trouble she had caused, however much the Earl had longed to be rid of her, the overseeing of her execution must have been not just a duty too far, but an agony.

Mary was dead, but as far as the Queen and her councillors were concerned, the Catholic menace remained very much alive, not just in Europe but at home. Despite the fact that English Catholics faced increasing penalties under Elizabeth, a small but resolute band remained, sustained by the seminary priests who had been arriving from Europe since the 1570s, and boosted by converts.* The Midlands in particular was something of a Catholic heartland – 'more danger-ously infected' than anywhere else in England according to Richard Topcliffe, the tireless persecutor of Catholics, a place where 'bad weeds will seek to shroud themselves under great oaks'.[25] Derbyshire had a considerable number of Catholic gentry families, such as the Babingtons. It was one of Shrewsbury's less enviable duties, as Lord Lieutenant of Yorkshire, Derbyshire and Nottinghamshire, to 'root out' Jesuit priests and their hosts, a task he performed with dogged determination. In 1582, he had been outraged to discover that a barrel stuffed with 'mass books' had been smuggled onto one of his ships at Hull.[26] 'Papist recusants' (those who refused to attend a Protestant service on Sunday) were gaoled and fined, though the fate of priests was much worse. In 1588, the Earl arrested Sir Thomas Fitzherbert and his family, together with two Catholic priests. All were sent to gaol in Derby, where Sir Thomas spent the last thirty years of his life; the priests were hanged, drawn and quartered.

When it came to hunting down recusants, the Earl employed a band of local men – John Harpur, Francis Leake, William and Thomas Kniveton among them – who entered suspect households, bearing

---

* Bossy estimated the number of English Catholics as 40,000 in 1603, less than 1 per cent of the population (J. Bossy, *The English Catholic Community: 1570–1850*, 1975).

warrants from the Earl, conducted searches and made any necessary arrests. John Harpur reported how he'd arrived at the house of a Mr Danyell early one morning, to find him still in bed and insisting that he was no recusant, whereupon Harpur bundled him and his wife off to church.[27] The Danyells were lucky. The Knivetons reported that a Constance Sherwin had offered to go to church and 'become a new woman', but they'd arrested her anyway, on the Earl's orders. However, they hadn't dared take her ninety-two-year-old bed-bound, blind and impotent husband, who, it was thought, would not survive without his wife; the Knivetons begged for mercy for the pair of them. There was no mercy for Lady Constance Foljambe, who was taken into custody on behalf of the Earl by her own grandson, Sir Godfrey.[28]

All this of course was immensely divisive, with families and neighbours informing on and betraying one another. Bess had friends and family on both sides – Francis Leake was a relation through her mother, Thomas Kniveton was married to her half-sister, Jane, and William was her nephew; the Babingtons and Foljambes she'd known all her life. Her daughter Frances had married into the Pierrepont family, a member of whom had sheltered the Jesuit priest Father Edward Campion, who brought the Jesuit mission to England in 1580. Frances herself was suspected of Catholicism and Mary Talbot was a known convert. Mary may have been turned by such as Campion, and she certainly knew the Derbyshire-born Jesuit priest Henry Garnett, who returned to England in 1586. Mary openly wore a crucifix around her neck and found herself in hot water in 1595 for holding Mass in her home.[29] Bess, who seems to have taken a characteristically pragmatic approach to matters of religion, showed no Catholic leanings; as to how she felt about the persecution of Catholic friends and acquaintances, we have no record. Nor indeed do we know how she felt about the death of the Queen of Scots, though since her stocks of sympathy for Mary had long been exhausted, it's unlikely that she was greatly moved. Besides, Mary's death meant that Arbella edged a little nearer to the English throne.

* * *

The winter of 1586–7 was particularly long and hard, and both Shrewsbury and Burghley suffered for it. In March 1587, Burghley told the Earl that he doubted 'not but a nosegay of cowslips or damask of roses of your own gathering shall recover all your strength lost this winter, as I am in good hope to recover the like for myself'.[30] Once again he urged Shrewsbury to help Gilbert with his debts, but the Earl, for all his regard for Burghley, was obdurate, and Gilbert was informed that he couldn't 'expect any more' at his father's hands. Shrewsbury still had plenty of affection for his son; his animosity was directed at Mary Talbot, on whose 'pomp and courtlike manner of life' he blamed Gilbert's penury.[31] Gilbert was welcome to come and visit, so long as he didn't bring his wife – the Earl couldn't stand the sight of her. Where Mary was concerned the Earl saw 'repentance in speeches, but not in actions'.[32]

Charles Cavendish reported on the progress, or lack thereof, of the Cavendishes' 'case', which he thought would soon be heard, since Burghley, Walsingham and the Queen herself were all anxious to see an end to it.[33] True to her word, the Queen made a final attempt to unite the Shrewsburys in April. Gilbert told John Manners how she had summoned Mary Talbot and questioned her as to what her mother wanted. Mary's reply was straightforward – Bess wished to live with her husband. Subsequently, in an audience with Shrewsbury, the Queen applied pressure, compelling him to agree to taking Bess to Wingfield, where they would 'keep house together', and to receiving her in his other homes. He was to give Bess £300 a year, and 'certain provisions for housekeeping', and to drop all legal suits for the return of the Chatsworth plate and furnishings. Before setting out for Wingfield, Bess was to join the Earl at his Chelsea house.[34]

From Chelsea, in April, Bess wrote her last (surviving) letter to her husband, a letter full of affection and humility: 'I longed greatly to hear from you and thank you most heartily for your letter which was a great comfort to me, next to your self there is not anything could be more welcome. I was in some fear that your early journey might bring you to some pain in your hands or legs. I have thought the time long since your going, you have been little out of my mind.' 'Bear sweetheart', read a postscript, 'with my bleating, of late I have used to write little with my own hand, but could not now forbear.'[35] Marital harmony had apparently been restored.

Not for long. By October, Bess was complaining to Burghley that since she had been at Wingfield, the Earl had visited a mere three times, never staying more than a day and appearing 'not unquiet, neither well pleased'. Having received a letter from Burghley, at which he'd taken offence – 'the more honourable and friendly it pleases your lordship to write of me, the more is he discontented' – he had been withholding Bess's provisions – firewood, beef, mutton and corn. And these provisions, as the Queen had assured Bess, were meant to be worth £700, 'over and beyond' her £300 allowance. 'I humbly beseech your Lord', she begged, 'that my long delayed matters may now receive end, till then my enemies will take great advantage to stir up my Lord against me and mine and still divide us.'[36]

The Shrewsburys remained divided, but by now energies were flagging, the heat had gone out of the battle and all parties were more or less willing to accept the status quo. Elizabeth had more pressing matters to hand. The execution of the Queen of Scots had left her feeling vulnerable – betrayed by her councillors (who she blamed for Mary's death) and apprehensive as to how Catholic Europe, and France in particular, would react or retaliate. The Earl, his health worsening – it was rumoured, in 1587, that gout had actually killed him – struggled to manage his affairs and spent much of his time at Handsworth Lodge, Sheffield, where he was consoled by his housekeeper and mistress Eleanor Britton. And Bess threw herself into her new building project – the transformation of her father's manor into Hardwick Old Hall.

16.

THE OLD HALL

Today, adjacent to Hardwick New Hall, looms the gaunt and blackened ruin of the Old, equally large and lofty, but awkward and ungainly beside its glamorous, perfectly formed sibling. It's little more than a shell, but you have only to climb the stairs to the fourth floor to get a sense of its former splendour. Here are not one, but two great chambers – the Hill Great Chamber and the Forest Great Chamber, both with vast windows, fine plasterwork, rooftop walks and glorious views. They would have been among the most spectacular rooms to be found in sixteenth-century England.

But in 1587, this was all to come. The existing house at Hardwick, the house in which Bess had spent her girlhood and to which she had retreated in July 1584 had originally been built by her grandfather, with additions by her father and brother, but what kind of state she found it in is impossible to determine. It was most probably a dilapidated half-timbered manor centred around an old hall, built by John Hardwick, Bess's father, with possibly some kind of wing to the east, begun by her brother James, and a scattering of outbuildings – a barn, a dovecote and some 'old lodgings'. It was certainly not at all the kind of house Bess had grown accustomed to, nor was it remotely sufficient for her needs – she had a large household to accommodate, as well as William Cavendish and his wife, who lived with her.

Bess was not exactly homeless – Wingfield was at her disposal, but Shrewsbury had made it clear that she was not welcome in any of his other properties and, thanks to his programme of harassment, made it impossible for her to live at Chatsworth, which for now, no doubt to her rage, was lost to her. She badly needed a home of her own, and a suitably large and grand one at that. After thirty years of working on Chatsworth, she had plenty of building know-how, but lacking the time or leisure to deliberate over the kind of house she wanted, she embarked on the Old Hall without any specific plan, or any one overseer. The house would evolve piecemeal, a collaboration between Bess and her craftsmen. During the building, she based herself at Wingfield, just six miles from Hardwick, and thus convenient for making site visits.

The building accounts for the Old Hall, kept by David Flood, known as 'Davy', don't begin until July 1587, but work was already in progress: Bess had replaced her father's hall with a two-storey transverse hall – running crossways, not lengthways – and had begun work on a new three-storey east wing.[1] Work continued on the east wing through the summer and autumn: old buildings and lodgings were demolished; masons and wallers erected walls that were then rough-cast and plastered; joists and lathes were laid for floors; interior walls were studded, windows glassed, roof trusses cut, slates laid; and a gallery was panelled and wainscoted. By December, the new wing, complete with gallery and a suite of rooms for Bess (a priority) on the third floor, had been roofed over – in time for winter – and connected to the main block by a staircase leading off the hall.

Why Bess decided on a transverse hall is interesting. Such halls were highly unusual in sixteenth-century England – medieval halls ran lengthways. It may have simply been a happy accident, dictated by pre-existing buildings, or the fact that the Old Hall was built on the edge of an escarpment, which imposed its own constraints. Equally she may have seen transverse halls illustrated in architectural books by Serlio, du Cerceau or Palladio. It's possible too that she might have visited the earliest known example in England, that in Sir Christopher Hatton's banqueting house – actually more of a lodge – built in the gardens of Holdenby sometime after 1580. Bess's only recorded visit to Holdenby didn't take place until 1592, though since it was but a short detour on her route from Derbyshire to London, it may not have been her first.

Historians have not been kind to Hatton, dismissing him as a somewhat ineffectual, effete figure. This is not quite fair. He was one of the principal sponsors of Sir Francis Drake's round-the-world voyage; when he became Lord Chancellor, in 1587, he proved himself perfectly competent; and he was the builder of two very fine houses. By 1578, work had started on Holdenby, Hatton's Northamptonshire family home. Three years earlier, he had bought the half-built Kirby Hall from Humphrey Stafford. Work continued on both Kirby and Holdenby well into the 1580s.

Hatton claimed that Holdenby, built around two large courtyards, with six great towers, was modelled on Burghley's Theobalds – a 'young Theobalds', though a poor relation. In 1579, in anticipation of a visit from Burghley, he wrote, full of apologies: 'I fear me that as your Lordship shall find my house unbuilt and very far from good order, so through the newness you shall find it dampish and full of evil air ... I humbly beseech you, my honourable Lord, for your opinion to the surveyor of such lacks and faults as shall appear to you in this rude building, for as the same is done hitherto in direct observation of your house and plot at Tyball's.'[2] In terms of layout, there were similarities between the two houses, but Holdenby, like Leicester's Kenilworth, was a 'lantern house', famous for its astonishing expanses of glass. 'As bright as Holdenby' went the local saying.

There is much that we don't know about Holdenby. Who designed it? And why was it so enormous? Was it simply to impress the Queen, who disappointed Hatton and never actually visited? Or was it intended not so much to imitate Theobalds as to outdo it? Burghley, writing with his usual urbane courtesy after he had made his visit, had nothing but praise: 'approaching to the house, being led by a large, long, straight fairway, I found a great magnificence in the front, or front pieces of the house, and so every part answerable to other, to allure liking. I found no one thing of greater grace than your stately ascent from your hall to your great chamber; and your chamber answerable with largeness and lightsomeness, that truly a Momus could find no fault. I visited all your rooms, high and low, and only the contentation of mine eyes made me forget the infirmity of my legs.'[3] At Holdenby he found those features so prized by Elizabethan builders – a sense of proportion and symmetry, large windows, an eye for the approach, both external (the drive to the house) and internal (the route from the great hall to the state rooms). All things that Bess would try and create at Hardwick, though in the case of the Old Hall, with very mixed results.

Since exterior work was impossible during the winter frosts, Bess laid off many labourers, rough-wallers and masons at the Old Hall in December 1587, though work on the interiors – carpentry and plastering, for example – carried on. During January, ninety-three loads of hair were delivered for the plasterers (animal hair acted as a binding agent). The 'plomer' (plumber) was paid for four and a half pounds of pitch, to fix lead flashing onto a roof. And 'stonebreakers' and 'stonegetters' cut and hauled sandstone from the quarry just below the Old Hall, in readiness for the spring.

It wasn't just stone that Bess had on her doorstep. Within a twenty-mile radius she could source all her own building materials: limestone from a quarry at Hardwick (now vanished), iron from her blast furnaces and glass from her glassworks (both at South Wingfield), timber from Heath and Stainsby, lime from Skegby and Crich, alabaster from Creswell, lead from Winster, Aldwark and Bonsall, slate from Whittington, East Moor, Walton Old Hay and Walton Spring, blackstone from Ashford and gypsum from Tutbury. The fact that the cost of building the Old and New Halls came to a modest £5,500 was largely because Bess was able to supply her own materials.[4]

By far her greatest outlay was labour. Finding unskilled local labour was easy enough, though at especially busy times extra men were drafted in from further afield – Sheffield, Edensor and Chesterfield. Bess was a fair and even generous employer. Labourers were well paid, at 6d a day, but the work was hard (quarrying and carting stone, clearing rubbish, making mortar, digging foundations). On top of that she provided food and drink – bread, made cheaply from dredge (a mix of oats and barley, grown together) and peas, butter, milk, oatmeal and, occasionally, herrings.

Wages stayed pretty much static during the second half of the sixteenth century, though they varied considerably from site to site, and within sites. At Wollaton, masons were paid between 9d and 14d per day, and labourers 6d, but without food, while at Longleat the majority of masons were on 10d, with some on 6d and the more skilled on 14d.[5] Masons and carpenters at William Dickenson's Sheffield house were paid 8d, and were fed by his wife. In the 1590s, Sir Thomas Tresham paid his rough-wallers 10d a day, and his labourers 6d, again without food. Bess's masons were on 6d, which sounds low, but these were 'board' wages, with food and lodging included. Masons had 'lodges' – simple lean-tos, made of wood – in which to work, while the plumbers had a 'plummery'. Valued craftsmen were some-times given their own rooms, as was the glazier at Shrewsbury House in 1575. The accounts for the Old Hall refer to the cleaning of the 'work folks chamber', which sounds like some kind of dormitory, but many probably just bedded down amongst the walls, in any corner that offered shelter.

The 1563 Statute of Artificers went some way towards regulating employment: day labourers were to work a six-day week, from 5 a.m. until 7 or 8 p.m. between mid March and September, and for the rest of the year 'from the spring of the day' until dusk; meals were to take up no more than two and a half hours; every additional hour's absence carried a 1d fine.[6] Extra pay was given for working on Sundays or 'holy days', and a candle allowance for interior work in winter. In practice, working hours must have varied according to employer, weather and season.

'Bargains' (contracts) were drawn up between Bess and Thomas Fogge, a carpenter, for making lathes and joists, Richard Snidall the glazier, for glass, John Beighton, a carpenter, for floors and roofs, and James Hindle, a plasterer, for rough-casting the gallery. Contract work was by its nature short-term and without any job security many craftsmen kept small agricultural holdings – a cow, a few sheep – to fall back on during lean times, when the work dried up. The lucky ones received an annual wage, paid every three or six months. One such was Abraham Smith, the great plaster modeller and stone carver, who first appears at Chatsworth in 1581, in a bargain for making plasterer's wooden moulds.[7] By 1589, he was on the payroll at the Old Hall.

Abraham Smith was not the only craftsman already known to Bess. John Hibard and John Rowarth, both carpenters, and Thomas Outram, a mason, had also worked at Chatsworth in the 1560s. John Balechouse, a painter – often referred to as John Painter, perhaps because no one could pronounce his Flemish or French name (he may have been Jehan Balechou, a painter recorded in Tours in 1557) – is first mentioned in the Chatsworth accounts in 1578; by 1589, he was at Hardwick, with a 'garate' in the Old Hall. Balechouse was a great deal more than a painter and would become crucial to the building of the New Hall, as a general supervisor; he may have played a similar role at the Old.[8]

Bess now had a suite of apartments in the east wing of the Old Hall, though the house was not yet large enough to accommodate William Cavendish and his family, not to mention Arbella. For much of the time Arbella was shunted between her aunts and uncles, Gilbert and Mary Talbot in particular. Whilst staying with the Talbots in 1587, she wrote, in a beautifully clear and regular italic hand, her first surviving letter to her 'Good Lady Grandmother': 'I have sent your ladyship the ends of my hair, which were cut the sixth day of the moon [for astrological purposes perhaps], on Saturday last, and with them a pot of jelly, which my servant made.'[9] Her cousin Mary (Talbot) had suffered 'three little fits of ague', but was now well and merry. Arbella was now twelve, and her immaculate handwriting bore testament to the expensive humanist education that Bess, ever mindful of her 'consanguinity' to the Queen, and ever hopeful of her prospects, had provided for her, an education superior to that of her mother, and certainly that of her grandmother. It was hardly surprising that, clever and accomplished as she was, Arbella also developed a powerful sense of entitlement.

In the summer of 1587, Arbella made her first appearance at court, at Theobalds, where the Queen was making a month-long visit as part of her summer progress. Elizabeth was now fifty-three, prospects of husbands and heirs had long receded and the question of the succession remained unresolved. With the death of the Queen of Scots, Arbella had moved up to second place in the line for the throne, after James VI. This was a fact to which the Queen seemed to attach little importance, though according to Arbella, she had pronounced her 'an eaglet of her own kind' and apparently told the wife of the French ambassador, 'Look to her well: she will one day be even as I am and a lady mistress.'[10] Bess may have been heartened by such pronouncements, but even if true, they counted for little. No one was more adept than the Queen at a policy of equivocation. Nevertheless, she was perfectly aware that Arbella's royal blood gave her currency in the marriage market: she was a commodity. Just as Elizabeth had once dangled the possibility of her own hand before a variety of European princes, so could Arbella be offered, a lesser prize to be sure, but still one endowed with a certain lustre, especially if named as the Queen's heir. Several candidates had been considered and rejected: Esmé Stuart, Duke of Lennox, his son

Ludovic, even James VI (this altogether too dangerous a prospect for Elizabeth). In 1587, the Queen and her councillors were discussing Rainutio Farnese, son of the Duke of Parma, who commanded the Spanish forces fighting the French in the Spanish Netherlands. Rainutio was a Catholic, but a marriage between him and Arbella might detach Parma from Philip II. It might bring an end to the Dutch wars too. There was an agenda behind Arbella's invitation to court – she was being looked over. Bess, knowing this, waited impatiently for news.

Charles Cavendish was also at 'Tibaldes', from where he wrote his mother a long letter, reporting on Arbella's reception: 'her majesty spoke to her twice, but not long and examined her nothing touching her book, she dined in the [royal] presence'. The dinner had taken place in Burghley's great chamber, and if the Queen's show of favour had hardly amounted to much, Burghley had made a point of praising Arbella, telling Sir Walter Ralegh, the dashing explorer, suppressor of Irish rebellions and new royal favourite, of her accomplishments in languages, music and dancing. If only, said Burghley, Arbella 'were twenty years old', whereupon he teasingly pulled Ralegh's ear. 'It would be a happy thing,' replied Ralegh, entering into the tease. The dinner ended with a royal compliment for Burghley – the Queen 'heartily prayed that god would lend her his life for 21 years for she desired not to live longer than she had him, which prayer was so kindly expressed that the good old lord could not return thanks nor other speech for tears'.

Charles himself thought highly of his niece: 'It is wonderful how she profits in her book, besides she will dance with an exceeding good grace and can behave herself with great proportion to every one in their degree.' In fact, behaving 'with great proportion' was not Arbella's strong suit. Just a year later, on visiting the court at Greenwich, she disgraced herself by insisting on taking precedence over ladies of higher rank as they walked to chapel. When asked to step back by the Master of Ceremonies, she replied haughtily that her chosen place was 'the very lowest position that could be given her'.[11] She was promptly ordered back to Derbyshire; it would be three years before she returned to court.

Charles continued his letter with news of the war in the Low Countries, snippets of court gossip and bulletins on family health: Mary Talbot still had a touch of jaundice, William Cavendish was in bed with a cricked neck; the King of Scotland was rumoured to be marrying a Spanish princess; at court, there was 'none in that height as my Lord of Essex'. The tall, handsome Essex was Leicester's twenty-one-year-old stepson Robert Devereux, a scholar-soldier, in whom Leicester took great pride – he 'striketh' Leicester 'marvellously', wrote Charles – and who was poised to succeed his stepfather in the Queen's affections. As for Ralegh, Charles thought him in fine form, 'yet labours to underprop himself by my Lord Treasurer and his friends'. Ralegh's rise to fame and fortune, and the arrogance with which he flaunted both, had made him extremely unpopular amongst the old guard at court, as Charles well knew: 'I see he is courteously used by my lord and his friends but I doubt the end considering how he hath handled himself in his former pride.'

But much of Charles's letter was taken up by describing the latest additions to Theobalds. The house was staggering in its scale, but it was the inventiveness of its interiors, the ways in which Burghley brought the outside in, that was a source of wonderment. Whimsy and frivolity are hardly qualities we associate with Burghley, yet his buildings had a playful quality: there is something of the fairy-tale castle about the 'roof-scape' of Burghley House, with its clusters of onion domes, turrets, chimneys and clock towers; and something of the enchanted forest about the interiors of Theobalds.

Charles (correctly) judged Burghley's 'fair gallery' to be 126 feet long, 21 feet wide and 16 feet high, with bay windows on one side.

---

* Only the Earl of Essex, according to Arbella, came to her defence. The pair were not dissimilar, both clever, self-dramatising and reckless.

A painted frieze, running above the panelling, showed the cities of the world. The long gallery was distinct from the green gallery, which was decorated as a kind of heraldic arboretum, with fifty-two trees, each representing an English county, the branches and leaves painted with the coats of arms of local dukes, earls and knights. But it was Burghley's great chamber that was particularly admired. This was on the second floor and looked out onto the 'great garden'. It was, as Charles told Bess, 60 feet long, 22 feet wide and 21 feet high, and had, at one end, 'a fair rock with ducks, pheasants, and divers other birds which serves for a cupboard' (this was a kind of grotto, complete with fountain). The ceiling was decorated with a sundial and the signs of the zodiac, beneath which a mechanised sun and planets rotated; at night stars shone through 'sky holes' cut into the roof. The 'old trees be there still' – six along each side, made of plaster and covered with natural bark, leaves and birds' nests, and so realistic, it was said, that birds flew in through the open windows, alighted on them and sang.[12]

It sounds as though Bess had instructed Charles to provide a detailed description of Theobalds though it would be surprising, given her friendship with Burghley and her interest in his house, if she never visited herself. She was on the lookout for ideas for Hardwick. The decoration of the Forest Great Chamber in the Old Hall and the High Great Chamber in the New, with their naturalistic plasterwork, clearly derive from the great chamber at Theobalds.

By the spring of 1588, building at the Old Hall was gearing up once again. In March, sieves and baskets were bought for the plasterers and the lime kilns were drawn. Work now began on another four-storey wing, to the west of the hall, with the kitchens on the ground floor, and a great chamber, the Hill Great Chamber, on the fourth, and it proceeded at an amazing rate. Thomas Hollingworth, a rough-waller, and his men were paid to erect the walls by the 'rood' (a measure of area), the higher the walls, the more per rood, a grand total of £73 for 290 roods when, by mid December, in just six months, the walls had risen to the top of the fourth storey. The labour was immense: over the summer, between early June and the end of August, seventy-three cartloads of timber, to make floors and roofs, were dragged in carts by oxen from Pentrich, eight miles away.[13] This was an operation fraught with difficulty and danger: wet weather made tracks, rudimentary at the best of times, virtually impassable, thus escalating costs; wheels could and often did break; harnesses wore out; the shoulders and necks of the oxen were rubbed raw by the wooden yokes and had to be eased with 'black soap', while their feet needed regular shoeing and their hooves treating with 'vergrease'.

Bess, at least in the early stages of the building of the Old Hall, seems to have tried to keep down costs, probably because she was still trying to extract money from Shrewsbury. Much of the Old Hall was walled – walls were built on a core of rubble and then rendered – by rough-wallers, who, at 4d a day, were cheaper than masons. However, her use of wallers may simply have been due to a lack of available masons. John and Christopher Rhodes and Thomas Accres, who would all be key to the building of the New Hall, were still employed at Wollaton in 1588.

As the walls of the west wing rose, the Spanish Armada prepared to set sail. After the death of the Queen of Scots, Philip II, who could claim descent from John of Gaunt and who had not forgotten his brief occupation of the English throne, fashioned himself as the restorer of the Catholic faith to England. The Armada was to join the Duke of Parma's army in the Netherlands, from where they would together invade England. At the end of May, 130 Spanish ships, carrying 19,000 soldiers and 7,000 sailors, left Lisbon. England braced itself, nervously, for invasion, without knowing exactly where or how that invasion would take place. In June, the Queen wrote to her lord lieutenants, including Shrewsbury – as Lord Lieutenant of Derbyshire and Staffordshire, he was to assemble the gentlemen of the county and ensure that they provided men for the defence of the country.[14]

On 18 July, the first sails were spotted off the Scilly Isles, and from there the Armada sailed purposefully up the English Channel, en route to meet Parma, an impressive and terrifying sight. However, the Spanish suffered setbacks from the off, thanks to bad weather and sickness, as Gilbert Talbot told his father in July, while assuring him that 'all our preparations for defence still hold'. Smaller, faster English ships did their work too (Shrewsbury's *Talbot* was used as a fire ship). That August, the Queen went to Tilbury to rally her troops. According to Leicester, her appearance 'so inflamed the hearts of her good subjects, as I think the weakest person among them is able to match the proudest Spaniard that dares land in England'.[15] In the event, not a single Spaniard landed – the great Armada scattered, destroyed by storms and English guns.

Whilst demonstrating all proper patriotic fervour, Shrewsbury was also keeping a close eye on his wife. In November 1588, Nicholas Kinnersley, one of Bess's servants, wrote to her from Wingfield to report that one of the Earl's men, Gilbert Dickenson, and a 'boy in a green coat' had come from Sheffield and nosed about, asking the Wingfield servants questions about Bess's whereabouts. What these questions meant, 'I know not except it be to bring my lord word of your absence here and so that he might come upon the sudden and find you away.' He thought Bess should return to Wingfield. Apart from foiling the Earl, Arbella needed taking in hand. She was 'merry' and eating 'her meat well' but hadn't been to school for the last six days.[16] Arbella's wilfulness, as displayed on her last visit to court, did not go unnoticed. Shrewsbury remarked that she 'was wont to have the upper hand of my wife and her daughter Mary, but now it is otherwise ... for that they have been advised by some of their friends at the court that it was misliked'.[17] A few months later, Kinnersley wrote to Bess again: he was sending her some of her 'principal jewels' and she was not to worry: 'take no thought but be merry for you shall find all things here I trust in good order as you left them for we neither will yield to commandment nor force except your honour's hand'.[18]

Why Shrewsbury was bothering to spy on Bess, or what he hoped to discover, is unclear. Perhaps he simply wished to make her feel uncomfortable at Wingfield, to maintain a vaguely threatening presence. In September 1589, he bought the Barley estate from Peter Barley, and with it Bess's dower from her first husband Robert, now worth about £100 a year. This made some sense in that the estate adjoined Talbot lands, and came with the Barley lead mines, but the Earl paid a high price – £8,000, with the estate encumbered with £7,000 worth of debt.[19] He hardly needed more debt; this sounds like a purchase made for reasons of control – over Bess's dower – rather than commerce. 'Queer what a dear purchase Barley is', wrote Gilbert Talbot later.

In March 1589, Thomas Hollingworth and his men were contracted to add a fourth floor to the east wing of the Old Hall, with a second great chamber – the Forest Great Chamber – a withdrawing chamber, bedchambers and a new staircase. Why Bess wanted another great chamber when she already had a very spectacular example in the west wing is curious, but the most likely explanation is that the west wing was to be made over to William Cavendish, while she herself would occupy the east wing, and she therefore needed her own suite of state rooms. In addition to the new storey, work began on the service buildings – brewhouse, bakehouse, stables, wash-house and dairy – on the west side of where the stable yard is today (a slaughterhouse, chandler house, still house and smithy came later).

By now, with her lands and rents secured, Bess felt able to spend. The walls of the new east wing were faced with ashlar (cut stone) rather than rendered, and there were no economies when it came to the decoration of the interiors. For the Forest Great Chamber, she ordered an elaborate frieze of forest scenes in three-dimensional painted plaster, inspired by Theobalds, and Abraham Smith was set to work carving his great overmantels. Plasterwork overmantels were first cast onto wooden frames, which, once set, were fastened to the walls with 'hicks' (hooks). Designs were frequently taken from

Flemish prints and engravings, as with Smith's very splendid over-mantel in the Hill Great Chamber (still intact today), which shows the giant muscular figures of Gog and Magog flanking the winged figure of Desire. It's based on an engraving, *The Triumph of Patience*, by Maarten van Heemskerck, published in 1559, of Desire and Hope leading Patience on a chariot, with Fortune shackled behind.[20] Both Patience and Fortune are missing from Smith's overmantel, but visitors would have been expected to recognise the allusion to Bess's situation – Patience triumphing over the ill fortune she has suffered at the hands of her husband, exactly the kind of device that would have appealed to Elizabethan tastes. Much of the decoration of both the Old and New Halls was inspired by Flemish prints, but whether these were supplied by one of Bess's craftsmen, such as John Balechouse, or whether she had a collection of her own, we don't know.

The Old Hall, when it was finally finished, was actually decorated more elaborately than the New would be, with gilded leather wall hangings (pricey and mostly imported from the Low Countries) and floor-to-ceiling panelling. It was perhaps with the adornment of the Old Hall in mind that Henry Cavendish was dispatched to Constantinople in 1589, though he may have been sounding out trading possibilities too. This, as Grace Cavendish rightly said, was a 'long and dangerous journey', and thanks to a journal kept by Henry's servant Fox, we have a record of it. Henry, together with a friend and three servants, sailed to north Germany at the end of March. From here, the party made their way south, by wagon, to Venice, took a boat to Dubrovnik and continued across Dalmatia, often on horseback, sleeping wherever they could – stables, hen coops – and eating bad food (a particular bugbear of Fox's). They arrived in Constantinople in June. Fox has disappointingly little to say about the city itself, beyond the 'evil build' of the houses and the 'rude and proud' inhabitants, and considering they'd spent nearly three months on the road, their stay was a brief two weeks. They returned via Poland, reaching England by the end of September, perhaps bringing with them some of the thirty-two 'turkie carpets' mentioned in the Hardwick inventory.[21]

By 1590, Bess had an impressive and very substantial house, yet an oddly incoherent and unbalanced one, with an irregular gabled central block flanked by two towering flat-roofed wings, the eastern set at an odd angle, possibly because it incorporated an existing building. Because of its position on the edge of an escarpment, the Old Hall faced north, rather than, more naturally, looking west across the valley, and the north front was left quite flat and unadorned. In its height and plainness it must have been reminiscent of Worksop, but it was also rather grim and forbidding. Inside, things were equally disorganised. Placing the kitchen in the west wing meant that the prevailing south-west wind would have carried cooking smells right through the house, as well as noise into the bedchambers above. Bess's bedchamber, on the third floor of the east wing, was on the cold north side of the house, while her withdrawing chamber was inconveniently on the floor above. Similarly, the long gallery was on the third floor and the Forest Great Chamber on the fourth. The Old Hall may have sufficed in terms of size and grandeur, but architecturally and practically it was far from perfect. It was a house built *in extremis* and it suffered as a result. Bess, however, would have another chance to rectify her mistakes.

While Bess shuttled between Wingfield and Hardwick, her children kept her abreast of events at court, and abroad. In July 1589, Gilbert Talbot told her how the Earl of Essex had been angling to get his hands on Tutbury, which was leased to Shrewsbury by the Queen, because it was very near his 'chief house', and had applied to the Queen, who had said that she wouldn't give it to anyone else. However, according to Gilbert, Essex had so much respect for his 'house' and such 'great good affection' for Gilbert himself that he was willing to 'surcease his suit'. He went on to provide a graphic account of the murder of Henry III, King of France, by a Dominican friar, or a man masquerading as a friar, in revenge for the killing of the Duke of Guise and his brother. The 'friar' had pulled 'a long, sharp pointed knife' out of his sleeve and stabbed the King, who had 'himself wrested the knife out of the villain's hand (some say he pulled it out of his own body)' and 'stabbed the varlet two or three times into the face and head therewith'. On the news of the King's death, Sir Christopher Hatton had been summoned to court from Holdenby, where he was celebrating the marriage of his nephew. In a postscript, Mary Talbot reported that the Queen had asked 'carefully' after Arbella, which could have meant something or nothing at all and would not have greatly satisfied Bess.[22]

Gilbert knew that Essex, as the new man at court, was not to be alienated. And so did Bess, though when, in 1590, he wrote to her recommending one of his former servants as a gentleman usher in her own household, she seems to have ignored the request.[23] The old guard were vanishing fast. Leicester had died in September 1588, on his way to Kenilworth, bloated and florid at fifty-five. Walsingham followed him in 1590, and Hatton a year later, owing £42,000 to the Crown, bankrupted by Holdenby, a house he had barely used. Their deaths meant the loss of Bess's friends and supporters at court, though she still had an ally in Burghley. Shrewsbury's health was failing too. He told Burghley, in January 1589, that he was unable to 'stir abroad', or take any exercise at all, and only warmth helped, something that was in short supply during a Yorkshire winter.[24]

The Queen wrote in December 1589 enquiring after the Earl's health, 'especially at this time of the fall of the leaf', and asking that Bess be allowed to see him occasionally, 'which she hath now of a long time wanted'. The chances of that were slim – Shrewsbury showed no sign of softening towards his wife, though, unexpectedly, he did towards Mary Talbot. In April 1590, he wrote to Mary with real affection: he was sorry to hear that she was unwell, which he felt could only have been caused by 'your extraordinary pains taken in visiting and comforting others ... good daughter let me hear from you more often'. He prayed God to bless her with good health; he himself could barely write his name and had to resort to the services of a clerk.[25] 'My father's kind letter to my wife', wrote Gilbert on the envelope, in surprise. This is one of the Earl's last surviving letters. On 18 November, aged sixty-two, he died at Handsworth Manor, Sheffield.

Of Bess's feelings on Shrewsbury's death we have no record. Theirs had been a marriage of more than twenty years, but one that had been over in all but name for the last five. Bess could not have had much sense of loss in November 1590; indeed, there must have been more relief than regret. She was now free from marital harassment. Free to enjoy Chatsworth. To buy more land. To do business. And free to devote herself to the building of the house she'd always wanted, in the place she loved best. By the time of Shrewsbury's death, work had already begun on Hardwick New Hall.

17.

SMYTHSON'S PLATT

'Your Lordship's kind letter is an exceeding comfort to me', wrote Bess to Burghley in December 1590, 'and your judgement therein of my late husband's disposition most true, as some circumstances before his death declared, with the general spoil of his goods by those bad instruments which continued the separation begun by a mightier hand.' By 'bad instruments' she meant the Earl's mistress, Eleanor Britton, and her nephew, who, on Shrewsbury's death, had promptly set about removing money, jewels, plate, furniture and bedding from Sheffield. One chest in the Earl's bedchamber had allegedly been emptied of £8,000 in silver and another of £10,000 in gold.[1] This, however, was a battle that Bess could leave to Gilbert Talbot, the new Earl of Shrewsbury. For her part, so she told Burghley, she now looked forward to a more peaceable future: 'I hope, my good Lord, that all disagreement (in this family) died with him, quiet is my principal desire and I shall rather suffer than enter into controversy.'[2]

Shrewsbury's body was embalmed, with the funeral finally taking place on 13 January 1591, at the church of Saints Peter and Paul in Sheffield. It was on a princely scale, with crowds of 20,000 and attendant casualties – three men were crushed by a falling tree. Shrewsbury had designed himself an elaborate tomb, with an epitaph – self-justifying till the end – that dwelt at length on his innocence of any impropriety towards the Queen of Scots and made no mention of Bess. The date of death was left blank, but, as the Earl had predicted, it was not supplied by his executors, who were busy fighting amongst themselves.

Shrewsbury had appointed Burghley as supervisor of his will, with Edward and Henry Talbot, his younger sons, as executors. When Edward and Henry declined – no doubt foreseeing trouble – Bess was approached. This met with immediate objections from Gilbert, who then became sole executor himself. As he soon discovered, the Talbot estates were cash poor – his father had left debts, as had his brother Francis (these still unpaid), while Gilbert had large debts of his own. He had Bess awaiting payment of her widow's jointure – the income from one third of the Talbot estates, for her lifetime – and Eleanor Britton merrily helping herself to Shrewsbury's valuables.

We know almost nothing of Eleanor Britton, other than the fact that in 1586 she put so much wine and spirit into her venison pasties that they disintegrated on the journey from Sheffield to London.[3] She may have brought some comfort and affection to Shrewsbury's last years, but, inevitably, she was regarded by his heirs as rapacious and venal, and perhaps she was. According to Gilbert, instead of nursing his father, Eleanor 'did continually lead him as all those who were about him did well know'. The Earl had 'suffered' her to embezzle his goods during his lifetime, and she had continued to do so after his death. Gilbert told Burghley that he would have indicted Eleanor and her nephew, these 'impudent, clamorous persons', but had refrained because he hoped they would confess. The Brittons, however, fought back and made accusations of their own: Gilbert had proceeded against them in a 'cruel and unlawful manner', including imprisoning them in his house.[4] Gilbert therefore decided to proceed with charges of felony, though not, it seems, with much success.

Like his father, Gilbert was thin-skinned and quick to take offence; like Bess, he was a committed feuder. He declared war on Eleanor Britton, his brothers, his neighbours and his mother-in-law. He claimed that Edward and Henry Talbot had behaved treacherously towards him – over the question of land and inheritance – both before and since their father's death.[5] When Edward accused him of trying to cheat him over a lease, Gilbert challenged him to a duel, which Edward flatly refused (subsequently Gilbert claimed that Edward had tried to murder him with poisoned gloves).[6] Gilbert famously conducted a long-running and pointless feud with the Stanhope family about a weir built, perfectly legitimately, over the River Trent, near the Stanhope home in Nottinghamshire, to which he objected ostensibly on behalf of local people, who were deprived of fish. Taunts and insults flew: Sir Thomas Stanhope, according to Gilbert, was 'one of the most ambitious, proud, covetous and subtle persons that ever I was acquainted with', and had long made trouble for him and Mary Talbot, telling his father that Mary and Bess 'did wholly rule and govern me in all things'.[7] The Stanhopes claimed Gilbert was a 'papist', an accusation that would have been more justly levelled at his wife.

Gilbert's enemies, as the Earl of Essex warned him, were only too happy to alarm the Queen with tales of his violent temper, 'which they tell her is dangerous in great men'.[8] The fact that Gilbert did not succeed to the high offices held by his father may simply have been because he was seen as too volatile and unstable. So he did not become Lord Lieutenant of Nottinghamshire, which, being Gilbert, he felt to be a slight and for which he blamed Thomas Stanhope – hence his campaign against the weir. Matters came to a head when Charles Cavendish, whose friendship Gilbert, almost uniquely, retained, challenged John Stanhope, Sir Thomas's son, to a duel, with rapiers, at Lambeth Bridge. This descended into farce when Stanhope appeared encased in a doublet so thickly padded as to repel any rapier. Charles offered to fight in shirtsleeves; Stanhope, claiming 'he had taken cold', refused, as he did the loan of Charles's waistcoat.[9] In the face of such unsportsmanlike behaviour, the duel was aborted.

Bess, hitherto Gilbert's ally and defender, now became his foe, as hostilities were transferred from father to son. Gilbert no longer required Bess's support; instead, she required him to pay her substantial sums of money. Hints that relations between Bess and the new Earl and Countess were not entirely amicable come through in a letter Bess wrote to Mary Talbot in February 1591, about the murder of one of her Leake cousins. Bess hoped that Mary would persuade Gilbert to bring the murderer to 'due judgement', though Gilbert was seemingly rather too friendly with a certain Sir John Berrone, who was thought to be protecting the murderer. 'I assure myself that you both would have right prevail and your cousin's blood so foully spilt requires your reasonable assistance to bring the murderer to his trial.'[10] It sounds like Bess was by no means sure that the Shrewsburys 'would have right prevail'. Behind Gilbert's failure to cooperate lay the question of Bess's jointure.

Extracting this from Gilbert was no easy matter. Gilbert's recalcitrance was hardly surprising. He faced the unwelcome prospect of paying his mother-in-law some £3,000 a year for the rest of her life, and given Bess's robust health, there was every indication that it might be a long life.[11] He saw his much-needed income draining away. Bess wrote to Burghley in April 1591, complaining of Gilbert's 'strange and unkind dealing ... in respect of my widow's part'. Gilbert had sent his man, 'Master Markham', who was bound by £6,000 to make sure the Earl met his obligations by the end of March, but, and this for the third time, he had not done so – Bess had still not received the money, cattle and lead that were her due and had heard that Gilbert intended 'to break off the agreement'. She felt that 'he will still seek to bring me in the end to nothing, but if this goes not forward I will be loath to talk the fourth time. What he will do yet rests uncertain.'[12] There was nothing uncertain about Bess's own course of action. Despite her claims to be looking forward to a quiet life, free of controversy, she was quite incapable of overlooking a wrong.

A portrait of Bess, probably painted around 1590, by or after Rowland Lockey, an apprentice to Hilliard, shows her with her red hair only a little faded, wearing a widow's cap and a black velvet gown, the splendidly starched ruff and cuffs much the same colour as her skin. She fingers a long five-stranded rope of pearls, her sole ornament, and her gaze is steady and a touch sardonic. This is Bess at sixty-nine, the sober widow, and a vastly wealthy one. As well as her jointure, when it finally came through, there were the lands made over to William and Charles by the deed of gift and lands subsequently purchased in the names of her sons. And then, under her marriage settlement, she had the use, for her lifetime, of Wingfield Manor with its ironworks and glassworks, Bolsover Castle with its coal pits, Shrewsbury House in Chelsea, and Chatsworth. Altogether this amounted to a very large collection of estates, concentrated in Derbyshire, Nottinghamshire, Staffordshire and Yorkshire, with the addition of the St Loe western lands in Gloucestershire and Somerset, to which Bess would go on adding. In 1590, her annual income stood at about £7,000; it continued to rise.[13]

Bess now had ample funds with which to build her new house. But why, when she already had the Old Hall, which was habitable but by no means finished in 1590, did she start work on another house a mere hundred yards away? Simultaneous building projects were not, as we have seen, so unusual: Lord Burghley embarked on Theobalds whilst still building Burghley House; Sir Christopher Hatton worked on both Kirby Hall and Holdenby, just twenty-five miles apart. Bess, however, was erecting two houses alongside each other.

She may have built the New Hall simply because she could; as a statement of proud confidence and independence. She could afford to be profligate. Dissatisfied with her existing house, she could put it to one side and start again. The Old Hall allowed her to experiment and try out ideas; it can be seen as a rehearsal for the New. Now she could reuse those features that pleased her and do away with those that did not. So she would keep the two-storey crossways hall, an arrangement that both allowed for greater symmetry and made it easier to have a compact building, two rooms deep, with no internal courtyard. So too would she once more have her state rooms on the second floor (as they also were at Chatsworth), rather than the first. And the plasterwork forest of the Forest Great Chamber would reappear, to even greater effect, in the New Hall's great chamber. On the other hand, she would make sure that her bedroom in the New Hall was on the warmer south side of the house, while the kitchens, and kitchen smells, were to be placed at the furthest possible distance, at the north end.

The New Hall was designed to correct the deficiencies of, but also to complement, the Old, which could now function as a very grand annexe, to accommodate guests and upper servants. With the Old Hall, and Chatsworth, Bess had built houses that were notable for their size and their richly decorated interiors, but not for any great architectural merit. The opposite is the case with the New Hall, which did not need to be particularly large – there are only six principal bedrooms – and whose interiors, on the whole, are relatively plain, rather as though Bess had begun to run out of energy when it came to interior decoration. Style, not size, was what counted now.

As a young woman in London, newly married to William Cavendish and mixing in humanist circles, Bess had acquired some understanding of architecture. Later, she commissioned inlaid wooden panels showing architectural scenes, probably derived from contemporary engravings, for Chatsworth (they hang on the stairs at Hardwick today). The noble women in the Virtues hangings are placed within architectural settings. And to a set of small appliqué hangings of female allegorical figures (these, like the noble women, were originally made at Chatsworth in the 1570s, but brought to Hardwick), personifying the seven Liberal Arts, she added an eighth: Architecture, who is shown holding a set square and a pair of dividers.[14]

The New Hall was to be an architecturally coherent house, and to that end, Bess needed design and draughtsmanship expertise. There is no absolute proof that Smythson designed Hardwick (the household accounts for 1590, which might have recorded payments to him, have vanished), but there is compelling evidence. Bess knew of him, from his work at Longleat and, more recently, at Worksop and Wollaton. She may have asked him to design the hunting tower at Chatsworth. Amongst the Smythson drawings that survive are three closely related to Hardwick, one an elongated version of the ground floor.[15] It was probably Smythson who drew up a design for Bess's splendid tomb, in Derby Cathedral, some years prior to her death. And his association with her continued afterwards, with his son John and grandson Huntingdon working for her children and grandchildren.

Smythson provided order and harmony for the New Hall – those very things that the Old lacked. Order – divine and social – so prized by the Elizabethans, was manifested in both the regularity of its exterior and the hierarchical arrangement of its interior, with the ground floor given over to the servants, the first to Bess and her family, and the second to the entertaining of guests – even, so Bess hoped, the Queen herself. Ceilings and windows rose corresponding-ly, culminating in the towering expanses of the High Great Chamber and the long gallery.* Changes were made to Smythson's design during the actual building – changes instigated or approved by Bess – but the result is a rigorously symmetrical building: the east front exactly matches the west, and the north the south. In the interests of symmetry, Smythson employed the crossways hall, already favoured by Bess; chimney flues carried up through internal walls, leaving the exterior free for glass; false windows, and windows that actually lit two floors rather than one.

Architectural devices, so coveted by Elizabethan builders, took many forms – houses built on geometric principles (like Hardwick), or

---

* By the 18th century, this arrangement would be reversed, with high-ceilinged reception rooms on the ground floor and servants and children tucked away in the attics.

inspired by biblical or religious symbolism. The seven pilasters on the porch of Kirby Hall were probably an allusion to the seven pillars of wisdom in the Book of Proverbs; the design of Wollaton may well have derived from King Solomon's Temple in Jerusalem.*[16] Sir Thomas Tresham took religious symbolism to new heights on his Northamptonshire estate at Rushton.

Tresham was a wealthy Catholic landowner, with a large architectural library, a particular interest in intellectual, richly symbolic buildings, and some design expertise. As a recusant, he suffered regular imprisonment and paid almost £8,000 in fines. However, such handicaps did not in any way deter him from a busy building programme, at times, during the 1580s and 90s, directed from his prison cell. Commitment to building equalled that to faith – the one informed the other. In 1593, after twelve years either in the Fleet prison, or under house arrest in his Hoxton house, Tresham returned to Rushton, where his Catholicism took concrete form: the Triangular Lodge, built in honour of the Trinity, using recurring multiples of three – three rooms on three floors, each of the three sides measuring thirty-three feet, with groups of three windows, under three gables, topped by a triangular chimney. The lodge walls are carved with emblems, numbers and letters, many of them highly obscure (some allude, obliquely since it was illegal, to the Mass), devised by Tresham, though he may have had help from a Cambridge mathematician and astrologer, John Fletcher.†[17]

---

* A reconstruction of Solomon's Temple was first published in 1481. It has also been suggested that Bess, trying to outdo Wollaton with the New Hall, may have been inspired by a woodcut of Solomon's Palace, by Jost Amman. The Palace features in one of the inlaid wood panels showing architectural scenes, commissioned by Bess for Chatsworth (Mark Girouard, 'Solomon's Temple in Nottinghamshire', *Town and Country*, 1992, pp.187–97).

† The Lodge was ostensibly built for Tresham's warrener, who was given the ground-floor room and the unsettlingly dungeon-like basement (for the storage of rabbit skins, perhaps), while Tresham kept the first floor as a place for meditation.

Tresham's lodge speaks of defiance, but also of ego. He may have dismissed his building projects as 'daubing, botching and bungling', but this was entirely false modesty. There is something self-regarding and precious about the man (he made much of the links between his name and the Trinity – he and his wife called each other 'Tres' and 'Tresse') and his buildings, for all their exquisite workmanship. And something of Sir John Thynne too – both were ruthless, demanding employers, obsessive micro-managers, slow to praise and quick to fault. Both got results.

Besides the Lodge, Tresham was making improvements to Rushton Hall, and in 1595, he began work on another house – the cross-shaped Lyveden New Bield, this time celebrating the Crucifixion. From prison in Ely, he sent detailed instructions about Lyveden and its gardens: measurements and stone were specified; walks, arbours and a bowling green were to be made, with due regard for boggy ground; particular varieties of roses, apple and pear trees planted.[18] When Tresham died, in 1605, Lyveden was still unfinished, so his friends never wound their way, as he intended, from his main house, a mile or so away, through meadows and orchards and moated gardens, complete with a labyrinth – its circular beds planted with roses – and grassy prospect mounds, until they came upon Lyveden, where they would have been entertained and refreshed and perhaps encouraged to contemplate the state of their souls. Lyveden sits today looking much as it would have done on Tresham's death – a roofless shell, starkly beautiful, a place of calm and quiet.

Tresham was able to supply most of his materials himself – he had 'redstone' and 'whitestone' quarries and timber – which is why his total building costs came to less than £2,000. However, Sir Christopher Hatton provided him with stone from his quarry at Weldon for another of Tresham's buildings, the Market House in Rothwell. In his letter of thanks in 1583, Tresham remarked that the Market House stood 'as a witness of the bounty of happy Holdenby to ruinous Rushton'.[19] In point of fact it was Hatton's finances that were 'ruinous', thanks to Holdenby.

There is no evidence that Bess ever visited Rushton, or had any dealings with Tresham, yet interestingly, and curiously, Tresham paid her (possibly Catholic) daughter Frances Pierrepont a twice-yearly annuity of £25.[20] Bess lacked Tresham's intellectualism, but she had quite as much ego, and she wanted the *effects* of an intellectual building. Here she looked to Smythson, who came up with a 'platt' that employed the simplest and yet most ingenious of devices – a rectangle encompassed by six rectangular turrets, two on each long and one on each short side, creating a kind of optical illusion, endlessly intriguing and surprising the eye. Sacheverell Sitwell, one of the house's many admirers, described how Hardwick's turrets mysteriously regroup themselves according to the position from which they're viewed – 'as though the building is shaped like a diamond on a playing card, more still, like the ace of clubs, so that the fourth tower is hidden, almost, behind the other three'.[21]

The Old and New Halls at Hardwick, wrote William Camden, 'by reason of their lofty situation show themselves afar off to be seen and yield a very goodly prospect'.[22] The importance of siting a house, both within a landscape and within gardens, was beginning to be recognised by the late sixteenth century. Burghley's house on the Strand, built in the early 1560s, had big gardens, divided into compartments, something that was recreated at Theobalds on a grander scale – the Great Garden and Privy Garden boasted a grotto, classical arcades, fountains, ponds and a 'great sea'. Hatton had huge gardens made around Holdenby. Tresham devoted a great deal of thought to the ways in which his grounds offset and enhanced his houses. The gardens at Chatsworth featured, like Worksop, elaborate waterworks.

Setting was clearly important to Smythson – he designed houses that commanded views from within and attention from without, and drew up plans both for and of gardens. So he positioned Wollaton on a hilltop, and, as can be seen in a surviving drawing, planned to encase the house within eight courts, containing gardens, outbuildings and courtyards, the whole forming a giant square (some, if not all, of this scheme was realised). He did something similar, albeit scaled down, at Hardwick, which is also set high and where symmetry extends from house to surroundings, with two walled orchards to the north and south and two walled courts to the east and west, an almost symmetrical scheme apart from one wall of the north orchard, which had to be set at an angle to accommodate the lie of the land.[23]

The architectural historian Mark Girouard, who has written so eloquently and elegantly about Hardwick, describes it as 'Worksop perfected and simplified, with the polish though not the exuberance of Wollaton ... It falls happily between the over-abundance of Wollaton and the severity of Worksop.'[24] For Hardwick, Smythson took the best of both houses – symmetry and setting from Wollaton, height, vast windows, recesses and bays from Worksop. Unlike Wollaton, exterior decoration is restrained, but the classical detail in the shape of the colonnades running along two sides, the entablatures between the storeys and the balustrade, and the Flemish ornament in the obelisks and strapwork along the courtyard wall, on the gatehouse and cresting the turrets is enough to soften what might otherwise be an uncompromisingly rectangular building.

By May 1591, the walls of the New Hall were high enough for William Carpenter to begin laying 'the new foundation floors', and fourteen sawpits were dug at Crich Chase, nine miles away.[25] Up to twenty-five wallers worked into the autumn. Work on the Old Hall continued alongside that on the New, with labourers and craftsmen shuttling back and forth between the two. Between April and August 1591, chimneys and moulding for windows in the Old Hall and steps and doors for the stable were hewn, the embroiderer's chamber and Bess's with-drawing chamber were panelled, all the windows were glassed, 'a great mashinge fatt' – a vat for mashing barley to make beer – was made for the brewhouse, and top soil was cleared to enlarge the quarry.

In November, a 'bargain' was drawn up between Bess and the mason John Rhodes for most of the stonework for the New Hall – walls, cornice, architrave, windows, door cases, stairs. He was paid by measure, according to the difficulty of the job: ashlar at 7½d per foot, windows at 4d, architrave at 7½d, and cornice at 6d, an enormous £890 in total. John Rhodes worked with his brother Christopher (Christopher left Hardwick in 1593, with 10s. from Bess), and they came to Hardwick from Wollaton, having previously worked on Shrewsbury's Turret House at Sheffield. Mason families were common – Thomas Tresham's Triangular Lodge was built by a father and three sons, Owlcotes by the four Plumtree brothers.

A house was found for John Rhodes and, in December 1591, enlarged by the addition of two bays, at Bess's expense. The New Hall was a huge job, and Rhodes, though he was illiterate and signed receipts with an 'X', must have been an extremely competent organiser and manager. In order to pay his men fairly, he needed to know who was responsible for what, and here masons' marks were key: the ashlar (cut stone) blocks bore two sets of marks – these can still be seen today – one made by the mason who cut the stone, the other by he who laid it. With the New Hall, there was no question of economies, and rather than being rendered, the house was entirely and expensively faced with ashlar, levelled on lime mortar beds with slivers of oyster shell, which acted as a setting agent (oysters appeared regularly on Bess's table). Lime, for the mortar, was burned in kilns in the north orchard that needed feeding and tending twenty-four hours a day.

Chatsworth provided some of the (finest) furnishings for the New Hall – hangings, tables, overmantels, beds and stools – but more were needed, tapestries and plate in particular. In the autumn of 1591, Bess decided to decamp to London for an eight-month shopping spree. Shopping aside, there was the question of her jointure to be settled – Gilbert was still prevaricating over payment and claiming that Bess was appropriating land that wasn't hers. There was to be a court case, and Bess was bent on ensuring that it was held in Derbyshire, where she could be confident of the outcome. She had good reason to remember the case brought against one of her Somerset tenants, Henry Beresford, in 1586, by Shrewsbury. This had been heard in York, with a jury entirely made up of Shrewsbury supporters, who naturally found against Beresford and proved that 'in this part great men may do what they list'.[26] Now Bess intended to do some jury-fixing of her own, and London lawyers needed to be courted and cajoled.

And then there was Arbella, now sixteen. Bess had not given up hope of persuading the Queen to increase her granddaughter's £200 allowance, nor of her making a great marriage. The possibility of Rainutio Farnese was under discussion once again. It was a match that both Bess and the Queen had reason to favour – Bess could provide Arbella with a well-connected husband (Farnese, like a great many European royals, could claim descent from John of Gaunt), who would take her granddaughter off her hands, while the Queen, who had no desire to keep supporting the French in what was proving a lengthy and costly war in the Netherlands, could expect peace. The promoters of the Rainutio match had recently requested a Hilliard miniature of Arbella – they wanted to size her up.

Towards the end of November, as Bess prepared to leave for London, the building works at Hardwick were scaled down: day labourers were greatly reduced and John Rhodes and his men were left with instructions to quarry and cut ashlar in preparation for the next storey of the New Hall. Other masons were diverted to the Old Hall, to plaster internal walls and finish off the Hill Great Chamber. While Bess was away, Sir Henry Jenkinson, the family priest, who had taken over the building accounts from David Flood, was to pay the workforce, apart from the carpenters, who were to be paid by John Balechouse. Balechouse was emerging as a key figure at the New Hall; he must surely have sent Bess reports of the progress of the building during her eight-month absence, but none such survive.

18

LONDON, 1591

Bess set out for London with an entourage of around forty: her personal servants, including her ladies, Timothy Pusey, her steward, and Edward Whalley, a lawyer; William and Charles Cavendish and their wives and servants; Arbella and her lady-in-waiting, Mrs Abrahall. Most were on horseback, though Bess and her ladies – Jane Kniveton (her half-sister) and Elizabeth Digby – travelled with Arbella in Bess's coach (recently introduced into England and, despite being unsprung and hideously uncomfortable, a coveted accessory), pulled by six horses. The journey must have been something of an ordeal for Elizabeth Digby, who was six months pregnant. Elizabeth was the most senior and trusted of Bess's four ladies, and also the highest paid, at £30 a year.*

Bess's coach rocked and rumbled its way towards London, via Nottingham, Leicester, Dunstable and Barnet, and as each came into view, the clerk comptroller rode on ahead to alert the townspeople to Bess's arrival so that church bells could be rung. This was a spectacle with all the hallmarks of a royal progress: 'the ringers' were given cash rewards; 'the poor' received 20s. (Bess was a generous tipper and this

---

* Elizabeth was given a generous £60 when she married John Digby, a gentleman servant, and £4 on the christening of her baby in April 1592 (Devonshire MSS, Chatsworth, HM/7, f.14).

was her standard handout); Bess's servants in their light blue Cavendish livery and velvet caps bearing her silver badge – an 'ES' topped with a coronet – swarmed about; the silver buckles on the horses' harnesses, also cut into 'ES's, flashed; food and drink was ordered; saddles stuffed, horses shod and coach wheels mended. On 25 November, after a week on the road, the party arrived at Shrewsbury House in Chelsea.[1]

Shrewsbury House had been little used, or maintained, since Shrewsbury's building works back in 1579, and stood in need of some refurbishment in order to comfortably accommodate Bess and her retinue. In advance of their arrival, a bricklayer, a carpenter and a smith had been engaged, loads of brick and sand had been delivered, the gallery had been boarded over, a stable turned into a dormitory – presumably for servants – and quantities of wood, for fuel, brought by barge. In addition, 'two fat oxen and forty sheep', a walking larder, had been driven from Bess's Leicestershire estate and pastured in fields around the house. Chelsea, in the 1590s, was little more than a village, but the river provided easy access to the royal palaces at Whitehall, Greenwich and Richmond, as well as to the City.

Visitors soon began to call, one of the first Mary Scudamore, a cousin of Bess's, an old friend of Gilbert and Mary Talbot, and a lady of the privy chamber to the Queen. Bess was probably eager to hear court gossip, to discover the lie of the land and to seek advice about her New Year's gift for Her Majesty – once again this was to be a 'garment', rather than cash. Her first important engagement was to attend court for the twelve days of Christmas, for which both she and Arbella (this would be Arbella's first visit to court since her disgrace three years earlier) urgently needed new clothes and jewels. The December accounts record payments for fifty yards of damask, fifty yards of velvet, forty yards of satin, black taffeta, black Spanish lace (these must have been for Bess, who now only wore black), blue and white starches for lace collars and ruffs (starch-making techniques, using wheat, had been introduced into England by a Dutch woman in the 1560s), several plain gold chains, gold bracelets, and a pair of bracelets set with diamonds, pearls and rubies (costing £21). William Jones, the royal tailor, was paid £59 14s. for making a gown for the Queen, and £50 went to John Parr, the Queen's embroiderer, for embroidering it.

The court, that Christmas, was at Whitehall, the largest of the Tudor palaces, a sprawling conglomeration of two thousand rooms covering twenty-three acres and decorated in medieval style, with Holbein's great portraits of Henry VII and Henry VIII and their queens looming from the walls of the privy chamber. Whitehall catered admirably for Elizabethan taste for colour and spectacle, with tennis courts, bowling alleys, a tiltyard, a cockpit, a pheasant yard, an orchard and gardens enlivened by thirty-four heraldic beasts mounted on brightly painted pillars, along with a sundial that told the time in thirty different ways and a multi-jetted fountain. Bess and Arbella enjoyed a round of feasts, masques, dancing, bear-baiting, plays and jesting. Ramsey, the court jester, must have pleased Bess, since she gave him 20s. at New Year. Other New Year's gifts were dispensed: the Queen had her gown and Bess received a 'great gilt bowl with a cover' in return.[2] Bess gave her usual cash gifts to family, servants and acquaintances: £100 to the Earl and Countess of Shrewsbury; £26 to William Cavendish and his wife; £20 apiece to Charles and Henry and their wives; £10 to Lady Cobham, in a purse of crimson silk, embroidered in gold, and another £10 to her son George, Bess's godson; £7 to Elizabeth Wingfield; £15 to Jane Kniveton; and 40s. to Mrs Digby.

In the five years or so since Bess had last visited, court had become a very different place, as a new generation of courtiers replaced the old. Bess needed to navigate the new ways, to cultivate the new favourites, on behalf of Arbella, if not herself. Her former friends and allies – Leicester, Walsingham, Hatton – all were no more. Burghley, whose much-loved wife Mildred had died in 1589, and who was himself increasingly frail and crippled by gout, was gradually handing over the reins to his equally clever and unscrupulous son, Robert Cecil. Cecil, who joined the Privy Council in

1591, headed one faction at court, Ralegh and Essex, who loathed each other almost as much as they loathed Cecil, others. All three jostled for power and position. Essex, having temporarily enraged the Queen by secretly marrying Walsingham's daughter (and Philip Sidney's widow), Frances, had just returned to court from France, where he'd spectacularly failed to capture Rouen from the Spanish and thus to win the military glory that he longed for. Whereas Walsingham, Burghley, Leicester and Hatton had worked more or less harmoniously together, held in place by the Queen, now the atmosphere at court was tense and febrile. Elizabeth herself was nearing sixty, her brilliant facade and her hold a little less sure. *Semper Eadem* (Always the Same) may have been her motto, but nothing *was* the same. The Virgin Queen was ageing. She still commanded the homage and admiration of her courtiers, but what had, in the past, been genuine enough now concealed frustration and impatience. And amongst her people there was apprehension. Who would succeed her?

Back in Chelsea, Bess entertained old friends (Anthony Wingfield, the husband of her half-sister Elizabeth, Roger Manners, a Shrewsbury cousin and Derbyshire neighbour, Lady Cobham), and courted new ones, such as Lord Buckhurst, the Lord Treasurer, Sir Fulke Greville, the statesman and poet, and Lord Howard, Admiral of the Fleet. A man like Howard, who was married to Kate Carey, one of the Queen's favourite ladies of the privy chamber, was very much worth cultivating (the Howards had a Chelsea estate, not far from Shrewsbury House). Fellow widows such as Lady Sheffield (Leicester's old love), Lady Walsingham, Lady Warwick, Lady Cheke and Lady Bacon (mother of Francis) came to gossip and, in the case of Ladies Bacon and Cheke, to borrow £50. The talk that spring would have been of the latest court scandal: Bess Throckmorton, one of the Queen's ladies, was discovered to have become pregnant by and to have subsequently married Ralegh; the baby was born in March and the pair were sent to the Tower, before being forgiven.

Bess also set about outmanoeuvring Gilbert Talbot. To win her case, she needed powerful allies: Sir William Cordell, the Master of the Rolls, who had already been warmed up with gifts ('a great standing cup' and venison pasties), was invited to dinner. Regular payments were made to Edward Whalley, for 'law matters'. Whalley and Timothy Pusey were hard at work securing Bess's titles to her lands, to avoid any dispute on her death, and thwarting Gilbert by engaging as many legal officers as they could in London, thereby preventing Gilbert from finding lawyers to represent him. Their efforts, and £430 in legal charges, paid off – the case was heard in Derbyshire and it found in Bess's favour.[3]

But much of Bess's time in London was devoted to shopping – for herself, for Arbella and for Hardwick. She spent £300 on clothes: Spanish leather shoes, a pair of pantables (overshoes), velvet shoes, looking glasses, perfumed gloves, a dress trimmed with red braid and a powdered ermine gown (these presumably for Arbella), yards of velvet, satin, damask, fustian, lawn and holland (for shifts), silver buttons and gold fringe. 'Five little jewels' were bought at 14s. 'a piece', and 'another little one of a bee' for 6s. 8d (again these sound too frivolous for Bess and were probably for Arbella), along with a ruby, 'a fair opal' and a pearl, 'a little jewel with 3 pearls and a whitestone in it', 'an agate with a man's face with a bunch of grapes hanging to it' and twelve rings.

Bess had a sumptuous new horse litter made (£11), upholstered in twenty-two yards of tawny velvet (£19 16s.), with a tawny silk fringe, windows of tawny and gold parchment and a felt-covered foot-stool. Shrewsbury House needed a few essentials: bellows and fire tongs and shovels, bedsteads and stools, close stools and pewter stool pots. But more importantly, huge quantities of plate and hangings were bought for the New Hall: silver-gilt bowls with covers (silver gilt being finer than plain silver), standing cups, casting bottles, chafing dishes (for keeping food warm), basins and ewers (for hand-washing before and after eating), a great porringer, gilt salts with covers, gilt candlesticks, gilt spoons, platters and flagons. Some silver plate came from Sir William Hatton, Christopher Hatton's nephew and heir, who, having inherited a pile of mortar and a pile of debt, was selling off the contents of Holdenby, offering bargains for Bess.

Since the rooms in the New Hall were only going to be panelled halfway, Bess needed a large acreage of tapestry to cover the remainder of her walls, and if she could acquire this inexpensively and second hand, then all the better. For £321 6s. she bought the thirteen-piece Gideon tapestry from Sir William Hatton, originally woven in 1578 for Holdenby. This was destined for the long gallery, and Bess insisted that £5 be knocked off the total to cover the cost of replacing Hatton's arms (these were eventually covered with her own, painted on felt, for just 30s. 4d). From Sir William too came the four Abraham tapestries for the state withdrawing chamber (now in the Green Velvet Room), bought piecemeal, some via the dealer Mulmaster, one piece for as little as £24 10s., and the set with 'personages with my ladies Armes' for Bess's own withdrawing chamber. All of these tapestries had been woven in Flanders, and their price, per Flemish ell, varied according to the complexity of the design (figures being more expensive than foliage) and the materials used (wool was cheaper than gold and silver thread). So the one piece of the Abraham tapestries that was woven with gold metal thread cost 20s. per ell, as opposed to 14s. for the rest.[4]

Three other sets of hangings were acquired, including five pieces of the 'Story of Tobit', for £38 17s., which were temporarily put up in Shrewsbury House but eventually hung in the Tobias Chamber of the New Hall. The story of Tobit, or Tobias, features elsewhere at Hardwick – in a table carpet, and an overmantel, brought from Chatsworth. It tells of Tobias setting out to recover money owed to his blind father Tobit, accompanied by his dog and, in disguise, the angel Raphael. On his journey, Tobias meets and marries Sarah, the daughter of a kinsman, undeterred by the fact that Sarah's seven previous husbands have been killed by a demon. Thanks to the good offices of Raphael,

Sarah's demon is exorcised, Tobit's sight is restored and Tobias and Sarah settle down to married life. As a tale of virtue rewarded, filial piety and the sanctity of marriage, it clearly appealed to Bess.

In April, Bess and Arbella joined the court at Whitehall, and in May at Greenwich, for which three boats were hired, with Bess's new litter taking up a boat of its own. The gardens at Greenwich must have particularly delighted her, since she gave several tips to the gardeners, and 20d to 'one who brought strawberries'. A second visit to Greenwich took place in June, with Bess staying until 19 July, leaving Arbella behind. Arbella had been sitting for Hilliard, who was paid 40s. for his portrait, with a 20s. tip. Another 40s. went to 'one Rowland' (this was Rowland Lockey, an apprentice to Hilliard), probably for a copy of the miniature. Whether Rainutio liked what he saw was immaterial, since the Duke of Parma died in December and the son without the father was quite worthless.

On 31 July, carried in relative comfort in her new litter, Bess left London for what would turn out to be the last time. She could count her visit a success – Gilbert defeated, Arbella still husbandless but reintroduced at court, a grand total of £6,360 spent on splendid furnishings for Hardwick, filling ten hired wagons, one with plate alone. Now she could look forward to seeing the progress of her new house, and she took the opportunity of her return journey to inspect the work of other builders, to gather ideas, to assess the competition. At Northampton, on what was possibly her first visit, she diverted to Holdenby, which sat vast, magnificent and empty. The housekeeper and gardener who showed her round had 20s. for their pains. From Holdenby she went on to stay with her daughter Frances Pierrepont at Holme Pierrepont, near Nottingham, a convenient base from which to visit Wollaton.

Robert Smythson would still have been living at Wollaton (he remained there after Sir Francis Willoughby's death in 1596, under the rather more harmonious regime of Sir Percival). Bess gave the Wollaton housekeeper 10s., but did Smythson act as her guide? Was

Hardwick discussed? Perhaps, though Smythson might well have been occupied elsewhere, drawing up 'platts' for other East Midlands houses, as he did during the early 1590s. Documentary evidence is lacking, but there's a strong case that such houses included Barlborough and Worksop Manor Lodge in Derbyshire, Pontefract in Yorkshire and Doddington in Lincolnshire.[5] Some of these survive – remnants of a lost world clinging on amid Midlands sprawl. Barlborough has become a school. Doddington, elegant in mellow red brick, with a long gallery taking up the top floor and octagonal cupolas, sits within earshot of the roar and rush of cars and cyclists. Worksop Manor Lodge, recently gutted by fire, has been renovated as a private house, surrounded by a suburban garden, with the town of Worksop creeping ever closer to its walls.

Manor Lodge, within a stone's throw of Shrewsbury's great house, was commissioned by Gilbert Talbot as a hunting lodge, and, like Worksop, it's immensely tall – four storeys, with originally a fifth, containing a gallery. Both houses, built of pale grey magnesian limestone, would have risen over and gleamed through the trees of Sherwood Forest. Manor Lodge had a crossways hall and a great chamber, with vast windows, on the fourth floor, while the rest was given over to lodgings for the huntsmen. Function and design were aligned in a surprisingly modern way – this was a house in which to sleep before a long day's hunting, but also to meet at the end of the day, for feasting and carousing in the great chamber. It's handsome, yet plain, with something, in its rows of small windows lighting the huntsmen's chambers, of the industrial buildings of the nineteenth century.[*]

Having inspected Wollaton, and eager to discover how her own house was progressing, Bess and her cavalcade reached Hardwick on

---

[*] A recent owner of Manor Lodge filled the great chamber with knitting machines, while the house has also had an incarnation as a hotel and pub, nods perhaps to its hybrid character.

5 August. The unusually hot summer of 1592 had fostered the plague that swept through London, but dry conditions aided building. In May, forty-one windows had been cut for the second storey of the New Hall, for which the scaffolding was erected and the cornice set in June. Bess must have been satisfied with what she found – both Rhodes and his men and Balechouse had 20s. cash rewards. She installed herself in the Old Hall, but here too work was still in progress. In October, escaping the dirt and dust and the relentless hammering of chisels and mallets, she and Arbella decamped to Chatsworth, which she was now free to use again.

The move to Chatsworth may have been for reasons of security too. In September, Bess had received a letter from Burghley warning her of the discovery of a Catholic plot to abduct Arbella. It was Arbella's curse to be the focus of Catholic plots to depose Elizabeth, and later James I. While no Catholic herself – although her grandmother, the Countess of Lennox, had been staunchly so, and her aunt was a convert – Arbella could always be furnished with a Catholic husband, who could then be placed on the English throne. Bess replied to Burghley, using her son William as a scribe since she was unable to write 'for fear of bringing pain to my head': she was doing all she could to thwart 'wicked and mischievous practices' and to protect her granddaughter. 'I will not have any unknown or suspected person to come to my house ... I have little resort to me, my house is furnished with sufficient company, Arbell walks not late, at such time as she shall take the air, it shall be near the house and well attended on. She goeth not to any body's house at all, I see her almost every hour in the day, she lyeth in my bed chamber.'

Bess had got wind of a Catholic priest who had been staying with his brother near Hardwick, and since Catholic priests were 'the likeliest instruments to put a bad matter in execution', it was as well to be vigilant. She had dismissed a certain Morley, who had acted as a tutor to Arbella for the last three years but had showed himself, ever since Bess's 'return into the country ... to be much discontented'. There was some reason to suspect Morley's religious leanings, though Bess admitted that she couldn't 'charge him with papistry'.[6] She assured Burghley that Arbella was 'loving and dutiful', but for how long would a strong-willed, intelligent seventeen-year-old be content to live under her grandmother's watchful eye, confined to her house, sharing her bedchamber?

Bess returned to Hardwick for Christmas. Living with her in the Old Hall, occupying the west wing, were William Cavendish, his wife Anne and their children (four of whom died young). Life in the Old Hall must have been noisy, crowded and, under the rule of Bess, not without its strains. William was making himself indispensable as Bess's second-in-command, but Anne may have felt rather differently about living with her mother-in-law. At any rate, the Cavendishes needed a home of their own. In January 1593, as part of her programme of land-buying around Hardwick, Bess bought the manors of Stainsby, Rowthorn, Heath and Oldcotes from Sir John Savage for £3,416 13s. Oldcotes – or Owlcotes – is three miles north-west from Hardwick, across the valley, just out of sight.[7] It became the site of a new house, Bess's last, built for William, and designed by Smythson.

All 'bargains' for the building of Hardwick Old and New Halls have vanished, but one survives for Owlcotes, and it gives a good idea of how such documents read and how the house looked. On 8 March, a bargain was drawn up between Bess and William Cavendish and six wallers, all of whom had been working at Hardwick – the four Plumtree brothers and two others. The wallers were to build a house 'from the bottom of the cellar, to the top of the roof and two turrets above the roof according to a plat already drawn'. The house was to be two rooms deep, with a twenty-foot-high hall. No ashlar was to be used, presumably for reasons of economy; instead, the walls were simply to be scappled (roughly finished) to match those of the old manor. The thickness and height of the walls, the details of the chimneys, the width of the ovens, all were specified. Bess and William were to supply the stone (sandstone), sand and water; the wallers were to make mortar and erect scaffolding at their own expense, the hurdles and poles (usually ash or elder) being provided. The wallers agreed 'to do what they can well and workmanlike, to work, scappel and finish all the said walls before All Hallows time next', i.e. in eight months' time. They were to be paid 'by measure' – 3s. 4d per rood of wall 'till they come to the height of 20 feet above the ground', 5s. for every rood above that, with extra for the two turrets, and 20s. for the two ovens. They would be lent six beds, which could be put up in the old house, and three cows, and provided with rye and oatmeal.[8]

William would never actually live in Owlcotes – it was not perhaps either large or grand enough for his liking – but he met most of its costs. Bess contributed too, with regular payments 'towards the building of Oulde Coats', a total of £300 in 1593. And she kept a close eye on progress, with inspections and site visits, on one such handing out £3 in tips.[9] When Owlcotes was finally finished, in 1600, it was Bess who provided the all-important furnishings.

Owlcotes was demolished in the late seventeenth or early eighteenth century and in its place today is a bleak-looking farmhouse, surrounded by rusting vehicles and sheds, occupied by men in boiler suits conducting mysterious business on mobile phones. The only trace of the old house is a scalloped alcove in a garden wall, but a drawing, thought to be Smythson's design for Owlcotes, survives. It shows an elegant Hardwick-in-miniature – a house with two towers, two storeys[*] and a flight of steps (Worksop Manor Lodge and Barlborough were also approached by steps) leading to a prettily colonnaded porch. It must have been one of Smythson's most enchanting buildings.

---

[*] From the evidence of a 17th-century survey, Owlcotes, once built, had three storeys (Durant, *Smythson Circle*, p.163).

19.

'MORE GLASS THAN WALL'

Alongside Owlcotes, work on the New Hall pushed ahead in 1593, helped by another long, dry summer. Plastering began in April and scaffolding for the third storey went up in June, whilst windows were hewn in July and set in October.[1] With the walls nearing completion and the shell of the house in place, a bargain was made with the slaters William and Peter Yates for the roof, and a further bargain with the plumber for leading the roof and making pipes. The Old Hall had been roofed with stone tiles, but the flat expanses of the New were to be leaded. This was expensive, but Bess had access to the lead works at Winster, Aldwark and Bonsall that she had made over to William Cavendish. The roof also required huge quantities of timber, including sixteen great oak trusses, each thirty-four feet, on which it would be supported. Tree-felling began in earnest at Teversal, at 3d a tree. The oaks for the trusses* – known as 'somers' – came from Chatsworth (3s. 4d for the 'felling and squaring' of each) and were dragged by oxen the sixteen miles or so to Hardwick, where they were hoisted into place using ropes and pulleys, and possibly some kind of wooden crane.

Remarkably few accidents seem to have occurred during the building of Hardwick, considering the hazards of manually lifting and

---

* Some of the oak at Hardwick was put in green – unseasoned – subsequently warping and shrinking, suggesting impatience on Bess's part.

manoeuvring lengths of timber and blocks of stone – just one payment is recorded in the accounts, 'to Hollingworth, when he was hurt'. However, at Owlcotes in 1597, a beam fell, taking two others with it, as Elizabeth Wingfield reported to Mary Talbot: 'there was a great beam fell at Oldcotes which broke two others and much shook the walls, but no men, but some a little bruised'.[2]

In May 1593, Bess moved to Chatsworth once again, where she remained for just over a year. Chatsworth would have been a great deal more peaceful and comfortable than Hardwick, and it was important that Bess exercise her rights of occupancy (she spent a month there in the summers of 1595 and 1596). Besides, it was a house to which she had devoted much time and attention, and of which she was rightly proud, and she made sure it wasn't neglected. In her absence, Ellen Steward, the Chatsworth housekeeper, was deputed to pay 'work folks' wages and for general repairs and improvements, such as fencing.

Burghley wrote in August, offering his congratulations on the marriage between Bess's granddaughter Grace Pierrepont and George Manners: 'I do persuade myself that your Ladyship shall take much comfort of their match, so as betwixt his father and your Ladyship the two young folks may be provided for to live without want.'[3] This sounds like a match of Bess's making – George's father was Sir John Manners, son of Thomas, 1st Earl of Rutland, and once brother-in-law of the Earl of Shrewsbury, whose first wife, Gertrude, had been Sir John's sister. It was a good marriage for Grace (from it would come the Dukes of Rutland), and as George would inherit Haddon Hall, near Chatsworth, it consolidated the family holdings in Derbyshire. Bess provided a dowry of £700 and gave George £100 to buy plate, with another £50 the following year for 'setting up' house.[4] Congratulations aside, Burghley added that he wished Bess would 'take more comfort by stirring abroad to visit your friends and children and not to live so solitary as it seems you do there in Chatsworth, amongst hills and rocks of stones'.

From London, Derbyshire seemed remote indeed. London, however, and court, no longer held much allure for Bess, who, now in her early seventies, was more interested in the short view, the view from Hardwick. Only Burghley survived of her allies of old, and he had more or less withdrawn from public life, making way for his son, Robert Cecil. In 1595, Bess wrote to Cecil congratulating him on his appointment as the Queen's 'principal secretary': 'the honourable remembrance, the whole realm retaineth, of your most noble father, placed in that room you are now in, will make every one expect no less good of you, carrying that name and being son to so worthy a counsellor'.[5] This was flattering, but carried with it the weight of expectation – Cecil had much to live up to and should be sure not to disappoint. Bess would have cause to appeal to him in the future, in regard to both her uncooperative son-in-law and her troublesome granddaughter.

Bess ruled over a court of her own making, among the hills and rocks and stones of Derbyshire. Here she was a great personage – rich, powerful and respected. She would seek to fight for and to further the interests – marital, territorial, financial – of her children and grandchildren, but she had no need of royal favour for her own sake. Which is not to say that she didn't hold out hopes of entertaining the Queen at Hardwick – the appearance of Diana, the huntress and virgin goddess, in the plasterwork of the High Great Chamber was intended as a tribute to Elizabeth, whose arms were also carved into the overmantel. Arbella, it was true, remained unmarried, and her prospects uncertain, but by now Bess was coming to accept that those prospects did not encompass the throne. The Queen was never going to recognise Arbella as her successor; those who counted at court increasingly looked to James VI as much the strongest claimant. Hardwick was surely not built for the glory of Arbella, who hardly features at all in the decoration of the house, other than her coat of arms in the room she called her 'quondam study'.

* * *

Financing the building of the New Hall was easy enough, given that during the 1590s, Bess's annual income averaged £8,300, rising to £10,000 by 1600.[6] Her business interests and estates were growing steadily, as she accumulated more land and property, most of it within twenty miles of Hardwick, some further afield. Three manors in Derbyshire were bought from a Mr Shackerly for £2,450 in 1596; other manors and rectories were bought in Lincolnshire, Nottinghamshire, Yorkshire and Leicestershire.[7] All were settled on William Cavendish. Several streams of revenue funded these acquisitions: rents and leases, sales of livestock, coal, wool, iron and glass, and interest on loans. Rents were collected by seventeen bailiffs, passed on, in canvas 'money bags', to Bess's receiver, William Reason, who in turn gave them to Timothy Pusey, her steward and right-hand man, before they ended up in Bess's coffers. Pusey was paid £10 a year, with, eventually, the lease of a farm and a mill, and was absolutely central to the running of Bess's affairs, his legal background being especially useful. Under him came Rowland Harrison, a gentleman servant and clerk comptroller, who acted as both a money collector and a keeper of the fortnightly household accounts. These were totalled by Pusey and finally signed off by Bess herself.

Key to Bess's business portfolio was moneylending, something she had practised successfully since the early 1580s. In the absence of banks, cash was both badly needed and in short supply in Tudor England. Bess offered the respectable face of usury. Like Shrewsbury, with his coffers at Sheffield allegedly emptied by Eleanor Britton, Bess kept eight coffers in her bedchamber, together with a pair of scales. She collected interest on her loans (the 1571 Act Against Usury fixed interest at 10 per cent), and as she frequently lent money on the security of land – mortgaging land being by far the easiest way of raising money – she collected land and property too. In 1581, for example, the Earl of Cumberland had mortgaged his land at Edensor to her for £500 (a sum that she managed to extract from Shrewsbury);

when the Earl defaulted on his loan, Edensor reverted to Bess, and is still owned by the Cavendishes today.[8]

In 1591, Sir Francis Willoughby, finding himself ever deeper in debt and hoping to generate some much-needed funds, had leased the ironworks at Oakmoor and the nearby woods at Alton, in Staffordshire, from Bess (both were Talbot properties and part of her marriage settlement).[9] Willoughby's ironmaster, Loggin, wanted to set up two new blast furnaces at Oakmoor, which would be fuelled by timber from the Alton woods, and it was he who initially approached Bess for a £400 loan, secured on Willoughby land. With this 'bargain' concluded, Bess received £172 a year in rent and from the sale of timber, and £40 interest on the loan. When Sir Francis, predictably, fell out with Loggin, Bess's own ironmaster, Sylvester Smith, stepped in to keep the operation running. Three years later, Sir Francis was applying for a loan once again, this time for £3,000 on the security of five manors. Bess, who didn't lend lightly, considered this expensive: 'for so great a sum I think it not a convenient portion. I know where for less than half this money you assured far more land', and she was only willing to enter into a deal 'for the security of them that are to disburse this money. Your land I do not desire. If I could be assured of your life, there should not need any mortgage at all to be made, but the youngest and healthfulest are subject to change.'[10]

Bess would have been perfectly aware that Willoughby was neither young nor healthy, nor in any position to repay his debts; she lent the £3,000, with annual interest of £300, and put the mortgage in her granddaughter Arbella's name. When Willoughby died in 1596 (possibly poisoned), the loan unpaid, the five manors, worth £15,000, became Arbella's. Bess's £3,000 initial outlay had brought a very substantial return. The accounts record a steady stream of loans: £200 to Mr Wright, £700 to Mr Perindle, £300 to Mr Sacheverell, £100 each to the Bishop of Coventry and Lichfield, Henry Leake, Mr Gilbert and Mr Hacker, £200 to William Kniveton, £200 to George Needham. She lent to family too, though they it seems were let off interest: £200 to Charles Cavendish to buy land, £200 to Henry Cavendish, £100 to Edward Talbot, £1,000 to William Cavendish, to be repaid 'upon my demand', £200 and £350 to Arbella, 'to be repaid when my lady shall command it'.[11]

That Bess should have become so successful and canny a business-woman, let alone as a woman in her seventies, is remarkable. She did not of course come to it entirely new. During her marriage to Shrewsbury, she had been buying land, in William Cavendish's name, as well as lending money. But widowhood brought independence and freedom to operate on her own terms. Her managing skills were applied to her businesses and estates. She had the good fortune, or good sense, to employ reliable and trustworthy servants, men like Pusey and Harrison who could offer sound advice. And she had William, with his thriftiness and legal training, at her side. Then too, over the years, she had had plenty of opportunity to observe and learn from others, husbands in particular. William Cavendish had made a fortune, and nearly lost it. William St Loe had demonstrated good husbandry. In Shrewsbury, who had struggled to manage his empire and racked up debts in the process, Bess had had an example of how *not* to manage one's affairs. And there were plenty of others – Gilbert Talbot, James Hardwick, Francis Willoughby, Christopher Hatton. Men from whose reckless borrowing, careless spending and grandiose speculating Bess profited.

With Bess at Chatsworth, Hardwick was left in the very capable hands of John Balechouse, who rode over every two weeks, taking the building accounts with him, and receiving a 10s. tip. Balechouse had an annual wage of £2, which seems surprisingly low for someone with his responsibilities, but this was substantially boosted by regular hand-outs from Bess: extra pay for working on 'holydays'; 10s. or 20s. tips for good service; £10 in 1599 simply 'of my goodwill'.[12] His wife too had regular gifts of 10s., and his son James worked with him. Balechouse also had a farm, within walking distance of Hardwick, at

Ault Hucknall, and his own room in the Old Hall, which he probably used as a kind of office. Around 1598, he built the New Inn – the Hardwick Inn today – at the entrance to the park, which was taken over by his son after his death. He was a highly skilled painter, but perhaps more importantly he acted as a foreman and overseer of the building work, and he was trusted to make important decisions in Bess's absence.

In February 1594, twenty turret windows were hewn, at which point Balechouse, taking a long, hard look at the turrets, Hardwick's crowning glory, decided that they needed some extra height and reported as much to Bess. On 20 April, John Rhodes was paid 'for the heightening of eight windows for two of the turrets upon the leads, viz for every window 25 foot at 4 and half d the foot'. By September, all the turrets had been raised by an extra pane of glass, adding just over six feet. Aesthetically this was doubtless the right decision, but the ratio of glass to wall brought structural problems for future generations, requiring much pinning and propping. Large windows tend to undermine walls, an eventuality that Smythson had tried to address by using the turrets as buttresses. However, the turrets themselves were weakened by their expanses of glass, and five of the six have no interior supporting walls; instead they are supported by concealed relieving arches to allow for the window bays on the top floor.

Glass had been manufactured in England since the thirteenth century, though of an inferior quality to that made in France, but it was transformed after 1567, when Jean Carré obtained a patent to make window glass in the Weald and brought over glass-makers from Lorraine and Normandy. By the 1590s, glass-making techniques were greatly improved and, as long as there were sufficient supplies of fuel, relatively straightforward, though most builders bought their glass ready-made, from the Weald in the south-east, or from Staffordshire in the Midlands.[13] For Hardwick, however, Bess, who had abundant timber, set up her own glassworks at South Wingfield, where she also had an ironworks, both under the management of Sylvester Smith.

Sixteenth-century glass was not completely clear, being mottled and greenish in colour, and windows were heavily leaded, which is why at a house like Hardwick, views were more readily admired from the roof or the loggias. But Hardwick's top-floor rooms would still have been flooded with light.

The heightening of the turrets was not the only alteration to Smythson's plan during the course of the building – changes were also made to the loggias and the stairs. Smythson had designed a loggia, or colonnade, to run right around the outside of the house. This was unusual – loggias, a classical feature, were more commonly found in interior courtyards, as at Burghley or Theobalds. At Hardwick they were clearly intended, despite the lack of balustrade, to be used as walks or viewing platforms accessed by doors on the first floor. In the summer of 1593, it was decided to abandon the side loggias (the rough stone where they were to be attached can still be seen), though it wasn't until 1595 that the redundant doors were blocked – Rhodes was paid 'for hewing 40 foots ashlar to make up two doors where the walks should have been'. In total, four doors leading onto the side loggias were blocked. The loggias may well have been abandoned to allow more light into the ground-floor rooms, but equally they may have simply not pleased Bess, who would hardly have used the ground floor herself.[14] Hardwick, entirely encased within a loggia, would have looked a very different house.

Two staircases – the 'great stone stairs' and the 'lesser stone stairs' – thread their way through the house, from the great hall to the top floor, emerging, in the case of the 'great' stairs, at the entrance to the High Great Chamber, and the 'lesser' at the north turret. According to Smythson's plan, however, the 'lesser' stairs would have come out into, and thus broken up, the long gallery. To avoid this, their course was altered in November 1594. What would have been a landing now became a small paved dining room, which was used by Bess and her ladies. Was Smythson consulted about these changes to his original plan – the turrets, the loggias, the stairs? Possibly, but Bess would certainly have felt no obligation to do so – Smythson had none of the status of an architect today, he was simply a draughtsman – and Bess and Balechouse between them were quite capable of making their own design decisions.

Bess returned to Hardwick in September 1594, in time to see the last of the twenty-four newly heightened turret windows set. By November 1594, the Yates brothers had completed their bargain for the roof, including the turrets, for £50. This meant that the scaffolding, which remained in place on sixteenth-century building sites for longer than you might expect because lime mortar was so slow to dry, could finally be removed and work could start on the loggias along the east and west fronts. In the spring of 1595, columns for the loggias were hewn, the plastering of the interiors began and John Mercer, a particularly skilled plasterer, put up the cornice in the gallery.

That year also saw Thomas Accres start work at Hardwick. Accres had long been known to Bess – he was at Chatsworth in 1576 on 5d a day and may well have gone on to Worksop, if Bess had acceded to Shrewsbury's request for him.[15] Between 1584 and 1588, he was at Wollaton, and after that he disappears from the record, most likely to some other Midlands house. By May 1595, he was at Hardwick, working with an apprentice, Luke Dolphin, and cutting the coat of arms over the entrance, many times renewed since. Accres brought his wife and family with him, lived on a rent-free farm and received a half-yearly wage of £6 13s. 4d (wages were paid biannually, at midsummer and Christmas). Apart from the coat of arms, the marble overmantel in the state bedchamber, and possibly those in the long gallery, we can't be certain what he was responsible for at Hardwick, but much of the marble work must have been his, and he was clearly highly valued by Bess, with the use of a ground-floor 'chamber' in which to work, and the chilly luxury of a turret room in which to 'lie'.

Accres and Abraham Smith were by far the most skilled and highly paid of the craftsmen working on the New Hall. Smith had been working on the Old Hall for several years, carving many of the great overmantels. By 1592, he, like Accres, was receiving a half-yearly wage of £6 13s. 4d, together with the income from *his* rent-free fifty-five-acre farm at Ashford, near Chatsworth and the blackstone quarries. Blackstone was used extensively in the New Hall, in fireplaces and overmantels, dragged to Hardwick by oxen – their driver received 2s. in 1594 for the oxen's grass and his own supper. Bess was well supplied, so much so that she gave Lord Cobham blackstone for his buildings in 1596.[16]

Smith carved some of the cartouches on the exterior of the New Hall, Bess's coat of arms (now vanished) on the east front, the stone around the great hall fireplace, and the 'terms' (figures) supporting the overmantel in Bess's bedchamber. It was also probably Smith, with assistants, who modelled at least some of the plasterwork frieze in the High Great Chamber. There were of course other masons at work: William Griffin hewed and laid the paving for the great hall and carved the hall screen (for £6), the balustrade on the chapel landing, the fireplace in Bess's withdrawing chamber and, together with James Adams, the columns for the loggias; Henry Nayll and Richard Mallory were responsible for the eighteen chimney shafts and the balustrade around the roof. But which of them carved the outsize 'ES's, each taking six days? We don't know.

Bess was an exacting employer: unreliable workers got short shrift; poor workmanship had to be put right. When in 1595 she was dissatisfied with the whitewashing of the walls, the plasterer was told that they must be 'whited' at his own charge (once plastered, walls were whitewashed using special white lime that came ready-burnt from nearby Crich; impurities in the lime resulted in an uneven colour). In September 1594, Bess complained to Richard Bagot, a sheriff and justice of the peace, about a 'lewd workman Tuft who hath dealt very badly and lewdly with me'. This was Richard Tuft, a slater, who had been working with the Yates brothers but had absconded before completing the job. He had, wrote Bess, 'greatly disappointed me and hindered my works.'[17]

William Bramley, a joiner, who was responsible for much of the panelling in the Old and New Halls, was also unsatisfactory. In October 1595, the panelling of the Hill Great Chamber in the Old Hall was pronounced as in 'many things yet imperfect', though Bramley had promised 'to mould them perfect'. He was in trouble again in January 1599, when he had to put right shoddy work in the New Hall's High Great Chamber: 'Bramley is to take up the window sills and a piece of the selling [panelling] in the great chamber at his own charges, to mend it as fair as conveniently he may.' But in the main, he must have been competent enough, since he worked continuously up until 1600, not just panelling, but making tables and benches and 'two little chairs' for Bess's grandson, her 'sweet James'.[18]

Yet if Bess was a hard taskmaster, she also believed in the value of praise and rewards for good work: in 1595, she rewarded Accres 'for the making of an engine for the sawing of blackstone' with 10s. The 'engine' was a form of water wheel, for the sawmill, and a year later, either because it worked so well, or perhaps had been improved, Accres' wife Grace was given 20s. 'in respect of her husband's device of sawing blackstone to buy her a gown withal'.[19] Balechouse was given 20s. when he painted Bess's arms onto the Gideon tapestries, and his wife the same when she sent Bess a basket of wardens.[20] Marriages generally brought a gift: Abraham Smith had 40s. on his marriage; the daughter of Thomas Accres 20s. on hers; and Mrs Cooper, one of Bess's ladies, was given £50 when she married Rowland Harrison.[21]

Bess's largesse went beyond her employees. The hot, dry summers of 1592 and 1593 gave way to a series of exceptionally wet and storm-ridden years – harvests failed, the price of wheat rocketed, and thousands starved. Bess, whose own revenues were down 25 per cent, did what she could.[22] Most weeks, 20s. were distributed among 'the poor about Hardwick'; sometimes they had money to buy winter coats. In the particularly cold winter of 1595, masons 'and others about Hardwick' were given 'a dish of meat' every day for the twelve days of Christmas. At Christmas 1600, the poor at Heath, Hucknall and

Tibshelf had £3, as well as beef, bread, beer and pease.[23] Those who appeared at the gates of Hardwick with an offering of some kind – 'a poor woman' who brought cakes, 'a poor boy' who brought a mallard – never left without a few pennies.

The rains would have made building difficult too. Just as lime mortar was slow to dry, so too were the lime ash floors – lime ash was mixed with water and laid on hay, over rushes nailed to the lathes and joints – on Hardwick's upper storeys. Once dry, the floors could be polished – much like concrete – but how that was ever achieved over a succession of wet summers and cold winters, with no source of heat but a fire, is hard to imagine. This is probably one reason why, while the basic construction of a sixteenth-century house was relatively quick, the finishing of its interior could be very lengthy indeed.

By 1595, work was going on outside the house as well as in: the building of walls around the orchards and courts; paving and fencing; a partridge house; 'corner turrets' in the entrance court; a turret originally intended as a banqueting house but turned into a still house in the north orchard; a gatehouse with gates and six great locks, made from Bess's iron; and a 'great gate' leading out of the gardens, hewn by 'Cutbeard the mason'.[24] We don't know what Hardwick's gardens looked like, but they were neither so large nor so elaborate as those at Chatsworth.

The end, however, was in sight. March 1596 brought the last payment of John Rhodes's bargain; in May, Bess's withdrawing chamber, on the first floor, was panelled; by October, the plastering was done. In the household accounts for the week ending 27 March 1597 comes the following entry: 'Given to Mr Smythson the surveyor 20s. and to his son 10s.'[25] It's possible that this was payment for some kind of actual surveying work undertaken by Smythson, but more likely that 'surveyor' was used loosely, in the sense of designer. Twenty shillings was Bess's standard tip; it sounds as though, with the New Hall nearing completion, Smythson had ridden north from Wollaton, bringing his son John* with him, to view the realisation of his 'platt', and had been rewarded by a delighted Bess.

For all her identification with Penelope, Bess did not find patience easy. After seven years of building, she must have longed to get into her house. At the very least, she was determined to have her own rooms – her withdrawing chamber and bedchamber – ready. The summer of 1597 saw a surge of activity: the completion of the glazing, the entrance court wall, the outside privies and the hall paving, the panelling of the great hall, and the window alcoves and door of Bess's bedchamber.

Work would continue on the New Hall for another few years, but it was habitable. And Bess had waited long enough. On 4 October, she was triumphantly played into her house by four musical members of her household – John Dodderidge (also known as John Good), James Starkey, the household chaplain – both of whom would become embroiled in Arbella's schemes – Francis Parker, a gentleman servant, and Richard Abrahall, whose mother had been one of Arbella's ladies.† They received 20s., with another £3 distributed to those whom Bess felt to be deserving.

---

* John Smythson trained, like his father, as a mason before graduating to architectural work. It's often difficult to distinguish between the work of father and son. Both Smythsons may, for example, have produced designs for Charles Cavendish's unfinished house at Kirkby-in-Ashfield, and Shireoaks in Derbyshire. John was responsible for parts of Welbeck Abbey. His greatest achievement is Bolsover Castle.
† Starkey, Dodderidge and Parker were versatile musicians – in 1601, they received 20s. for their singing (Devonshire MSS, Chatsworth, HM/8, f.150).

20.

'HOUSHOLD STUFF'

Few letters, to or from Bess, survive from the late 1590s, reflecting, perhaps, a period of relative calm as she settled into her new house. The 'quiet' she had longed for. A time for taking stock. She had built a house to glory in, a house to be wondered at, a house, above all, that proclaimed just how far she had come, from Derbyshire squire's daughter to Dowager Countess. In the place of her father's ramshackle, unremarkable manor stood not one but two very large, very grand and, in the case of the New Hall, architecturally thrilling houses, financed and built by Bess herself.

She no longer needed her day labourers, who were dismissed, but, as with all building projects, work dragged on – rooms that needed finishing, work that needed to be redone, repairs that needed to be made. Key craftsmen were retained: John Balechouse, Thomas Accres, Abraham Smith, Richard Snidall, William Bramley and John Mercer. Over the next few years, the Low Great Chamber, the long gallery, the state withdrawing chamber and the High Great Chamber were panelled; Balechouse stained the cloth hangings for the chapel, painted the frieze in the long gallery, the plasterwork in the High Great Chamber and Bess's arms on felted wool, covering over those of Christopher Hatton on the Gideon tapestries, which were hung in July 1598. Yards of sweet-smelling rush matting for the gallery floor came from Shropshire and Leicestershire, at 4d per yard, stitched together with 'pack thread' (rush matting still covers Hardwick's floors). Bramley made a table of marble and blackstone, and sluices for the fish ponds that Bess had dug below the house, Mercer mended windows and stairs, paling (fencing) was put up around the orchard and park, Snidall replaced glass in the turrets and cellars.[1]

The first letter that we have written by Bess from the New Hall is to the Earl and Countess of Shrewsbury in February 1598. She had been 'exceedingly troubled' to hear of Mary's 'sickness' and asked anxiously after her and the 'three jewels', her granddaughters. She herself had been 'troubled with a cold' at Christmas and then 'much grieved' for her 'daughter Cavendish' – Anne Cavendish, William's wife, who had died after giving birth to a son, James – but she was now well and took 'the air often abroad'. 'I desire that I may some times hear from you', she finished, 'both how you do have your healths, and when you mean to come into the country, this air is better for you both than London, and especially for you sweetheart after your ague.'[2] This is an affectionate letter, though it's clear enough that there had been little in the way of communication between Bess and the Shrewsburys, a breakdown of relations that went back to Gilbert's recalcitrance when it came to paying Bess's jointure and his continued appropriation of lands that, as Bess maintained, rightfully belonged to her sons. Gilbert had long ceased writing his mother-in-law newsy letters from London; Bess, as in the letter above, tried to stay on some kind of terms with Mary (she gave her £100 in 1599 and £5 to each of the 'three jewels'), but privately she seethed.

When it came to championing her cause at court and seeking redress in matters such as the payment of her jointure, Bess had always turned to Burghley, who – this a credit to his gifts of diplomacy – had somehow managed to steer a course between the warring Shrewsburys. In August 1598, Burghley died, aged seventy-seven, a very great blow for the Queen, who visited him during his last days at his house on the Strand and spoon-fed him broth, but a loss for Bess too. Now she could only look to Burghley's son and heir, Robert Cecil, who had all his father's ruthlessness but no particular loyalty to his father's old friend.

While we don't know how Bess *felt* about Hardwick, we do know something about how she lived there. The household accounts for the 1590s illuminate daily life – the comings and goings of servants and neighbours, the buying of foodstuffs, fabric and plate, the loans made and lands purchased, the sales of cattle and sheep, the ongoing work in the house and gardens. Blue cloth was bought to make livery cloaks and caps; new shoes came from Chesterfield; Gilbert Talbot, in a rare conciliatory moment, sent a 'fat stag'; a neighbour sent three apricot trees; another artichokes and flowers for planting out; Bess's Pierrepont son-in-law sent oysters; the carrier brought a portrait of the Queen, commissioned by Bess, from London; a woman brought plums; labourers started 'grubbing' around the fish ponds; a bull, oxen, steers and wethers were all delivered; 'one that brought plovers' was given 6d; an Anthony Glossop, who brought partridges, had 2d a bird; Sir Thomas Stanhope, who evidently didn't include Bess in his feud with Gilbert, sent two salmons; a great many consignments of 'red deer pies' (venison pasties) went up to London; yet more plate was bought, and gold fringe, lawn, velvet, taffeta and lace to make furnishings and clothes.

There would have been plenty of home-grown, -reared and -made food and drink at Hardwick, from the home farm, the gardens, the bakehouse and the brewery, but shopping needed to be done. William Jenkinson, the clerk of the kitchen, was sent to Hull to buy herrings, salt salmons, oysters, stockfish, sturgeon, salad oil, sprats, eels, hops, bay salt, 'a topknot' of figs, sack, 'gasgone' wine, hogsheads of claret, firkins of soap, cod and sprats, all of which were taken by boat, on the River Trent, to Stockwith, then up the River Idle to Bawtry, then on by wagon to Worksop before finally reaching Hardwick. From Stourbridge Fair – one of the largest fairs, held in September outside Cambridge – came ling, stockfish (this was dried and generally a poor man's fish – useful for feeding servants perhaps), soap, corks and candlewicks. While in London, Timothy

Pusey bought imported goods – pepper, cinnamon, nutmeg, sugar loaves, ginger and currants. Nearer home, Lenton Fair, outside Nottingham, held over eight days at the feast of St Martin in November, provided fine sewing silk and 'Venice gold' (gold metal thread).

Through the 1590s, Bess's household stood at between sixty and seventy, including those craftsmen kept permanently on the payroll like Accres, Smith and Snidall. Most servants apart from Bess's ladies, and the laundry and nursery maids, were male and the fact that many remained in her service for years bears testament to their good treatment. Bess's insistence on justice, as regarded her own affairs, extended to those dependent on her – she was quite prepared to defend the interests and fight the causes of her employees. Back in 1576, for instance, she had written to Lord Thomas Paget, who was presiding over the trial of one of her servants, Robinson. Robinson was accused of murder, but, insisted Bess, he was innocent of all charges.[3] When John Clarkson, a labourer at Hardwick, was 'robbed', he was given 10s., and John Balechouse's wife had 20s. when she suffered similarly.[4]

Bess looked after her own, be they servants or family, so long, that is, as they showed themselves deserving. John Dodderidge (Good), a gentleman servant, with the lease of a farm, and 'Hatfield of Alton', a bailiff, had 40s. and £5 a year respectively, to pay for their sons' schooling. John Hardwick, the illegitimate son of Bess's brother James, was always treated kindly: he had a £40 annuity, £5 to buy sheep in 1594, and a year later a loan of £8, apparently without security. Bess's younger half-sister Margaret was regularly given 20s. Anne Baynton, Bess's step-daughter by William Cavendish, who had married Sir Henry Baynton, had £20 a year. And who was Mary Norton, who enjoyed a substantial £100 annuity? We can't be sure.* But Bess made a clear distinction between rewards for good service and charitable

---

* Margaret St Loe, Sir William St Loe's daughter by his first marriage, married a Thomas Norton. Could Mary have been her daughter? Was Bess trying to make amends for depriving her stepdaughters of their inheritance?

handouts: a servant called Gurney was given 40s. 'at her going away, not for good service but for charity'. George Kniveton, Bess's nephew, whom she had taken into her household, proved unsatisfactory and had to be dismissed. However, he left with an extremely generous £600, 'not in respect of his services but for his mother's sake over above his wages at his go—' and here Bess corrected herself: 'my putting him away'.[5]

The impact and drama of Hardwick's interior lies in the use of space and proportion – the turns and sweeps of the wide, shallow steps of the stone stairs, passing through light and shadow, leading you upwards towards the astonishing, profligate and entirely impractical expanses of the High Great Chamber and the long gallery. Decoratively, the interior is fairly restrained – the exception being the monumental marble and blackstone overmantels.* There is no inlaid panelling, no plasterwork ceilings (that in the long gallery was probably put in later, by William Cavendish), no heraldic glass. Such restraint may have been due to Bess's dislike of excess, more ingrained now with age, but equally it may simply have been a lack of suitable craftsmen.

Where Bess did not hold back was in her deployment of textiles and soft furnishings – hangings, tapestries, carpets, cushions, uphol- stered chairs and stools. Some of these had been brought, or removed by William Cavendish, from Chatsworth (the Virtues and Liberal Arts hangings), some acquired in London (the Gideon, Abraham and Tobias tapestries), some from further afield – 'a quilt of India stuff', Turkish carpets, silk damask from China for backing cushions (a pair survive, of 'crimson satin embroidered with strawberries and worms with blue silk fringe and tassels and lined with blue damask').[6] There's no evidence that Bess herself was directly engaged in trade with the

---

* The 6th Duke of Devonshire described the Green Velvet Room as a 'wilderness of a bedroom, with a quarry of marble in one corner'.

Far East, but she had had access to its spoils via Shrewsbury, she had sent Henry Cavendish to Constantinople, and William Cavendish was involved in the founding of the East India Company in 1600, subscribing £200 to its inaugural voyage and receiving a ton and a half of pepper in return.[7]

Hardwick's interiors are remarkably unchanged, though little of the original Elizabethan furniture survives and Bess's huge collection of plate has entirely vanished. Also, and crucially, lost are colour and light. Today, Hardwick's windows are shrouded, in the interests of conservation, and paintwork, tapestries and hangings have faded.* Traces of brightly coloured plasterwork remain, but the overall effect is muted and sombre. However, we have only to look to the inventory of the contents of Chatsworth and Hardwick Old and New Halls, made in 1601 as an adjunct to Bess's will, to get a sense of the brilliancy of Elizabethan Hardwick. The 'houshold stuff' in each and every room is carefully listed – the inlaid tables, the Turkey carpets, the hangings, the gold and silver plate, the beds and chairs and stools and long cushions gorgeously upholstered in cloth of gold and silver, in mulberry, orange, purple and green velvets, in watchet (pale blue) satin, in crimson damask, all fringed and tasselled and spangled, and laid about with gold twist and silver lace.[8] A house of shimmering light and colour.

At Hardwick, a mini court revolved around Bess, its rituals shaped, indeed enforced, by the house's stratified interior. On the ground floor, the great hall was a place of noise and bustle, where lower and outdoors servants, and whichever of Bess's craftsmen were working, milled about, ate at long tables and benches and warmed themselves by the fire. Also here were rooms for Jane Kniveton, Bess's half-sister, and William Cavendish, and a nursery for William's children. But in the

---

* The Virtues hangings are in the process of being restored – reds, greens and golds once more vivid and glowing against a black and white velvet background.

main, the ground floor, and basement, housed the service rooms: kitchen, 'surveying place' (serving area), between the kitchen and hall, where food was set out, pantry, buttery, dry larder, pastry, scullery, wine cellars and boiling house (here, the hard graft of cooking took place, using ten spits, a grid-iron, brass pans, chopping and mincing knives and a cleaver). The Old Hall's brewhouse, bakehouse, wash-house, dairy, slaughterhouse and chandler's house also serviced the New. Lower servants weren't provided with bedchambers and simply bedded down wherever they could, all over Hardwick, within calling distance (this before the invention of the bell). Throughout the house were bedsteads 'to turn up like chests' and mattresses, feather beds, bolsters and blankets, tucked into corners or stored in pallets. The night darkness would have been thick with the rustling and shifting, the sighing and snoring of sleeping servants.

Upper servants slept in the Old Hall, but ate in the New Hall's Low Great Chamber on the first floor, which also functioned as a kind of common room, a place for sitting about, gossiping and card-playing, while Bess, her ladies – Mrs Digby, Mrs Cooper, Mrs Skipwith and Mary Steward – and Arbella used the 'little dining chamber' created from a landing when the course of the stairs was altered. At the southern end of the first floor were Bess's rooms: a withdrawing chamber and bedchamber, with an adjoining maid's room and, beyond that, a room for a gentlewoman.

For everyday purposes Bess kept to her first-floor rooms, emerging for a walk along the colonnades perhaps, a coach drive in the park, a visit to neighbours or an inspection of a new property. Days began and finished early: breakfast, a simple meal of manchet and beer, was followed by lunch at 11 a.m., and supper at 5 or 6 p.m. Bess received family, visitors and employees in her withdrawing chamber: William Cavendish come to discuss further acquisitions of land and property; Charles with news of his building projects; grandchildren, for whom there were 'two little chairs'; Timothy Pusey reporting on Bess's various business affairs; William Reason bringing rent money and news of troublesome tenants; John Balechouse seeking approval for work in the house; Edward Whalley reporting on ongoing legal suits; Rowland Harrison bringing the household accounts; William Jenkinson come to collect the money to pay the weekly household bill (generally between 17s. and 22s.); neighbours begging for favours or loans or help in brokering a marriage.[9]

Today, Bess's bedchamber seems surprisingly small, especially given the quantity of furniture with which it was crowded, but originally it was probably larger. Equally surprising is the overmantel, supported by two naked figures – the 'terms' carved by Abraham Smith. There is more nudity above the mantel in the shape of chubby putti, Adam and Eve cavorting astride a rope, and the head of a Hardwick stag with a long, red, lascivious tongue. It's playful, sensual and oddly anarchic, and unlike all the other Hardwick overmantels, there are no arms – not entirely what you might expect for a woman in her late seventies with a reputation for severity.

Besides two beds, one for Bess and one for Arbella, there was an upholstered chair, several stools and long 'quitions' (cushions), a looking glass, an hourglass, fire irons, an iron chest and five trunks for storing valuables. 'Two pieces of tapestry hangings with person-ages and forest work' hung on the walls, and 'two foot carpets of turkie worke' (a knotted pile fabric, made in England, as opposed to imported 'Turkey carpets') lay on the floor.[10] However, Bess's bedchamber doubled as an office and counting-house. She had one large and two small leather-covered desks and 'a little desk to write on', and, for storing gold and silver coins, 'two trussing coffers bound with iron', with three further 'little coffers' and three 'flat coffers', which may have been used for jewels as well as money (in the maid's room were four more iron coffers, brass weights and scales). The New Hall had close-stools – luxury chamber pots, with box-like seats and hinged lids – rather than garderobes; Bess had hers in a tiny room off her bedchamber, tastefully covered in blue and white cloth, with a red and black silk fringe, and equipped with three pewter basins.

When not in use, the second floor could be easily shut off, but on formal occasions, and for important guests, it came into its own. The great suite of state rooms – High Great Chamber, long gallery, withdrawing chamber and best bedchamber – was for show, expressly designed to astonish and awe. We don't know how much entertaining went on at Hardwick – there's a sense of retreat on Bess's part by the late 1590s, of her choosing to lead a retired life at Hardwick, removed from London and court, of concentrating her energies on local affairs, on consolidating her empire and planning for its future. Which is not to say that she wouldn't have relished showing off her house. Approach and anticipation were all – Hardwick reveals itself slowly. Guests, having passed through the gatehouse and the court, would have come into the great hall, a modest enough entrance, giving little hint of what was to come. From the hall they would have climbed the stairs, winding upwards, emerging at the door of the High Great Chamber, a cathedral of a room, a room to make you catch your breath.

The glory of the High Great Chamber is the three-dimensional plaster frieze depicting the court of Diana and woodland hunting scenes. As at Theobalds and in the Forest Great Chamber in the Old Hall, real tree trunks and branches were nailed to the wall, then plastered over. It's fantastic and fantastical: boar and deer mingle with more exotic creatures – unicorns, camels, elephants, lions. The frieze is probably the work of Abraham Smith and his men, who would of course have never seen such animals and looked to Flemish prints and woodcuts.* Once finished and dried, the plasterwork was painted, in 1599, by Balechouse, in vivid reds and greens and yellows.[11]

Here meals were served in great splendour and according to strictly prescribed ceremony. Food, following a similar progression to guests, was carried (rapidly cooling) from the 'surveying place' by the kitchen,

---

* The hunting scenes are taken from engravings by Philips Galle, after designs by Johannes Stradanus, first published in 1578 (Wells-Cole, p.270).

Allegorical figure of Architecture, from the Liberal Arts hangings, *c.* 1580

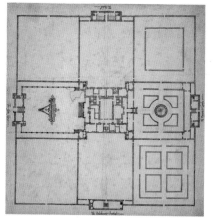

Smythson's plan for the house,
gardens and courts at Wollaton

Wollaton Hall

Smythson's design for a hall screen at Worksop

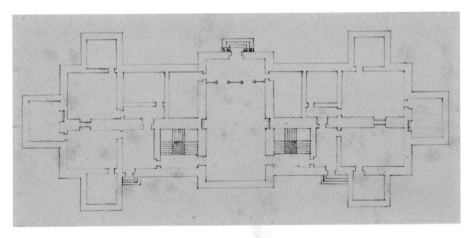

A variant plan, by Smythson, for Hardwick's ground floor,
showing the 'lesser' stairs in their original position

Hardwick, north elevation, 1831 sketch, with the ruins
of the Old Hall on the right

Long gallery at Hardwick, 1839, watercolour by David Cox

Detail of the plasterwork frieze of the court of Diana, in the High Great Chamber

William Cavendish, 1576,
1st Earl of Devonshire

Arbella Stuart, aged two, 1577,
commissioned by Bess

Gilbert Talbot, 7th Earl of Shrewsbury

Mary Talbot, Countess of Shrewsbury

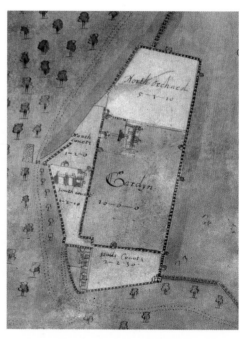

The saucy overmantel in
Bess's bedchamber

William Senior's map of Hardwick, 1610,
showing the Old and New Halls and gardens

Hanging showing Faith (looking rather like Elizabeth I) and Muhammad,
made from 15th-century ecclesiastical vestments collected by William St Loe

Smythson's drawing of Owlcotes, Bess's final house

Bess's silver livery and almshouse badge,
with a countess's coronet

Smythson's design for Bess's tomb,
All Saints' Church, Derby

Bess fingering her pearls, 1590s, attributed to Rowland Lockey

through the hall, where all stood to attention and the gentleman usher, carrying a rod, called for silence, then up the stairs to the High Great Chamber. Having dined, guests would adjourn to the withdrawing chamber, or the long gallery, so the High Great Chamber could be cleared, for music perhaps, or a play. The Queen's players came at least twice to Hardwick, in 1593 and 1600, performing, in all likelihood, Shakespeare (they might also have used the great hall, with Bess watching from the gallery above). On other occasions the players of Admiral Lord Thomas Howard, Lord Ogle, the Earl of Huntingdon and the Earl of Pembroke all performed. And there was plenty of music. William Cavendish was a music-lover, regularly buying song books, by such as Thomas Tallis and William Byrd, books of madrigals and sheet music in London.[12] Bess had competent musicians amongst her own household, but those belonging to the Earls of Rutland and Essex played, as did the waits (singers) of Nottingham, Lincoln, Derby and Newark.

The ceiling of the withdrawing chamber was lowered in the eighteenth century to create rooms for servants, but in Bess's day it was as high as that of the other state rooms, and from its walls loomed almost life-sized heroines from the Ancient World – Penelope, Cleopatra, Lucretia, Zenobia and Artemisia – the five Virtues hangings.[*] The withdrawing chamber, intended to function as a very grand waiting room, had little in the way of furniture, apart from a splendid carved walnut table, brought from Chatsworth, along with some stools and long cushions. In the adjoining best bedchamber hung the second set of appliqué hangings, showing a virtue and its opposite vice. Here there was a magnificent bed with a valance of cloth of gold and silver and 'six curtains of blue and red satin striped with gold and silver and laid with gold lace about the edges and a gold twist down the seams and fringed about with gold fringe'.

---

* The Abraham tapestries were used as a substitute set.

The roof at Hardwick, as at Longleat or Burghley or Wollaton, functioned as a kind of extra storey, a place for eating dessert (in the south turret's banqueting room), for strolling, viewing, even sleeping. The four middle turrets, all with fireplaces, were evidently intended as bedchambers, though only one was furnished as such, and this very grandly, with white damask and mulberry velvet embroidered hangings and a bed with a black velvet valance embroidered with Hardwick stags and Talbot hounds. It would have been a romantic but fantastically cold room to sleep in, despite four curtains of 'tufted sacking' for the windows and a great many blankets and quilts. The remaining turrets were simply used for storage, piled with feather beds, mattresses, pewter-ware and kitchen utensils.

Bess's building days were not quite over. Besides ongoing work on the New Hall and Owlcotes, and repairs to the Old, she began building almshouses in Derby in 1597. A bargain was drawn up with Hall, a carpenter, 'for the setting, squaring, framing, rearing and perfect finishing of all the timber work for the almshouse at Derby', as well as bargains with a mason and a slater.[13] By 1599, the almshouses, now nearing completion, were kitted out with blankets, sheets, shovels, tongs, iron candlesticks, brass pots, pewter dishes, skillets, cups and spoons.[14] The first twelve residents (eight men and four women) moved in a year later; each was given a livery of Cavendish blue, and every year thereafter three yards of blue cloth with which to make new livery, a silver 'ES' badge, and 2s. 6d per week.[15] In May 1601, some kind of building work restarted at Chatsworth too – John Mercer, the Plumtree brothers, carpenters and stone-getters were all employed for several months.[16]

Owlcotes, though a good deal smaller than Hardwick, took much the same time to build. In 1599, Bess gave William Cavendish £200 'for the full finishing', and a year later it was, finally, finished.[17] In October 1600, John Dodderidge was paid for installing bedsteads, furnishing rooms and matting the gallery.[18] William, however, never made Owlcotes his home. After the death of his first wife in 1598, he preferred to remain at Hardwick. Owlcotes became a kind of satellite house, used occasionally by William and Bess herself, sometimes as a staging post en route to Chatsworth, sometimes to temporarily house a recalcitrant granddaughter (Arbella), sometimes as a refuge for William's second wife Elizabeth, when she wished to escape her mother-in-law.[19]

Bess supported Charles Cavendish's building projects too. Charles had a Derbyshire home, Stoke Manor, but in 1597 he started building a house at Kirkby-in-Ashfield, a few miles from Hardwick, towards which Bess contributed £400. It's possible that Robert Smythson provided plans for Kirkby, as he did for several houses belonging to members of the Talbot and Cavendish families during the 1590s, not just Owlcotes, and Pontefract (for Edward Talbot), but, also for Charles, the never-built Slingsby, on a moated island in Yorkshire, and Welbeck Abbey, which Charles leased from Gilbert Talbot in 1597 and bought ten years later, of which only a small section of Smythson's plan was realised. Plans for Slingsby and Welbeck and for a Pontefract-type house survive.[*20] However, Charles's house at Kirkby came to nothing: while inspecting progress in June 1599, he was attacked by twenty men on horseback, led by Sir John Stanhope, son of Thomas – a flare-up of the old feud. Charles was shot in the leg, and consequently abandoned his semi-built house, later using the stone to build Bolsover Castle.

The new century found the Queen debilitated and depressed. Now sixty-seven, she was suffering from insomnia and migraines; her thinning hair disguised by wigs; her teeth blackened stumps; her complexion destroyed by toxic face creams and whiteners. She was still smarting from the Earl of Essex's insubordination. The previous

---

* Other identifiable houses amongst the Smythson drawings are Blackwell-in-the-Peak, Derbyshire, and Burton Agnes Hall, Yorkshire.

year he'd persuaded her to send him to Ireland, with orders to subdue the Earl of Tyrone. Instead he had made a truce and returned to England, without the Queen's permission, in September, an act of defiance for which he'd been punished by banishment from court.

Bess, on the contrary, though entering her eighth decade, was still in remarkably good health (presumably with the exception of her teeth) and showing little sign of slowing down, especially when it came to further acquisitions of land and property. 'Parsonages and rectories in divers counties' were acquired from the Queen in 1599 for £12,855.[21] In 1600, Hercules Foljambe, a neighbour and recipient of loans, was paid £1,500 for land at Chesterfield, Moorhall and Whittington.[22] Over just one year, between 1602 and 1603, William received £16,916 from Bess, to buy land.[23] These were very substantial purchases. And given the notoriously and fiendishly complicated Elizabethan land laws, such purchases involved lawyers, a team of whom, including Edward Whalley and George Chaworth (a cousin of Bess's), were more or less permanently engaged in pursuing lawsuits brought by or against Bess. The accounts record countless payments (£100 here, £200 there) to be 'laid out' on 'law causes', many of these to do with 'concealments' – the illegal withholding of land.

And many such 'causes' involved Gilbert Talbot. In June 1600, Bess appealed to Robert Cecil: 'I am wronged by those who in reason should seek my comfort. The Earl of Shrewsbury under pretence of a grant of concealed lands, goeth about to overthrow the estate of some lands formerly conveyed to my children and dearly obtained by me and upon great considerations, the matter I have caused to be briefly set down, which my son William Cavendish will present to you.'[24] Cecil seemingly took little action, since four months later, Bess was writing again: Gilbert, she complained, was 'most unconscionably and unnaturally' appropriating lands that belonged not to him, but to Henry Cavendish.[25] In November, William, who was in London, acting as Bess's representative and attending the Star Chamber, where 'concealment' cases were heard, reported on progress, or rather lack of it, since Bess's cases had been postponed. He thanked her 'for the hands of the three little honest folks [his children] subscribed in your Ladyship's letter. I know by James writing where he learned his skill.'[26]

As far as Gilbert was concerned, Bess was wilfully trying to thwart his perfectly legitimate acquisitions of land, and in his own appeals to Cecil, he made no attempt to hide his feelings: 'I perceive my dear good mother-in-law (dear I may justly term her) means quite to overthrow me in the late purchase I made, wherein I am resolved to stand so far as I may justify in honour, conscience and law, the particulars shall be hereafter at large opened unto you and in the meantime I beseech you suspend your judgement notwithstanding all the fair shows that are made on the contrary side.'[27]

The building of the almshouses in Derby was no mere act of charity – by 1601, Bess was thinking of, and preparing for, her own death. There was no question of her taking her place in the Shrewsbury vault at Sheffield, or indeed of joining any husband. She wished to orchestrate her own burial. She commissioned Smythson to design a very splendid tomb, of blackstone and marble, for All Saints church, Derby (now Derby Cathedral). Payments were made to labourers for preparing the site, to stone-getters, and for teams of horses to drag forty loads of stone to Derby; by April 1601, it was 'finished and wanting nothing but the setting up'. Three years later, a vault was added.[28]

In the same year, Bess drew up a will – eleven large, densely written vellum pages. Chatsworth was entailed on Henry Cavendish, while she had ensured that William and Charles were amply provided with land and property; however, her goods and chattels could be distributed as she wished. To William Cavendish went the contents of the Old and New Halls and Owlcotes, and to Henry those of Chatsworth; William's children, Frances, James and William, had £1,000 each; Henry's wife Grace was left 100 angels* to buy a mourning ring, and

---

* An angel was a gold coin, worth 10s.

the Pierrepont grandchildren also had money with which to buy rings; to Arbella, 'my very loving grandchild', went Bess's 'crystal glass trimmed with silver and gilt' and set with lapis lazuli and agates, her sables – one with a gold enamelled head – her pearls and jewels and £1,000; to Bess's daughter Frances went the book, set with stones, given to her by William Cavendish, 'with her father's picture and mine drawn in it'; £1,000 was to be distributed between the servants, who were to have 'meat, drink and lodging' at Hardwick for one month after the funeral; the almshouse residents were to get mourning gowns and 20s. apiece; Anne Baynton, Bess's stepdaughter, was to go on receiving an annual legacy of £5; and to the Queen, who was asked to be good to Arbella, 'the poor orphan', went £200 in gold to buy a cup. Due to the 'unkindness offered me by my son-in-law the Earl of Shrewsbury and my daughter his wife, and likewise my son Charles Cavendish', Mary and Charles received nothing more than Bess's blessing.[29] Subsequently, as beneficiaries rose and fell in favour, the will would be revised.

21

'A SCRIBBLING MELANCHOLY'

—|—

Though Bess had not been to court since 1592, she still had her court informants. One such, Lady Dorothy Stafford, a friend of old, and now the longest serving of the Queen's ladies of the privy chamber, wrote in January 1601 to report on the reception of Bess and Arbella's New Year's gifts to the Queen. Bess had simply given £100, but Arbella had gone to more trouble – 'a scarf or head-veil of lawn cutwork, flourished with silver and silks of various colours', quite possibly worked by Arbella herself, to which the Queen had 'taken an especial liking', although apparently that did not signify any 'especial liking' towards Arbella herself. Bess had not given up hope of a good match for Arbella, and had continued to write to the Queen to that effect, urging 'that she might be carefully bestowed'. However, the Queen, true to form, had refused to commit herself beyond assuring Lady Stafford, vaguely, that 'she would be careful of her'. Her New Year's 'token' for Arbella (a piece of plate) was not, felt Lady Stafford, 'so good as I could wish it, nor so good as her La. deserveth in respect of the rareness of that which she sent unto her Majesty'. It was a case of gift disparity. But Lady Stafford, nervous that she had said too much, begged Bess to keep this to herself.[1]

The Queen, at nearly seventy, was increasingly reliant on artifice – cosmetics, jewels, ever more fantastic frocks – to disguise the ravages of age, and still refusing to nominate a successor. Arbella's claim was no longer taken seriously. Nor was that of Lord Beauchamp – the son of Katherine Grey and the Earl of Hertford – by reason of his illegitimacy and the fact that he'd married a commoner. Philip III of Spain was pushing his half-sister, the Infanta Isabella, but the strongest candidate remained James VI of Scotland. James was the closest blood heir; he was a Protestant; he had not one but two healthy sons; and he was a man – after nearly fifty years of female rule, there was appetite for a king. Robert Cecil, who was secretly corresponding with James, claimed that he was simply acting in Elizabeth's best interests whether she knew it or not: 'If her Majesty had known all I did … her age and orbity, joined to the jealousy of her sex, might have moved her to think ill of that which helped to preserve her.'[2]

After several peaceful years, as Bess settled into and perfected her new house, drama erupted at Hardwick, charted in an avalanche of letters. By 1602, relations between Bess and Arbella had broken down. The 'dearest jewel' and 'loving grandchild' was, at twenty-seven, somewhat tarnished and distinctly less loving. Shortly before his death, the Earl of Shrewsbury had predicted that Arbella 'would bring much trouble to his house by his wife's and her daughter's devices'.[3] He was right, though trouble came thanks to Arbella's own devices.

Bess had certainly treated Arbella liberally – cash, land, jewels, all came her way. In January 1594, she had had £2,000 from Bess and £1,360 from William Cavendish (this was Elizabeth Lennox's £3,000 dowry, finally paid to Arbella with interest).[4] There were the five manors acquired from Francis Willoughby; £500 in 1599 towards buying a 'piece of land' in Lincolnshire and £640 to buy a property at Skegby; £10 for a set of viols; £100 to buy a pearl 'to enlarge her chain'; 'a bone grace with thirty pearls for a coronet', taken out of Bess's 'jewel coffer'.[5] But such gifts carried obligations and only served to bind Arbella more closely.

It was Arbella's misfortune to be educated for sovereignty, but overeducated for her lot. Thanks to Bess, she had had the benefit of a fine humanist education: she could read, write and speak in French and Latin,* she was familiar with Italian, Spanish, Greek and Hebrew, she was almost as skilled a needlewoman as her aunt the Queen of Scots; she was an accomplished viol and lute player; her letters, scattered with biblical and classical allusions, are testament to her scholarship. However, raised with the highest expectations – 'in exile with expectation' as she put it – possibly of a throne, certainly of a great match, Arbella was disappointed of both. At an age when most young women would have been long married, she was leading the life of an unmarried dependant, immured in Derbyshire under the rule of her grandmother. Although she had a room of her own at Hardwick – her 'study' – this could only be accessed via Bess's rooms. She still slept in Bess's bedchamber.

An already combustible situation was made more so by the fact that apart from sharing a very powerful will, grandmother and granddaughter were otherwise two very different, and incompatible, personalities. Where Bess was pragmatic, controlled and prudent, Arbella was romantic, impulsive and reckless. As with Shrewsbury, Bess misjudged a character whose passions were quite alien to her own. Arbella wanted to be able to select her own servants, to see whom she wished, to have 'the company of some young lady or gentlewoman for my recreation and scholars, music, hunting, hawking'. 'Many infants' were able to choose 'their own guardian'; at twenty-seven, she simply wanted the liberty to choose her 'place of abode'.[6] Here was a clever, articulate young woman, desperate for autonomy, longing to 'be my own woman' and to 'shape my own coat according to my cloth'.[7] One way, indeed the only way, to liberate herself from Hardwick, and Bess, was marriage.

---

* In November 1602, William Cavendish drew up an agreement promising his 12-year-old son a rapier, a dagger, an embroidered girdle and a pair of spurs if he spoke Latin until the following Lent Assizes with his cousin Arbella (Devonshire MSS, Chatsworth, H/143.12).

Arbella's choice of groom was curious: sixteen-year-old Edward Seymour, a youth she had never set eyes on. Seymour was the son of Lord Beauchamp and grandson of the Earl of Hertford. For marrying in secret, Hertford and Katherine Grey had been sent to the Tower, where Lord Beauchamp had been born. Arbella was a romantic, and this tale of doomed love, far from warning her off, seemed to exert an irresistible lure. She later claimed that the marriage had initially been proposed by Hertford, who, she understood, had 'desired and well liked' the idea; he had approached Bess through one of her servants, David Owen Tudor, whose son Richard was Arbella's page, but the plan had been rejected by Bess as not having the approval of the Queen. If this was the case, nobody, least of all Hertford or Bess, ever admitted to it. Since a marriage between Seymour and Arbella would unite two, admittedly tentative, claims to the throne, it would indeed be highly unlikely to win the approval, let alone the consent, of the Queen.

To put her plan into action, Arbella needed help. She first appealed to James Starkey, the chaplain at Hardwick and former tutor to William Cavendish's children. Starkey was disgruntled – he had been promised a living by William, which had then been withheld. Arbella offered to help Starkey get his living, and he to deliver letters for her. According to Starkey, Arbella would often burst into tears while 'at her book' and felt that 'she was hardly used ... in despiteful words, being bobbed and her nose played withal'.[8] In the summer of 1602, Starkey left Hardwick and Arbella sent money and jewels to Yorkshire for safe keeping, after Bess had threatened to take them away. Arbella then approached John Dodderidge (Good), an old and trusted servant at Hardwick – he had witnessed Bess's will and Bess had paid for his son's education. Would Dodderidge, asked Arbella, 'go a little way for her'? In fact she wanted him to go a rather long way – as far as London, to deliver a message to the Earl of Hertford. Dodderidge was to say that he was representing Henry and William Cavendish and to request that Edward Seymour come to Hardwick, in disguise, accompanied by some 'grave, ancient man', on the pretext of selling land (this being bait, Arbella calculated, that Bess would be unable to resist). They were to bring with them some form of identification such as 'some picture or handwriting of the Lady Jane Grey, whose hand I know'.[9]

Surprisingly, Dodderidge agreed to this fanciful plan and on Christmas Day 1602 set off for London on a horse provided by Henry Cavendish. He arrived on 30 December, only to be received 'contrary to all expectation'. An alarmed Hertford immediately alerted Cecil, and Dodderidge was marched off to the Gatehouse gaol at Westminster. It was clear enough that all was not well at Hardwick, and this at a moment when the Queen, as her godson John Harington wrote, was in a 'most pitiable state', sunk in 'melancholy', her memory failing, refusing food, unable to sleep, spending her days hunched on cushions on the floor. There was still great uncertainty as to what would happen in the event of Elizabeth's death. Cecil may have been paving the way for James's accession, but James was not recognised by the Queen, nor was he necessarily the popular choice. The support of the Privy Council was no guarantee in itself without the backing of the people, as had been proved by the ill-fated attempt to put Jane Grey on the throne. There was talk of France and Spain favouring Arbella as less objectionable than James. And Arbella's proposal to Edward Seymour alarmed the Queen – she'd become a loose cannon. Sir Henry Brounker, a Queen's commissioner with a reputation for tact and experience, was dispatched to Hardwick.

On the morning of 7 January, Brounker arrived at Hardwick, un-announced. He was taken up to the long gallery, where he found Bess, Arbella and William Cavendish walking. Bess's gallery, at 167 feet, stretching the length of the top floor, was one of the longest in England, only surpassed by Montacute in Somerset and probably by Worksop. Like the withdrawing chamber, it was sparsely furnished (a couple of inlaid tables covered with Turkish carpets, a few chairs and stools, long cushions for the window seats), a room for strolling and admiring the portraits – fewer than there are today – the two great chimney-pieces, with their alabaster figures of Justice and Mercy, carved by Thomas Accres,* and the great thirteen-piece Gideon tapestry. On a January morning the gallery would have been flooded with clear, thin winter light from its wall of east-facing windows, inadequately warmed by two fires, and smelling faintly of grass from the rush matting covering the floor (Bess was fussy about her matting – Arbella commented, sourly, that she and her cousin Mary walked in the adjoining great chamber 'for fear of wearing the mats in the gallery', which was 'reserved' for important guests).[10] Brounker might well have been struck by the gallery, but he had not travelled at speed from London to admire Hardwick's interiors.

For Bess, and Arbella, the sudden appearance of an officer from court must have caused consternation. Brounker began by drawing Bess to one end of the gallery – a long gallery being conducive to confidences – and giving her a letter from the Queen, which, without revealing the whole story, was quite alarming enough to provoke an instant 'change of countenance' and make Bess attempt to fall to her knees (no easy matter for an eighty-two-year-old). Brounker then took Arbella to the other end of the gallery and confronted her. When she denied all, he produced Dodderidge's confession. The following day, Arbella wrote a statement, a nonsensical document – 'confused, obscure and in truth ridiculous', thought Brounker, who asked for another draft. He considered 'her wits were throughout disordered, either through fear of her grandmother or conceit of her own folly'.

Bess, when told of Arbella's proposal to Seymour, took it so badly 'as with much ado she refrained her hands'. In private, with Arbella, she may not have refrained. While sentimental on occasion, she rarely allowed herself to be swayed by sentiment. Justice and Mercy may

---

* Mark Girouard has suggested that the chimney-pieces were designed by Smythson, his only contribution to Hardwick's interiors (Girouard, *Elizabethan Architecture*, p.388).

have graced her fireplaces, but they were not virtues to be practised in the case of an ungrateful and disobedient granddaughter. Bess now wished to be rid of Arbella quite as much as Arbella wished to be rid of Bess. Brounker left Hardwick with a letter from Bess to the Queen, in which she begged that Arbella 'be placed elsewhere, to learn to be more considerate'.[11] Removal, however, did not find favour at court. Cecil and Sir John Stanhope (vice-chamberlain of the royal household, son of Sir Thomas and enemy of Gilbert and Mary Talbot) informed Bess that the Queen chose not to make too much of Arbella's marriage proposal, putting it down to 'base companions' and her own foolishness. Arbella was to be pardoned, and though she should be watched, it was important that she shouldn't be seen to be a prisoner, nor subject to 'any extraordinary restraint'. The Queen could think of no 'other place so fit for her' as Hardwick.[12]

This was not what Bess wanted to hear. 'The bad persuasions of some', she told the Queen, had 'so estranged her [Arbella's] mind and natural affection from me, that she holds me the greatest enemy she hath'. Now far from holding out for a husband worthy of Arbella, *any* husband would do; she had 'little care how meanly soever she were bestowed', as long as it was 'not offensive' to the Queen.[13] Cecil and Stanhope may have argued against 'extraordinary restraint', but Bess was all in favour. Having been informed that Arbella 'could go away at her pleasure and against my will', she employed whatever measures were necessary to ensure that 'she should not'. Bess's 'ancient gentlewomen' became Arbella's guards.[14] Arbella had been sending and receiving letters through her servants. Now her letters – to John Hacker, for example, a servant of Mary Talbot's, asking Mary to come to Hardwick – were intercepted by Bess, who dictated false answers, written by Timothy Pusey, to encourage further correspondence.

Hardwick had become a battleground, as Bess and Arbella squared up to each other, and as with Bess and Shrewsbury, the servants took sides. Bess could deploy her 'ancient gentlewomen', but Arbella had the support of her own 'regiment', as well as that of some of Bess's servants whom, according to Bess, she had 'corrupted', such as John Dodderidge and James Starkey (Starkey was the first casualty – after being interrogated by Cecil's men, he hanged himself). When Arbella sent her page to fetch some books from her room, he wasn't allowed to enter. When she went to ask for Bess's blessing after dinner, she received a 'volley of most bitter and injurious words' and retreated to her chamber, only to be followed by Bess, whereupon 'another skirmish' ensued, accompanied by a 'storm' of threats.[15]

Immured at Hardwick, Arbella grew desperate and turned to invention – a mystery lover, 'a noble gentleman whose name I conceal'. Her romantic hopes were, she wrote, resorting to architectural metaphor, built on rock: 'let the winds and billows and tempests show that though my building be low yet it is not builded upon the sand for then I had been ruined, but like the wise Architect who first draws his platt and after makes an estimate of the charges, giving some allowance more than he thinks will be needful, and then finding himself able to go through cheerfully, sets his workmen to their several works'.[16] Bess had no patience with such fancies – 'what truth there is in this new matter I know not. I have found her to swerve so much from the truth, and so vainly led in the first practice that I cannot give any credit to her'.[17]

Watched by Bess and William Cavendish, Arbella sat 'scribbling' her letters. Letter-writing had become a refuge and a release. Her letters to Brounker, to Bess, to the Queen are immensely long and frequently incomprehensible. Contemporary opinion held Arbella to have lost her wits – 'I think she has some strange vapours to her brain', wrote Cecil in the margin of one of her outpourings – but there was method to her madness. Her longest letter, written to Brounker on 9 March, ran to 7,000 words, and though incoherent in parts, it's also strikingly eloquent, a plea to be heard. She was writing on the second anniversary of Essex's execution for treason (Arbella had always claimed a special relationship with Essex, who had taken her part when she'd been disgraced at court back in 1588): 'they are dead whom I loved, they have forsaken me in whom I trusted ... doth her Majesty favour the Lady Catherines husband [the Earl of Hertford] more than the Earl of Essex friend?.' She was perfectly sensible of Brounker's view that the more she wrote, 'to the less purpose it was', but she offered a persuasive explanation for her writing mania: 'being allowed no company to my liking and finding this the best excuse to avoid the tedious conversation I am bound to, I think the time best spent in tiring you with the idle conceits of my travelling mind till it make you ashamed to see into what a scribbling melancholy (which is a kind of madness and there are several kinds of it) you have brought me'.[18] For Arbella, letter-writing became the only means she had of making sense of her predicament both to herself and to others, of honouring her 'travelling mind'. At times she *was* nonsensical and rambling – 'a kind of madness' – but her later letters, after her departure from Hardwick, are perfectly lucid, indeed concise.

Such was the impasse at Hardwick that both Bess and Arbella begged for Brounker to return. On 21 February, Bess told Cecil that Arbella had been suffering from 'extreme pain of her side', which Bess considered, no doubt rightly, as being all in 'her mind', and that she had now resorted to hunger strike: 'she is so wilfully bent that she has made a vow not to eat or drink in this house at Hardwick or where I am till she may hear from her Majesty'. At the end of her tether, Bess had sent Arbella, accompanied by William Cavendish, to Owlcotes.[19] By 2 March, Brounker and Arbella were back at Hardwick. When questioned as to the identity of her mystery lover, Arbella at first remained silent and then, resorting to farce, came up with a name: James VI. Once again, Bess begged Cecil and Stanhope to remove her granddaughter: 'she is so wilfully bent and there is so little reason in most of her doings that I can not tell what to make of it. A few more such weeks as I have suffered of late will make an end of me.'[20]

But with the Queen steadily sinking – she had now contracted bronchitis – this was a critical moment. If James was to succeed peacefully, it was important to prevent Arbella from causing trouble, or simply drawing attention to herself, especially in London. Brounker and Cecil insisted that she remain at Hardwick, safely out of sight. Arbella, frustrated and with nothing to lose, made one last bid for freedom. Neither Gilbert nor Mary Talbot had come to her aid – Bess made sure of that – and an appeal to Edward Talbot had been swiftly passed on to Cecil, by Edward himself, who wanted no part of Arbella's schemes. However, Henry Cavendish, who always welcomed an opportunity to thwart or irritate his mother, had shown himself more amenable. Despite Bess's vigilance, Arbella managed to communicate with Henry and concoct a plan for her escape.

On 10 March, Henry and Henry Stapleton, a local Catholic recusant priest, attempted to station themselves in the church tower at Ault Hucknall, a mile or so from Hardwick, from where they were to look out for Arbella when she emerged for her daily exercise. But when they failed to get the key for the church from the vicar, and then received a message, brought by Arbella's page Richard Owen and 'old Freake', Bess's embroiderer, that she was unable to walk out, they decided to come to the gates of Hardwick. Bess described what happened next. Arbella wished to speak to Henry, so Bess let him in, with the proviso that he couldn't stay for more than two hours, though 'Master Stapleton' was refused entry because she 'disliked him of long'. It was easy enough for Bess to monitor the comings and goings across the entrance court from her rooms, and when she saw Arbella and Henry approaching the porter's lodge, she had them stopped. Arbella 'asked if she were a prisoner and said she would see and so went to the gates and would have gone out but was not suffered'. She had to content herself with speaking to Stapleton through the gates, before he and Henry departed. Since then, Bess had learned that there were more than forty armed horsemen secreted around Hardwick, at Hucknall and Rowthorne, waiting to spirit Arbella away. Arbella was now forbidden to walk 'abroad' and spent her time 'writing and sending up and down in the country and to London'.[21] Her escape had been foiled, but only thanks to Bess's cool head.

This brought Brounker back to Hardwick for a third time. He arrived on 17 March and interviewed all those involved in the escape plot, except for Henry Stapleton. He finally decided that Arbella must be removed, both for her own sake – 'so settled is her mislike of the old lady' – and for that of Bess, who was growing 'exceeding weary of her charge, beginneth to be weak and sickly by breaking her sleep and cannot endure long this vexation'. The Queen was dying, and it now seemed unwise to leave Arbella in the Catholic heartland of the Midlands; so fearful indeed was William Cavendish that he'd laid in supplies of gunpowder, arms and armour, in case of possible attack.[22] Towards the end of March, Arbella left Hardwick for Wrest Park in Bedfordshire, the home of Henry Grey, Earl of Kent, who was married to Gilbert and Mary's daughter, Elizabeth. Her departure came as a relief to Bess. On 20 March, she added a codicil to her will cutting out both Arbella, a 'loving grandchild' no longer, and Henry, her 'unnatural son'. She could not prevent Chatsworth from going to Henry, but a house without its contents was useless to a poor man. Effectively Bess was preventing Henry from ever living there.

The Queen died peacefully at Richmond Palace in the early hours of 24 March 1603. Later that morning, Robert Cecil, together with his privy councillors, proclaimed James VI King of England, before riding to London to read the proclamation at Whitehall. Whether or not Elizabeth signalled her approval of James in her dying moments is a matter of debate. It made little difference either way. The decision had been made for her. Thanks to Cecil and his behind-the-scenes manoeuvring (a draft of the proclamation had been sent to James on the 19th, the ports had been closed within hours of the Queen's death, and, as had been prearranged, a messenger, bearing a ring as proof of death, had been dispatched to Scotland), James's accession was accomplished with remarkable ease and lack of bloodshed.

In early April, Frances Pierrepont wrote to tell Bess that she had heard that the new King was nearing Berwick, on the border, and that 'all things in the southern parts proceed peaceably, only my Lord Beauchamp is said to make some assemblies'. It was hoped that these would 'suddenly dissolve into smoke, his force being so feeble'.[23] And so they did. On 20 April, James reached Worksop, where he was entertained by Gilbert Talbot. In a state of high excitement at the impending royal visit (Elizabeth had never graced any Shrewsbury property), Gilbert had written to local friends, requesting their 'company' and, always keen to make a saving, adding that he would 'not refuse any fat capons, or hens, partridges or the like'.[24] At Worksop, James enjoyed some fine hunting (one of his great passions, along with young men) in Sherwood Forest, as well as some 'most excellent soul-ravishing music'.[25] Gilbert could congratulate himself.

James was still making his way south when the Queen's funeral took place on 28 April at Westminster. Bess did not attend – the journey to London was by now too long and hard – though the death of the Queen whom she had known for over fifty years, and who was some twelve years her junior, must have been a strange and sombre moment. James had put forward Arbella, his closest living relative, as chief mourner, but Arbella felt that 'since her access to the queen in her lifetime might not be permitted, she would not after her death be brought upon the stage for a public spectacle'.[26]

22

'IT DOTH STICK SORE IN HER TEETH'

By 1603, Bess was eighty-three. Her knees gave her trouble (she kept a 'pair of pullies lined with black taffeta' – knee protectors – in her bedchamber) and, inevitably, given the damp and chill of Hardwick, she suffered from arthritis, but her mental powers, her appetite for business and her energy for feuding – all were undiminished. She was still lending money, still bringing legal suits, still expanding her estates, still adjudicating and advising in the disputes of neighbours and acquaintances and still matchmaking. But given her age, those around her, those hoping for a slice of the cake, watched closely. Bess was, variously, deferred to, grovelled before, resented and feared; the 'olde ladie' behind her back; 'your Ladyship's ever most humble and ready to be commanded', from those looking for favour.[1]

One such was Henry Cavendish, whose fortunes were entirely dependent on Bess. Henry and Grace were living, wretchedly, in gloomy Tutbury, and in desperate straits financially. In reply to a letter from Robert Cecil in April 1603, pleading Henry's case, Bess remained unmoved: 'I wish he had lived so that he were clear of all faults imputed to him … I have been so hardly and unnaturally dealt withal by him and others who I take it specially sought my overthrow.' Since Henry had set out to 'hurt and hinder' her and had conscripted others in his cause – some of them supposedly loyal members of Bess's own household – she begged Cecil's pardon if she declined to come to her son's aid.[2] By behaving so 'unnaturally', by entering into Arbella's schemes, Henry had once again proved himself unworthy of trust and undeserving of help.

It probably came as no surprise to Bess to learn that Henry was implicated in the Bye Plot, one of two plots in 1603 to depose the new King. English Catholics, like Mary Talbot, had high hopes of a new, tolerant regime under James, whose wife after all was a recent convert, who was the son of a Catholic mother (not a consideration that carried much weight with James), and who had not hitherto showed any particular enthusiasm for persecuting Catholics. But although James claimed that he was willing to turn a blind eye to Catholic worship so long as it was 'quiet and decently hidden', religious toleration was not on the cards. Disappointed Catholics started scheming.

The Bye Plot, in July, which involved both Catholics and Puritans, proposed to kidnap James and force him to introduce religious toleration. The more serious Main Plot, a few months later, went further: James was to be killed, along with Prince Henry and Robert Cecil, and Arbella, who was not actually consulted, was to be put on the throne. Once again, freedom of worship for Catholics was the aim. Three of the principal Main Plot conspirators were known to Bess: Henry Brooke, Lord Cobham (son of her old friend, described as 'a most silly Lord, but one degree from a fool'); his brother George – Bess's godson; and Sir Griffin Markham, a Derbyshire neighbour. Cobham had tried to enlist Spanish help, and had written to Arbella, who promptly handed over his letter to the King. When the treason trials took place at Winchester, in November, Henry Cavendish's name came up and he was summoned to court.[3] Henry was exonerated. Not so the conspirators, who were found guilty and sentenced to death, although three, including Lord Cobham and Griffin Markham, received a last-minute reprieve from the King.

Arbella too was cleared of any involvement. Far from wishing to supplant James, she had every reason to be grateful to him. Shortly after his accession, James had written to the Earl of Kent: 'we are desirous to free our cousin the Lady Arbella Stuart from that unpleasant life which she hath led in the house of her grandmother with whose severity and age she, being a young lady, could hardly agree'.[4] Arbella, as she'd long wanted, came to court, with a pension of £800 (somewhat short of the £2,000 she'd hoped for) and a position as carver to the Queen. Court, as she soon discovered, was both ruinously expensive – all the gifts, all the dressing up – and for a serious-minded bluestocking not especially congenial. In letters to Gilbert and Mary, she complained of the lack of courtesy and refinement, the 'everlasting hunting', the tiresome round of entertainments and 'court sports' beloved by James – children's games, for example, played until two or three in the morning.[5] The hectic frivolities of James's court proved just as distasteful as life at Hardwick; one form of imprisonment had merely been exchanged for another.[*]

While Bess remained very much in charge of her affairs, she increasingly looked to William Cavendish, her second son and second-in-command, to take care of day-to-day business. In 1604, William married again, this time Elizabeth Wortley, the widow of a wealthy Yorkshire landowner. Elizabeth, it was said, did not always see eye to eye with her mother-in-law and, as a woman of expensive tastes, would probably not have been delighted by William's rather

---

[*] Arbella's fate was not a happy one. In 1610, in an act of wilful self-sabotage, she secretly, without seeking royal permission, married William Seymour, younger brother of Edward, for which both parties were imprisoned. They escaped the following year and attempted to flee to France. Arbella was recaptured and sent back to the Tower, as was Mary Talbot, who had tried to help her. In 1615, still a prisoner, she died, apparently of starvation.

gloomy bachelor bedchamber on the ground floor of the New Hall.* The newly-weds spent about two thirds of their time in London, where William was much engaged in business on his own and Bess's behalf, as well as, after 1605, with the House of Lords. When in Derbyshire, they stayed at either Owlcotes or Hardwick, but it was the latter that William used as his business headquarters. Next to his bedchamber was an office, and beyond that, the 'Evidence House'. In the early 1600s, this was furnished with 492 drawers, with tasselled pulls, made by William Bramley, while the door was reinforced with tin plate, and iron bars, from Bess's forge at Wingfield, were fitted onto the windows.

Exactly how Bess and William coexisted at Hardwick, not to mention how the Old and New Halls operated together, is a puzzle. It might have been expected that William and Elizabeth would have based themselves in the Old Hall, where they could have had their own suite of very grand rooms. But that was not the case. The Old Hall seems to have been used to accommodate occasional guests and upper servants – John Digby and William Reason, for example, both had rooms there. There's also evidence that it became something of a party house, where, free from Bess's control, a lot of illicit sex and drinking went on (of which more later). William had his own servants at Hardwick, some with wonderfully Shakespearean names – Smout and Nodin – together with Freake, a 'running' footman, who may have been the son of Old Freake, and Newsam the carrier, who was kept busy carting shopping back from London. And he regularly bought foodstuffs – eggs, oatcakes made by 'Millington's wife', and quantities of fish (sole, plaice, herrings, skate, thornback, haddock, crab, lobster,

---

* Once married to Elizabeth, presumably at her urging, William became an extravagant shopper, buying, for example, in 1605, a fine suite of upholstered walnut furniture and expensive furnishing fabrics – 46 yards of crimson damask for £31 – from Sir Baptist Hicks and Thomas Henshaw (Riden (ed.), *Household Accounts*, Part 3, pp. 324 and 402).

turbot) from two fishmongers, Dixon and Boothby.[6] Yet food was apparently cooked in one kitchen, by one set of staff.

If Bess and William's households were to some degree interchange-able, so too were their interests. Henry Travice, William's main man of business, also worked for Bess, and Edward Whalley and George Chaworth, Bess's lawyers, were also used by William. Timothy Pusey reported to both mother and son. In April 1604, he informed William that Bess had agreed to lend one Francis Needham £500, 'upon good security' and for the express purpose of buying a castle; that Jones of Bampton had failed to repay his loan; and that there was 'no good agreement' between Henry and Grace Cavendish – 'he hath charged her to be a harlot to some of his men and named the men to her.'[7] Grace told her brother, Edward Talbot, who passed it on to Bess, that she and Henry felt very 'hardly dealt with', by both Bess and Gilbert – Bess was not prepared to help them unless Gilbert did too, and Gilbert, with huge debts of his own, was neither willing nor able to do so. 'The Earl's jewels and plate are laid to pawn', wrote Edward, 'and there is as many suitors every day at his chamber as at the most noble men in the Court, but they come only to crave their debts.'[8] Bess was fond of Grace, and remembered her in her will, but she remained resolute in her determination not to bail Henry out. A New Year's gift of £20 was as much as he could hope for, as in 1605, when he thanked her for her 'bountiful goodness' and, with a show of abasement, sent some 'poor and homely things', all that 'this place can afford.'[9]

By 1605, Bess, hitherto robust, seemed decidedly less so, as those with a vested interest – those in need of or counting on her money – were quick to note. For Gilbert Talbot and Henry and William Cavendish, much depended on her death: the reversion of Talbot lands that constituted Bess's jointure would provide Gilbert with a badly needed stream of income; Henry still hoped that she might leave him the contents of Chatsworth, or money to relieve his debts; William, the sole executor of her will, was simply anxious to keep as much of her estate as possible to himself, to the exclusion of his siblings.

Since Bess preferred not to communicate with Gilbert, he relied on his own network of supporters and informers to keep him abreast of developments at Hardwick. Derbyshire neighbours like Sir John Harpur and Sir Francis Leake* supplied him with news, while he supplied them with gifts of venison. So from Francis Leake, Gilbert learned that William Cavendish's wife Elizabeth was very sick at Owlcotes and that it was said that 'my old lady and she have had some discontenting speeches'.[10] William took the line of least resistance with Bess, but Elizabeth was possibly less willing to dance to the tune of her powerful mother-in-law.

In February 1605, John Harpur sent Gilbert a bulletin: Bess's 'old infirmity' had returned and 'takes more hold of her as it seems than formerly it hath done'; she hadn't left her chamber for the last month, during which time, with William Cavendish in London, Sir John Bentley had been 'disposing of her worldly business' (Bentley, a lawyer, made himself useful, and in return Bess was 'very bountiful' in the shape of loans). Gilbert and his supporters regarded Bentley as a 'meddler'. Bess, continued Harpur, had sent for Henry Cavendish a few times, which had given Henry reason to hope that she might go to Chatsworth 'and furnish the house there and then give him present possession thereof and of much land thereunto adjoining'. Harpur thought otherwise: 'I assure myself that her end is to draw him to make some further assurance of his lands.' He would wait for Henry to come to Hardwick in the next week or so, as expected, and then ride over to Tutbury, to discover 'how far and upon what terms

---

* Sir Francis lived at Sutton Scarsdale – today the site of an 18th-century ruin – near Owlcotes, and was on friendly terms with William Cavendish, though William and Bess engaged in numerous lawsuits with members of the Leake family, who were related to Bess through her mother.

her Lady's bounty will extend'.[11] Not far at all was the answer. Bess had no intention of extending her bounty to Henry and every intention of preventing him from occupying Chatsworth.

Rumours of Bess being 'exceeding sick and in danger of death' had reached Arbella too. Despite the breakdown of her own relations with her grandmother, Arbella made some efforts to reconcile Bess and the Shrewsburys, offering to be 'mediator, moderator and peacemaker'. However, this was largely for Gilbert and Mary's sakes – 'you know I have cause only to be partial on your side, so many kindnesses and favours have I received from you and so many unkindnesses and disgraces have I received from the other party'.[12] But with 'the other party' thought to be dying, and mindful of the pearls and jewels and £1,000 that had been denied her, Arbella hurried to Hardwick. She came armed with a letter from the King asking Bess to treat her kindly, and an offer that she felt confident would restore her to favour.

On the occasion of the christening of his daughter Princess Mary, to whom Arbella was asked to be godmother, the King, in expansive mood, let it be known that he would be dispensing peerages: Arbella was offered a patent for a peerage, to fill in as she wished. On arriving at Hardwick in March, she was able to tell Bess that it was in her power to award a baronetcy to William Cavendish. The elevation of her son and designated heir could only have delighted Bess, but she was under no illusions about Arbella's motives. She found it strange, she told Dr James Montague, Dean of the Chapel Royal, and one of her court informers (he had been given £300 to keep him sweet and was left £20 in Bess's will), that Arbella had been so anxious to visit her, 'from whom she had desired so earnestly to come away'. She felt that she'd done quite enough for her granddaughter already – lands bringing in £700 a year, with another £100 on top of that – and besides, she had other grandchildren in greater need.[13] Nevertheless, Arbella came away from Hardwick with a gold cup worth £100 and £300 in cash.

Back at court, William was reported as waiting 'hard on my Lady Arbella for his Barony', though some thought that he'd be disappointed since he was 'very sparing in his gratuity', and while he 'would be glad if it were done', he 'would be sorry to part with anything for the doing of it'. This was not how things worked at court, where the rules of the marketplace applied and there was 'an equal proportion' between 'liberality' and 'courtesy', a fact that William was forced to acknowledge – having stumped up £2,000, he became Baron Cavendish.[14]

That her grandchildren should marry well was a matter of the highest importance for Bess. In 1603, she had sounded out George Clifford, Earl of Cumberland, about a match between his daughter and her grandson, William Cavendish's son 'Wylkyn'.[15] Two years later, this was still under discussion, but it had now become a double match: Wylkyn and Cumberland's daughter, and William's sister and Cumberland's nephew, the son of his brother George Clifford.[16] Large-scale entertaining was now rare at Hardwick, but the Cumberlands needed to be wooed. In July 1605, they were invited to Hardwick.

The Earl, his brother and their entourage were 'greatly entertained', as John Harpur reported to Gilbert. Their days were spent hunting, with hounds, in the park and – a particular prize – a 'great stag which had been long preserved' was killed. In the evenings they gathered for dinner in the High Great Chamber. They would have sat at the 'long table of white wood', covered with damask tablecloths, on benches upholstered in pale blue satin, embroidered with cloth of gold and needlework flowers, with black silk fringes and needlework stools. The table would have been laid with some of the best pieces from Bess's enormous collection of plate – the 'great gilt standing cup like a gourd' perhaps, the gold standing cups, the six candlesticks 'wrought with stags and talbots', or the six 'like galleys', the gold cups and spoons, the gilt basins and ewers, salts and porringers, with Bess presiding in her needlework chair with a gold silk fringe and a footstool made of watchet (light blue) velvet.[17]

Having dined, and this being high summer and the evenings long, the Cumberland party might have proceeded to the rooftop banqueting house for a dessert course. At Hardwick there was, unusually, a banqueting room on the ground floor and a small banqueting house in the south orchard, but by far the grandest and most thrilling was, as at Longleat and Wollaton, on the roof. Whether or not Bess's arthritic knees were up to climbing the 'lesser stairs' – its oak steps dramatically sloping today – is doubtful, but her guests would have done so, emerging into the north turret and from there making their way across the leads to the south turret, with its painted plasterwork ceiling and walls almost entirely made of glass. Here, bathed in golden evening light, they would have been served assorted sweetmeats: 'suckets' (preserved fruits), marchpane (made of ground almonds), jellies (made from boiled calves' feet flavoured with sugar, spice and wine), 'caraway comfits' and 'sweet fennel comfits' (bought ready-made), whilst surveying spectacular views.[18]

Bess's hospitality notwithstanding, the double marriages came to nothing. If this was a disappointment, Bess could, and did, take satisfaction in the very fine matches made by her granddaughters Mary and Alethea Talbot – Mary married William Herbert, Earl of Pembroke, in 1604, and two years later, Alethea married Thomas Howard, Earl of Arundel.

Fifteen long years after Shrewsbury's death, Bess's battles with Gilbert over her jointure continued, conducted on much the same lines as her battles with his father – both parties entrenched in their respective positions, both refusing to give an inch. Gilbert hardly needed further reason to infuriate Bess, but such was provided in 1604, when she discovered that, in order to repay a debt, he had borrowed £5,000 from Sir Fulke Greville, Treasurer of the Navy and poet, secured on Talbot lands that had been settled on Bess. When Greville demanded his £5,000, Bess found herself having to assure him that she and Gilbert would, if necessary, sell land in order to raise the money.[19] Whether it was necessary, we don't know, but it's not hard to imagine Bess's indignation.

Gilbert smarted under the 'manifold injuries' that he felt he'd suffered at Bess's hands: the 'spoil and waste' of land that was not rightfully hers, by felling timber and mining coal; the bringing of suits; the 'foul maintenance' of Gilbert's 'most base and paltry enemies'. Bess claimed that the land in question was part of her jointure, that Gilbert owed her £4,000, that he was buying land 'over her head' and supporting those who were bringing suits against her.[20] All of which, as one of Gilbert's informants put it, 'doth stick sore in her teeth.'[21]

There were some, however, who felt that Bess's campaign against Gilbert was hardly in her own interests, given that he was her son-in-law and the father of her granddaughters. In April 1605, one Thomas Woodward, reporting a conversation with John Bentley, wondered at Bess's 'injurious course against so noble a person and her own progeny', especially given the 'rising of her happy fortunes'. Bentley had pointed out that Bess had a 'good estate' for her lifetime, and if the lands bought by Gilbert 'should come to her own issue what cause hath she to complain'? It seemed 'unnatural' to Bentley for Bess to 'contend' with Gilbert when he 'placeth in great honour her grandchildren' (the marriages of Alethea and Mary Talbot). But for Bess, injustice trumped familial ties. She admitted that she was 'glad of the good bestowing' of Alethea and Mary, but claimed that Gilbert had simply been acting in his own interests, not 'for her sake'. However, she softened somewhat and told Bentley that since there were currently no suits between her and Gilbert, she didn't rule out reconciliation.[22]

That was off the cards just two months later, when Gilbert brought yet another suit against Bess for the recovery of estates held as part of her jointure (a suit that would be won by Bess).[23] In August, Roger Manners told Gilbert that he'd tried to talk to Bess of 'pacification', but had 'found her far off from any agreement' and unwilling to listen to him. 'What I said, she told me that she had heard by others and I seeing her so resolved left her to her own wisdom.'[24] It's doubtful that Bess had ever much listened to well-meaning advice, and she certainly didn't wish to do so now. As always, she preferred to trust to 'her own wisdom'.

23.

'NOT OVER SUMPTUOUS'

Feuding between Bess and Gilbert took a back seat with the eruption of another Catholic conspiracy, the Gunpowder Plot, in November 1605. Led by Robert Catesby (Francis Tresham, eldest son of Sir Thomas, was also involved), the plotters intended to blow up the House of Lords, along with the King and his sons, at the State Opening of Parliament. Their cover blown, the conspirators fled to the Midlands. This, presumably, explains why the Privy Council – rather curiously, considering that Arbella was no longer at Hardwick – instructed the Derbyshire justices to look out for Bess: 'as Lady Shrewsbury, Dowager, dwelling at Hardwick is a widow and solitary, we request you to have a care of her safety and quietness and if Lord Cavendish shall have occasion to ask your assistance in her behalf that you will aid and assist him for securing her safety.'[1]

Eight surviving conspirators came to trial on 27 January and were sentenced to be hanged, drawn and quartered. Bess, at Hardwick, was avid for news and James Montague duly supplied it: 'for the late executions of the traitors, I am sure your Honour hath heard how they died. There was but 2 of the 8 that would freely confess their fact to be a sin against God.' He went on to tell of the 'apprehension' of Henry Garnet, who had been found in a priest hole at Hindlip Hall on the same day as the trial. Garnet, a prominent Jesuit, who certainly knew of the plot, thanks to the confession box, without actively furthering it, was nevertheless regarded by Montague and a great many others as 'the most dangerous man to this state that liveth'.[2] In March, Montague reported that Garnet was in the Tower, awaiting execution, and that Parliament was busy with anti-Catholic legislation: 'to compel every man to the communion ... within the space of two years or else they shall be in the nature of recusants.'[3]

There was no suggestion of Gilbert Talbot being involved in the Gunpowder Plot, but he was implicated by association: Garnet was known to Mary; and Gilbert's cousin, John Talbot, had hidden one of the conspirators. Gilbert himself would have preferred his wife not to flaunt her Catholicism, telling Cecil that he wished she could follow 'the rare and excellent example' of those who were 'resolute against crosses' (Mary openly wore hers around her neck). But he was no more successful than had been his father when it came to controlling his wife.

For Mary's sake, Bess made occasional friendly overtures towards the Shrewsburys, as in January 1606 when she wrote affectionately to her 'very good son and daughter'. A visit, it seemed, was in the offing. Bess insisted that she would be 'heartily glad' to see them at Hardwick; indeed, there was nowhere they would be 'more welcome'. Gilbert, as usual, was engaged in a lawsuit, and Bess claimed to be 'as desirous it should go well as your selves can be'. 'I shall think it long till I see you both', she finished, and added a postscript – Mary was to tell her brother Charles, who had been unwell, 'to keep good diet.'[4]

But the visit to Hardwick was never made and Gilbert and Bess were soon at loggerheads once more, with new suits brought against Bess. John Harpur told Gilbert in June that Bess was looking 'well for her [eighty-five] years', but suffering from an arthritic hip and walking with a stick. Her temper was not of the best either – she was 'very impatient at every occasion or word which any speaketh', and Gilbert's suits were called to mind 'very often'. Harpur added that William Cavendish and 'his Lady' had returned to Hardwick recently and Bess had 'used them well, which was not expected by some about her.'[5] It seems that even William couldn't count on his mother's favour.

Of Bess's children, only Charles Cavendish, who was living at Welbeck Abbey, which he bought outright from Gilbert in 1607, seems to have successfully distanced himself from his mother – both her tongue-lashings and her control. Crucially, he had no need of her money. Equable, contented and rich, he was free to pursue his own interests – music and architecture in particular. Charles was an enthusiastic amateur architect* and in letters to Gilbert and Mary Talbot, in the spring of 1607, he set out something of an architectural manifesto, balancing aesthetics with practicalities. Gilbert had asked him to come up with a 'platt' for a house. Charles was not entirely happy with his 'first draft', partly because he had not been the 'drawer', but 'if the general convenience be liked the rest will easily be amended, as windows, chimneys, doors and such like. I have kept myself to the proportion of lodgings your lordship gave me, which was 6 or 7, only I have lodged the builder conveniently besides, which few think of. If you or my sister were to build I would advise you to this platt, some small things corrected.' He went on to outline the 'imperfections' in another 'platt' by a rival 'inventor': the hall had too many doors and would fill the house with 'noise and smell'; the great chamber only had windows on one side; there was no chapel or gallery; and the chimneys would smoke.[6]

In a further letter to Mary, Charles assured her that his plan would result in a 'sweet and fair and easy house', one fit for entertaining royalty. The kitchen would be separate from the main building, the gallery 'most fair' with the addition of two vaults, no room would be 'annoyed with any stair except servants' chambers', and there would be 'fair vaults on the garden side'. For Charles, a house 'without such singularities' would be 'greatly defective'. He had thought about site and positioning too. As he didn't know 'the seat', he might have erred 'in placing the principal rooms', but this could easily be altered. He felt that it was important to angle a house so 'all sides ... have the sun and yet not in a direct line.'[7]

---

* In 1612, he started work on Bolsover Castle, just along the ridge from Hardwick.

Although it sounds as if Charles was designing a house for Gilbert and Mary – and they may well have led him to believe so – the fact that both letters ended up at Hatfield makes it more likely that Gilbert was procuring plans on Cecil's behalf. In 1607, Cecil, who had become Lord Salisbury in 1605, exchanged Theobalds for the King's Hatfield and was casting about for ideas for a new house. In 1608, he would request a plan of Chatsworth from Arbella and one of Hardwick from Gilbert.[8] Writing to thank Gilbert for the 'platt' of Hardwick and 'more for the hand that guided the pencil', Cecil hoped to see him one day 'at the house, which is as yet but in fancy and (for ought I know) shall be so far from beauty or greatness as it shall make amends for my precedent vanity'.[9] Cecil's Hatfield, completed in 1612, at a cost of a staggering £40,000, had plenty of beauty and greatness, though it owed little, in the end, to Charles's platt.[*][10]

The event of the summer of 1607 was the christening of Bess's great-grandson, James Howard (Lord Maltravers), the first son of Alethea and Thomas Howard, Earl and Countess of Arundel, which brought about a rapprochement between Bess and the Shrewsburys. Bess was asked to be a godmother, though had to withdraw when the Queen proposed herself.[11] However, she sent Mary Talbot a lavish present in honour of the event – a 'fair and well wrought ermine'. Mary thanked her profusely: she would treasure the ermine 'as a great jewel both in respect of your ladyship and of her from whom your ladyship had it, there can nothing be wrought in metal with more life'.[†] The christening, she continued, would take place that July at Whitehall, with Their Majesties in attendance, and she was glad to hear that Bess's hip pain had improved.[12] A few months later, Mary received an affectionate note from her mother: 'my good sweet daughter. I am very desirous

---

[*] The principal architect behind Hatfield was Robert Lemynge, with contributions from Simon Basil, the Surveyor of the Royal Works, and Inigo Jones.
[†] It may have been a gift from Queen Elizabeth.

to hear how you do. I trust your Lord is well now of the gout, and I desire to hear how all ours do at London and the little sweet Lord Maltravers. I pray God ever to bless you dear heart and them all with his good blessings and so in haste I cease at Hardwick this last of November.'[13] It was to be her last letter to Mary: Bess's health was finally failing.

This brought the Shrewsburys together with Charles Cavendish to Hardwick in early December, the first time, as Gilbert told Cecil, that he'd visited in a decade. He 'found a lady of great years, of great wealth and a great wit, which yet still remains'; moreover, there was no word 'of any former suits or unkindness, neither was there any motion on either side, but only compliment, courtesy and kindness'.[14] Admittedly they only stayed a day, and Gilbert probably wanted to present a united front to Cecil – at such a critical time it was important to be seen to be behaving well. He wrote more frankly to Henry Cavendish: Bess was hardly eating and couldn't walk the length of her chamber, even when supported by two people.

As the new year dawned, with the country still in the grip of a great freeze (the Thames froze solid) and Arbella appearing at court in Ben Jonson's *Masque of Beauty* (masques were a feature of court life and courtiers' participation compulsory), Bess grew weaker.[15] On New Year's Eve, Mary Talbot had sent her mother a gift – a cushion on which to kneel for her daily prayers, though Bess must have been long past kneeling – and as Gilbert told Henry, 'the messenger told us she looked pretty well and spoke heartily, but my Lady wrote that she was worse than when we last saw her and Mrs Digby sent a secret message that her Ladyship was so ill that she could not be from her day or night'.[16] Gilbert had heard that the order had been given to 'drive away all the sheep and cattle at Ewden instantly upon her ladyship's death' – Ewden, in Yorkshire, was land that formed part of Bess's marriage settlement and would revert to Gilbert on her death, but William could at least prevent him from taking possession of the livestock that grazed there.* Gilbert had words of warning for Henry: he should look out for William, whose 'principallest means is to keep us all so divided one from another', and who, he suspected, had been hoping to see Henry's 'end' before Bess's. 'They' – i.e. William and his supporters – had been doing their best to persuade Bess that Henry intended to 'enter the house and seize all' on her death.[17] Gilbert thought that Henry would receive an offer from William, an offer he should certainly refuse. He was right. Bearing in mind the delicate state of both Bess's health and Henry's finances, William calculated that Henry might be tempted to relinquish Chatsworth in return for ready cash and offered him £5,000 and £500 a year for Bess's lifetime.[18] Henry turned this down – he was holding out for £6,000 and £500 a year 'for four years certain.'[19]

While her children hovered, Bess lay cocooned in her bed. This was splendid enough – its posts encased in 'scarlet' (woollen cloth) edged with silver lace, with a scarlet valance embroidered with gold studs and thistles, gold and silver lace and a gold fringe – but, during one of the coldest winters on record, primarily designed for warmth. It was hung with three curtains of scarlet and five curtains of purple 'bays' (also woollen cloth), and covered in three pairs of fustian blankets and six Spanish (finest-quality) blankets, and banked around with eight 'fledges' – wool mats. Curtains were rare in Tudor homes, but this was a corner room and, in the interests of excluding draughts, two red curtains and three coverlets hung over the windows, with another for the door.[20]

Bess was suffering from abdominal pain, and when this grew worse, the two ladies attending her, Mary Cartwright and Elizabeth Digby,

---

* This was common practice in the event of death: in 1602, Bess had stepped in to prevent goods from being removed and cattle and sheep being 'stolen out of the pastures' of a Master Beresford. Those sent to guard Beresford's belongings found 'a good portion of wool that was hid in a rock', by his heirs presumably (BHL, ID 241 and 44).

'held her stomach' to give her some relief. But she remained in full possession of her wits, perfectly aware of the manoeuvrings of her family, and perfectly attuned to falsehoods and insincerity. She 'showed herself to be very offended with some, for that the well was poisoned and yet breath was made with that water.'[21] The fire, burning steadily through the long January nights, cast shadows across the naked torsos of the 'terms' carved by Abraham Smith, supporting the mantel, and illuminated the cavorting couple and the red-tongued stag above. Perhaps Bess looked back to her younger, lusty, firm-fleshed self. To the days of her marriage to William Cavendish, when all was ahead of her.

Looking to the future, beyond her death, to her acquisitive, quar-relsome, litigious children and stepchildren, there were real grounds for apprehension. Bess could only put her trust in William: 'she lay awake much of the night thinking of matters that might concern him much and which perhaps he never thought of and that it stood upon him to look about him'. William didn't need telling. He was jealously guarding access to his mother, anxious lest Mary Talbot in particular, still a favourite daughter, should have 'any private conference' with Bess; Elizabeth Digby was instructed to use whatever means she could to keep Mary away.

On the last day of January, Bess dragged herself from her bed, seated herself in her chair of 'russet satin striped with silver' and sent for William. She declared that 'she found herself extreme sick at heart' and had 'no hope of life'. The following day, she instructed Timothy Pusey to make some revisions to her will: she wished Mary Talbot to have the Pearl Bed (the marriage bed she had shared with William Cavendish), 'but she would give no hangings' (a bed with no hangings, like Chatsworth without its contents, was practically worthless); Elizabeth Digby was to have £100 and Bess's other ladies £20 apiece; £100 was to go to the Derby almshouses; and 4,000 marks to Charles Cavendish to buy land for his two sons.[22] Last-minute amendments were just what William had dreaded, but though Charles and Mary had received some recognition, there was nothing here to give much cause for alarm.

On 2 February, Dr Hunton, the Cavendish family doctor, was summoned from Newark and moved into Hardwick. He applied a plaster to Bess's back and a few days later dosed her with treacle. But she was beyond plasters and treacle. Bess died on 13 February, as darkness fell, with her 'sense and memory even to the end'.[23] Dr Hunton was paid 40 marks (£13 6s.) for his pains and sent away. Because the time involved in organising a countess's funeral usually meant a delay of several weeks between death and burial, embalming, by an apothecary, was essential. Bess's body was drained of blood, disembowelled and embalmed, then sealed in wax.[24] On the 17th, it was transported in a litter to Derby and placed in a lead coffin in the Cavendish vault that Bess had had constructed in 1601.[25] She had chosen to lie with future generations of Cavendishes, not Talbots.

William quickly took charge. Gilbert Talbot told Cecil that both he and Arbella had been 'made strangers to all my Lord Cavendish's proceedings'; he knew nothing of either the will or the funeral.[26] The will variously brought disappointment, relief and satisfaction. Gilbert and Henry had nothing. Charles had 4,000 marks for his sons, and Arbella, who came to Hardwick in March, had her £1,000. John Bentley, despite his many services to Bess, including travelling all the way from London to witness the codicil made in 1603, went empty-handed. 'Yesterday's experience breeds this day's wisdom', he commented ruefully, and promptly set about offering his services to Gilbert Talbot.[27] Of Bess's children, only Mary Talbot, with her pointedly compromised bequest, took her mother's death very 'sorely' and gave herself up to 'extreme grief'.[28] Gilbert expressed surprise at his wife's distress – she was still 'melancholy' in August – and hoped to 'set some workmen' on a building project soon to distract her.[29] Gilbert himself was busy reclaiming his Talbot properties. Just five days after Bess's death, he ordered all except those servants authorised by himself to be expelled from Wingfield.[30]

In April, before Bess's funeral, William Cavendish's eighteen-year-old son, 'Wylkyn', was married to Christian Bruce, the twelve-year-old sister of Lord Kinloss, a match of which Bess would certainly have approved, and which she may have helped engineer, though Arbella took the credit. Christian was a 'pretty, red-haired wench', but Wylkyn was a reluctant groom, in large part because he'd succumbed to the attractions of one of his stepmother's ladies, Margaret Chatterton.[31] Margaret, who came from an apparently respectable family of Staffordshire gentry and was seven years Wylkyn's senior, had seduced him back in 1605, and then claimed that a marriage had taken place. It soon emerged that she had been enjoying drunken orgies in the Old Hall with William Cavendish's male servants and his wife's laundry maid.[32] A twelve-year-old virgin bride held little appeal for Wylkyn, though he would have reason to be grateful to Christian, who did much to rescue the family fortunes from his own extravagances.

Henry Cavendish, reporting on the wedding, told Gilbert that the young couple 'were bedded together to his [Wylkyn's] great punishment some 2 hours'. William Cavendish was bringing a bill against Henry – 'something touching my entail' – and Henry, being 'so unfit and so unapt for these law matters', knew all too well that he was no match for his 'wily politic' and 'too skilfully experimented' brother.[33] Since Henry had no legitimate heir, Chatsworth would revert to William on Henry's death, but William was unwilling to wait and banked on Henry's need for money. Sure enough, in 1610, Chatsworth became his, for £8,000.

When Bess first made her will in 1601, she expressed a wish, with her usual dislike of waste and excess, that her funeral 'be not over sumptuous or otherwise performed with too much vain and idle charges'. However, this was somewhat at odds with the very substantial £5,102 that was put into bags, in a coffer, to cover cash legacies and funeral expenses.[34] She must have known that as a dowager countess, a heraldic funeral, with all attendant ceremony and display, was inevitable. And indeed her due.

It took place on 4 May at All Saints church, Derby, which was extravagantly swathed in black cloth for the occasion.[*][35] We have no contemporary accounts, but the procession into the church would have been headed by a mourning knight, carrying a banner painted with Bess's arms, followed by heralds from the College of Arms, then the coffin, and behind that two hooded gentleman ushers carrying white rods, Mary Talbot, as lady chief mourner, supported by two hooded barons, and Bess's family and servants, with the twelve residents of the almshouses and fifty-eight 'poor women' bringing up the rear.

Inside All Saints, the coffin would probably have been laid on a huge thirty-foot-tall hearse, like a four-poster bed, made of timber, with a canopy, all covered in black velvet. Bess's funeral sermon was preached by Tobie Matthew, the Archbishop of York and a committed Protestant. Matthew, who was famed for his sermons, took his text from the Book of Proverbs, 31:25: 'Strength and honour is her clothing, and in the latter day she shall rejoice.' Aside from black cloth, the greatest expense was the funeral feast. Glasses and plates had been bought in London, as well as delicacies such as two pounds of green lemons, three barrels of pickled oysters, two firkins of sturgeon, twenty-five gallons of 'reinish' wine, eighteen dried tongues, a firkin of quinces, six gammons of Westphalia bacon, three pounds of Polonia sausage, three pounds of dates, four pounds of ginger, four pounds of figs, pickled cucumbers, pickled lemons and anchovies. The total cost of the occasion came to £3,257, a sum that Bess would certainly have regarded as excessive.[36]

'The old Countess of Shrewsbury died about Candlemas this year, whose funeral was about Holy Thursday. A great frost this year. A hot

---

* Biographers of Bess have suggested that the hall, chapel and High Great Chamber at Hardwick were also draped in black cloth. This, disappointingly, has no factual basis.

fortnight about James's tide. The witches of Bakewell hanged.' So read the 1608 entry in the *National Records of Derby*.[37] Bess's death is a detail of no greater significance than the fate of the Bakewell witches or the vagaries of the weather. Yet her legacy has been far-reaching and long-lasting. She is remarkable not just by the standards of her age, but by those of *any* age. Remarkable for her eighty-seven years and for outliving four husbands and most, if not all, of her friends and contemporaries – Sir John Thynne, Frances Grey, the Earl of Leicester, Lord Burghley, Margaret Lennox, Lady Cobham, Queen Elizabeth herself. Remarkable for being able to remember the Dissolution, yet living to see the first Stuart monarch ascend the throne. Remarkable for amassing a fortune that no woman in sixteenth-century England, bar Elizabeth I, came even close to. Nor many men for that matter.

When Robert Cecil said that Elizabeth 'had been more than a man and, in troth, sometimes less than a woman', he could just as well have been referring to Bess. The Earl of Shrewsbury certainly felt that he suffered from his wife's unwomanly behaviour. And he was eaten away by the belief that the Cavendishes were enriching themselves at his expense, a reversal of fortunes that would continue: while Gilbert Talbot sank deeper into debt, a survey of the estates of William and Charles Cavendish, begun in 1608 and finished in 1627, reckoned each at 100,000 acres.[38] The Talbot fortunes have declined further (though the Shrewsbury title survives); those of the Cavendishes, founded on land and property originally accumulated by Bess, have, largely, flourished. There is hardly an English duke who doesn't have Bess's blood running in his veins: descended from her, directly and indirectly, are the Dukes of Devonshire (Bess's great-great-grandson, William Cavendish, 4th Earl of Devonshire, became 1st Duke in 1694), Newcastle, Portland, Kingston and Norfolk. This is her achievement. But so too is her visible memorial, her greatest and only surviving house, Hardwick.

It would be unusual, indeed eccentric, for an elderly widow today to build a complicated, ambitious house, right alongside a more than adequate existing house, and then to display her initials all over it, writ large, in stone. 'Builder of Chatsworth, Hardwick and Oldcotes, highly distinguished by their magnificence' – so Bess is described in the inscription on her tomb. According to local legend, she would live so long as she continued to build: the exceptionally cold winter of 1608 meant that the mortar at Owlcotes froze, whereupon Bess ordered her masons to use boiling water; when that proved ineffectual, ale was substituted; when this too failed, she drew her last breath. In point of fact, Owlcotes was long finished by 1608, and masons would not have been making mortar in February, but the sentiment rings true – Bess had been engaged in building of one sort or another for nearly fifty years; it was her lifeblood. Energy, creativity, ambition, pride, vast wealth and resources, all found expression in and were lavished on her houses, and none more so than Hardwick, which not only stands as a monument to a brilliantly managed marital and business career, but proclaims one woman's triumphant survival and her desire for immortality.

HARDWICK POST BESS

Many of the great Tudor houses built by Bess's contemporaries – Kenilworth, Theobalds, Holdenby, Worksop – have vanished: burnt down, pulled down, abandoned. But Hardwick has survived: architecturally intact, its interiors largely unchanged, its collection of sixteenth-century textiles unsurpassed. Though today under the management of the National Trust, it is still very much Bess's house. This would not be the case if Henry Cavendish had been rather more like his brother William; it was because Henry sold Chatsworth to William in 1610 that Hardwick became a secondary house for the Cavendishes and so, unlike Chatsworth, escaped rebuilding according to more fashionable tastes.

William Cavendish, who became 1st Earl of Devonshire in 1618, was keen, like most heirs, to make his mark and spent a substantial £1,163 on building works (supervised by John Balechouse) at Hardwick. What exactly these works consisted of is unclear, but they probably included the moulded plaster ceiling in the long gallery. In 1611, Hardwick had its first royal visit (something that would have gratified Bess) – Prince Charles (the future King), who came whilst his father was touring and hunting in the Midlands. When William died in 1626, his son, 'Wylkyn', became the 2nd Earl, inheriting Hardwick and Chatsworth. Young William was as profligate as his father had been parsimonious, leaving debts of £38,000 on his death in 1628, aged just thirty-eight.

During the 1600s, Hardwick was used as an alternative to Chatsworth, but towards the end of the century Chatsworth was demolished and completely rebuilt, to designs by William Talman; thereafter it became the principal home of the Cavendishes. Through the eighteenth century, Hardwick was regarded as a romantic curiosity, visited occasionally, but frequently empty. It was the 1st Duke of Devonshire who took the decision to abandon the Old Hall, for reasons of economy, and parts were demolished in 1756, with the west wing surviving, but steadily decaying, into the nineteenth century (the young Princess Victoria, visiting Hardwick in 1833, had to be dissuaded, on the grounds of safety, from climbing the stairs to the Hill Great Chamber). The 5th Duke, and his wife Georgiana, stayed regularly at Hardwick in the 1780s, and authorised various works, including the lowering of the ceiling of the state withdrawing chamber, thus diminishing one of Hardwick's great spaces. A few months before the 5th Duke's death, in 1811, a legendary party took place at Hardwick, to celebrate the coming-of-age of his son and heir, Lord Hartington.

The 6th Duke, known as the Bachelor Duke, had to pay off the considerable debts left by his parents, but became an extravagant spender himself. He transferred quantities of furniture, paintings and tapestries from his other houses to Hardwick, and carried out various improvements, including blocking up the windows at either end of the long gallery, to reduce glare. He adored the house, dining in the High Great Chamber, despite the extreme cold, and sleeping, and eventually dying, in Bess's corner bedchamber. The Bachelor Duke was succeeded by his second cousin, who built the two-storey service wing, with bedrooms for servants, at the north end of the house.

The 6th and 7th Dukes also left huge debts, but the 8th and 9th Dukes did much to recoup them. Under the 9th Duke, extensive repairs to Hardwick's structure and stonework (which had been badly damaged by pollution from local coal mines) were carried out, but it was his wife, Duchess Evelyn, a woman of whom Bess would have approved, who took on the task of preserving the house. After she was widowed in 1938, the Dowager Duchess came to live at Hardwick, making Bess's rooms her own and devoting herself to the repair and restoration of Bess's tapestries and hangings. Except for the war years, she remained at Hardwick until her death in 1960, three years after Hardwick had been given to the nation in lieu of death duties, and two years after it had been made over to the National Trust.

ACKNOWLEDGEMENTS

This book has been a long time in the making and there are many to whom I am grateful for their scholarship, help and patience. Anyone interested in Bess of Hardwick has reason to thank Alison Wiggins and her team at Glasgow University, who have collected, and made available online, Bess's entire correspondence. Similarly, the task of deciphering early modern English has been made immeasurably easier by the work of David Durant, biographer of Bess, whose papers and transcriptions of Bess's household and building accounts can be read at Nottingham University Library. Philip Riden has also done much painstaking research into and work on Bess's accounts and papers, correcting a few misconceptions in the process. I'm very grateful to him for supplying articles and patiently answering questions. I feel greatly indebted to Mark Girouard for his invaluable works on Robert Smythson and Elizabethan architecture, and I thank him for conversations about Bess and Hardwick, for reading parts of the book and for correcting architectural errors.

Thanks to Dr Kate Harris, archivist at Longleat House, and to James Towe and Aidan Haley, archivists at Chatsworth. Quotations from the Thynne papers are included by permission of the Marquess of Bath, Longleat House, and from the Chatsworth archives, by kind permission of the Duke of Devonshire and the Chatsworth House trust. Also thanks to the staff at the British Library, Lambeth Palace Library, Nottingham University Library and the London Library. For permission to reproduce drawings and photographs I am grateful to those institutions credited in the list of illustrations, and to Clare Broomfield, Megan Evans, Jonathan Makepeace and Diane Naylor in particular. Many thanks to Tim Wales, for battling with the Earl of Shrewsbury's handwriting, to John Goodall at *Country Life,* for talking to me about Hardwick, and to Andrew Barber at the National Trust. At Hardwick, Nigel Wright and Elena Williams kindly showed me around, answered questions and allowed me to wander about after hours. Thank you to the late Alexander Chancellor, for accompanying me on a tour of Elizabethan houses in Northamptonshire. For their hospitality at Doddington Hall, thanks to James and Clare Birch, and to Antony Jarvis, for sharing his immense knowledge of and enthusiasm for the house. For showing me Shireoaks, taking me to Worksop Manor Lodge, and conversation about Smythson, I am extremely grateful to Leo Godlewski.

I would like to thank Mary Miers, for all her help, and Rebecca Nicolson and Aurea Carpenter at Short Books, for whom I first wrote about Bess. For chat and excellent advice on Tudor matters, thanks to Jessie Childs. Also to Victoria Millar, who read an early draft and made many useful suggestions. And to Georgia Garrett, my agent. I feel lucky in my friends and family: thank you to all those who offered advice, support and good cheer along the way, including Lucy Baring, David and Emma Craigie, Miranda Creswell, Phil Eade, Alexa de Ferranti, Catherine Gibbs, Ed and Nicole Hubbard, Max and Lucas Hubbard, Caryl Hubbard, Ben Macintyre, Flora McDonnell, Adam Nicolson, Karen Richards, Ben Rogers, Sweetpea Slight, Simon and Alexa Tiffin, Daryl Weldon and Caddy Wilmot-Sitwell. I have been lucky too in my publishers. My editors – Juliet Brooke at Chatto & Windus and Jennifer Barth at Harper Collins US – waited patiently for this book and pushed me, gently, to make it better. Juliet's successor, Charlotte Humphery, guided it through its final stages with the greatest efficiency and care. The team at Chatto – Jane Selley (copy-editor), Alison Rae (proofreader), Kris Potter (designer) and Emmy Lopes (map-drawer) did a fine job. My thanks to all of them.

NOTES ON SOURCES

All letters to and from Bess can be viewed online: http://www.bessofhard-wick.org, Bess of Hardwick's Letters: The Complete Correspondence, c.1550–1608, ed. Alison Wiggins, Alan Bryson, Daniel Starza Smith, Anke Timmermann and Graham Williams, University of Glasgow, web development by Katherine Rogers, University of Sheffield Humanities Research Institute (April 2013).

Transcriptions of Bess's household and building accounts, made by David Durant, are held at Nottingham University Library (David Durant Papers).

The Folger Shakespeare Library, Washington DC, holds the Cavendish-Talbot MSS (X.d. 428), the account book of Sir William and Lady Cavendish, 1548–50, (X.d. 486) and Edward Whalley's London account book, 9 September 1589–12 July 1592 (V.b. 308).

The Talbot and Shrewsbury MSS are in Lambeth Palace Library.

The Devonshire MSS are at Chatsworth.

The Thynne Papers and the Longleat building accounts are at Longleat. The Thynne Papers are also on microfilm in the British Library.

The Cecil Papers, Hatfield House, are available online in the British Library.

Abbreviations

BHL	Bess of Hardwick's Letters: The Complete Correspondence, *c.* 1550–1608
BL	British Library
CP	Cecil Papers
CSP Domestic	Calendar of State Papers, Domestic
CSP Scotland	Calendar of State Papers relating to Scotland
HMC	Historical Manuscripts Commission
L&P	Letters and Papers Foreign and Domestic, Henry VIII
LPL	Lambeth Palace Library
TNA	The National Archives

Introduction

1 Furnivall (ed.), Vol. I, p.130.
2 'Of Building', Bacon, p.111.
3 Quoted in Summerson, *Architecture in Britain*, p.38.
4 Quoted in Stone, *Family, Sex and Marriage*, p.198.
5 Goodall.
6 Howard, *Building of Elizabethan and Jacobean England*, pp.159–61.
7 Strachey, p.10.
8 Hunter, p.84
9 Lodge, Vol. I, p.xvii.

Prologue: Hardwick Hall, 1590

1 Durant and Riden (eds), *Building of Hardwick Hall: Part I*, p.114.
2 Durant, *Smythson Circle*, p.138.

1. Derbyshire Beginnings

1 For a discussion of Bess's birth date, see Riden, 'Hardwicks of Hardwick Hall', p.150.
2 TNA E 150/743/8.
3 Crook, 'Hardwick Before Bess', pp.41–54.
4 Hey, p.12.
5 Levey and Thornton (eds), p.53.
6 For libraries at Hardwick, see Adshead and Taylor (eds), pp.177–86.

7   TNA E 150/743/8.

8   Riden, 'Hardwicks of Hardwick Hall', p.157.

9   Ibid., pp.153 and 155.

10 Thurley, p.39.

11 Furnivall (ed.), Vol. II, p.268.

12 Girouard, *Elizabethan Architecture*, p.25.

13 Airs, p.72.

14 Riden, 'Hardwicks of Hardwick Hall', p.154.

15 Johnson, Vol. V, p.259.

16 Riden, 'Hardwicks of Hardwick Hall', p.152.

17 TNA CI/1101/17.

18 TNA C1/1101/17.

19 Devonshire MSS, Chatsworth, H/144.

2. Sir William Cavendish

1   Collins, p.11.

2   John Maynard Keynes, *A Treatise on Money*, Vol. II, Harcourt Brace, 1930, p.159.

3   BL, SP1/104.f.197.

4   Richardson, p.55.

5   CSP L&P Henry VIII, May 1542, p.182.

6   Folger X.d.428 (13).

7   Devonshire MSS, Chatsworth, HM/1, f.2.

8   Levey, *Embroideries at Hardwick Hall*, p.14.

9   Simon Thurley, 'Somerset House: the palace of England's queens, 1551–1692', London Topographical Society, No.168 (2009).

10 Howard, *Early Tudor Country House*, p.188.

3. Acquisition

1   All details in this chapter of the Cavendishes' life in London and at Northaw are taken from the household accounts in Devonshire MSS, Chatsworth, HM/1, and Folger X.d.486.

2   Collins, p.11.

3 David Durant, notes on HM/1, University of Nottingham, Manuscripts and Special Collections (MS 663/2).

4 CSP Domestic, Edward VI, 1547–53, p.61.

5 Riden, 'Hardwicks of Hardwick Hall', p.151.

6 Riden, 'Sir William Cavendish', p.245.

7 Ibid.

8 Furnivall (ed.), Vol. II, p.341.

9 Girouard, *Robert Smythson*, p.116.

10 'Of Building', Bacon, p.109.

11 Devonshire MSS, Chatsworth, HM/1, f.5v.

12 Ibid., f.10.

13 Quoted in Summerson, *Architecture in Britain*, p.19.

14 Christopher Hussey, *Country Life*, 3 December 1953.

15 Listed in the 1601 inventory, this is still at Hardwick.

16 Girouard, *Robert Smythson*, p.34.

17 Ibid., p.116.

18 Folger X.d.428 (82).

4. 'Every man almost is a builder'

1 Thynne Papers, Longleat, Vol. II, f.227.

2 Devonshire MSS, Chatsworth, H/143/6.

3 Thynne Papers, Longleat, Vol. II, f.85.

4 Quoted in Girouard, *Robert Smythson*, p.41.

5 Building Records, Longleat, Vol. I, f.73.

6 Ibid., f.111.

7 Ibid., f.237.

8 Building Records, Longleat, Vol. II, f.27.

9 Building Records, Longleat, Vol. I, f.339.

10 Building Records, Longleat, Vol. II, f.23.

11 Ibid., f.145.

12 Thynne Papers, Longleat, Vol. II, f.250.

13 Ibid., f.252.

14 Devonshire MSS, Chatsworth, H/143/2. Also see Levey, *Elizabethan Inheritance*, p.11.
15 TNA E 101/424/10.
16 Ibid. Also see Riden, 'Sir William Cavendish'.
17 Devonshire MSS, Chatsworth, HM/3, f.1v.
18 Ibid., f.2v, 4v.
19 Collins, p.12.

5. 'My honest swete Chatesworth'

1 Durant, *Bess of Hardwick*, p.33.
2 Thynne Papers, Longleat, Vol. III, f.9.
3 Ibid., f.15.
4 Thynne Papers, Longleat, Vol. V, f.246.
5 Ibid., f.243.
6 Devonshire MSS, Chatsworth, HM/3, f.20.
7 Devonshire MSS, Chatsworth, HM/3, ff.24–32.
8 Ibid., f.42.
9 For more on William St Loe and the St Loe family see Lovell, Chapter 7. Also Philip Riden, 'Bess of Hardwick and the St Loe Inheritance', in Riden and Edwards (eds), p.80–106.
10 Quoted in Starkey, p.140.
11 Durant, *Bess of Hardwick*, p.34.
12 Thynne Papers, Longleat, Vol. III, f.27.
13 Folger X.d.428 (133).
14 Lovell, p.123.
15 BHL, ID 59.
16 BHL, ID 47.
17 Devonshire MSS, Chatsworth, H/143/43.
18 See Mark Girouard, *Country Life*, 22 November 1973.
19 Devonshire MSS, Chatsworth, HM/2, f.5.
20 BHL, ID 61.
21 Folger X.d.428 (83).

22 BHL, ID 113, Bess to John Thynne.

23 Thynne Papers, Longleat, Vol. II, f.29.

24 Building Records, Longleat, Vol. III, f.115.

25 Girouard, *Elizabethan Architecture*, p.167.

26 Folger X.d.428 (84).

27 Folger X.d.428 (83).

28 Devonshire MSS, Chatsworth, HM/2, f.10.

29 Ibid., f.12.

30 Ibid., f.23.

31 Devonshire MSS, Chatsworth, H/143/2.

32 Devonshire MSS, Chatsworth, HM/2, ff.13–17.

6. 'This devil's devices'

1 See Philip Riden, 'Bess of Hardwick and the St Loe Inheritance', in Riden and Edwards.

2 Devonshire MSS, Chatsworth, H/143/3, Copy of Replication of Sir William St Loe, 1561.

3 Lovell, p.140.

4 BHL, ID 58.

5 Quoted in Durant, *Bess of Hardwick*, p.39.

6 Devonshire MSS, Chatsworth, H/143/3.

7 Ibid., H/144/2.

8 Devonshire MSS, Chatsworth, William St Loe account book, 8 August – 31 December 1560.

9 BHL, ID 59.

10 BHL, ID 61.

11 Devonshire MSS, Chatsworth, William St Loe account book.

12 BHL, ID 60.

13 Devonshire MSS, Chatsworth, William St Loe account book.

14 BHL, ID 61.

15 BHL, ID 54.

16 BHL, ID 55.

17 BHL, ID 62.

18 Devonshire MSS, Chatsworth, H/143/6, Chatsworth inventory, *c.*1566.

19 Folger X.d.148 (16).

20 See Riden and Fowkes, also Riden, 'Hardwicks of Hardwick Hall'.

21 BHL, ID 30.

22 BHL, ID 31.

23 BHL, ID 40.

24 Durant, *Bess of Hardwick*, p.53. Riden and Fowkes suggest that the figure could have been as much as £2,500.

7. Countess of Shrewsbury

1 TNA C3/170/13. See also Philip Riden, 'Bess of Hardwick and the St Loe Inheritance', in Riden and Edwards (eds).

2 BHL, ID 158.

3 BHL, ID 17.

4 BHL, ID 18.

5 BHL, ID 28.

6 CSP Domestic, Elizabeth I, Addenda 1566–79, p.39.

7 CP 155/22.

8 Thynne Papers, Longleat, Vol. III, f.59.

9 'In Search of Smythson', *Country Life*, 19 December 1991.

10 Quoted in Girouard, *Elizabethan Architecture*, p.28.

11 BHL, ID 114.

12 Folger X.d.148 (129).

13 Stone, *Crisis of the Aristocracy*, p.299.

14 'Of Riches', Bacon, p.88.

15 See Kiernan.

16 Lodge, Vol. II, p.69.

17 Talbot MSS, LPL, 3200, f.39.

18 Stone, *Crisis of the Aristocracy*, p.352.

19 CP 164/92.

20 Devonshire MSS, Chatsworth, H/278/1.

21 See Hunter, p.84, also Johnson, Vol. V, p.259.
22 BHL, ID 64.
23 BHL, ID 65.

8. The Scots Queen
1 BHL, ID 66.
2 CSP Scotland, Vol. II, p.609.
3 BHL, ID 107.
4 CSP Scotland, Vol. II, p.606.
5 BHL, ID 164.
6 Strickland, Vol. II, p.161.
7 Quoted in Guy, *My Heart is My Own*, p.443.
8 Quoted in Weir, p.125.
9 Devonshire MSS, Chatsworth, 'Given by the Scotys quene to my lorde and me'.
10 CSP Scotland, Vol. II, p.648.
11 Ibid., p.649.
12 Ibid., p.612.
13 Levey, *Embroideries at Hardwick Hall*, p.22.
14 Levey, *Elizabethan Inheritance*, p.47.
15 Ibid., p.58.
16 CSP Scotland, Vol. II, p.638.

9. A Dubious Honour
1 Lodge, Vol. II, p.192.
2 Ibid., p.180.
3 Ibid., p.39.
4 Ibid., p.655.
5 BHL, ID 220.
6 Quoted in Rawson, p.56.
7 CSP Scotland, Vol. II, p.695.
8 BHL, ID 68.
9 BHL, ID 25.

10   BHL, ID 170.

11   Talbot MSS, LPL, 3205, f.58.

12   CP 157/50.

13   Quoted in Rawson, p.80.

14   HMC Salisbury, Vol. I, p.499.

15   BHL, ID 225.

16   CSP Scotland, Vol. IV, p.17.

17   BHL, ID 26.

18   CSP Scotland, Vol. IV, p.65.

19   Quoted in Rawson, p.90.

20   Ibid., p.97.

21   Lodge, Vol. II, p.14.

22   Ibid., p.19.

23   CSP Scotland, Vol. V, p.95.

24   BHL, ID 36.

25   Talbot MSS, LPL, 3205, f.70.

26   BHL, ID 71.

27   BHL, ID 75.

28   Indenture 1572, see Devonshire MSS, Chatsworth, H/143.

10. 'Close dealing'

1   Lodge, Vol. II, p.49.

2   BHL, ID 71.

3   Folger X.d.428 (123).

4   Quoted in Rawson, p.102.

5   Furnivall (ed.), Vol. II, p.347.

6   Lodge, Vol. II, p.231.

7   Quoted in Girouard, *Robert Smythson*, p.118.

8   Rawson, p.179.

9   BHL, ID 72.

10   Talbot MSS, LPL, 3206, f.653.

11   Leader, p.146.

12   Wigfull, 'Extracts from the Notebook'.

13 BHL, ID 43.

14 BHL, ID 244.

15 Folger X.d.428 (50 and 51).

16 Howard, *Collection of Letters*, p.235.

17 BL Lansdowne, 40/41.

18 BHL, ID 27.

19 BHL, ID 73.

20 Quoted in Rawson, p.152.

21 Howard, *Collection of Letters*, p.235.

22 TNA State Papers Supplement, 46/30/333.

23 CSP Scotland, Vol. V, p.30.

24 Lodge, Vol. II, p.43.

25 BHL, ID 76.

26 CSP Scotland, Vol. V, p.202.

27 Folger X.d.428 (127).

28 Folger X.d.428 (128).

29 Folger X.d.428 (130).

30 Labanoff, Vol. IV, p.360.

31 HMC Longleat, Talbot Papers, Vol. II, p.98.

11. 'Great turmoil doth two houses breed'

1 Lodge, Vol. II, p.33.

2 Quoted in Airs, p.93.

3 Summerson, *Building of Theobalds*.

4 Skelton and Summerson (eds).

5 Quoted in Girouard, *Robert Smythson*, p.295.

6 Airs, p.123.

7 Lodge, Vol. II, p.53.

8 Ibid., p.69.

9 Folger X.d.428 (136).

10 BHL, ID 218.

11 Ibid.

12 BHL, ID 77.

13 Robert Laneham, quoted in Girouard, *Robert Smythson*, p.19.
14 Wells-Cole, Kenilworth inventory 1588, p.297.
15 BHL, ID 109.
16 Ibid.
17 HMC Longleat, Talbot Papers, Vol. II, f.113.
18 Quoted in Rawson, p.101.
19 Details of building work at Chatsworth in 1577 from Devonshire MSS, Chatsworth, HM/4.
20 HMC Salisbury, Vol. II, p.154.
21 Folger X.d.428 (137).
22 BHL, ID 94.
23 TNA State Papers Scotland, 53/10, f.84.
24 BHL, ID 172.
25 Talbot MSS, LPL, 3206, f.837.
26 BHL, ID 188.
27 Talbot MSS, LPL, 3205, f.66.
28 BHL, ID 84.
29 BHL, ID 85.
30 CSP Scotland, Vol. V, p.235.
31 Ibid., p.236.

12. 'The old song'

1   BHL, ID 83.
2   BHL, ID 122.
3   CP 10/77.
4   BHL, ID 166.
5   BHL, ID 174.
6   Lodge, Vol. II, p.143.
7   Shrewsbury MSS, LPL, 697, f.111.
8   Talbot MSS, LPL, 3205, f.72.
9   Ibid., f.64.
10 BL Lansdowne, 99/274.

11 BHL, ID 195.

12 Folger X.d.428 (51).

13 HMC Longleat, Talbot Papers, Vol. V, p.22.

14 BHL, ID 110.

15 Durant, *Bess of Hardwick*, p.106.

16 BHL, ID 10.

17 Folger X.d.428 (7).

18 Durant, *Bess of Hardwick*, p.79.

19 Riden (ed.), *Household Accounts*.

20 BHL, ID 74.

21 BHL, ID 228.

22 BHL, ID 227.

23 BL Lansdowne, 40/41.

24 BHL, ID 105.

25 Talbot MSS, LPL, 3198, f.172.

26 Talbot MSS, LPL, 3206, f.957.

27 BHL, ID 33.

28 BHL, ID 189.

29 Lodge, Vol. II, p.182.

30 BHL, ID 78.

31 Folger X.d.428 (3).

32 HMC Longleat, Talbot Papers, Vol. V, p.25.

33 Talbot MSS, LPL, 3198, f.97.

34 BHL, ID 78.

35 Lodge, Vol. II, p.155.

36 CSP Scotland, Vol. VI, p.77.

37 Ibid., p.90.

38 TNA SP 12/154, f.122.

39 Gristwood, p.54.

40 TNA SP 12/152, f.30.

41 Ibid., f.36.

42 BL Lansdowne, 34/143.

43 TNA SP 12/153, f.85

13. 'Send me Accres'

1 BHL, ID 79.
2 Quoted in Girouard, *Robert Smythson*, p.113.
3 Talbot MSS, LPL, 3189, f.92.
4 Camden, p.482.
5 Friedman, p.26.
6 Quoted in ibid., p.55.
7 Camden, p.482.
8 Durant, *Smythson Circle*, p.94.
9 Talbot MSS, LPL, 3198, f.225.
10 Summerson, *Architecture in Britain*, p.25.
11 Talbot MSS, LPL, 3198, f.308.
12 Ibid., ff.87 and 282.
13 Lodge, Vol. II, p.201.
14 HMC Longleat, Talbot Papers, Vol. V, p.39.
15 Talbot MSS, LPL, 3198, f.311.
16 HMC Longleat, Talbot Papers, Vol. V, p.40.
17 Lodge, Vol. II, p.239.
18 HMC Middleton 69, p.152.
19 Talbot MSS, LPL, 3198, f.142.
20 For letters between Baldwin and Shrewsbury, see Lodge, Vol. II.
21 HMC Longleat, Talbot Papers, Vol. V, p.44.
22 CSP Scotland, Vol. VII, p.356.
23 BHL, ID 148.
24 BHL, ID 229.
25 Talbot MSS, LPL, 3198, f.256.
26 BHL, ID 86.
27 Talbot MSS, LPL, 3198, f.300.
28 Ibid., f.124.
29 TNA SP 12/170/10.

14. 'Civil wars'

1 BL Add. CH 73965.

2 HMC Salisbury, Vol. III, p.162.

3 BL Lansdowne, 40/41.

4 See Riden, 'Hardwicks of Hardwick Hall', p.163.

5 Leader, p.551.

6 Lodge, Vol. II, p.244.

7 HMC Longleat, Talbot Papers, Vol. V, p.50.

8 BL Lansdowne, 40/63.

9 TNA SP 12/172/64.

10 Talbot MSS, LPL, 3151, f.58.

11 BHL, ID 116.

12 HMC Rutland, Vol. I, p.200.

13 CSP Scotland, Vol. II, p.49.

14 Shrewsbury MSS, LPL, 698, f.39

15 CSP Scotland, Vol. VII, p.5.

16 Leader, p.551.

17 Johnson, Vol. V, p.271.

18 Labanoff, Vol. VI, p.51.

19 CSP Scotland, Vol. VII, p.54.

20 HMC Rutland, Vol. I, p.168.

21 Ibid., p.169.

22 CSP Scotland, Vol. VII, p.514.

23 BL Lansdowne, 40/88–146.

24 Devonshire MSS, Chatsworth, HM/5.

25 See Riden, 'Sir William Cavendish', p.249.

26 Talbot MSS, LPL, 3198, f.277.

15. Mocking and Mowing

1 Lodge, Vol. II, p.223.

2 HMC Longleat, Talbot Papers, Vol. V, p.65.

3 Ibid., p.80.

4 HMC Longleat, Talbot Papers, Vol. I, p.11.

5 Lodge, Vol. II, p.272.

6 TNA SP 12/183/7.

7   BHL, ID 230.
8   BHL, ID 229.
9   Quoted in Friedman, p.63.
10 BHL, ID 229.
11 BHL, ID 117.
12 Folger X.d.428 (131).
13 HMC Longleat, Talbot Papers, Vol. V, p.67.
14 Ibid., p.70.
15 Lodge, Vol. II, p.410.
16 TNA SP 12/207/23.
17 HMC Salisbury, Vol. III, p.165.
18 HMC Rutland, Vol. I, p.199.
19 Ibid., p.204.
20 CP 164/91.
21 Talbot MSS, LPL, 3198, f.331.
22 HMC Salisbury, Vol. III, p.152.
23 TNA SP 12/207/29.
24 HMC Longleat, Talbot Papers, Vol. V, p.75.
25 Lodge, Vol. II, p.430.
26 Ibid., p.240.
27 Ibid., p.342.
28 Ibid., p.343.
29 Talbot MSS, LPL, 3200, f.212.
30 HMC Longleat, Talbot Papers, Vol. I, f.11.
31 Lodge, Vol. II, p.302.
32 Talbot MSS, LPL, 3198, ff.386 and 337.
33 Devonshire MSS, Chatsworth, H/143/16.
34 HMC Rutland, Vol. I, p.212.
35 Talbot MSS, LPL, 3205, f.73.
36 TNA SP 12/207/23.

16. The Old Hall

1　All details for the building of the Old Hall, unless stated otherwise, are taken from Durant and Riden (eds), *Building of Hardwick Hall: Part I.*

2　Quoted in Read, p.216.

3　Quoted in Girouard, *Robert Smythson*, p.19.

4　Durant, *Bess of Hardwick*, p.193.

5　Airs, p.198.

6　Ibid., p.171.

7　Stallybrass, p.376.

8　Wells-Cole, p.286.

9　BHL, ID 106.

10　Quoted in Gristwood, p.100.

11　Ibid., p.97.

12　Devonshire MSS, Chatsworth, H/143/16, and Summerson, 'Building of Theobalds'.

13　Durant, *Smythson Circle*, p.118.

14　HMC Longleat, Talbot Papers, Vol. V, p.91.

15　Lodge, Vol. II, p.345.

16　BHL, ID 37.

17　Quoted in Gristwood, p.107.

18　BHL, ID 38.

19　Portland Papers, Nottingham Record Office, DDP 51/19 and 42/27.

20　Worsley.

21　Fox's journal is at Chatsworth, with a transcript in *The Camden Miscellany*, Vol. XVII, Office of the Royal Historical Society, 1940.

22　BHL, ID 88.

23　BHL, ID 24.

24　Talbot MSS, LPL, 3198, f.544.

25　Talbot MSS, LPL, 3200, f.67.

17. Smythson's Platt

1 Stone, *Crisis of the Aristocracy*, p.352.
2 BHL, ID 231.
3 Shrewsbury MSS, LPL, 698, f.55.
4 Talbot MSS, LPL, 3200, f.110.
5 Ibid., f.204.
6 Ibid., f.186, and Lodge, Vol. II, p.464.
7 CP 168/21.
8 Lodge, Vol. II, p.469.
9 HMC Longleat, Talbot Papers, Vol. V, p.106.
10 BHL, ID 233.
11 Durant, *Bess of Hardwick*, p.152.
12 BHL, ID 159.
13 Riden and Fowkes, p.29.
14 This is based on an engraving by Étienne Delaune. See Levey, *Embroideries at Hardwick Hall*, p.124.
15 Girouard, *Robert Smythson*, p.147
16 See Nicholas Cooper, *Country Life*, 15 October 2014.
17 Girouard, *Elizabethan Architecture*, p.236, and 'Tresham Papers'.
18 See 'Tresham Papers, belonging to T.B. Clarke-Thornhill'.
19 Ibid., p.33, and BL Add. MS 39832.
20 Riden (ed.), *Household Accounts*, p.292.
21 Sitwell, p.26.
22 Camden, p.555.
23 Pete Smith suggests that Smythson may have drawn up the scheme for the courts after his original plan for the house. See Pete Smith, '"Whear the walks should hav bene": The Unfinished Hall at Hardwick', in *National Trust Historic Houses and Collections Annual 2015*, pp.50–6.
24 Girouard, *Robert Smythson*, p.149.
25 All details for the building of the New Hall are taken from Durant and Riden (eds), *Building of Hardwick Hall: Part I and Part II*.
26 BHL, ID 235.

18. London, 1591

1 All details of London visit 1591–2, unless stated otherwise, are taken from Devonshire MSS, Chatsworth, HM/7, and also Edward Whalley's account book, Folger V.b. 308.

2 Devonshire MSS, Chatsworth, H/143/41.

3 Durant, *Bess of Hardwick*, p.169.

4 Levey, *Elizabethan Inheritance*, p.24.

5 See Girouard, *Robert Smythson*, p.124.

6 BHL, ID 163.

7 Devonshire MSS, Chatsworth, HM/7, f.50.

8 Durant and Riden (eds), *Building of Hardwick Hall: Part II*, Appendix 1.

9 Devonshire MSS, Chatsworth, HM/7, f.58.

19. 'More glass than wall'

1 All details for the building of the New Hall, unless stated otherwise, are taken from Durant and Riden (eds), *Building of Hardwick Hall: Part II*.

2 Quoted in Kettle, p.19.

3 BHL, ID 108.

4 Devonshire MSS, Chatsworth, HM/7, f.66.

5 BHL, ID 124.

6 Durant, *Bess of Hardwick*, p.182.

7 Devonshire MSS, Chatsworth, HM/7, f.154.

8 Devonshire MSS, Chatsworth, HM/5.

9 Talbot MSS, LPL, 3199, f.353, and BHL, ID 215.

10 BHL, ID 102.

11 For loans see Devonshire MSS, Chatsworth, HM/7 and H/143/43.

12 Payments to Balechouse in Devonshire MSS, Chatsworth, HM/7 and HM/8.

13 Airs, p.127.

14 See Pete Smith, *National Trust Historic Houses and Collections Annual 2015*, pp.50–6.

15 Stallybrass, p.378.

16 BHL, ID 16.

17 BHL, ID 1.

18 Devonshire MSS, Chatsworth, HM/8, ff.59 and 81.

19 Devonshire MSS, Chatsworth, HM/7, f.152.

20 Ibid., f.76.

21 Ibid., f.37, and Stallybrass, p.379.

22 Durant, *Bess of Hardwick*, p.185.

23 Devonshire MSS, Chatsworth, HM/8, f.111.

24 Devonshire MSS, Chatsworth, H/143/44.

25 Devonshire MSS, Chatsworth, HM/7, f.189.

20. 'Houshold stuff'

1 All details for life at Hardwick, unless stated otherwise, are taken from Bess's household accounts, Devonshire MSS, Chatsworth, HM/7 (1591–97) and HM/8 (1598–99).

2 Talbot MSS, LPL, 3205, f.75.

3 BHL, ID 103.

4 Stallybrass, p.383.

5 Stallybrass, p.389.

6 Levey, *Elizabethan Inheritance*, p.29.

7 Riden (ed.), *Household Accounts*, Part 2, p.272, and Part 3, p.103.

8 Levey and Thornton (eds).

9 Devonshire MSS, Chatsworth, H/143/43.

10 The tapestry hangings may have been acquired by Sir William Cavendish (Levey, *Elizabethan Inheritance*, p.26).

11 Balechouse was supplied with white lead, red lead, yellow ochre, chalk and varnish (Devonshire MSS, Chatsworth, HM/8, f.45).

12 Riden (ed.), *Household Accounts*, Part 2, p.124.

13 Durant and Riden (eds), *Building of Hardwick Hall: Part II*, p.243.

14 Devonshire MSS, Chatsworth, HM/8, f.63.

15 Adshead and Taylor (eds), p.150.

16 Devonshire MSS, Chatsworth, HM/8, f.127.

17 Devonshire MSS, Chatsworth, HM/7, f.58.

18 Riden (ed.), *Household Accounts*, Part 2, p.254.

19 Ibid., p.354.

20 See Girouard, *Robert Smythson*, p.176.

21 Devonshire MSS, Chatsworth, HM/8, f.69.

22 Ibid., f.117.

23 Devonshire MSS, Chatsworth, H/143/40.

24 CP 80/9.

25 CP 250/16.

26 BHL, ID 20.

27 CP 250/8.

28 Riden (ed.), *Household Accounts*, Part 3, p.103.

29 Bess's will: TNA PROB 11/111, ff.188–193. Also see Collins, p.15, and White, Appendix 4.

21. 'A scribbling melancholy'

1 Folger X.d.428 (120).

2 Quoted in Guy, *Elizabeth*, p.368.

3 Quoted in Durant, *Arbella Stuart*, p.60.

4 Devonshire MSS, Chatsworth, HM/7, ff.83 and 88.

5 Devonshire MSS, Chatsworth, HM/8, ff.60 and 79, and HM/7, f.140.

6 Steen (ed.), p.135.

7 Ibid., p.168.

8 HMC Salisbury, Vol. XIV, p.254.

9 Steen (ed.), p.121.

10 Ibid., p.153.

11 BHL, ID 128.

12 BHL, ID 136.

13 BHL, ID 129.

14 BHL, ID 130.

15 Steen (ed.), p.153.

16 BHL, ID 141.

17 BHL, ID 130.

18 Steen (ed.), p.158.

19 BHL, ID 132.

20 BHL, ID 134.

21 BHL, ID 135.

22 Riden (ed.), *Household Accounts*, Part 3, p.17.

23 BHL, ID 53.

24 Folger X.d.428 (116).

25 Nichols, *The Progresses of King James I*, Vol. I, p.17.

26 Quoted in Gristwood, p.257.

22. 'It doth stick sore in her teeth'

1 BHL, ID 35.

2 BHL, ID 140.

3 Talbot MSS, LPL, 3205, f.124.

4 Quoted in Durant, *Arbella Stuart*, p.117.

5 Steen (ed.), pp.184 and 193.

6 Riden (ed.), *Household Accounts*.

7 Devonshire MSS, Chatsworth, H/143/14.

8 BHL, ID 63.

9 BHL, ID 11.

10 Talbot MSS, LPL, 3205, f.300.

11 Talbot MSS, LPL, 3202, f.327.

12 Steen (ed.), p.202.

13 Talbot MSS, LPL, 3202, f.7.

14 Ibid., f.13.

15 BHL, ID 19.

16 Talbot MSS, LPL, 3203, f.308.

17 Levey and Thornton (eds), p.47.

18 Devonshire MSS, Chatsworth, HM/7, f.96.

19 Talbot MSS, LPL, 3202, f.266.

20 Ibid., f.44.

21 Quoted in Rawson, p.343.

22 Talbot MSS, LPL, 3203, f.290.

23   Talbot MSS, LPL, 3202, f.44.

24   Ibid., f.310.

23. 'Not over sumptuous'

1   Quoted in Durant, *Bess of Hardwick*, p.220.

2   Folger X.d.428 (59).

3   Ibid. (60).

4   Talbot MSS, LPL, 3205, f.62.

5   Talbot MSS, LPL, 3203, f.349.

6   CP 121/25.

7   CP 121/24.

8   Talbot MSS, LPL, 3202, f.149.

9   Ibid., f.151.

10   Stone, *Family and Fortune*, p.32.

11   BHL, ID 4.

12   BHL, ID 89.

13   Talbot MSS, LPL, 3205, f.59.

14   CP 123/123.

15   See John Chamberlain, 8 January 1608, in *The Letters of John Chamberlain*, Philadelphia, 1939.

16   BHL, ID 90.

17   Quoted in Rawson, p.346.

18   Talbot MSS, LPL, 3202, f.482.

19   Talbot MSS, LPL, 3205, f.481.

20   Levey and Thornton (eds), p.53.

21   Shrewsbury MSS, LPL, 710, f.61.

22   Devonshire MSS, Chatsworth, H/143/17, Shrewsbury MSS, LPL, 710, f.61, and White, Appendix 4.

23   HMC Salisbury, Vol. 20, p.67.

24   Devonshire MSS, Chatsworth, HM/29, f.4.

25   Johnson, Vol. V, p.398.

26   HMC Salisbury, Vol. XX, p.96.

27   Talbot MSS, LPL, 3202, f.143.

28 HMC Salisbury, Vol. XX, p.67.

29 Talbot MSS, LPL, 3205, f.384.

30 Shrewsbury MSS, LPL, 707, f.112.

31 Talbot MSS, LPL, 3202, f.155.

32 For details of the Chatterton scandal, see TNA STAC 8/13/8.

33 HMC Longleat, Talbot Papers, Vol. V, p.134.

34 TNA C/1123 and TNA PROB 11/111, ff.188–193.

35 For funeral expenses, see Devonshire MSS, Chatsworth, HM/29, f.27.

36 Burghley's funeral cost £1,000 and that of Leicester £3,000. See Stone, *Crisis of the Aristocracy*, Appendix XXV.

37 Quoted in Rawson, p.347.

38 Durant, *Bess of Hardwick*, p.226.

SELECT BIBLIOGRAPHY

Unless stated otherwise, the place of publication is London.

Books

Adshead, David, and Taylor, David A. H. B. (eds), *Hardwick Hall: A Great Old Castle of Romance*, New Haven, Yale, 2016

Airs, Malcolm, *The Tudor and Jacobean Country House: A Building History*, Stroud, Sutton, 1995

Bacon, Francis, *The Essays*, Macmillan, 1900

Brigden, Susan, *New Worlds, Lost Worlds: The Rule of the Tudors 1485–1603*, Allen Lane, 2000

Brotton, Jerry, *This Orient Isle: Elizabethan England and the Islamic World*, Allen Lane, 2016

Camden, William, *Britannia*, 1789

Childs, Jessie, *God's Traitors: Terror and Faith in Elizabethan England*, Bodley Head, 2014

Collins, A. C., *Historical Collections of the Noble Families of Cavendish, Holles, Vere, Harley and Ogle*, Withers, 1752

Cooper, Nicholas, *Houses of the Gentry, 1480–1680*, New Haven & London, Yale, 1999

Cowell, Ben, 'Hardwick Hall: An Archival Survey', unpublished report, National Trust, 1997, Chatsworth

Crook, David, 'Hardwick Before Bess: The Origins and Early History of the Hardwick Family and Their Estate', *Derbyshire Archaeological Journal*, Vol. 107, 1987

Daybell, James, *Women Letter-Writers in Tudor England*, Oxford University Press, 2006

Durant, David N., *Arbella Stuart: A Rival to the Queen*, Weidenfeld and Nicolson, 1978

Durant, David N., *Bess of Hardwick: Portrait of an Elizabethan Dynast*, Peter Owen, 1977

Durant, David N., *The Smythson Circle: The Story of Six Great English Houses*, Peter Owen, 2011

Durant, David, and Riden, Philip (eds), *The Building of Hardwick Hall: Part I, The Old Hall, 1587–91*, Derbyshire Record Society, Vol. IV, 1980

Durant, David, and Riden, Philip (eds), *The Building of Hardwick Hall: Part II, The New Hall, 1591–98*, Derbyshire Record Society, Vol. IX, 1984

Erickson, Amy Louise, *Women and Property in Early Modern England*, Routledge, 1993

Friedman, Alice T., *House and Household in Elizabethan England: Wollaton Hall and the Willoughby Family*, Chicago & London, University of Chicago, 1989

Frye, Susan, *Pens and Needles: Women's Textualities in Early Modern England*, Philadelphia & London, University of Pennsylvania, 2010

Furnivall, F. J. (ed.), *Harrison's Description of England in Shakespeare's Youth*, 1877

Girouard, Mark, *Elizabethan Architecture: Its Rise and Fall 1540–1640*, New Haven & London, Yale, 2009

Girouard, Mark, *Robert Smythson and the Elizabethan Country House*, New Haven & London, Yale, 1983

Goodall, John A., *Lady Anne Clifford and the Architectural Pursuit of Nobility*, Yorkshire Archaeological Society, 2009

Gristwood, Sarah, *Arbella: England's Lost Queen*, Bantam, 2003

Guy, John, *Elizabeth: The Forgotten Years*, Viking, 2016

Guy, John, *My Heart is my Own: The Life of Mary Queen of Scots*, Fourth Estate, 2009

Harris, Barbara J., *English Aristocratic Women, 1450–1550: Marriage and Family, Property and Careers*, Oxford University Press, 2002

Henderson, Paula, *The Tudor House and Garden: Architecture and Landscape in the Sixteenth and Early Seventeenth Centuries*, New Haven & London, Yale, 2005

Hey, David, *Packmen, Carriers and Packhorse Roads: Trade and Communications in North Derbyshire and South Yorkshire*, Leicester University Press, 1980

Howard, Leonard, *A Collection of Letters from the Original Manuscripts*, E. Withers, 1753

Howard, Maurice, *The Building of Elizabethan and Jacobean England*, New Haven & London, Yale, 2007

Howard, Maurice, *The Early Tudor Country House: Architecture and Politics, 1490–1550*, George Philip, 1987

Hunter, Joseph, *A History of Hallamshire*, 1869

Innocent, C. F., *The Development of English Building Construction*, Cambridge University Press, 1916

Ives, Eric, *Lady Jane Grey: A Tudor Mystery*, Wiley-Blackwell, 2009

Johnson, Nathaniel, *A History of the Lives of the Earls of Shrewsbury*, 7 vols, 1692–3, unpublished, Chatsworth

Jones, Norman, *God and the Moneylenders: Usury and Law in Early Modern England*, Oxford, Blackwell, 1989

Kettle, Pamela, *Oldcotes: The Last Mansion Built by Bess of Hardwick*, Cardiff, Merton Priory Press, 2000

Kiernan, David, *The Derbyshire Lead Industry in the Sixteenth Century*, Derbyshire Record Society, Vol. XIV, 1989

Labanoff, Prince A., *Letters of Mary Stuart*, 1845

Langham, Mike, and Wells, Colin, *Buxton Waters: A History of Buxton the Spa*, J. H. Hall & Sons, 1986

Leader, J. D., *Mary Queen of Scots in Captivity*, Sheffield, 1880

Levey, Santina M., *An Elizabethan Inheritance: The Hardwick Hall Textiles*, National Trust, 1998

Levey, Santina M., *The Embroideries at Hardwick Hall: A Catalogue*, National Trust, 2007

Levey, Santina M., and Thornton, Peter K. (eds), *Of Household Stuff: The 1601 inventories of Bess of Hardwick*, National Trust, 2001

Levy, Allison (ed.), *Widowhood and Visual Culture in Early Modern Europe*, Ashgate, 2003

Lisle, Leanda de, *The Sisters Who Would Be Queen: The Tragedy of Mary, Katherine and Lady Jane Grey*, Harper, 2008

Lisle, Leanda de, *Tudor: The Family Story*, Chatto & Windus, 2013

Lodge, Edmund, *Illustrations of British History, Biography and Manners*, 3 vols, John Chidley, 1838

Lovell, Mary S., *Bess of Hardwick: First Lady of Chatsworth*, Little, Brown, 2005

Newcastle, Duchess of, *The Life of William Duke of Newcastle*, 1906

Nichols, John, *The Progresses and Public Processions of Queen Elizabeth*, 1823

Nichols, John, *The Progresses, Processions and Magnificent Festivities of King James I*, 4 vols, 1828

Picard, Liza, *Elizabeth's London*, Weidenfeld and Nicolson, 2003

Rawson, Maud, *Bess of Hardwick and her Circle*, Hutchinson, 1910

Read, Conyers, *Lord Burghley and Queen Elizabeth*, Jonathan Cape, 1960

Richardson, Walter C., *History of the Court of Augmentations, 1536–54*, Baton Rouge, Louisiana State University Press, 1961

Riden, Philip, 'The Hardwicks of Hardwick Hall in the Fifteenth and Sixteenth Centuries', Derbyshire Archaeological Journal, Vol. 130, 2010

Riden, Philip (ed.), *The Household Accounts of William Cavendish, 1597–1607*, Derbyshire Record Society, 2016

Riden, Philip, 'Sir William Cavendish: Tudor Civil Servant and Founder of a Dynasty', *Derbyshire Archaeological Journal*, Vol. CXXIX, 2009

Riden, Philip, and Edwards, David G. (eds), *Essays in Derbyshire History*, Derbyshire Record Society, Vol. XXX, 2006

Riden, Philip, and Fowkes, Dudley, *Hardwick: A Great House and its Estate*, Phillimore, 2009

Rowse, A. L., *The England of Elizabeth: The Structure of Society*, Macmillan, 1951

Sitwell, Sacheverell, *British Architects and Craftsmen*, Stroud, B.T. Batsford, 1945

Sim, Alison, *Food and Feast in Tudor England*, Sutton, 1997

Skelton, R. A., and Summerson, John (eds), *A Description of Maps and Architectural Drawings in the Collection made by William Cecil*, The Roxburgh Club, 1971

Stallybrass, Basil, 'Bess of Hardwick's Buildings and Building Accounts', *Archaeologia*, Vol. LXIV, 1913

Starkey, David, *Elizabeth: Apprenticeship*, Chatto & Windus, 2000

Steen, Sara Jayne (ed.), *The Letters of Lady Arbella Stuart*, Oxford University Press, 1994

Stone, Lawrence, *The Crisis of the Aristocracy, 1558–1641*, Oxford University Press, 1965

Stone, Lawrence, *Family and Fortune: Studies in Aristocratic Finance in the Sixteenth and Seventeenth Centuries*, Oxford University Press, 1973

Stone, Lawrence, *The Family, Sex and Marriage in England, 1500–1800*, Weidenfeld and Nicolson, 1977

Strachey, Lytton, *Elizabeth and Essex*, Chatto & Windus, 1929

Strickland, Agnes, *Letters of Mary Queen of Scots*, 2 vols, 1844

Summerson, John, *Architecture in Britain 1530–1830*, Penguin, 1963

Summerson, John, 'The Building of Theobalds, 1564–85', *Archaeologia*, Vol. XCVII, 1959, pp. 107–126

Thurley, Simon, *The Royal Palaces of Tudor England: Architecture and Court Life, 1460–1547*, New Haven & London, Yale, 1993

Thurley, Simon, *Somerset House: The Palace of England's Queens, 1551–1692*, London Topographical Society, No. 168, 2009.

'The Tresham Papers, belonging to T. B. Clarke-Thornhill Esq.', HMC 55: *Report on Manuscripts in Various Collections*, Vol. III, 1904

Weir, Alison, *Elizabeth the Queen*, Jonathan Cape, 1998

Wells-Cole, Anthony, *Art and Decoration in Elizabethan and Jacobean England: The Influence of Continental Prints, 1558–1625*, New Haven & London, Yale, 1997

White, Gillian, '"That whyche ys nedefoulle and nesesary": The Nature and Purpose of the Original Furnishings and Decoration of Hardwick Hall Derbyshire', unpublished PhD thesis, University of Warwick, 2005

Whitelock, Anna, *Elizabeth's Bedfellows*, Bloomsbury, 2013

Wigfull, J. R., 'Extracts from the Notebook of William Dickenson', *Transactions of the Hunter Archaeological Society*, Vol. II, 1921

Wigfull, J. R., 'House Building in Queen Elizabeth's Days', *Transactions of the Hunter Archaeological Society*, Vol. III, 1925

Williams, E. C., *Bess of Hardwick*, Longman, 1959

Worsley, Lucy, *Hardwick Old Hall*, English Heritage, 1998

INDEX